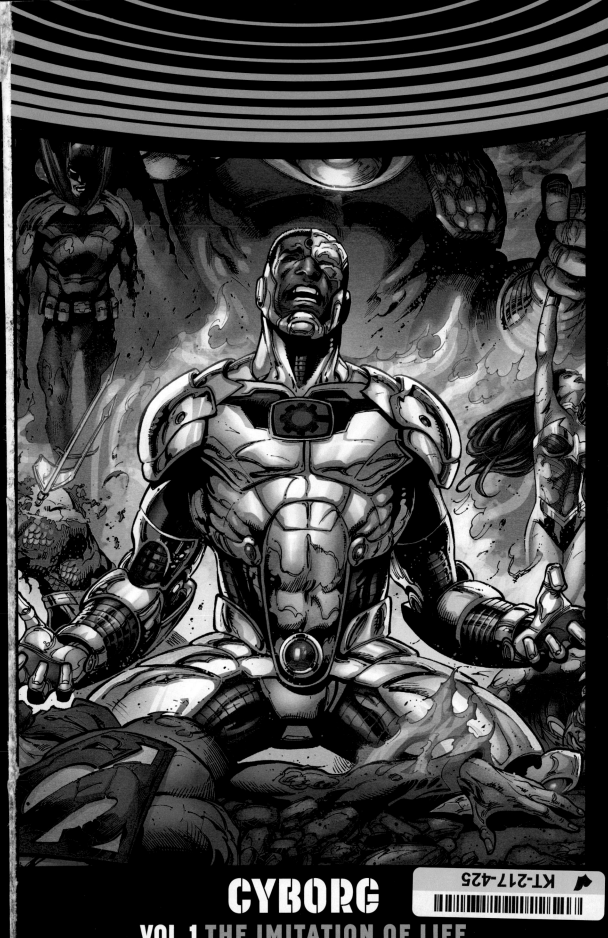

CYBORG
VOL.1 THE IMITATION OF LIFE

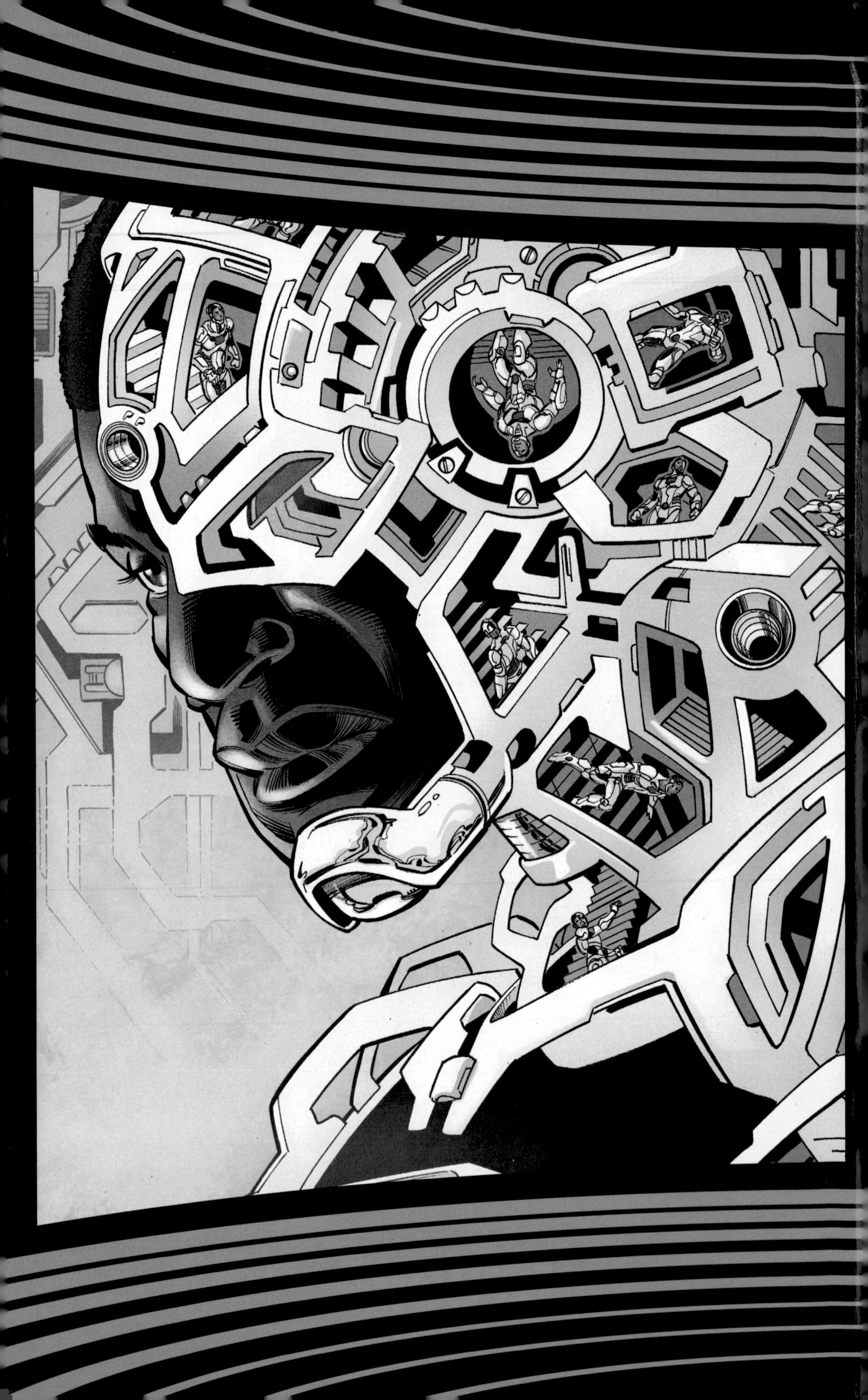

"Refreshes the reader on the titular character while establishing the cast and setting. And it does that in particularly magnificent fashion." **COMICOSITY**

"...it's packed with surprises from the start." **NEWSARAMA**

IT'S WAR BETWEEN MAN AND MACHINES... AND CYBORG IS TRAPPED IN THE MIDDLE!

Cyborg is a member of the Justice League. He is one of Earth's greatest heroes. But is Cyborg really who he thinks he is?

When a shocking discovery about his own origin makes Victor Stone question everything he thought he knew about his identity and his humanity, it seems Cyborg might be more machine than man after all. But if that's the case, which side will Cyborg take when a mysterious cybernetic entity starts a war between man and machines?

Now the people Victor Stone cares about the most are caught in the crossfire, and the choices he makes may mean the difference between the survival of mankind and an artificially intelligent future. Can Cyborg display the heart of a hero...or will he be torn in two by his dual nature?

CYBORG VOL. 1: THE IMITATION OF LIFE is the perfect new jumping-on point as Cyborg is reborn for DC Rebirth, thanks to animation writer **JOHN SEMPER JR.** (*Spider-Man: The Animated Series*) and artists including **PAUL PELLETIER** (AQUAMAN), **WILL CONRAD** (NIGHTWING), **TIMOTHY GREEN II** (RED HOOD AND THE OUTLAWS) and more! **CYBORG VOL. 1: THE IMITATION OF LIFE** collects issues #1-5 and CYBORG: REBIRTH #1.

9 781401 267926 51699 >

$16.99 USA $22.99 CAN ISBN: 978-1-4012-6792-6 dccomics.com

"There's just something about the idea of Dick Grayson returning to the role of Nightwing that feels right." – IGN

"Equally weighted between pulse-pounding and heartfelt drama."
– NEWSARAMA

DC UNIVERSE REBIRTH

NIGHTWING

VOL. 1: BETTER THAN BATMAN

TIM SEELEY
with JAVIER FERNANDEZ

VOL.1 BETTER THAN BATMAN
TIM SEELEY * JAVIER FERNÁNDEZ * CHRIS SOTOMAYOR

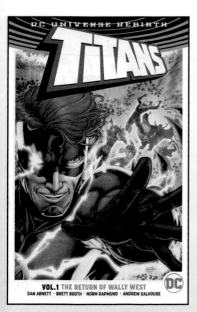

TITANS VOL. 1:
THE RETURN OF WALLY WEST

BATGIRL VOL. 1:
BEYOND BURNDSIDE

BATMAN VOL. 1:
I AM GOTHAM

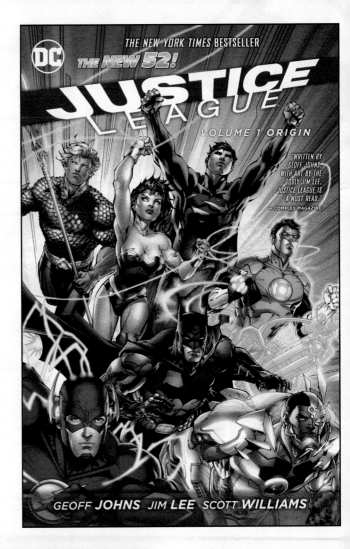

DC UNIVERSE REBIRTH
JUSTICE LEAGUE
VOL. 1: The Extinction Machines

BRYAN HITCH
with TONY S. DANIEL

VOL.1 THE EXTINCTION MACHINES
BRYAN HITCH • TONY S. DANIEL • SANDU FLOREA • TOMEU MOREY

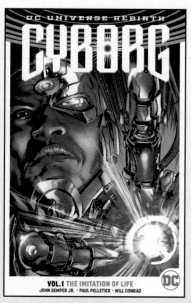

CYBORG VOL. 1:
THE IMITATION OF LIFE

GREEN LANTERNS VOL. 1:
RAGE PLANET

AQUAMAN VOL. 1:
THE DROWNING

Get more DC graphic novels wherever comics and books are sold!

CYBORG #5 COVER SKETCHES

by Paul Pelletier

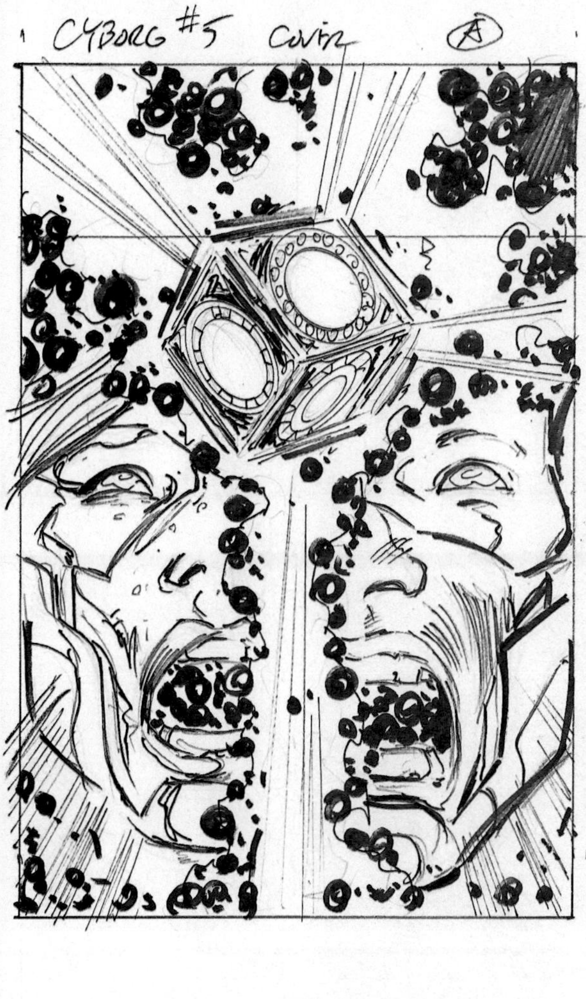
CYBORG #5 COVER A

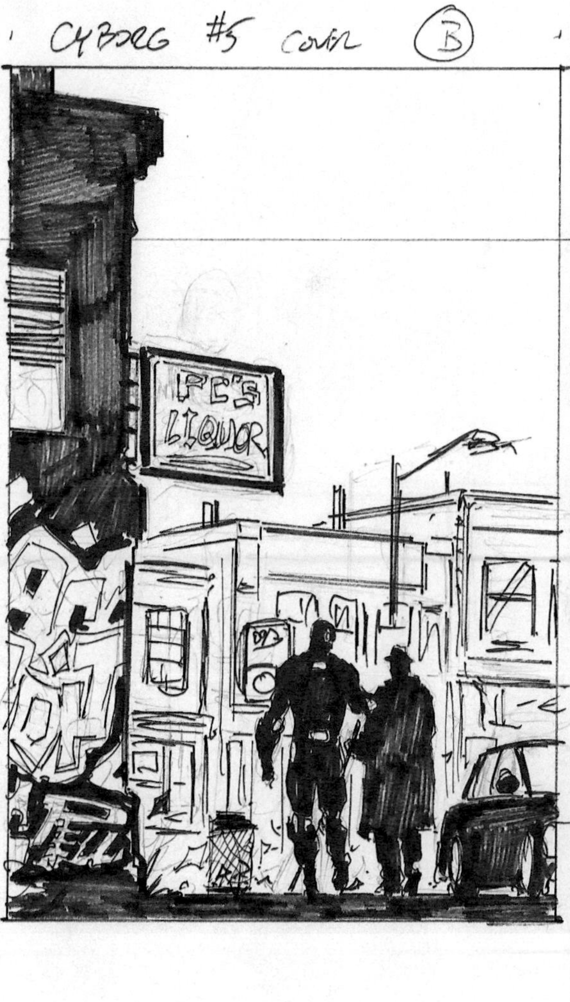
CYBORG #5 COVER B
PC'S
LIQUOR

CYBORG #3 PENCILS
by Paul Pelletier

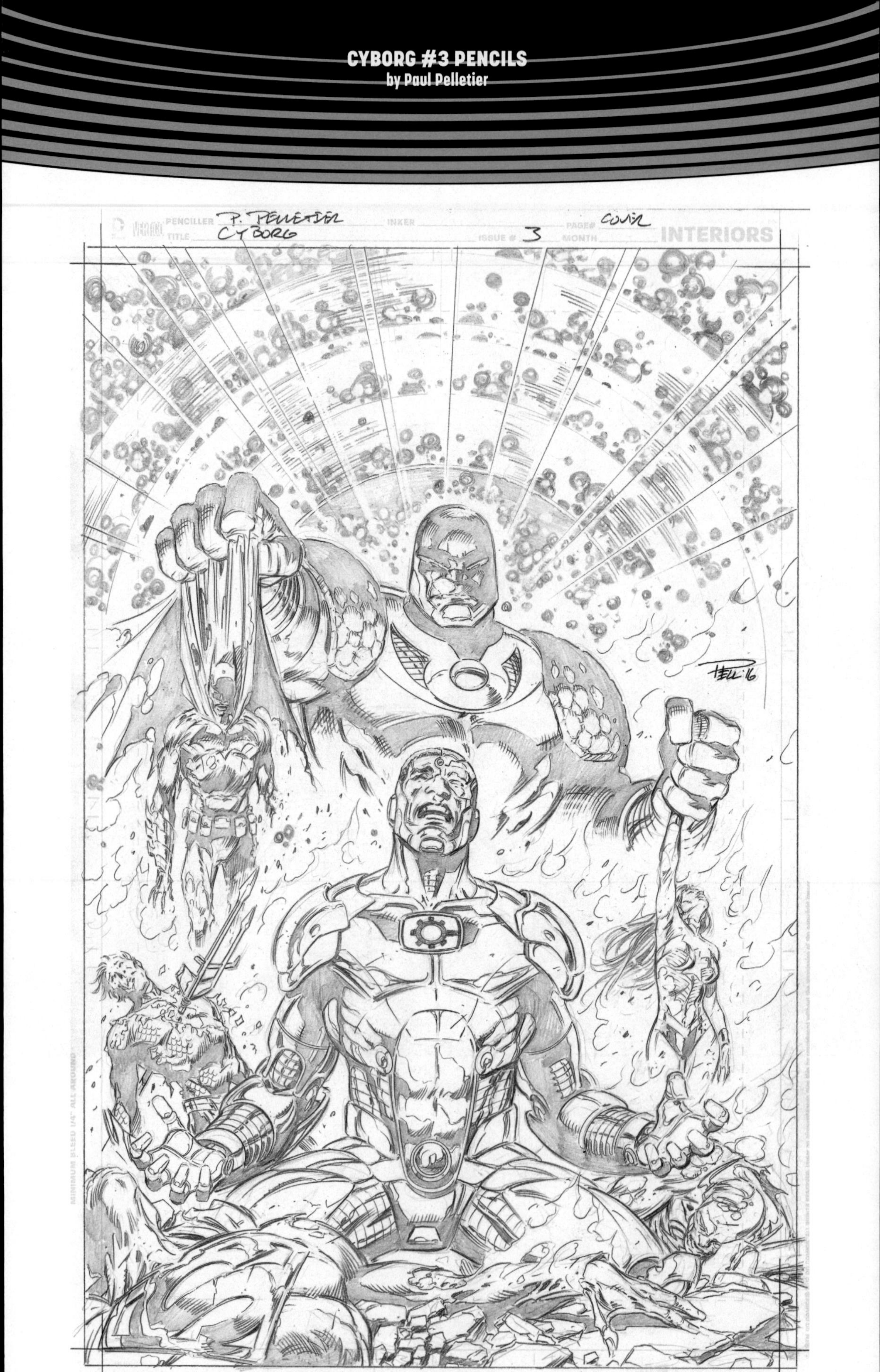
PENCILLER P. PELLETIER
TITLE CYBORG
INKER
ISSUE # 3
PAGE# COVER
MONTH
INTERIORS
PELL '16

CYBORG #2 COVER LAYOUT
by Will Conrad

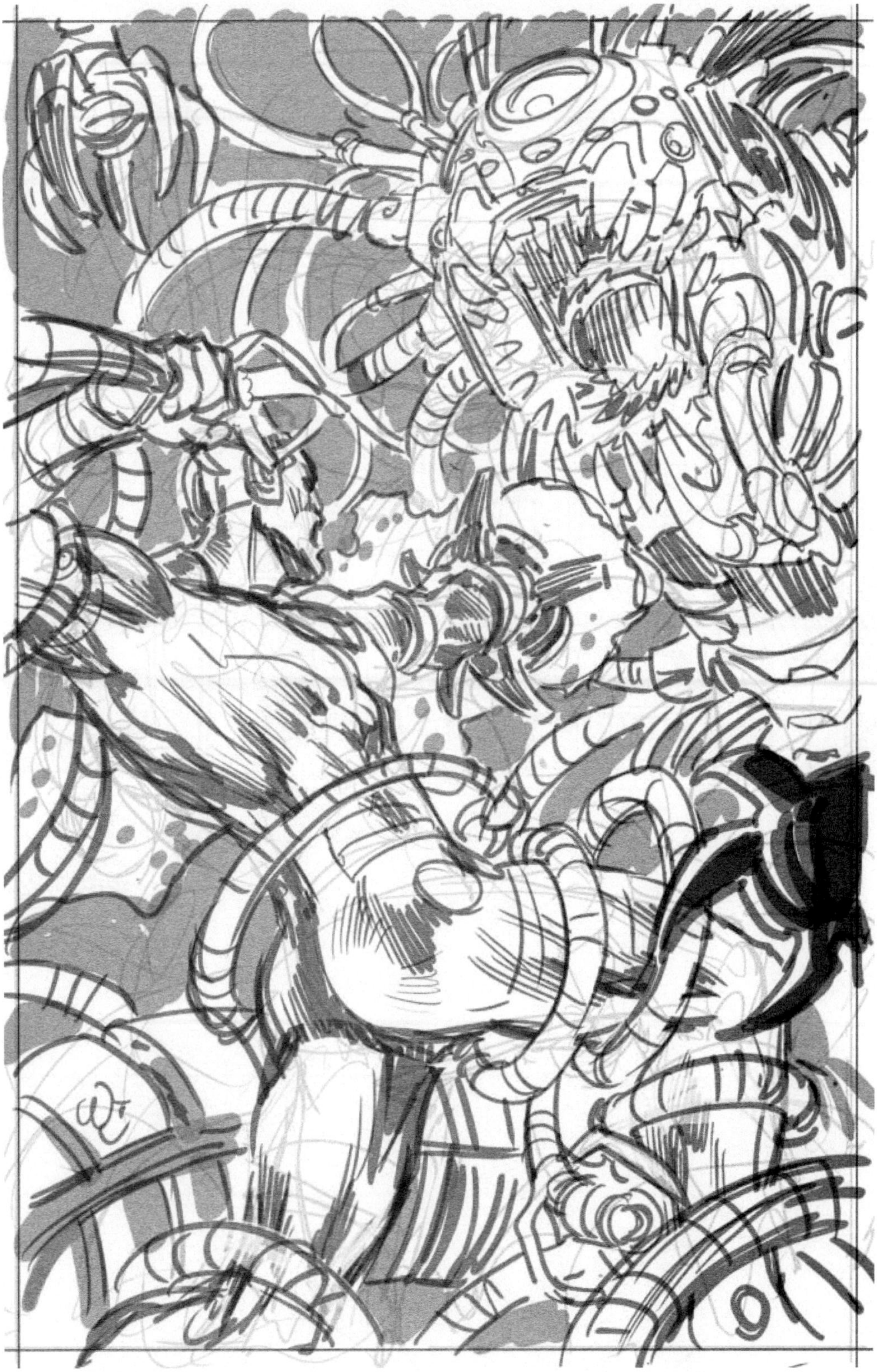

S.T.A.R. LABS CONCEPT SKETCH
by Paul Pelletier

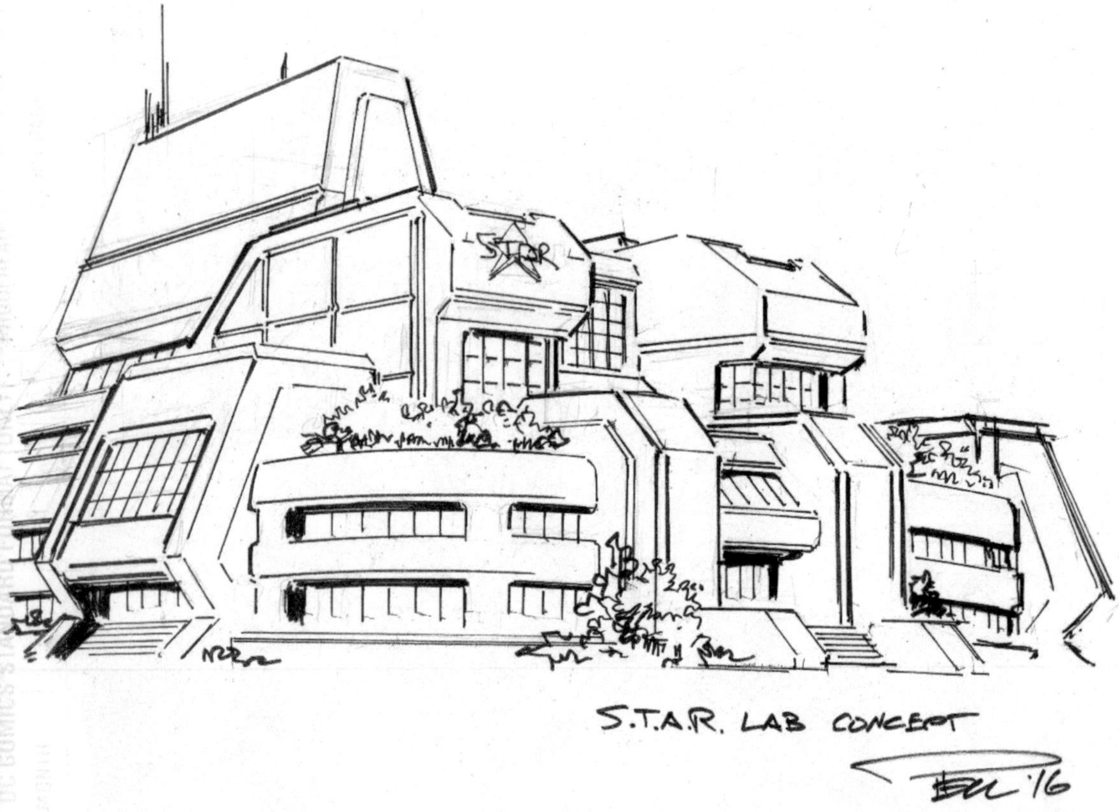
S.T.A.R.
S.T.A.R. LAB CONCEPT

MALWARE DESIGN
by Paul Pelletier

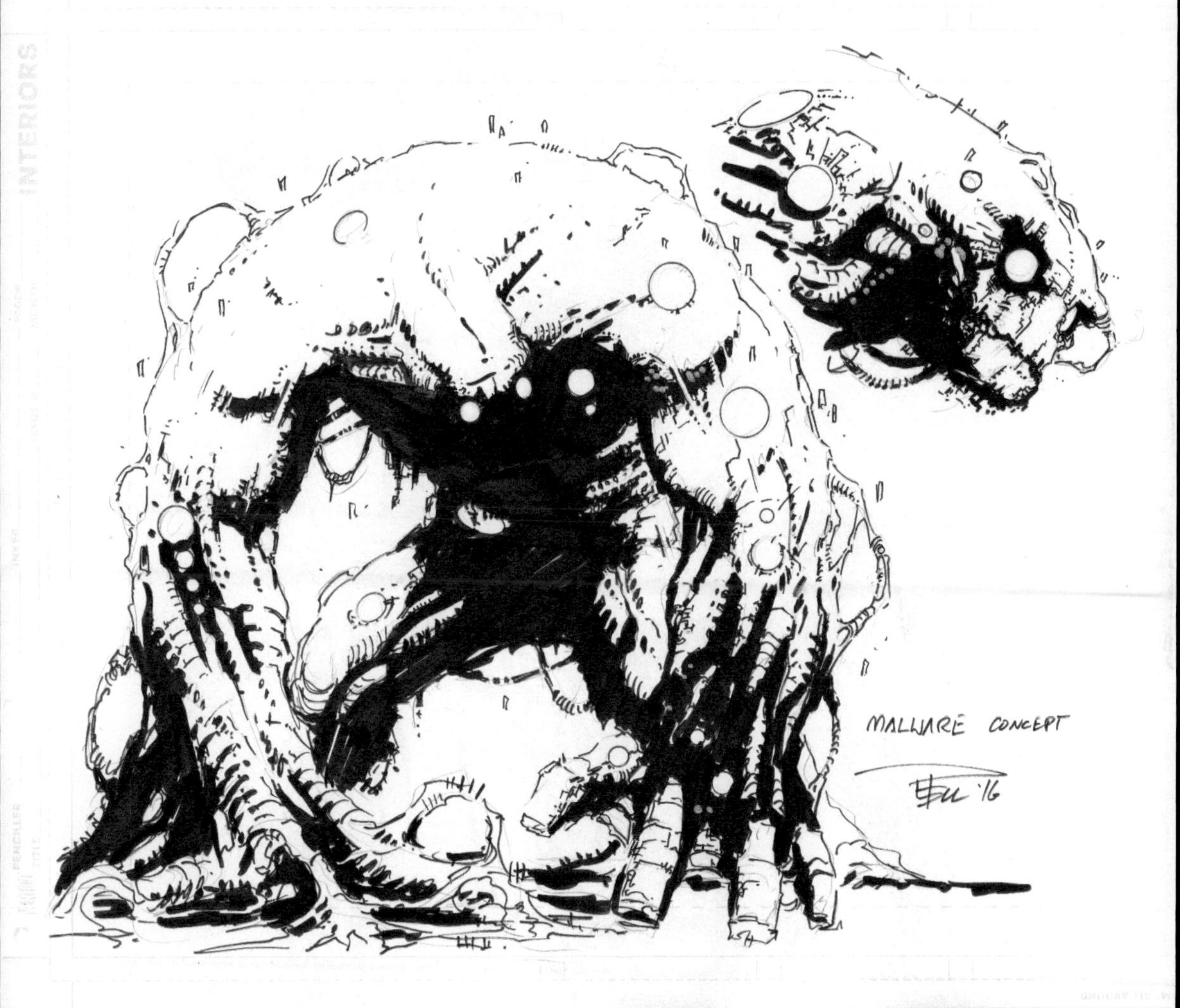
MALWARE CONCEPT
'16

CYBORG REBIRTH DESIGN
by Paul Pelletier

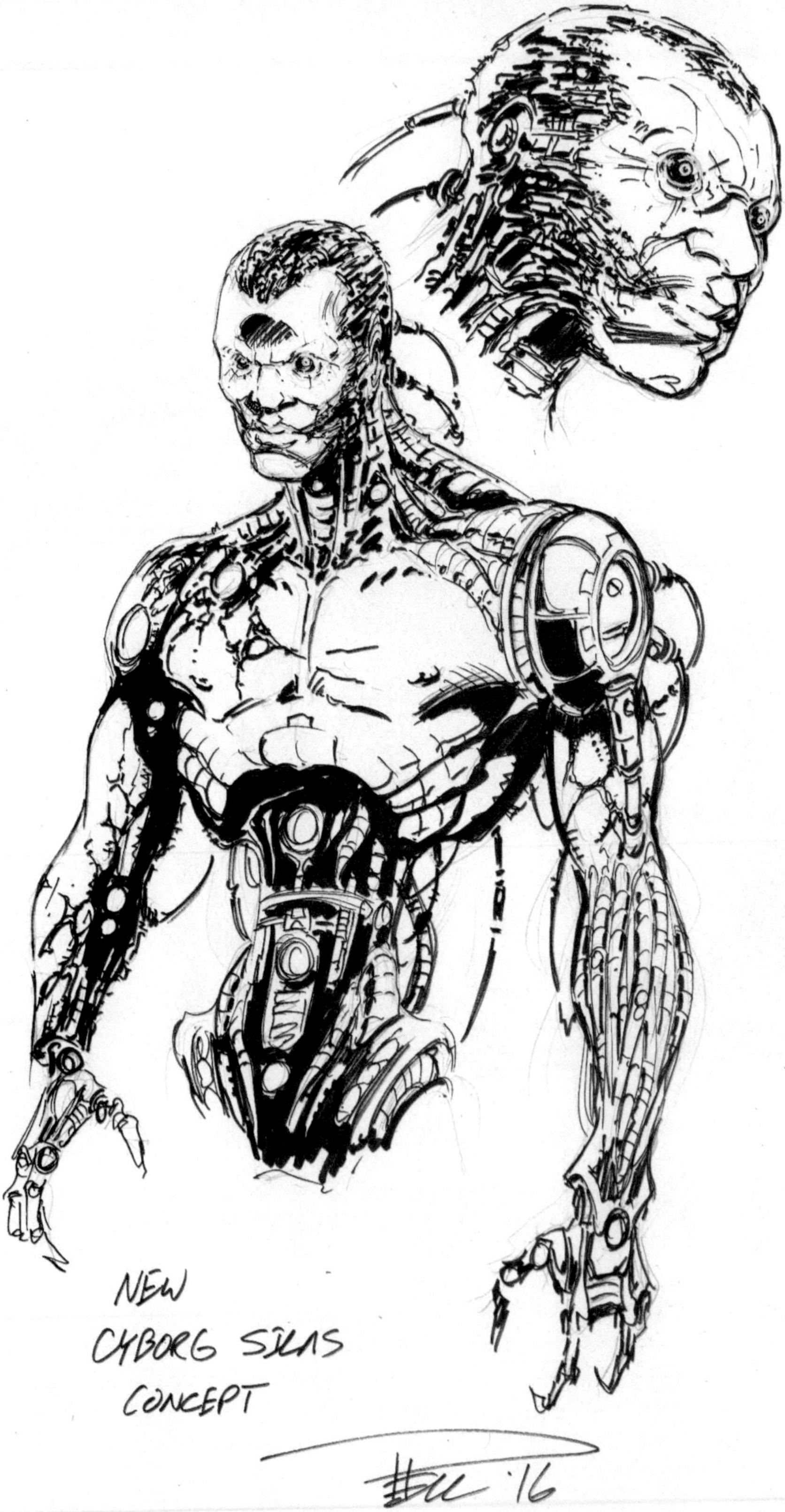
NEW
CYBORG SILAS
CONCEPT
'16

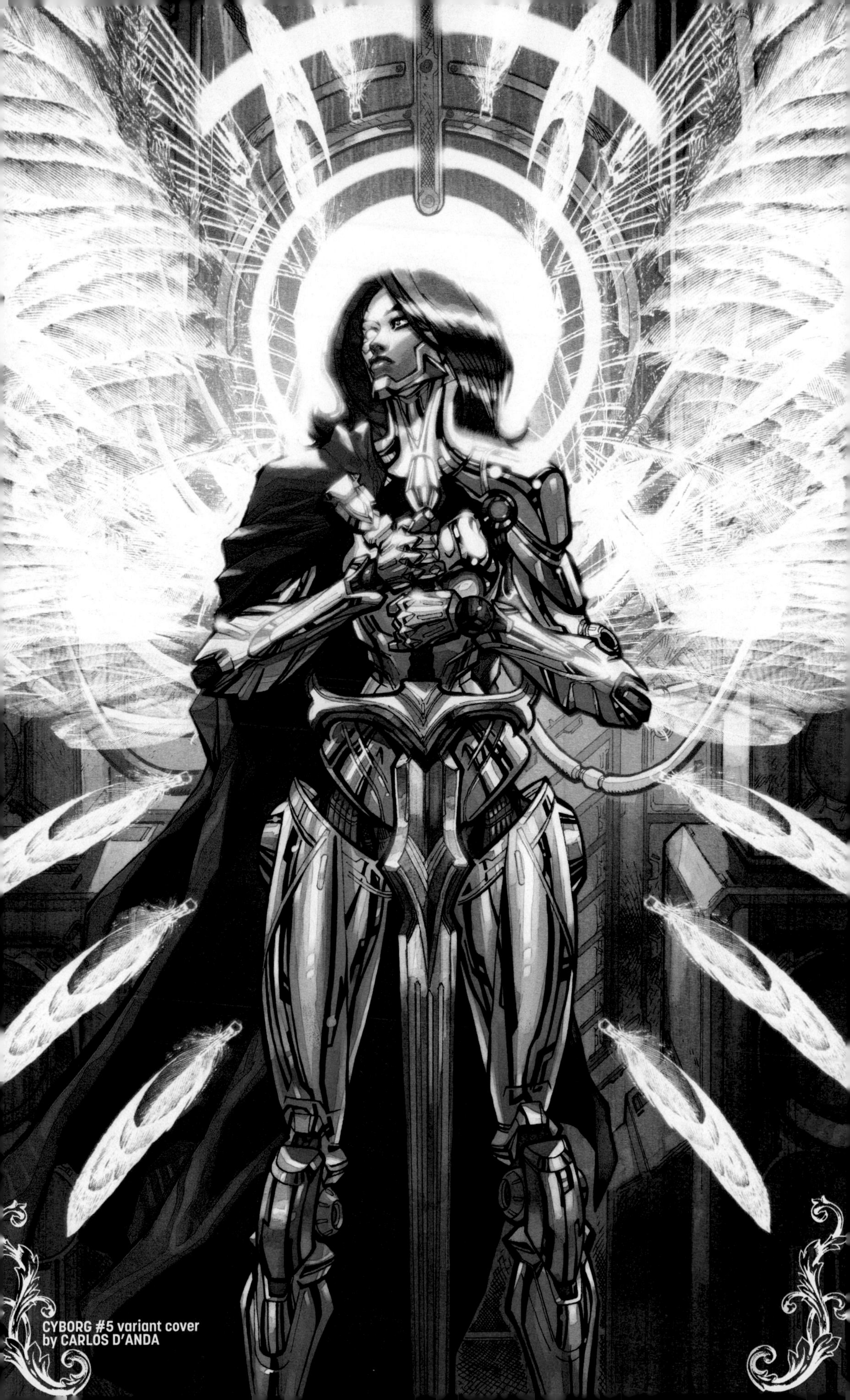

CYBORG #5 variant cover
by CARLOS D'ANDA

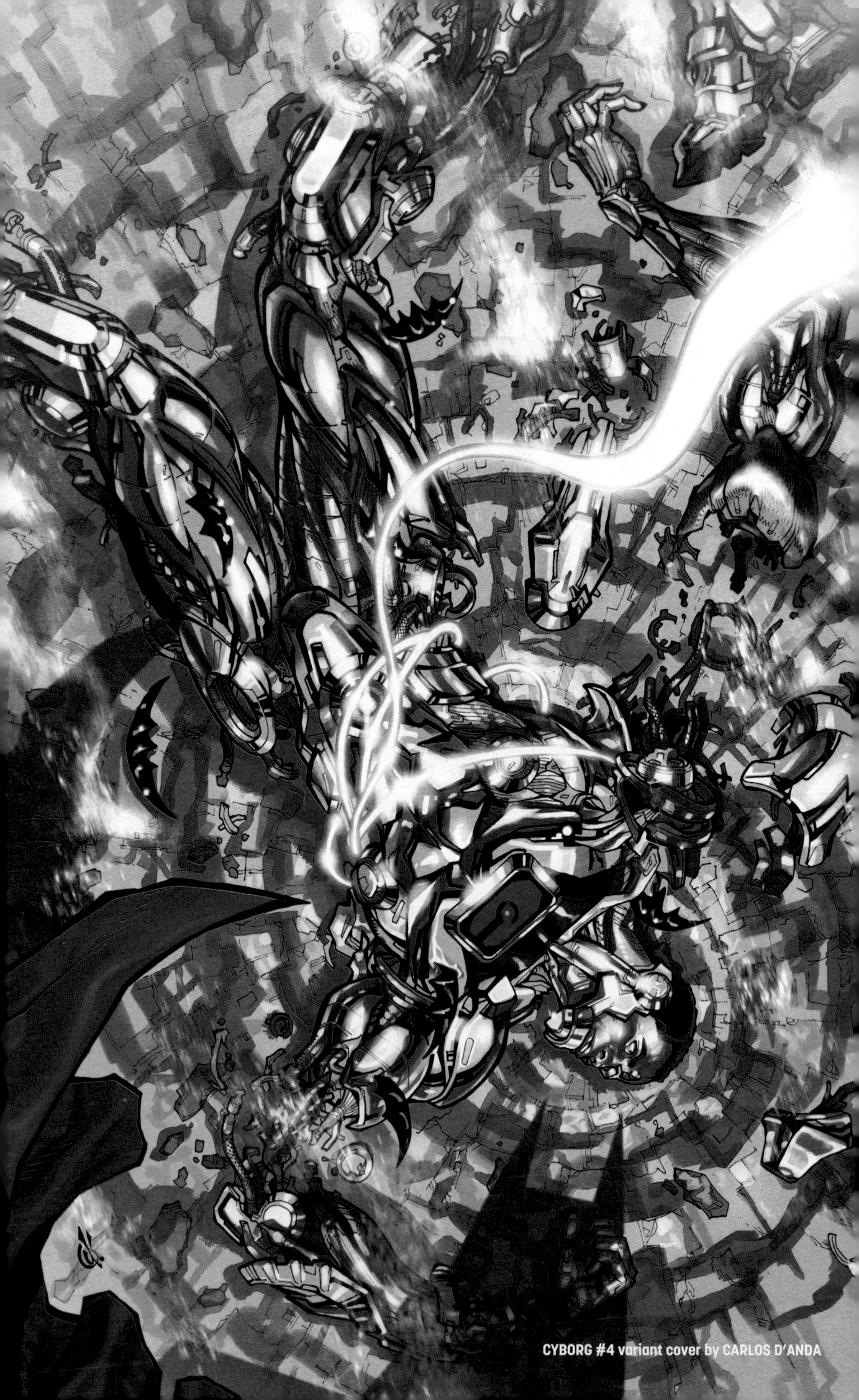

CYBORG #4 variant cover by CARLOS D'ANDA

CYBORG #3 variant cover by CARLOS D'ANDA

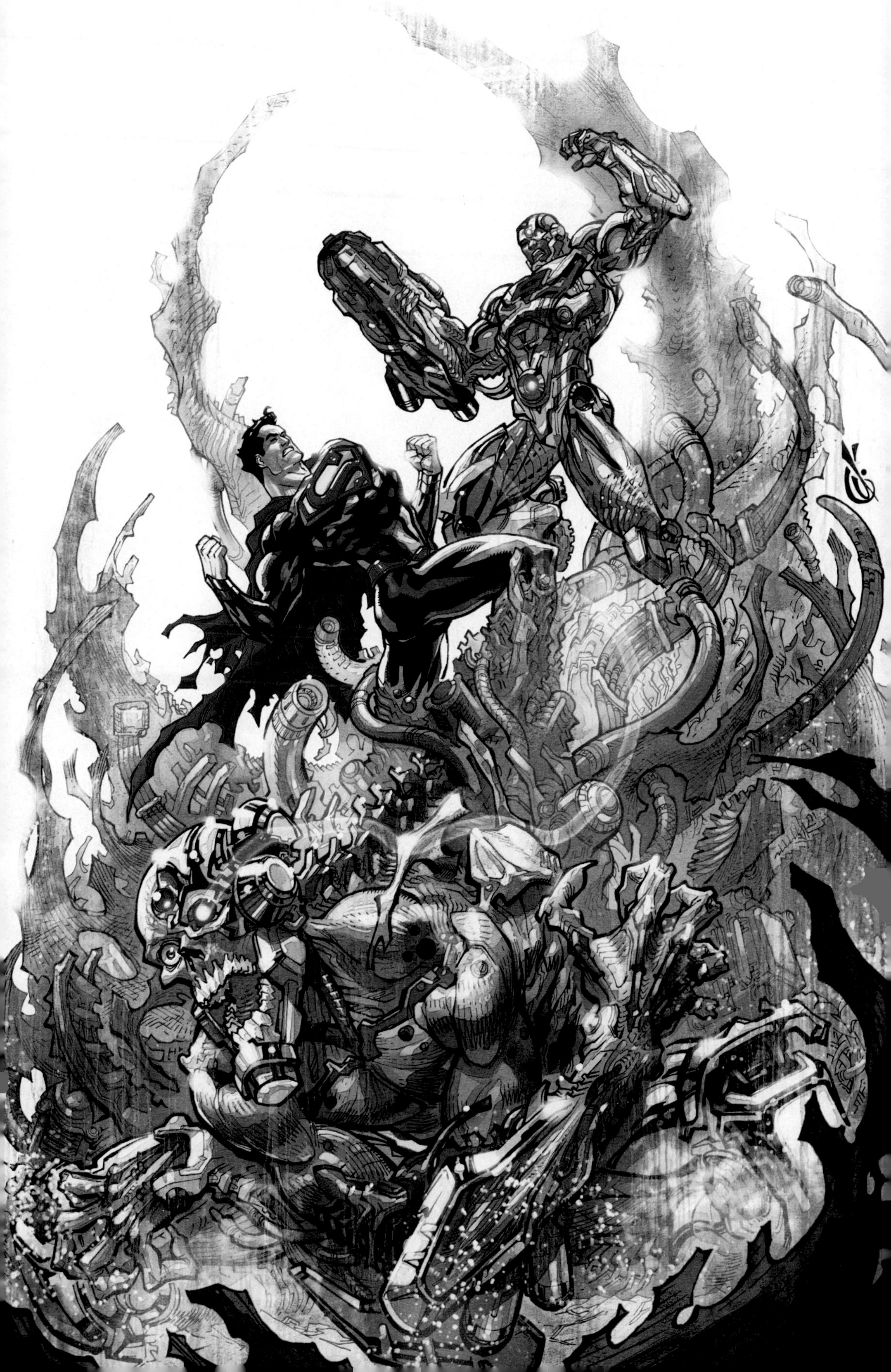

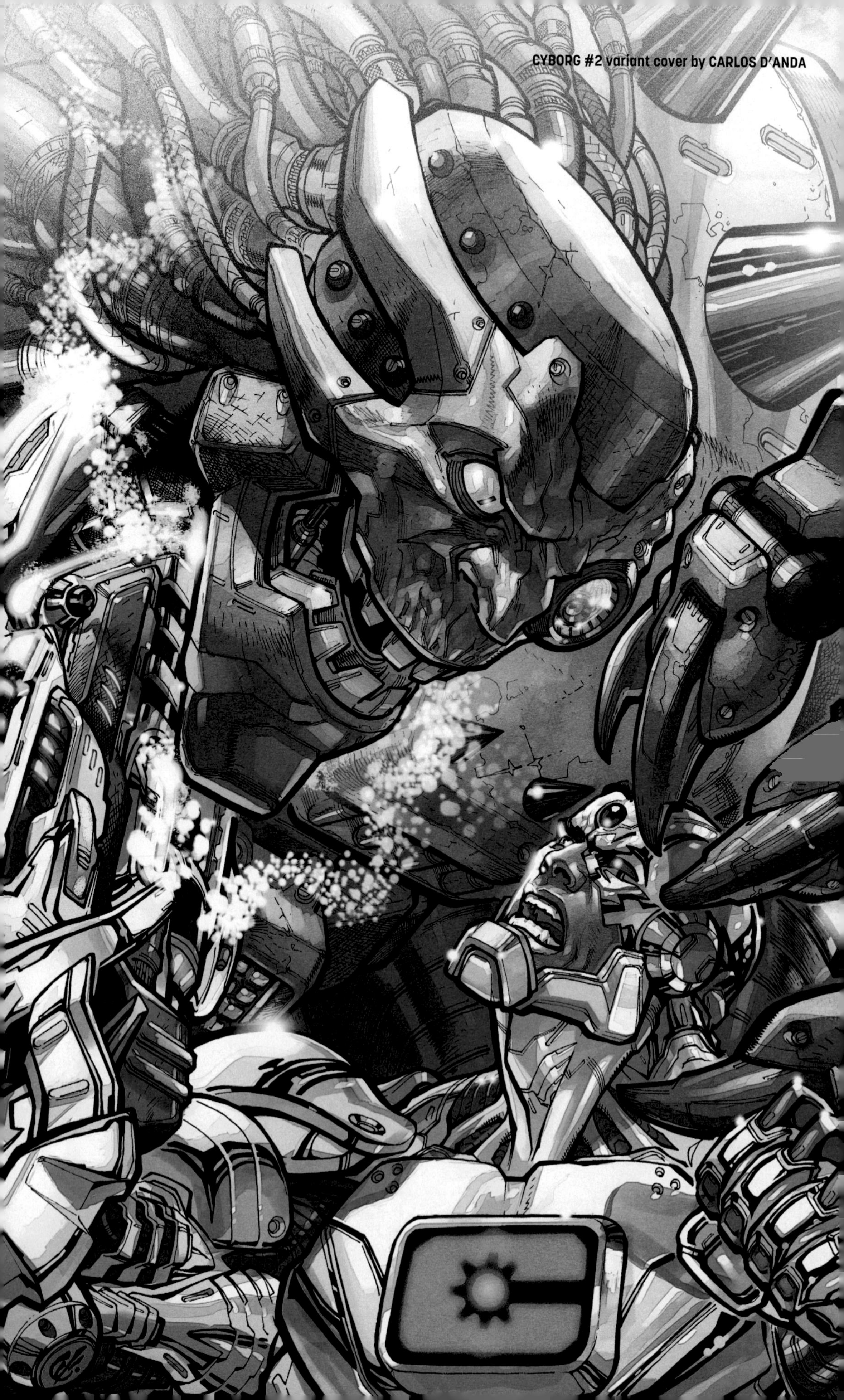
CYBORG #2 variant cover by CARLOS D'ANDA

CYBORG #1 variant cover by CARLOS D'ANDA

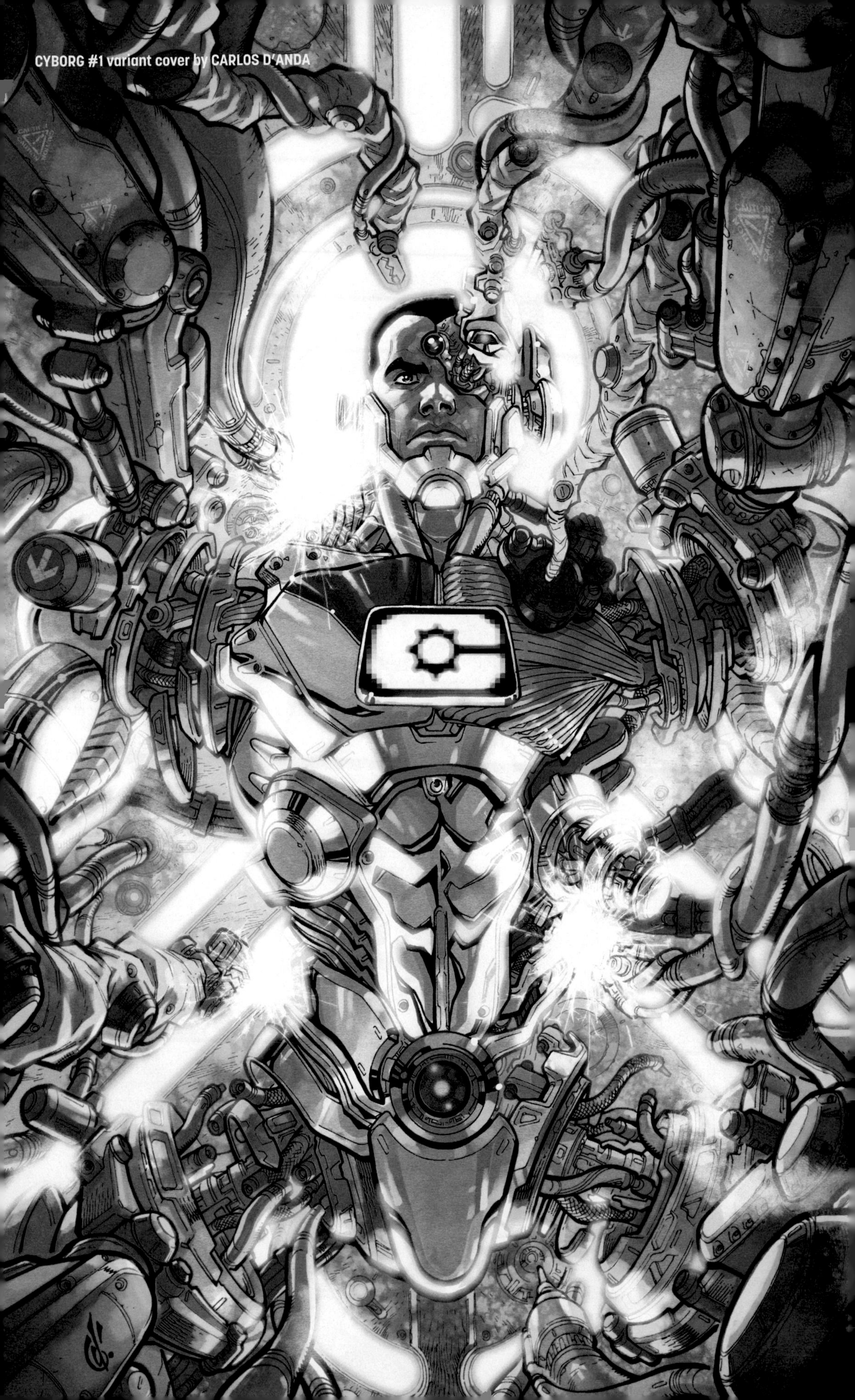

CYBORG: REBIRTH #1 variant cover by CARLOS D'ANDA

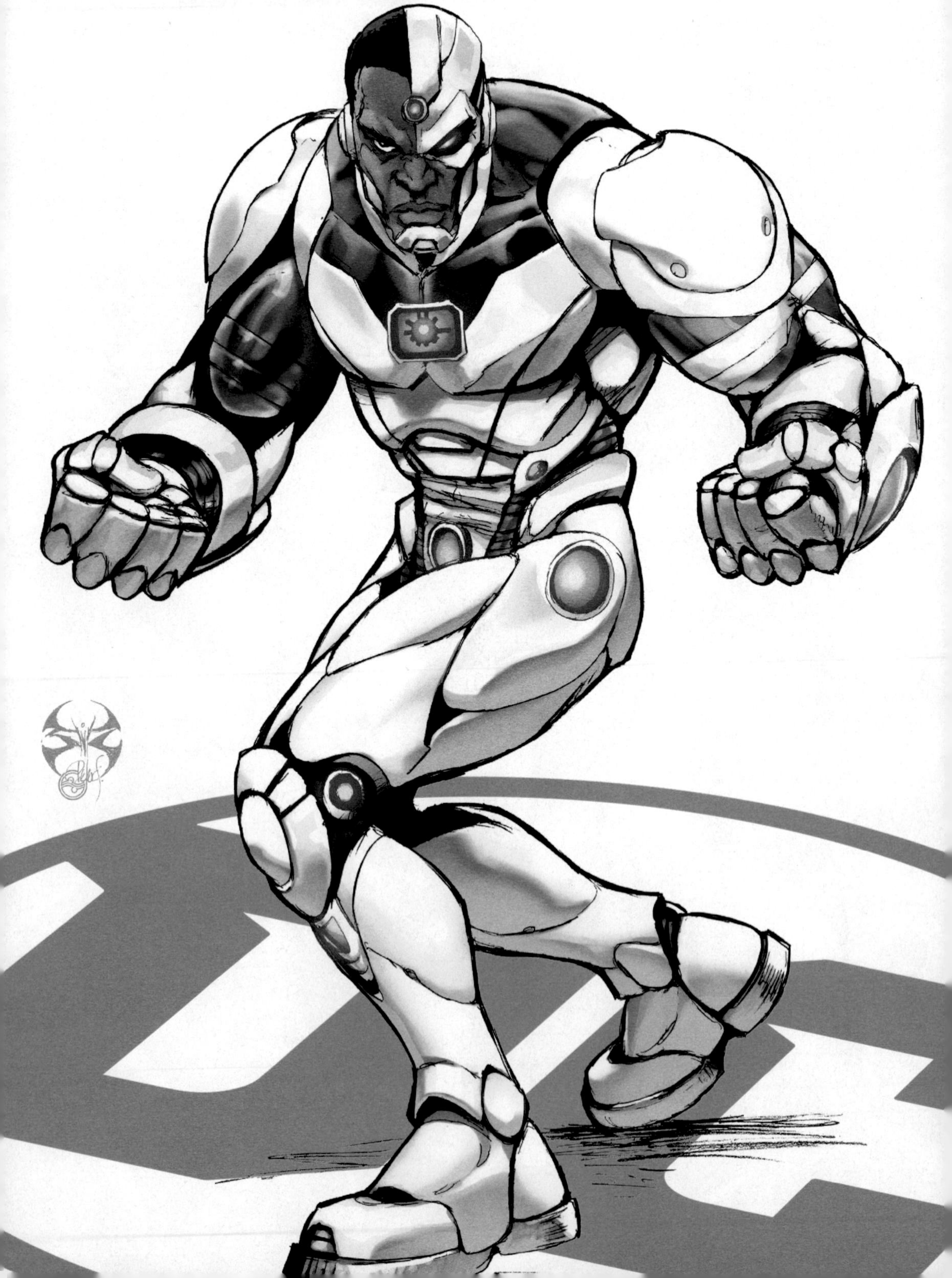

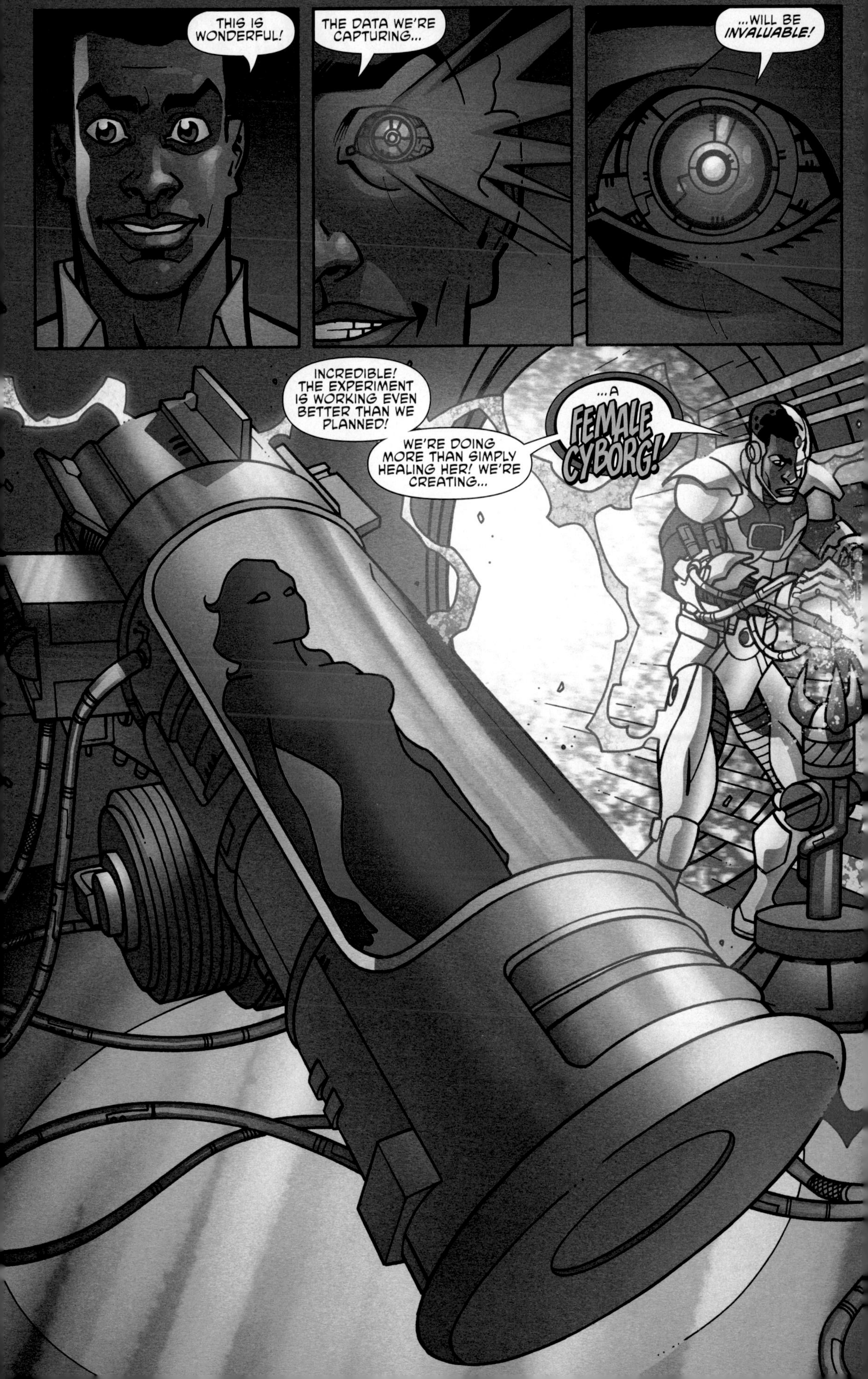
THIS IS WONDERFUL!
THE DATA WE'RE CAPTURING...
...WILL BE INVALUABLE!
INCREDIBLE! THE EXPERIMENT IS WORKING EVEN BETTER THAN WE PLANNED!
WE'RE DOING MORE THAN SIMPLY HEALING HER! WE'RE CREATING...
...A FEMALE CYBORG!

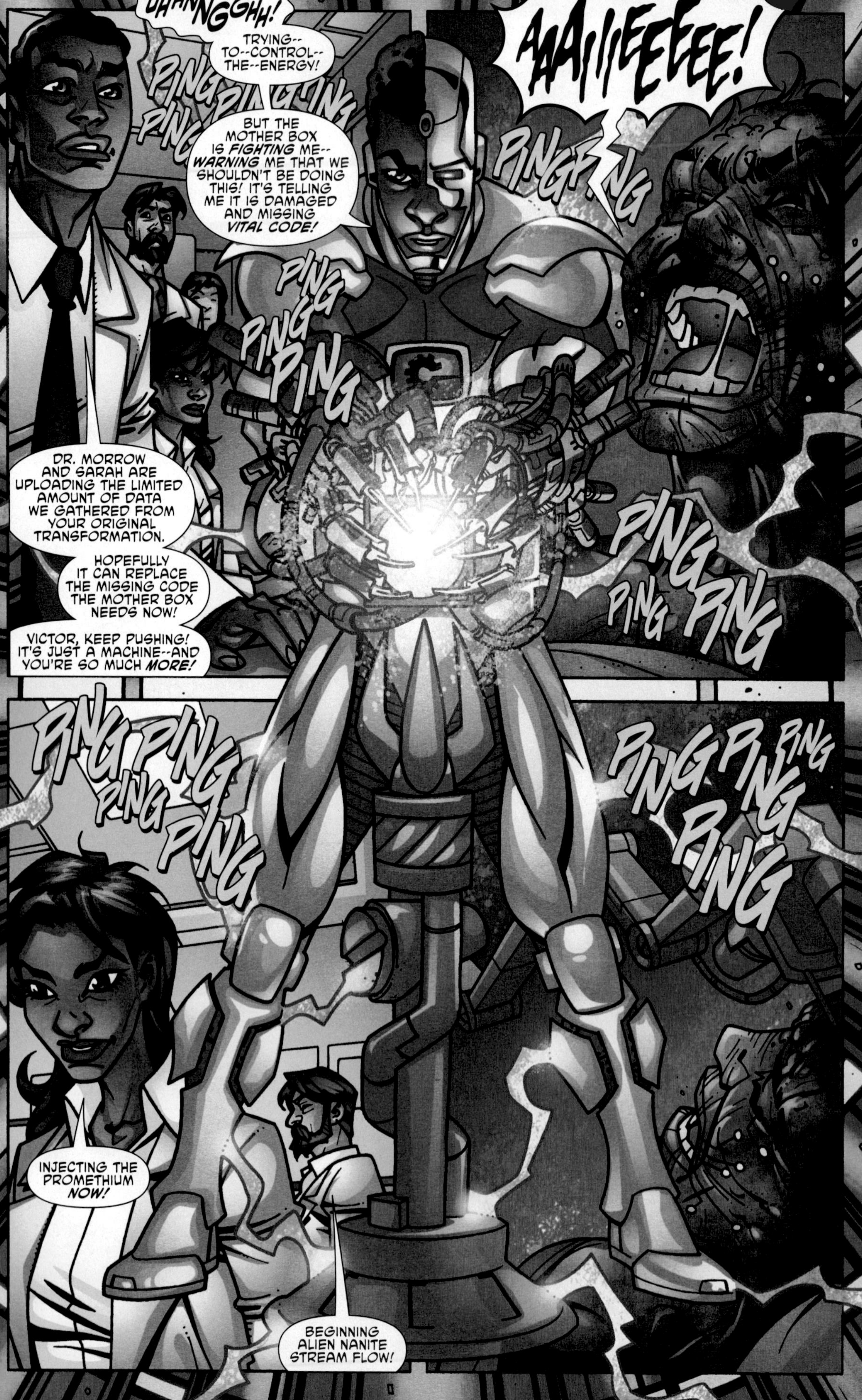

UHHNNGGHH!
TRYING-- TO--CONTROL-- THE--ENERGY!
BUT THE MOTHER BOX IS *FIGHTING* ME-- *WARNING* ME THAT WE SHOULDN'T BE DOING THIS! IT'S TELLING ME IT IS DAMAGED AND MISSING *VITAL CODE!*
AAAIIIEEEEEE!
PING PING PING PING
PING PING PING
DR. MORROW AND SARAH ARE UPLOADING THE LIMITED AMOUNT OF DATA WE GATHERED FROM YOUR ORIGINAL TRANSFORMATION.
HOPEFULLY IT CAN REPLACE THE MISSING CODE THE MOTHER BOX NEEDS NOW!
VICTOR, KEEP PUSHING! IT'S JUST A MACHINE--AND YOU'RE SO MUCH *MORE!*
PING PING PING
PING PING PING PING
PING PING PING PING PING
INJECTING THE PROMETHIUM *NOW!*
BEGINNING ALIEN NANITE STREAM FLOW!

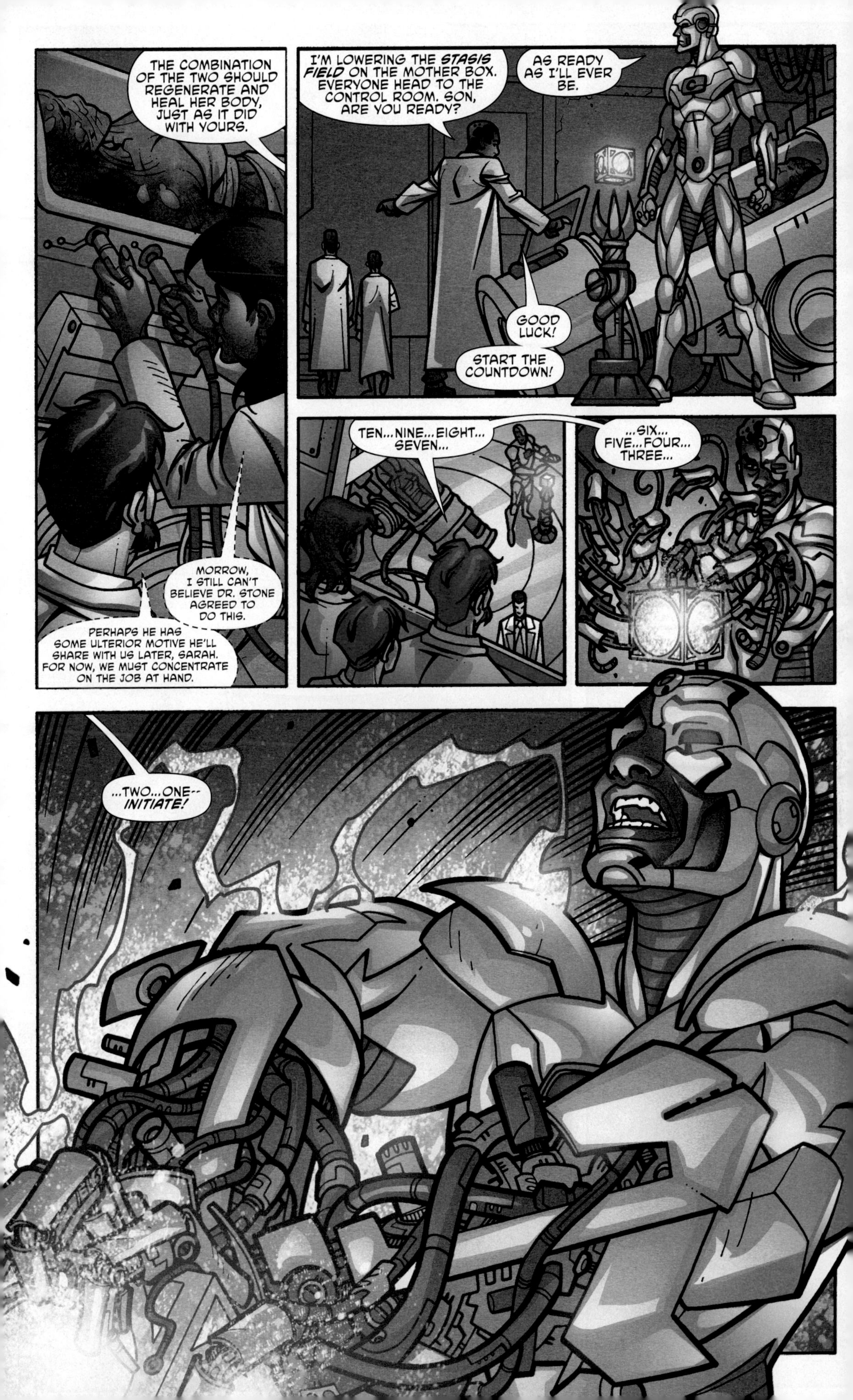

THE COMBINATION OF THE TWO SHOULD REGENERATE AND HEAL HER BODY, JUST AS IT DID WITH YOURS.
MORROW, I STILL CAN'T BELIEVE DR. STONE AGREED TO DO THIS.
PERHAPS HE HAS SOME ULTERIOR MOTIVE HE'LL SHARE WITH US LATER, SARAH. FOR NOW, WE MUST CONCENTRATE ON THE JOB AT HAND.
I'M LOWERING THE *STASIS FIELD* ON THE MOTHER BOX. EVERYONE HEAD TO THE CONTROL ROOM. SON, ARE YOU READY?
AS READY AS I'LL EVER BE.
GOOD LUCK!
START THE COUNTDOWN!
TEN...NINE...EIGHT... SEVEN...
...SIX... FIVE...FOUR... THREE...
...TWO...ONE-- *INITIATE!*

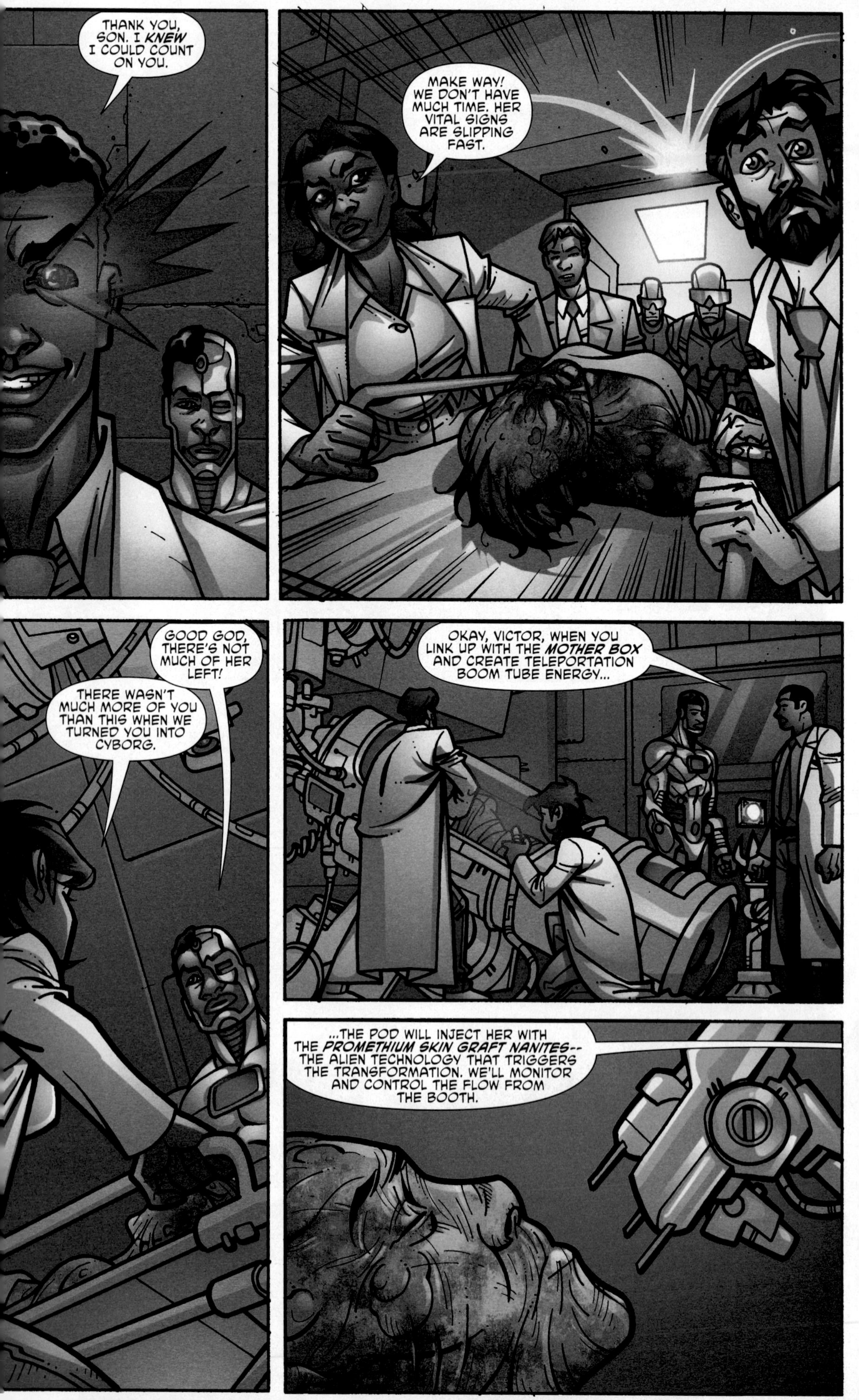
THANK YOU, SON. I *KNEW* I COULD COUNT ON YOU.
MAKE WAY! WE DON'T HAVE MUCH TIME. HER VITAL SIGNS ARE SLIPPING FAST.
GOOD GOD, THERE'S NOT MUCH OF HER LEFT!
THERE WASN'T MUCH MORE OF YOU THAN THIS WHEN WE TURNED YOU INTO CYBORG.
OKAY, VICTOR, WHEN YOU LINK UP WITH THE *MOTHER BOX* AND CREATE TELEPORTATION BOOM TUBE ENERGY...
...THE POD WILL INJECT HER WITH THE *PROMETHIUM SKIN GRAFT NANITES*-- THE ALIEN TECHNOLOGY THAT TRIGGERS THE TRANSFORMATION. WE'LL MONITOR AND CONTROL THE FLOW FROM THE BOOTH.

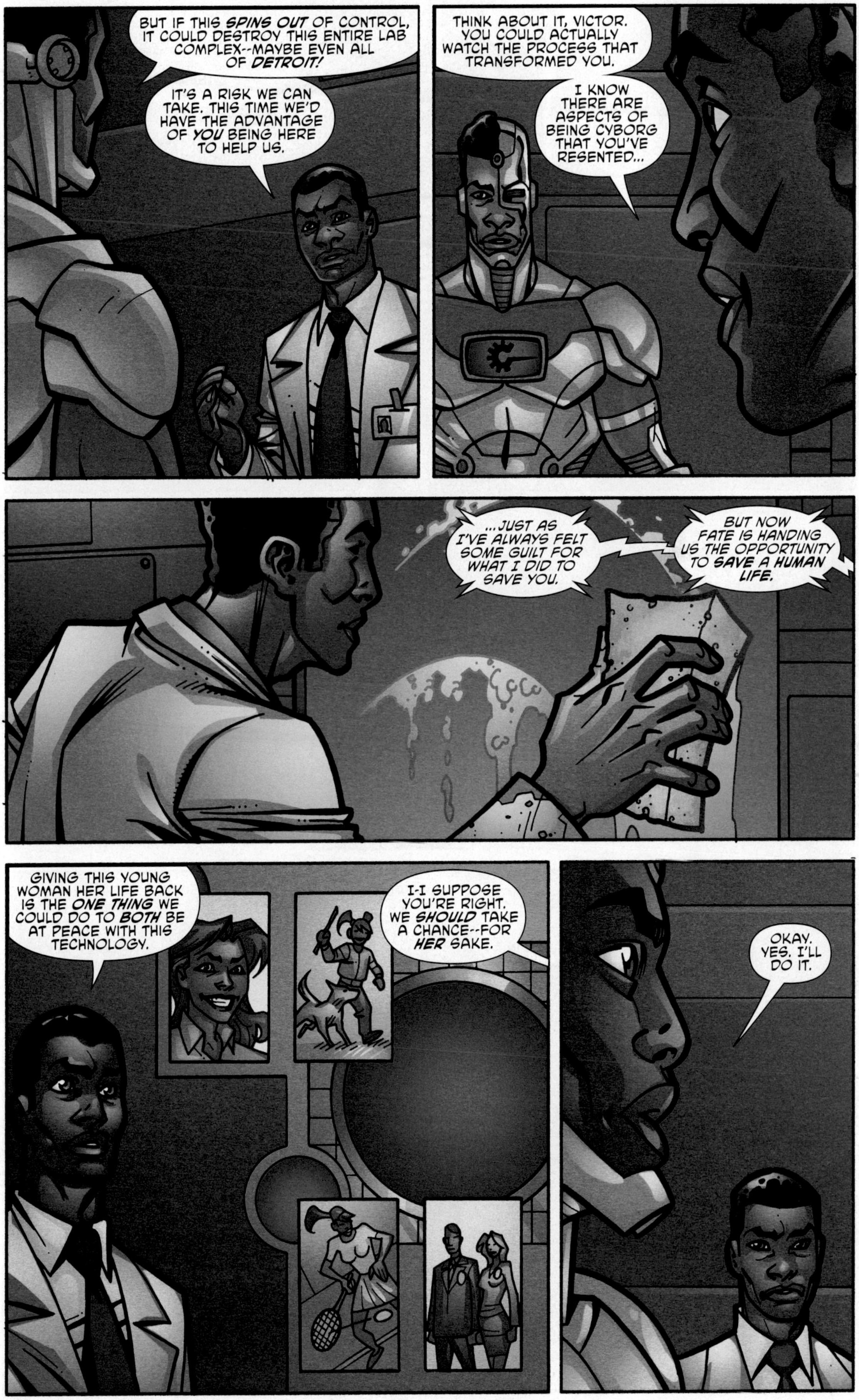
BUT IF THIS SPINS OUT OF CONTROL, IT COULD DESTROY THIS ENTIRE LAB COMPLEX--MAYBE EVEN ALL OF DETROIT!
IT'S A RISK WE CAN TAKE. THIS TIME WE'D HAVE THE ADVANTAGE OF YOU BEING HERE TO HELP US.
THINK ABOUT IT, VICTOR. YOU COULD ACTUALLY WATCH THE PROCESS THAT TRANSFORMED YOU.
I KNOW THERE ARE ASPECTS OF BEING CYBORG THAT YOU'VE RESENTED...
...JUST AS I'VE ALWAYS FELT SOME GUILT FOR WHAT I DID TO SAVE YOU.
BUT NOW FATE IS HANDING US THE OPPORTUNITY TO SAVE A HUMAN LIFE.
GIVING THIS YOUNG WOMAN HER LIFE BACK IS THE ONE THING WE COULD DO TO BOTH BE AT PEACE WITH THIS TECHNOLOGY.
I-I SUPPOSE YOU'RE RIGHT. WE SHOULD TAKE A CHANCE--FOR HER SAKE.
OKAY. YES. I'LL DO IT.

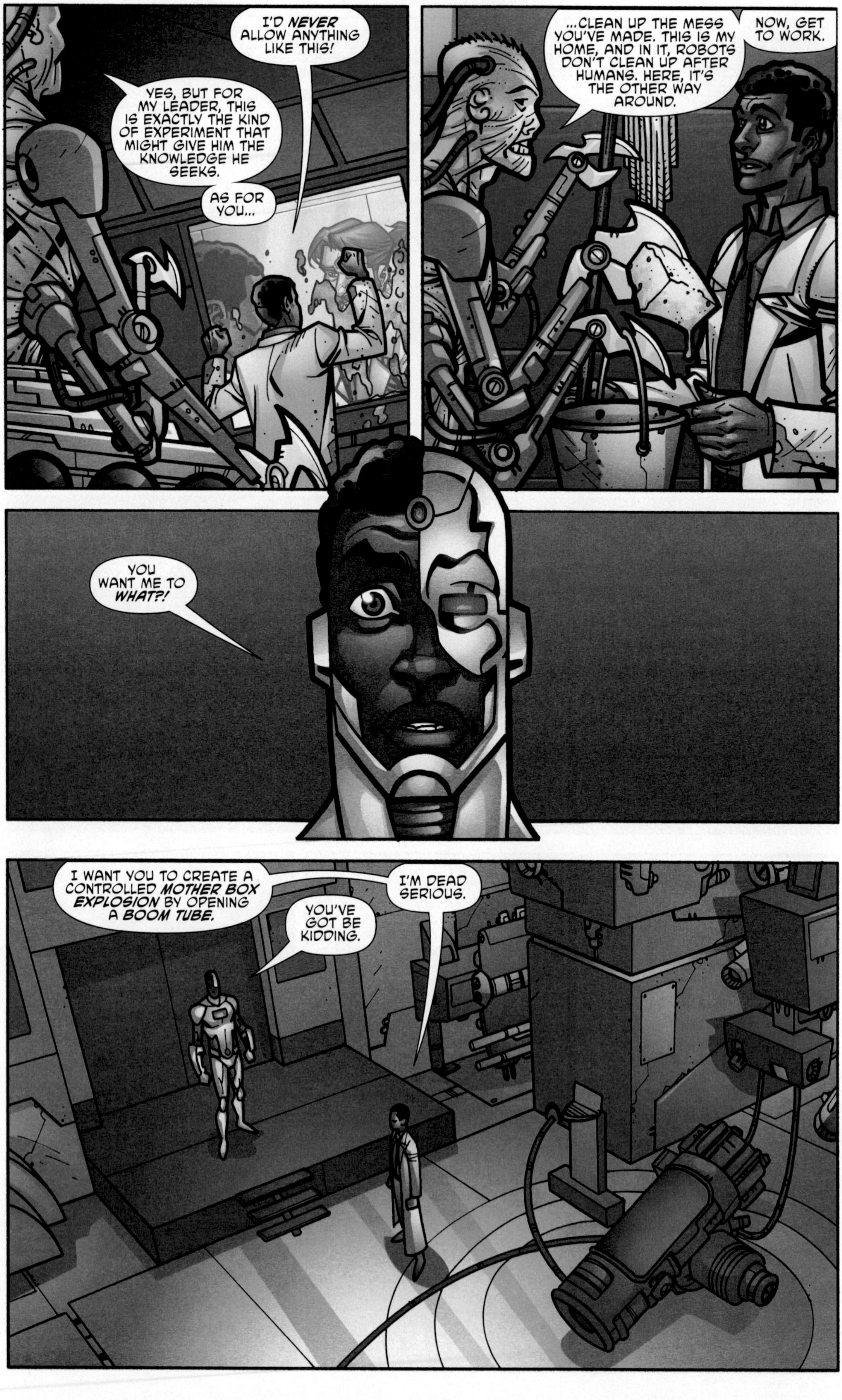
YES, BUT FOR MY LEADER, THIS IS EXACTLY THE KIND OF EXPERIMENT THAT MIGHT GIVE HIM THE KNOWLEDGE HE SEEKS.
I'D NEVER ALLOW ANYTHING LIKE THIS!
AS FOR YOU...
...CLEAN UP THE MESS YOU'VE MADE. THIS IS MY HOME, AND IN IT, ROBOTS DON'T CLEAN UP AFTER HUMANS. HERE, IT'S THE OTHER WAY AROUND.
NOW, GET TO WORK.
YOU WANT ME TO WHAT?!
I WANT YOU TO CREATE A CONTROLLED MOTHER BOX EXPLOSION BY OPENING A BOOM TUBE.
YOU'VE GOT BE KIDDING.
I'M DEAD SERIOUS.

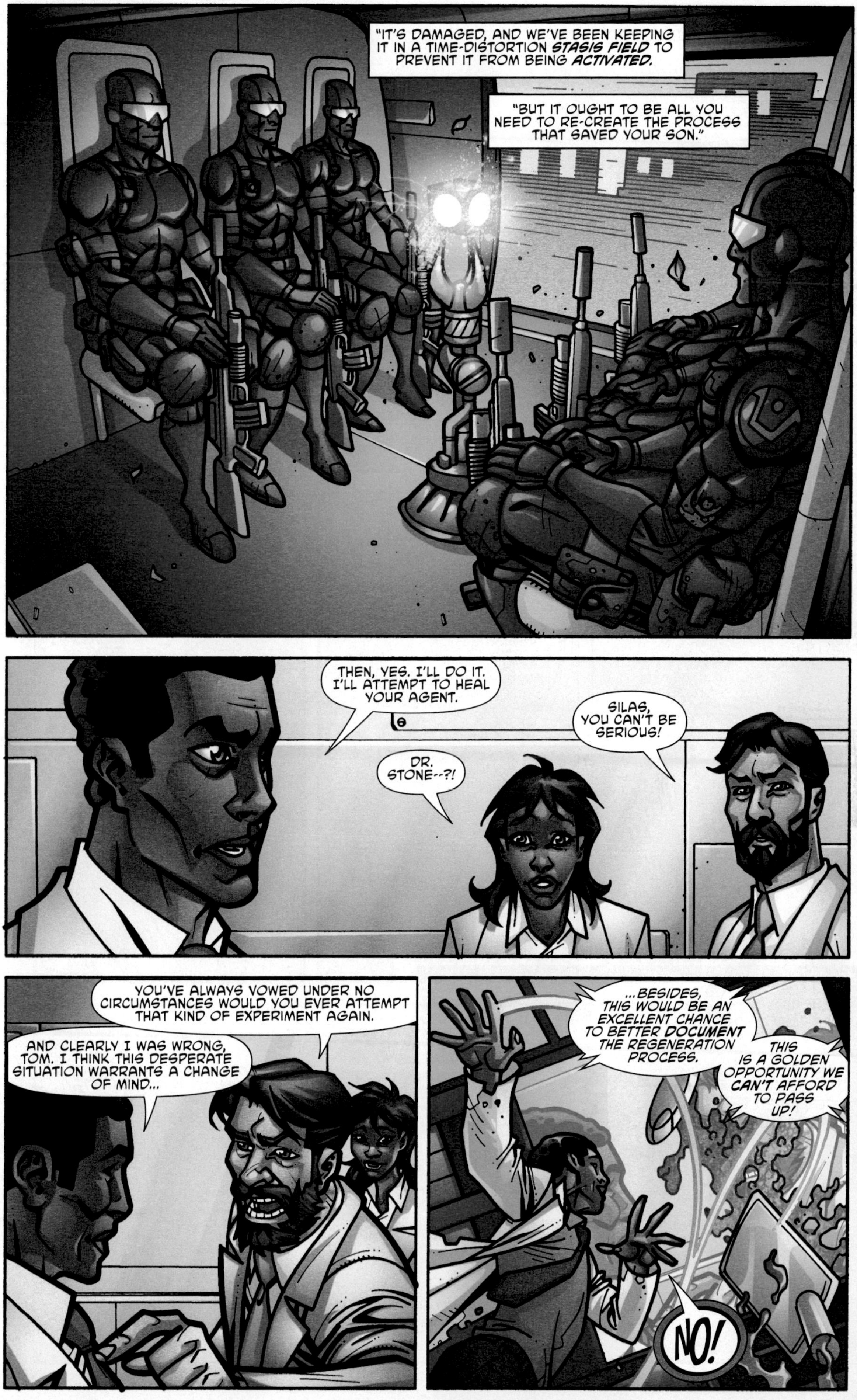
"IT'S DAMAGED, AND WE'VE BEEN KEEPING IT IN A TIME-DISTORTION *STASIS FIELD* TO PREVENT IT FROM BEING *ACTIVATED.*
"BUT IT OUGHT TO BE ALL YOU NEED TO RE-CREATE THE PROCESS THAT SAVED YOUR SON."
THEN, YES. I'LL DO IT. I'LL ATTEMPT TO HEAL YOUR AGENT.
SILAS, YOU CAN'T BE SERIOUS!
DR. STONE--?!
YOU'VE ALWAYS VOWED UNDER NO CIRCUMSTANCES WOULD YOU EVER ATTEMPT THAT KIND OF EXPERIMENT AGAIN.
AND CLEARLY I WAS WRONG, TOM. I THINK THIS DESPERATE SITUATION WARRANTS A CHANGE OF MIND...
...BESIDES, THIS WOULD BE AN EXCELLENT CHANCE TO BETTER *DOCUMENT* THE REGENERATION PROCESS.
THIS IS A GOLDEN OPPORTUNITY WE *CAN'T* AFFORD TO PASS UP!
NO!

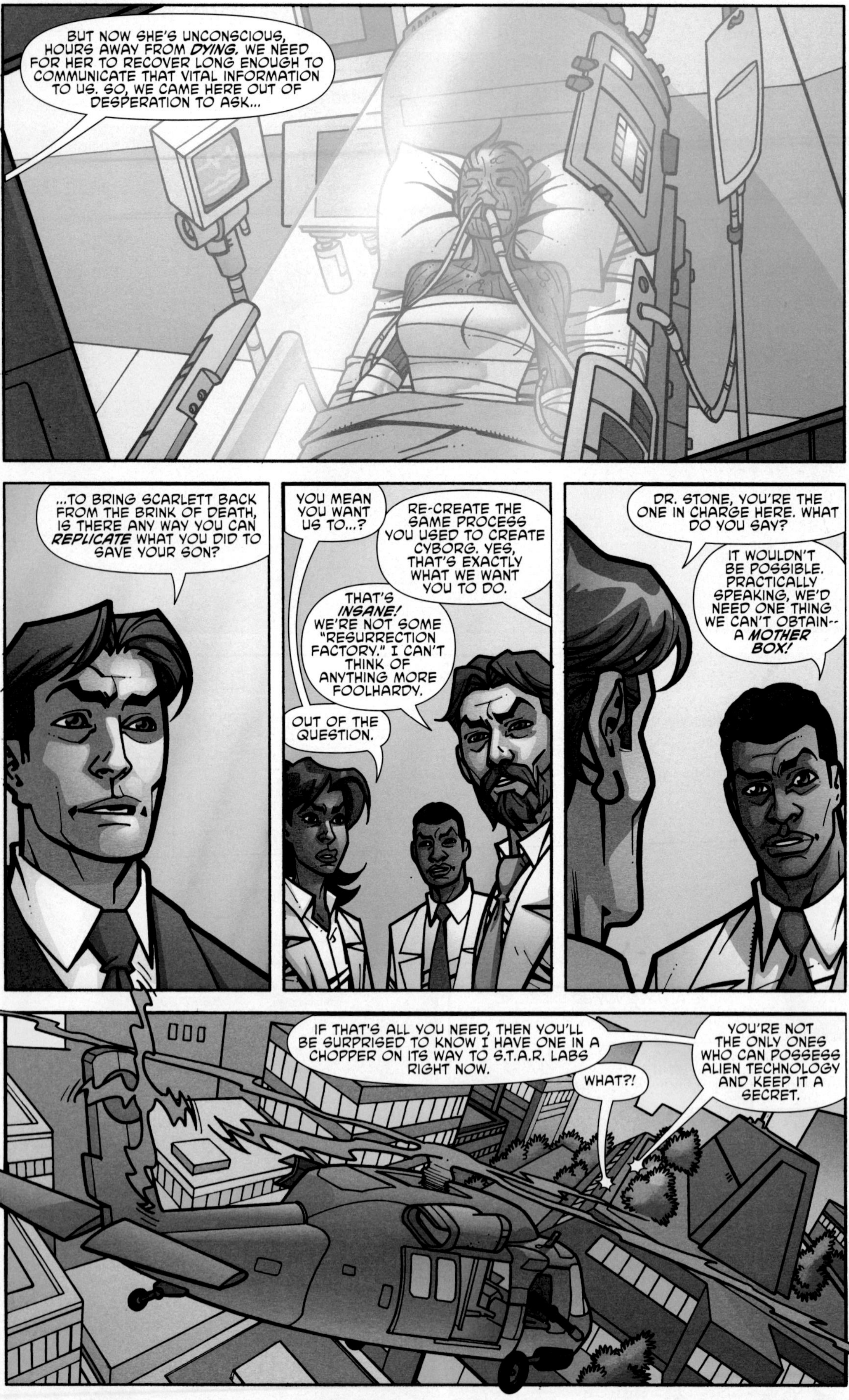
BUT NOW SHE'S UNCONSCIOUS, HOURS AWAY FROM *DYING.* WE NEED FOR HER TO RECOVER LONG ENOUGH TO COMMUNICATE THAT VITAL INFORMATION TO US. SO, WE CAME HERE OUT OF DESPERATION TO ASK...
...TO BRING SCARLETT BACK FROM THE BRINK OF DEATH, IS THERE ANY WAY YOU CAN *REPLICATE* WHAT YOU DID TO SAVE YOUR SON?
YOU MEAN YOU WANT US TO...?
RE-CREATE THE SAME PROCESS YOU USED TO CREATE CYBORG. YES, THAT'S EXACTLY WHAT WE WANT YOU TO DO.
THAT'S *INSANE!* WE'RE NOT SOME "RESURRECTION FACTORY." I CAN'T THINK OF ANYTHING MORE FOOLHARDY.
OUT OF THE QUESTION.
DR. STONE, YOU'RE THE ONE IN CHARGE HERE. WHAT DO YOU SAY?
IT WOULDN'T BE POSSIBLE. PRACTICALLY SPEAKING, WE'D NEED ONE THING WE CAN'T OBTAIN-- A *MOTHER BOX!*
IF THAT'S ALL YOU NEED, THEN YOU'LL BE SURPRISED TO KNOW I HAVE ONE IN A CHOPPER ON ITS WAY TO S.T.A.R. LABS RIGHT NOW.
WHAT?!
YOU'RE NOT THE ONLY ONES WHO CAN POSSESS ALIEN TECHNOLOGY AND KEEP IT A SECRET.

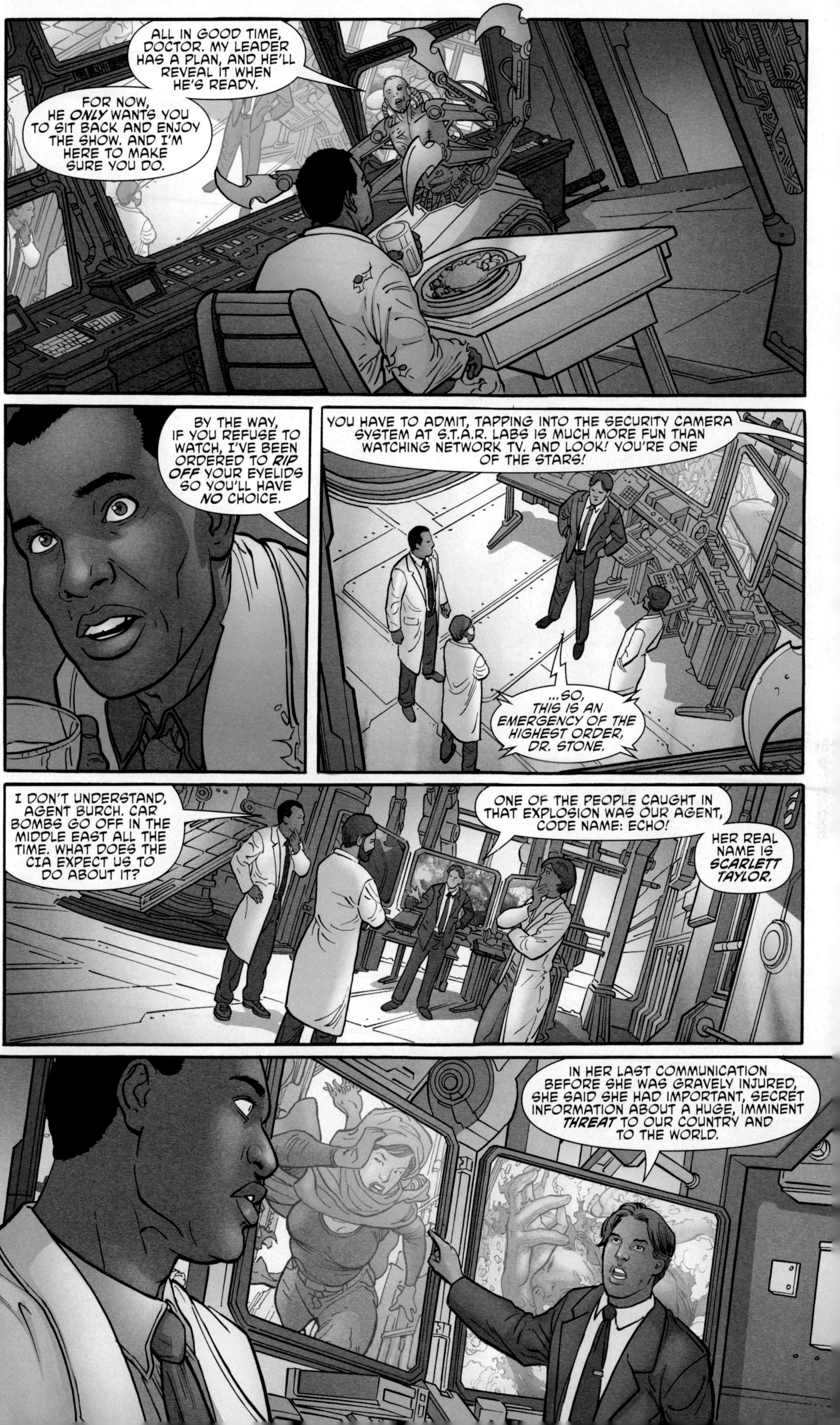
ALL IN GOOD TIME, DOCTOR. MY LEADER HAS A PLAN, AND HE'LL REVEAL IT WHEN HE'S READY.
FOR NOW, HE ONLY WANTS YOU TO SIT BACK AND ENJOY THE SHOW. AND I'M HERE TO MAKE SURE YOU DO.
BY THE WAY, IF YOU REFUSE TO WATCH, I'VE BEEN ORDERED TO RIP OFF YOUR EYELIDS SO YOU'LL HAVE NO CHOICE.
YOU HAVE TO ADMIT, TAPPING INTO THE SECURITY CAMERA SYSTEM AT S.T.A.R. LABS IS MUCH MORE FUN THAN WATCHING NETWORK TV. AND LOOK! YOU'RE ONE OF THE STARS!
...SO, THIS IS AN EMERGENCY OF THE HIGHEST ORDER, DR. STONE.
I DON'T UNDERSTAND, AGENT BURCH. CAR BOMBS GO OFF IN THE MIDDLE EAST ALL THE TIME. WHAT DOES THE CIA EXPECT US TO DO ABOUT IT?
ONE OF THE PEOPLE CAUGHT IN THAT EXPLOSION WAS OUR AGENT, CODE NAME: ECHO!
HER REAL NAME IS SCARLETT TAYLOR.
IN HER LAST COMMUNICATION BEFORE SHE WAS GRAVELY INJURED, SHE SAID SHE HAD IMPORTANT, SECRET INFORMATION ABOUT A HUGE, IMMINENT THREAT TO OUR COUNTRY AND TO THE WORLD.

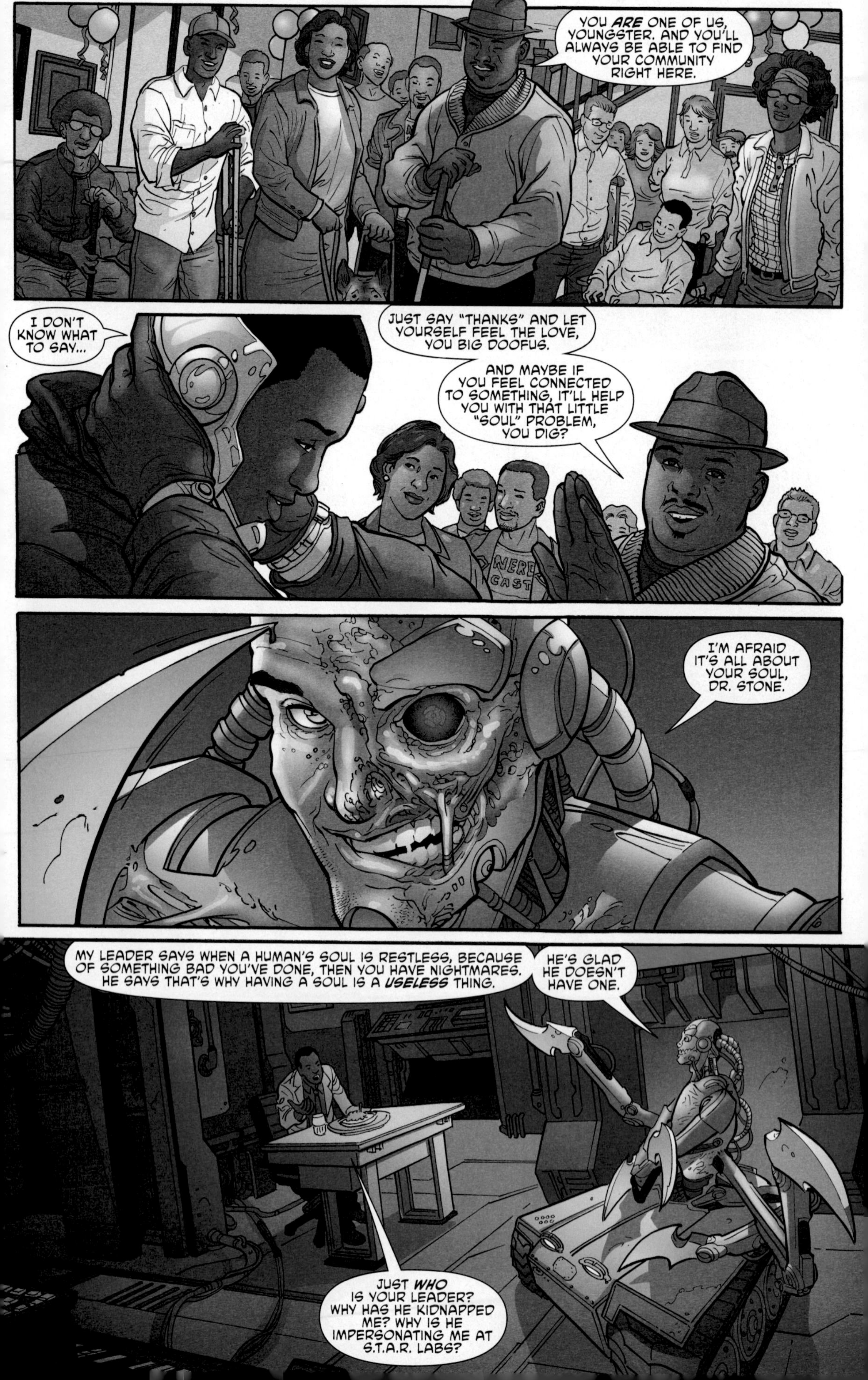

YOU ARE ONE OF US, YOUNGSTER. AND YOU'LL ALWAYS BE ABLE TO FIND YOUR COMMUNITY RIGHT HERE.
I DON'T KNOW WHAT TO SAY...
JUST SAY "THANKS" AND LET YOURSELF FEEL THE LOVE, YOU BIG DOOFUS.
AND MAYBE IF YOU FEEL CONNECTED TO SOMETHING, IT'LL HELP YOU WITH THAT LITTLE "SOUL" PROBLEM, YOU DIG?
NERD CAST
I'M AFRAID IT'S ALL ABOUT YOUR SOUL, DR. STONE.
MY LEADER SAYS WHEN A HUMAN'S SOUL IS RESTLESS, BECAUSE OF SOMETHING BAD YOU'VE DONE, THEN YOU HAVE NIGHTMARES. HE SAYS THAT'S WHY HAVING A SOUL IS A USELESS THING.
HE'S GLAD HE DOESN'T HAVE ONE.
JUST WHO IS YOUR LEADER? WHY HAS HE KIDNAPPED ME? WHY IS HE IMPERSONATING ME AT S.T.A.R. LABS?

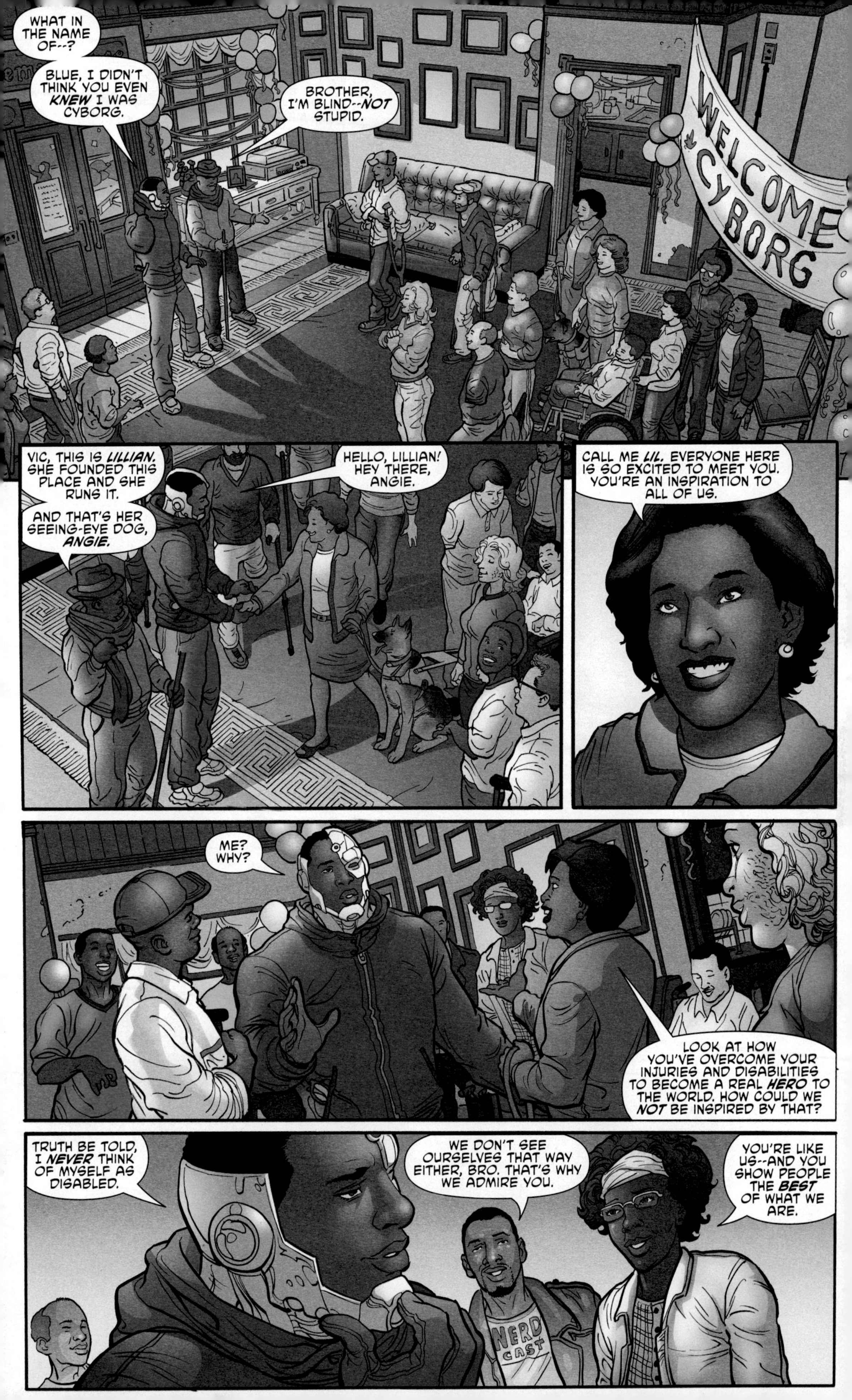
WHAT IN THE NAME OF--?
BLUE, I DIDN'T THINK YOU EVEN *KNEW* I WAS CYBORG.
BROTHER, I'M BLIND--*NOT* STUPID.
WELCOME CYBORG
VIC, THIS IS *LILLIAN.* SHE FOUNDED THIS PLACE AND SHE RUNS IT.
AND THAT'S HER SEEING-EYE DOG, *ANGIE.*
HELLO, LILLIAN! HEY THERE, ANGIE.
CALL ME *LIL.* EVERYONE HERE IS SO EXCITED TO MEET YOU. YOU'RE AN INSPIRATION TO ALL OF US.
ME? WHY?
LOOK AT HOW YOU'VE OVERCOME YOUR INJURIES AND DISABILITIES TO BECOME A REAL *HERO* TO THE WORLD. HOW COULD WE *NOT* BE INSPIRED BY THAT?
TRUTH BE TOLD, I *NEVER* THINK OF MYSELF AS DISABLED.
WE DON'T SEE OURSELVES THAT WAY EITHER, BRO. THAT'S WHY WE ADMIRE YOU.
YOU'RE LIKE US--AND YOU SHOW PEOPLE THE *BEST* OF WHAT WE ARE.
NERD CAST

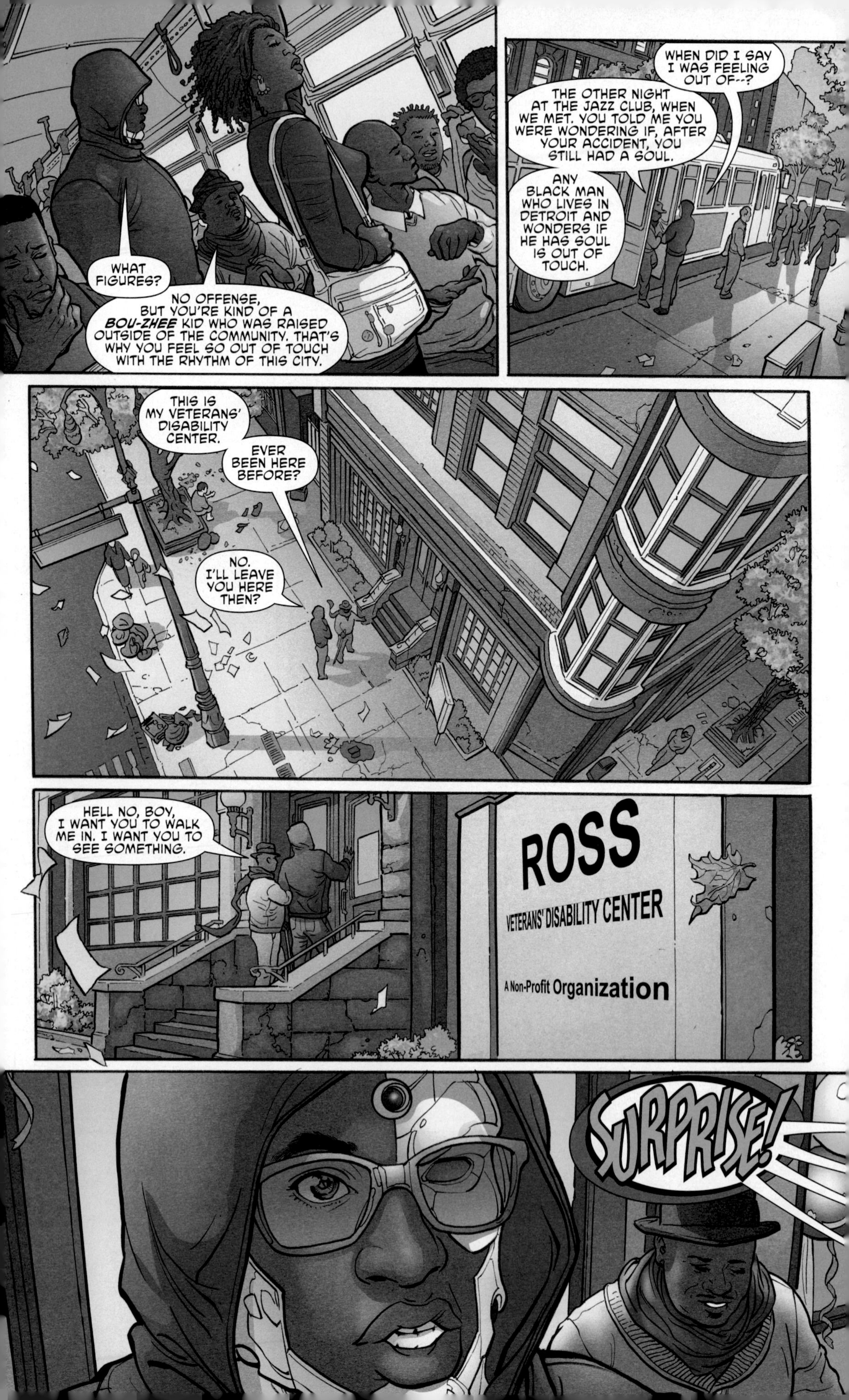
WHAT FIGURES?
NO OFFENSE, BUT YOU'RE KIND OF A BOU-ZHEE KID WHO WAS RAISED OUTSIDE OF THE COMMUNITY. THAT'S WHY YOU FEEL SO OUT OF TOUCH WITH THE RHYTHM OF THIS CITY.
WHEN DID I SAY I WAS FEELING OUT OF--?
THE OTHER NIGHT AT THE JAZZ CLUB, WHEN WE MET. YOU TOLD ME YOU WERE WONDERING IF, AFTER YOUR ACCIDENT, YOU STILL HAD A SOUL.
ANY BLACK MAN WHO LIVES IN DETROIT AND WONDERS IF HE HAS SOUL IS OUT OF TOUCH.
THIS IS MY VETERANS' DISABILITY CENTER.
EVER BEEN HERE BEFORE?
NO. I'LL LEAVE YOU HERE THEN?
HELL NO, BOY, I WANT YOU TO WALK ME IN. I WANT YOU TO SEE SOMETHING.
ROSS
VETERANS' DISABILITY CENTER
A Non-Profit Organization
SURPRISE!

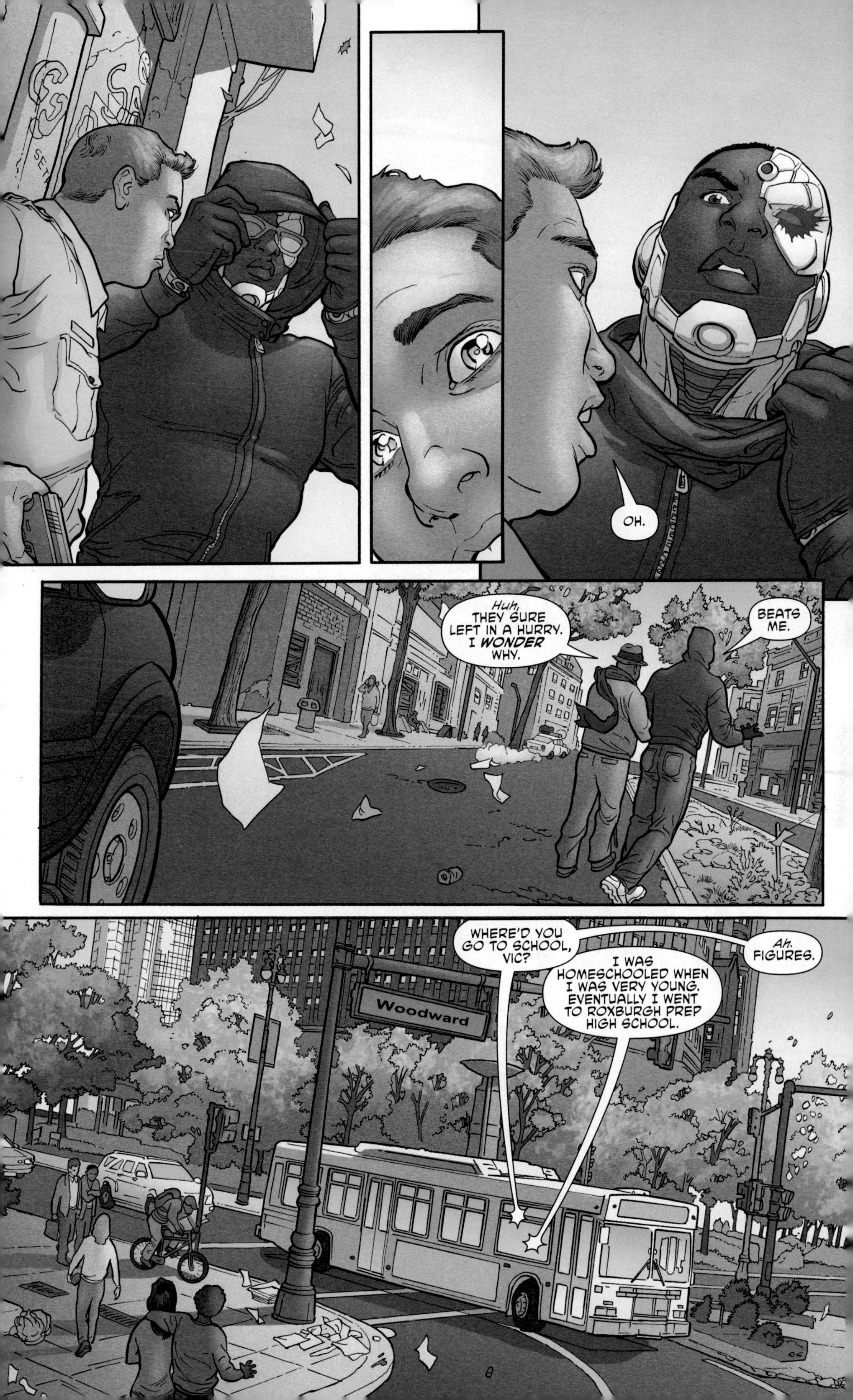
OH.
Huh, THEY SURE LEFT IN A HURRY. I WONDER WHY.
BEATS ME.
Woodward
WHERE'D YOU GO TO SCHOOL, VIC?
I WAS HOMESCHOOLED WHEN I WAS VERY YOUNG. EVENTUALLY I WENT TO ROXBURGH PREP HIGH SCHOOL.
Ah. FIGURES.

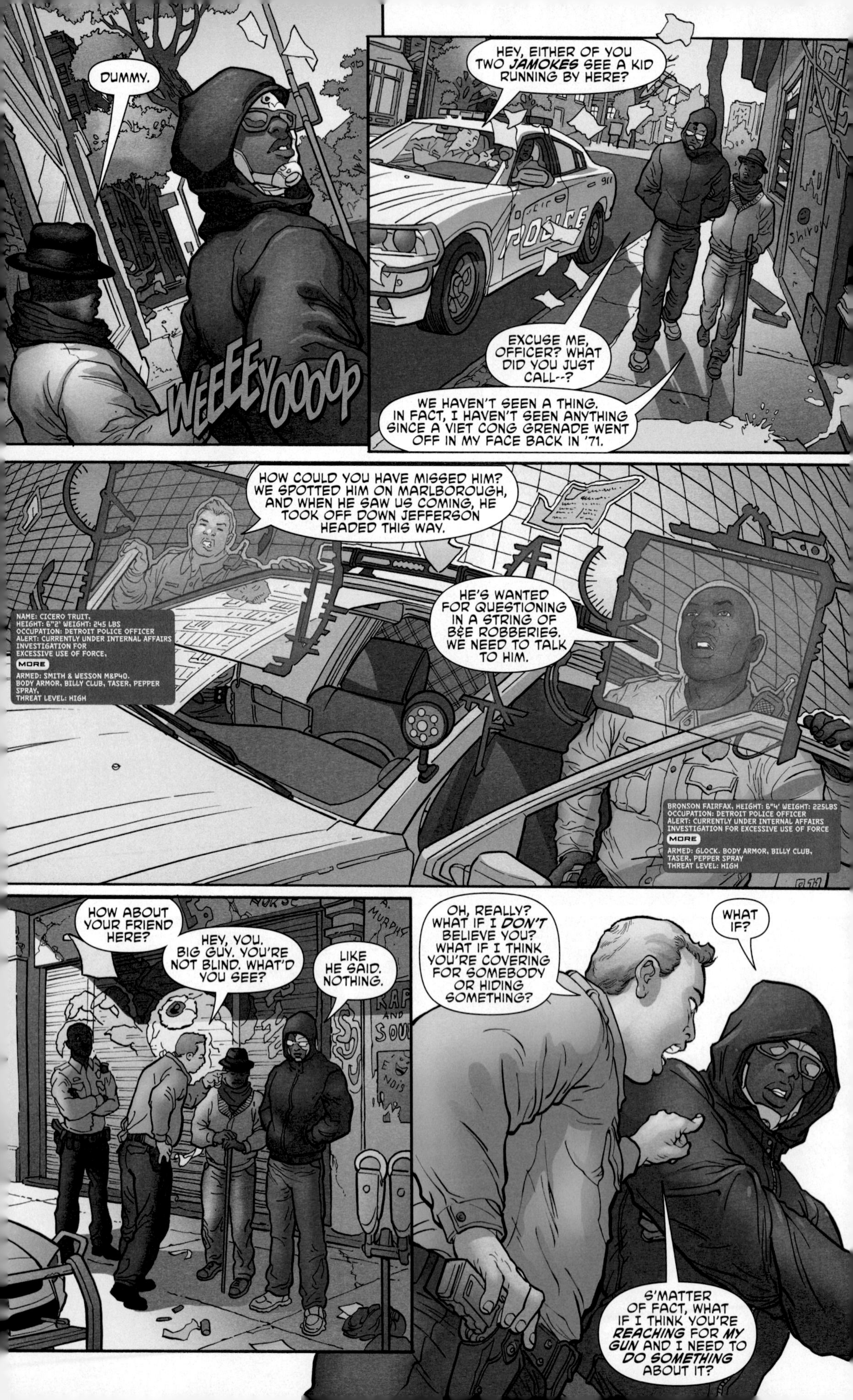
DUMMY.
WEEEEYOOOOP
HEY, EITHER OF YOU TWO JAMOKES SEE A KID RUNNING BY HERE?
EXCUSE ME, OFFICER? WHAT DID YOU JUST CALL--?
WE HAVEN'T SEEN A THING. IN FACT, I HAVEN'T SEEN ANYTHING SINCE A VIET CONG GRENADE WENT OFF IN MY FACE BACK IN '71.
HOW COULD YOU HAVE MISSED HIM? WE SPOTTED HIM ON MARLBOROUGH, AND WHEN HE SAW US COMING, HE TOOK OFF DOWN JEFFERSON HEADED THIS WAY.
NAME: CICERO TRUIT,
HEIGHT: 6"2' WEIGHT: 245 LBS
OCCUPATION: DETROIT POLICE OFFICER
ALERT: CURRENTLY UNDER INTERNAL AFFAIRS INVESTIGATION FOR EXCESSIVE USE OF FORCE,
MORE
ARMED: SMITH & WESSON M&P40.
BODY ARMOR, BILLY CLUB, TASER, PEPPER SPRAY,
THREAT LEVEL: HIGH
HE'S WANTED FOR QUESTIONING IN A STRING OF B&E ROBBERIES. WE NEED TO TALK TO HIM.
BRONSON FAIRFAX, HEIGHT: 6"4' WEIGHT: 225LBS
OCCUPATION: DETROIT POLICE OFFICER
ALERT: CURRENTLY UNDER INTERNAL AFFAIRS INVESTIGATION FOR EXCESSIVE USE OF FORCE
MORE
ARMED: GLOCK. BODY ARMOR, BILLY CLUB, TASER, PEPPER SPRAY
THREAT LEVEL: HIGH
HOW ABOUT YOUR FRIEND HERE?
HEY, YOU. BIG GUY. YOU'RE NOT BLIND. WHAT'D YOU SEE?
LIKE HE SAID. NOTHING.
OH, REALLY? WHAT IF I DON'T BELIEVE YOU? WHAT IF I THINK YOU'RE COVERING FOR SOMEBODY OR HIDING SOMETHING?
WHAT IF?
S'MATTER OF FACT, WHAT IF I THINK YOU'RE REACHING FOR MY GUN AND I NEED TO DO SOMETHING ABOUT IT?

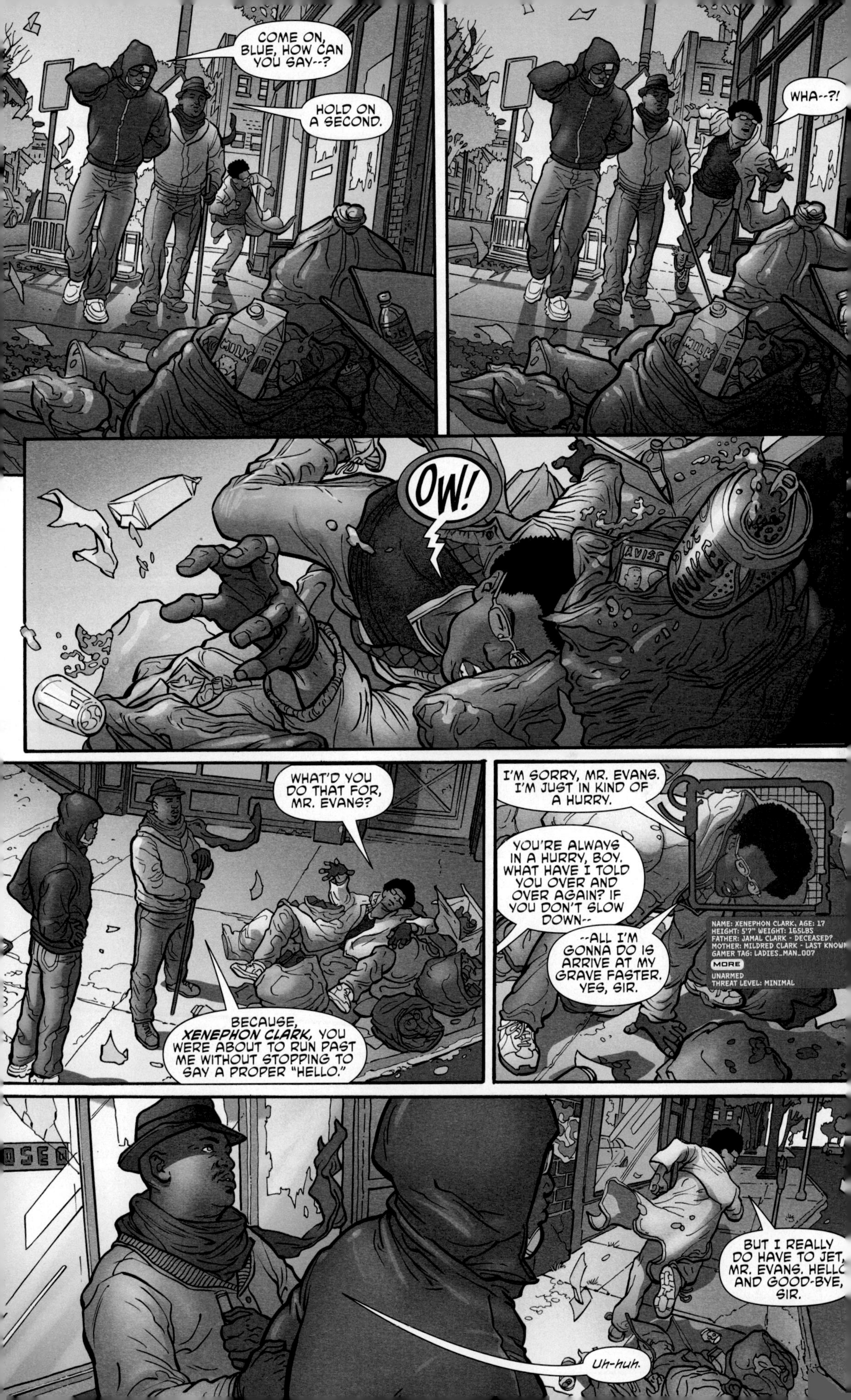

COME ON, BLUE, HOW CAN YOU SAY--?
HOLD ON A SECOND.
WHA--?!
OW!
WHAT'D YOU DO THAT FOR, MR. EVANS?
BECAUSE, *XENEPHON CLARK,* YOU WERE ABOUT TO RUN PAST ME WITHOUT STOPPING TO SAY A PROPER "HELLO."
I'M SORRY, MR. EVANS. I'M JUST IN KIND OF A HURRY.
YOU'RE ALWAYS IN A HURRY, BOY. WHAT HAVE I TOLD YOU OVER AND OVER AGAIN? IF YOU DON'T SLOW DOWN--
--ALL I'M GONNA DO IS ARRIVE AT MY GRAVE FASTER. YES, SIR.
NAME: XENEPHON CLARK, AGE: 17
HEIGHT: 5'7" WEIGHT: 165LBS
FATHER: JAMAL CLARK - DECEASED?
MOTHER: MILDRED CLARK - LAST KNOWN
GAMER TAG: LADIES_MAN_007
MORE
UNARMED
THREAT LEVEL: MINIMAL
BUT I REALLY DO HAVE TO JET, MR. EVANS. HELLO AND GOOD-BYE, SIR.
Uh-huh.

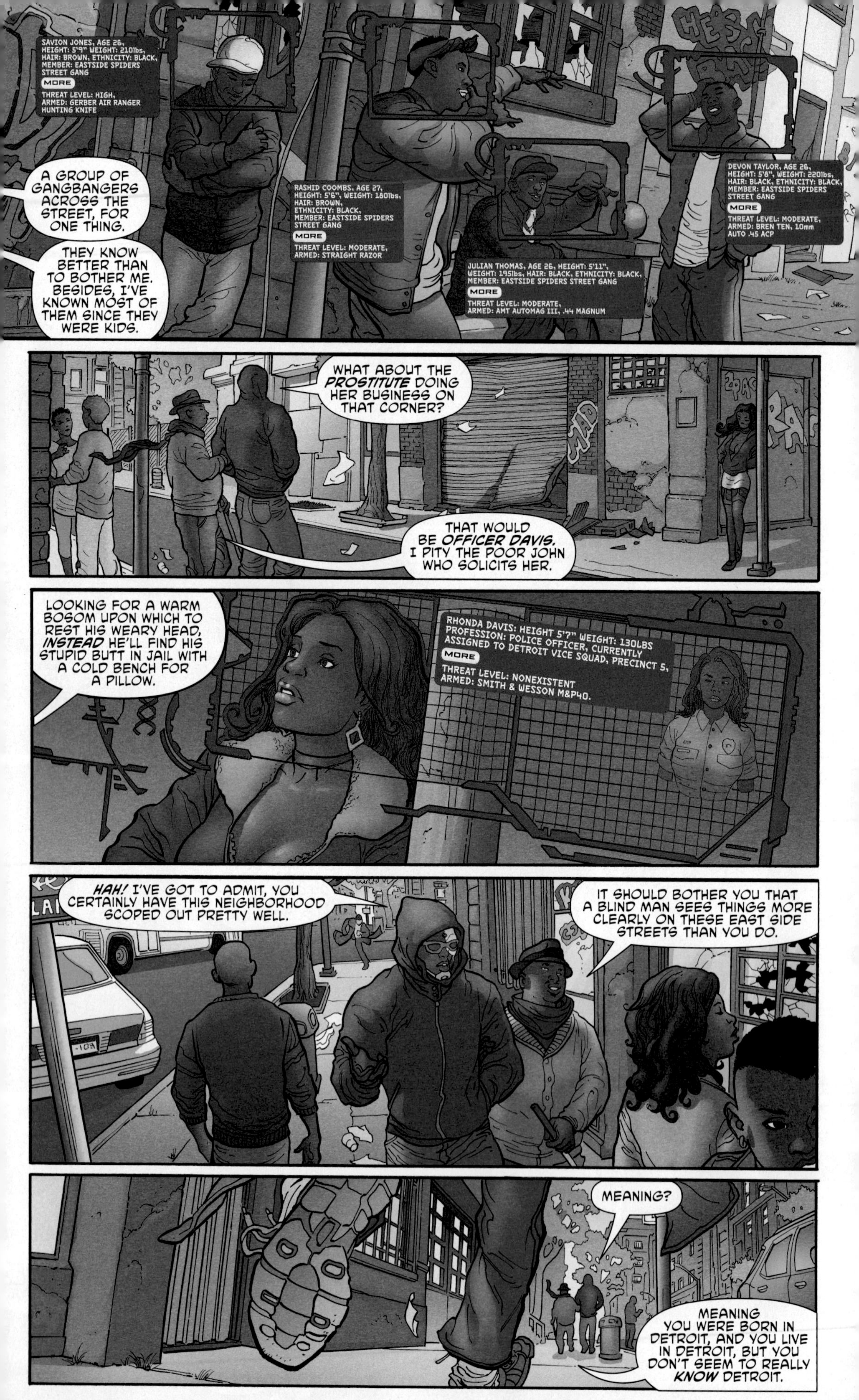
SAVION JONES, AGE 26, HEIGHT: 5'9" WEIGHT: 210lbs, HAIR: BROWN, ETHNICITY: BLACK, MEMBER: EASTSIDE SPIDERS STREET GANG
MORE
THREAT LEVEL: HIGH, ARMED: GERBER AIR RANGER HUNTING KNIFE
A GROUP OF GANGBANGERS ACROSS THE STREET, FOR ONE THING.
THEY KNOW BETTER THAN TO BOTHER ME. BESIDES, I'VE KNOWN MOST OF THEM SINCE THEY WERE KIDS.
RASHID COOMBS, AGE 27, HEIGHT: 5'6", WEIGHT: 180lbs, HAIR: BROWN, ETHNICITY: BLACK, MEMBER: EASTSIDE SPIDERS STREET GANG
MORE
THREAT LEVEL: MODERATE, ARMED: STRAIGHT RAZOR
JULIAN THOMAS, AGE 26, HEIGHT: 5'11", WEIGHT: 195lbs, HAIR: BLACK, ETHNICITY: BLACK, MEMBER: EASTSIDE SPIDERS STREET GANG
MORE
THREAT LEVEL: MODERATE, ARMED: AMT AUTOMAG III, .44 MAGNUM
DEVON TAYLOR, AGE 26, HEIGHT: 5'8", WEIGHT: 220lbs, HAIR: BLACK, ETHNICITY: BLACK, MEMBER: EASTSIDE SPIDERS STREET GANG
MORE
THREAT LEVEL: MODERATE, ARMED: BREN TEN, 10mm AUTO .45 ACP
WHAT ABOUT THE PROSTITUTE DOING HER BUSINESS ON THAT CORNER?
THAT WOULD BE OFFICER DAVIS. I PITY THE POOR JOHN WHO SOLICITS HER.
LOOKING FOR A WARM BOSOM UPON WHICH TO REST HIS WEARY HEAD, INSTEAD HE'LL FIND HIS STUPID BUTT IN JAIL WITH A COLD BENCH FOR A PILLOW.
RHONDA DAVIS: HEIGHT 5'7" WEIGHT: 130LBS PROFESSION: POLICE OFFICER, CURRENTLY ASSIGNED TO DETROIT VICE SQUAD, PRECINCT 5.
MORE
THREAT LEVEL: NONEXISTENT ARMED: SMITH & WESSON M&P40.
HAH! I'VE GOT TO ADMIT, YOU CERTAINLY HAVE THIS NEIGHBORHOOD SCOPED OUT PRETTY WELL.
IT SHOULD BOTHER YOU THAT A BLIND MAN SEES THINGS MORE CLEARLY ON THESE EAST SIDE STREETS THAN YOU DO.
MEANING?
MEANING YOU WERE BORN IN DETROIT, AND YOU LIVE IN DETROIT, BUT YOU DON'T SEEM TO REALLY KNOW DETROIT.

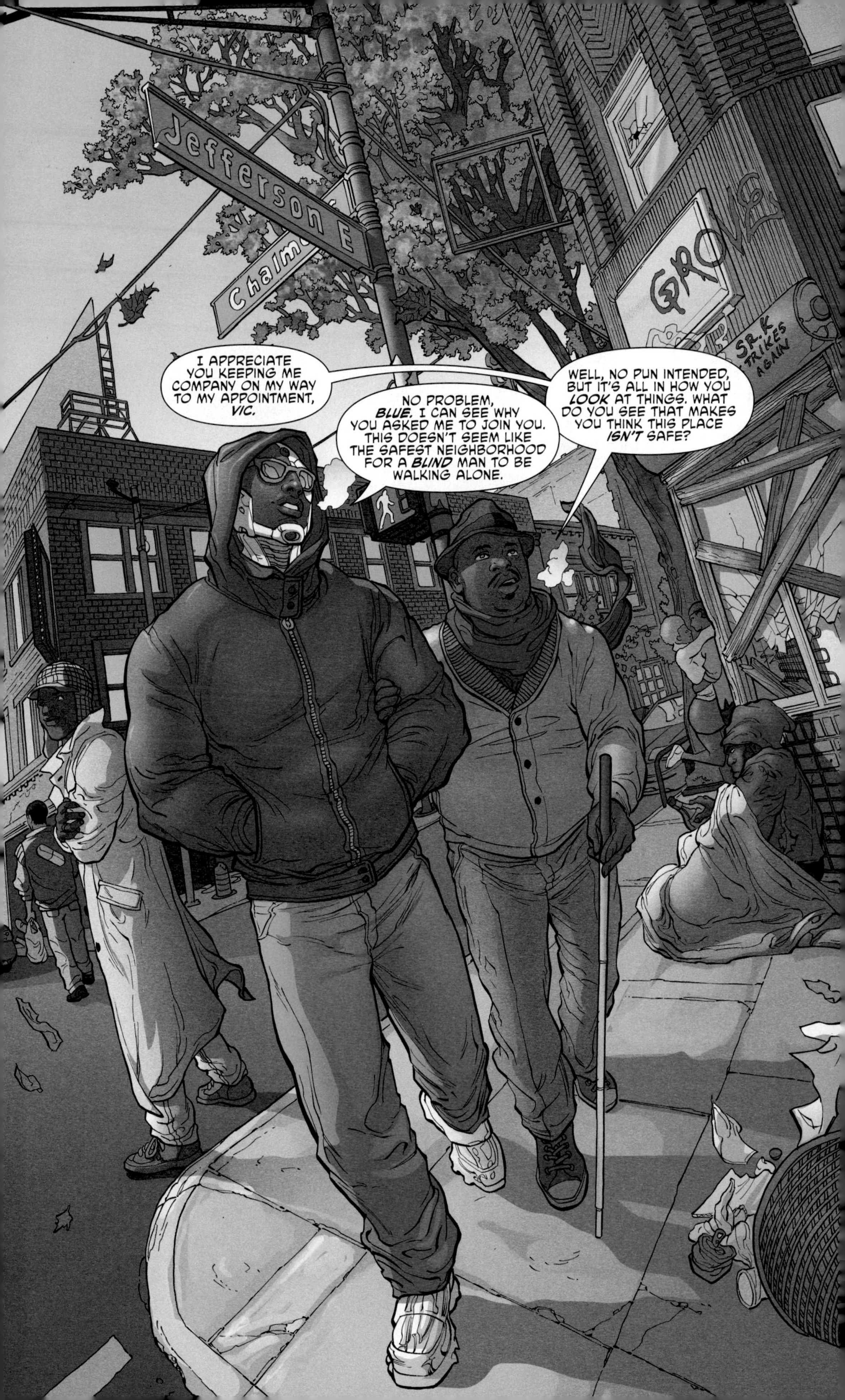
Jefferson E
Chalm
GROVE
SR. K TRIKES AGAIN
I APPRECIATE YOU KEEPING ME COMPANY ON MY WAY TO MY APPOINTMENT, VIC.
NO PROBLEM, BLUE. I CAN SEE WHY YOU ASKED ME TO JOIN YOU. THIS DOESN'T SEEM LIKE THE SAFEST NEIGHBORHOOD FOR A BLIND MAN TO BE WALKING ALONE.
WELL, NO PUN INTENDED, BUT IT'S ALL IN HOW YOU LOOK AT THINGS. WHAT DO YOU SEE THAT MAKES YOU THINK THIS PLACE ISN'T SAFE?

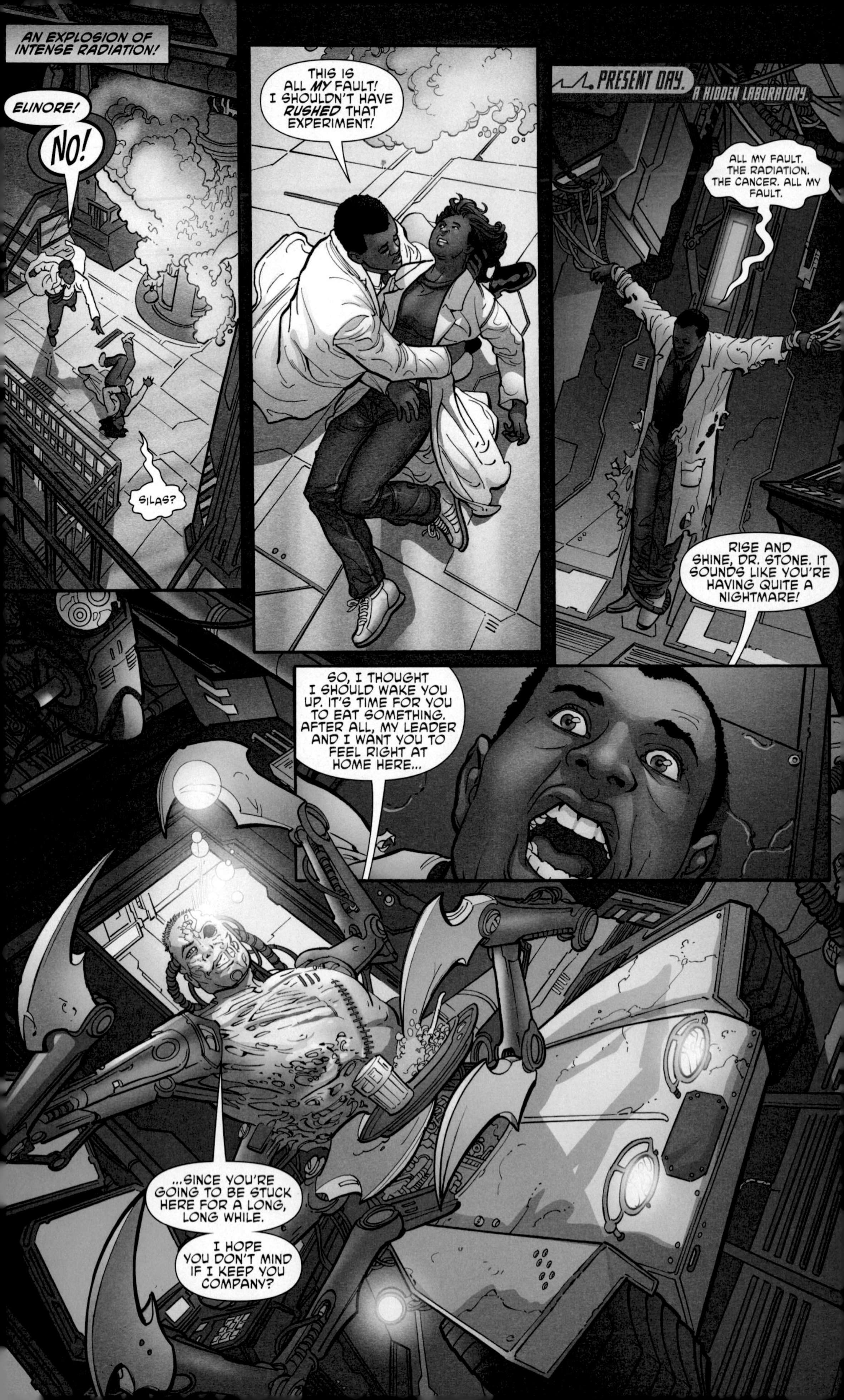
AN EXPLOSION OF INTENSE RADIATION!
ELINORE!
NO!
SILAS?
THIS IS ALL MY FAULT! I SHOULDN'T HAVE RUSHED THAT EXPERIMENT!
PRESENT DAY.
A HIDDEN LABORATORY.
ALL MY FAULT. THE RADIATION. THE CANCER. ALL MY FAULT.
RISE AND SHINE, DR. STONE. IT SOUNDS LIKE YOU'RE HAVING QUITE A NIGHTMARE!
SO, I THOUGHT I SHOULD WAKE YOU UP. IT'S TIME FOR YOU TO EAT SOMETHING. AFTER ALL, MY LEADER AND I WANT YOU TO FEEL RIGHT AT HOME HERE...
...SINCE YOU'RE GOING TO BE STUCK HERE FOR A LONG, LONG WHILE.
I HOPE YOU DON'T MIND IF I KEEP YOU COMPANY?

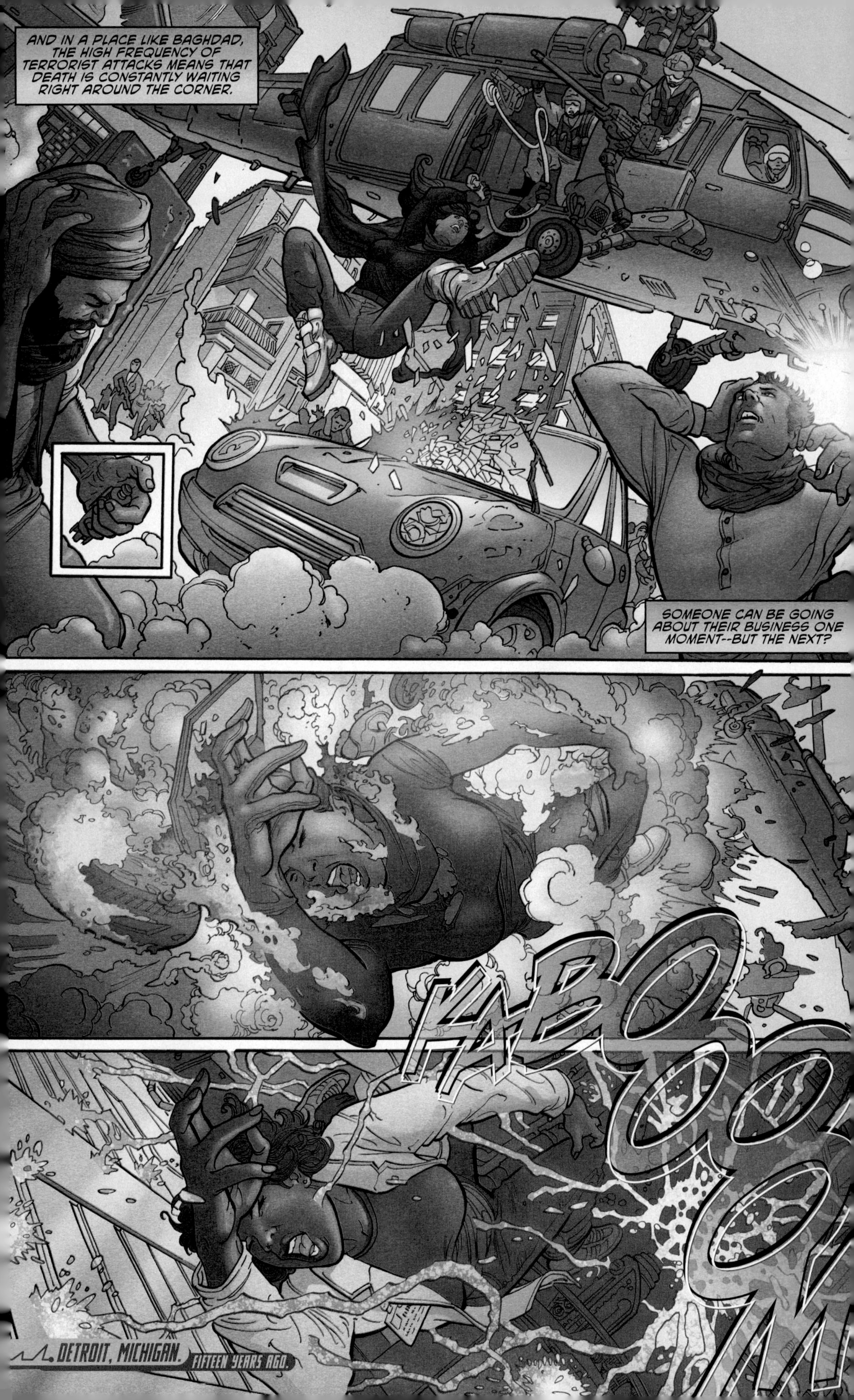
AND IN A PLACE LIKE BAGHDAD, THE HIGH FREQUENCY OF TERRORIST ATTACKS MEANS THAT DEATH IS CONSTANTLY WAITING RIGHT AROUND THE CORNER.
SOMEONE CAN BE GOING ABOUT THEIR BUSINESS ONE MOMENT--BUT THE NEXT?
KABOOOM
DETROIT, MICHIGAN.
FIFTEEN YEARS AGO.

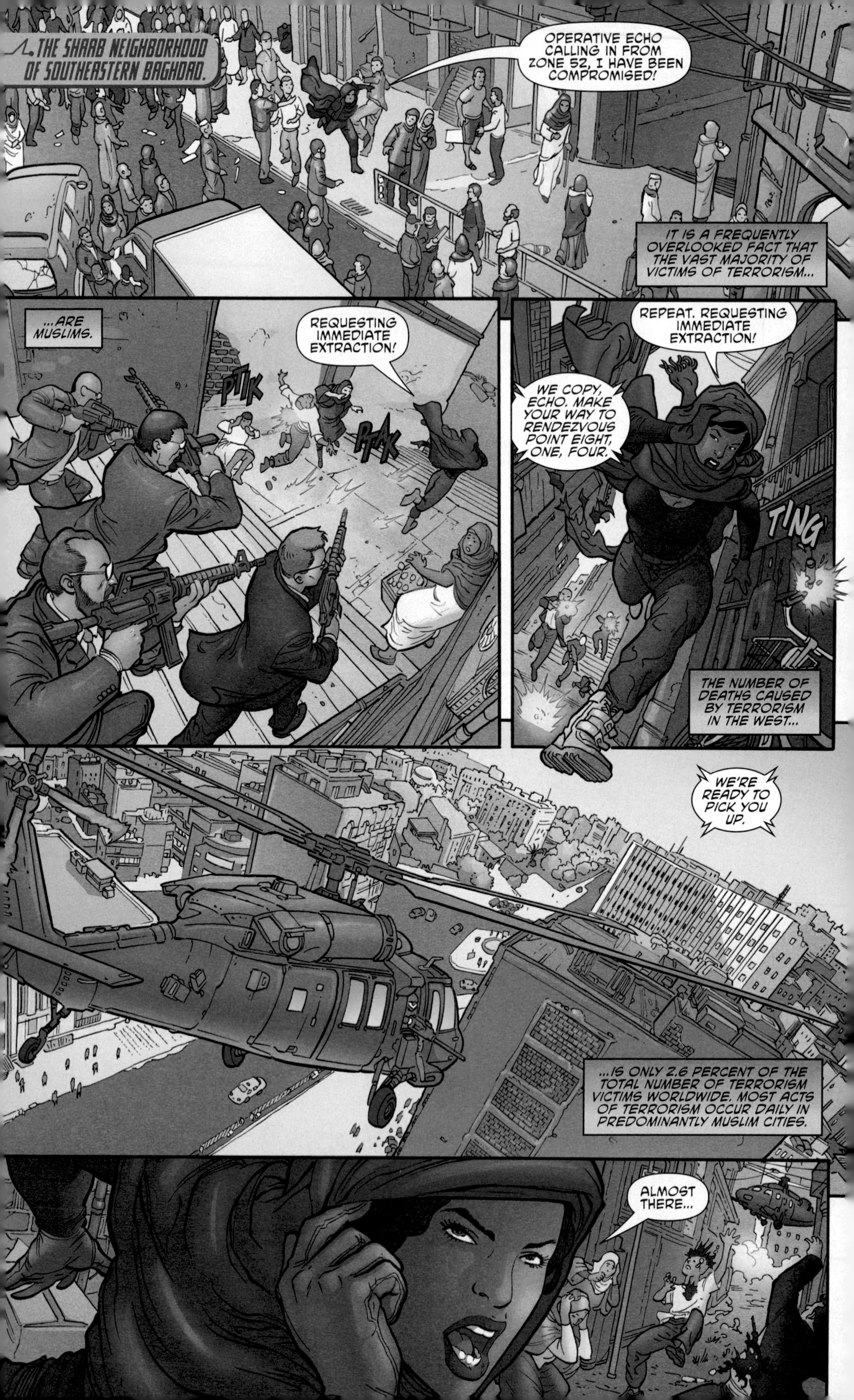
THE SHAAB NEIGHBORHOOD OF SOUTHEASTERN BAGHDAD.
OPERATIVE ECHO CALLING IN FROM ZONE 52, I HAVE BEEN COMPROMISED!
IT IS A FREQUENTLY OVERLOOKED FACT THAT THE VAST MAJORITY OF VICTIMS OF TERRORISM...
...ARE MUSLIMS.
REQUESTING IMMEDIATE EXTRACTION!
PTIK
PTAK
REPEAT. REQUESTING IMMEDIATE EXTRACTION!
WE COPY, ECHO. MAKE YOUR WAY TO RENDEZVOUS POINT EIGHT, ONE, FOUR.
TING
THE NUMBER OF DEATHS CAUSED BY TERRORISM IN THE WEST...
WE'RE READY TO PICK YOU UP.
...IS ONLY 2.6 PERCENT OF THE TOTAL NUMBER OF TERRORISM VICTIMS WORLDWIDE. MOST ACTS OF TERRORISM OCCUR DAILY IN PREDOMINANTLY MUSLIM CITIES.
ALMOST THERE...

PART FIVE: REGENERATION

JOHN SEMPER JR. writer * ALLAN JEFFERSON and DEREC DONOVAN pencillers
SCOTT HANNA and DEREC DONOVAN inkers
Cover by PAUL PELLETIER and SCOTT HANNA with GUY MAJOR

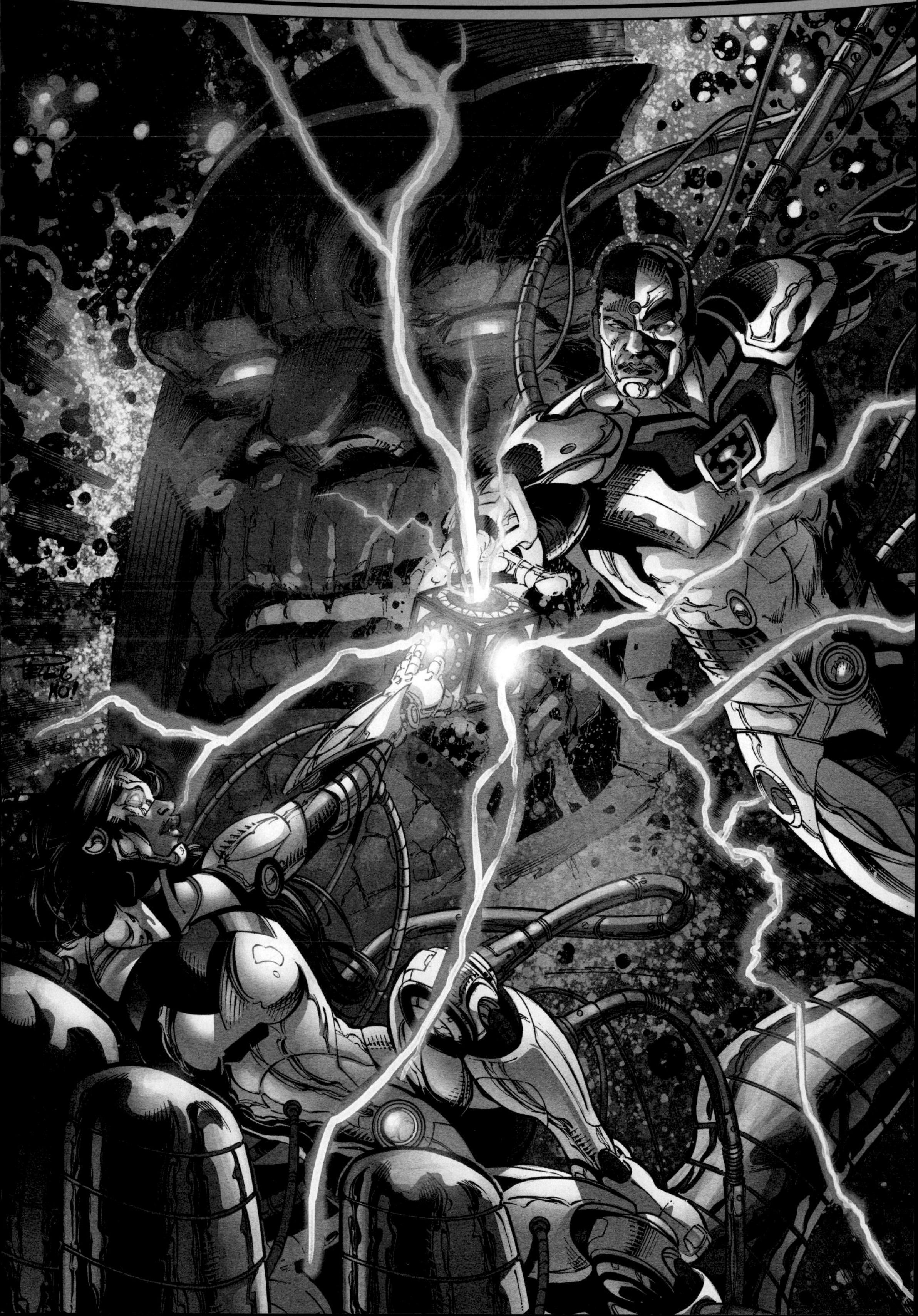

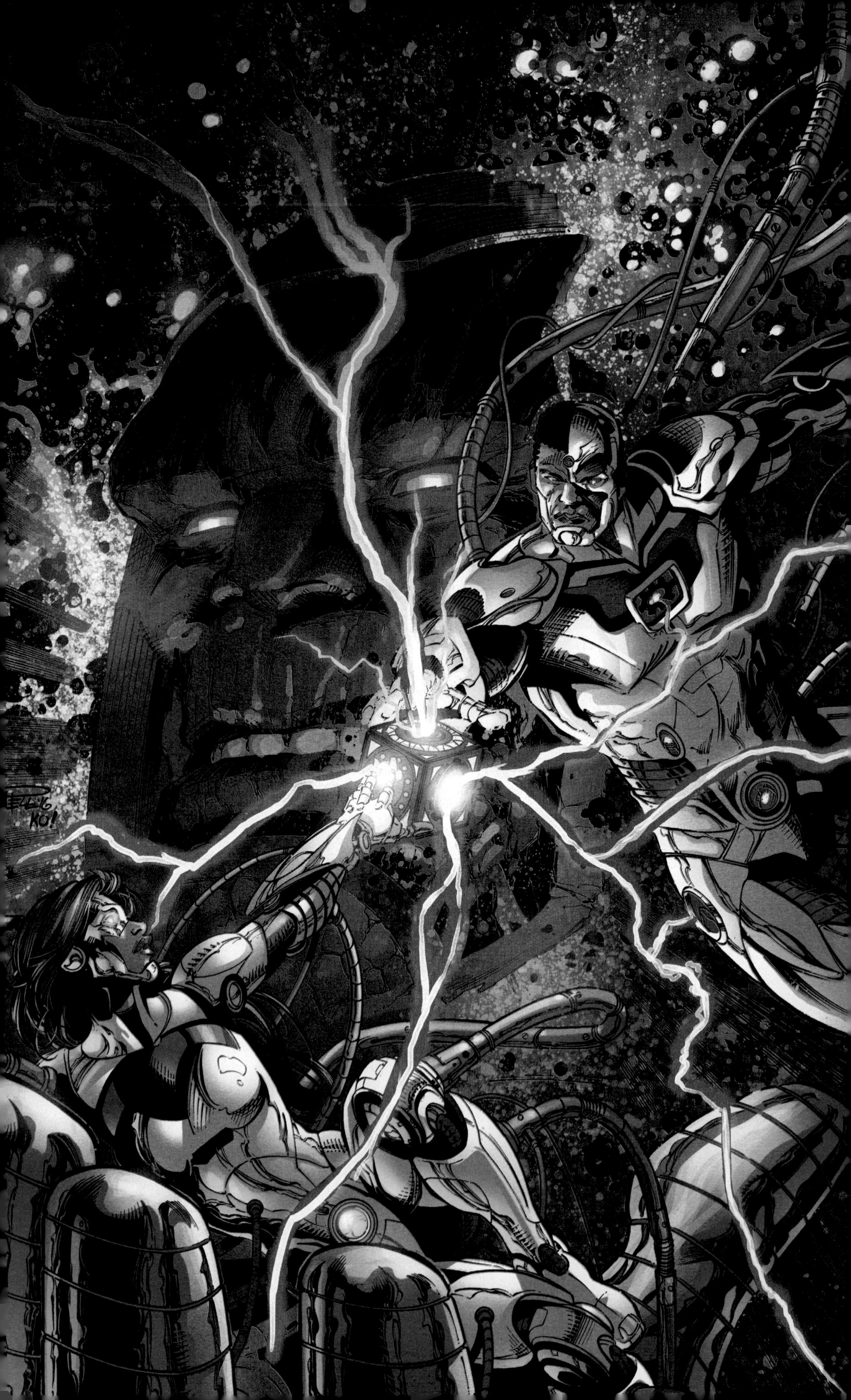

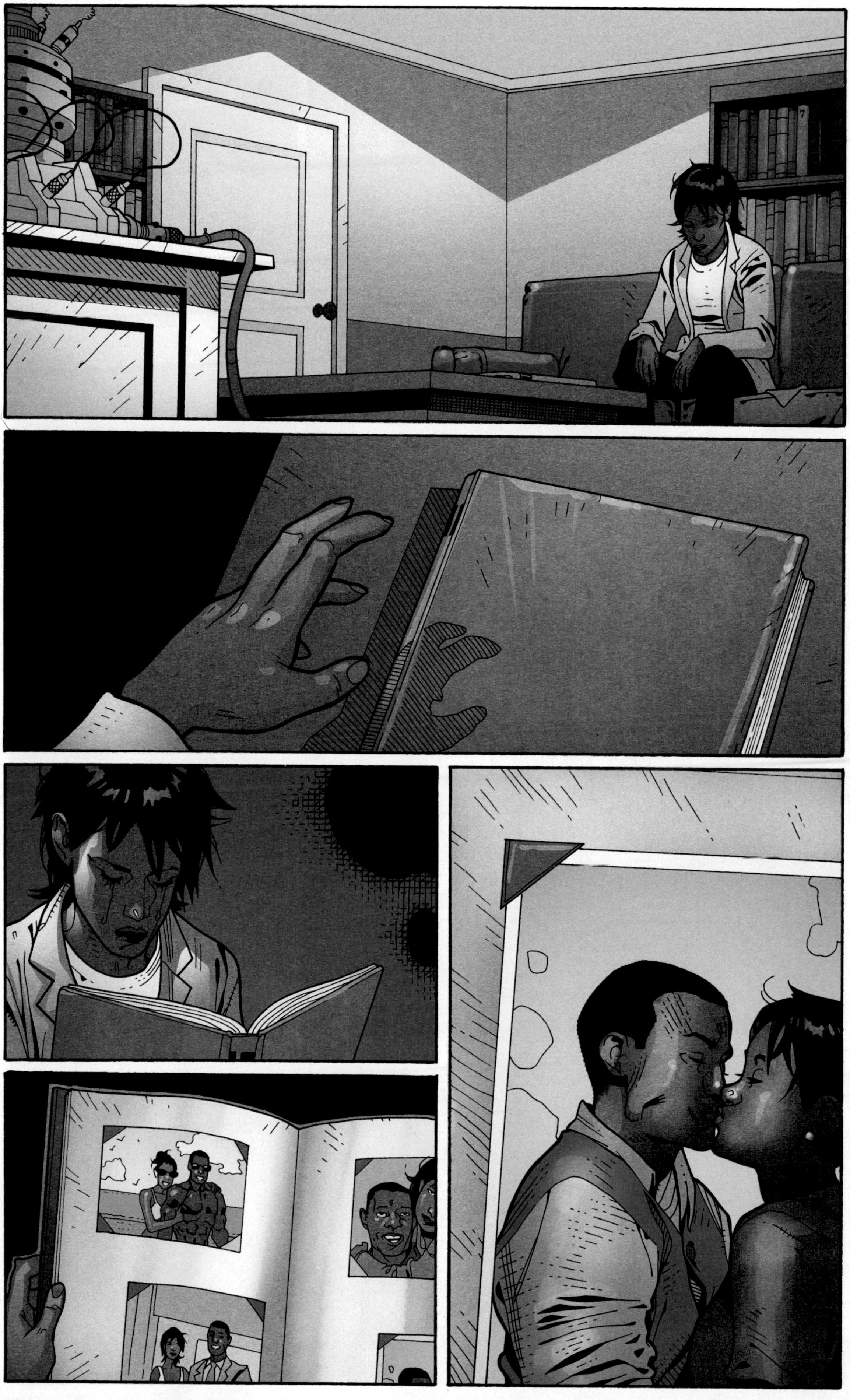

WHY *NOT?*

I THINK I MIGHT HAVE BLOCKED IT FROM MYSELF--FOR *HER* PROTECTION.

BUT JUST *KNOWING* THAT SOMEBODY ONCE LOVED ME THAT MUCH--AND THAT I ONCE LOVED THAT *INTENSELY*--GAVE ME ENOUGH STRENGTH TO GET THROUGH ANY ORDEAL.

THAT SOUNDS WONDERFUL, VIC. I'M *VERY* HAPPY FOR YOU.

Ah, WELL, FOR NOW, IT'S MEANINGLESS. AFTER ALL, I HAVE *NO* IDEA *WHO* SHE WAS, OR IF SHE'D STILL EVEN CARE ABOUT ME AS I AM TODAY.

I'M SURE THAT IF SHE LOVED YOU THAT DEEPLY, SHE'D PUT UP WITH *ALL* OF THIS TO BE BY YOUR SIDE.

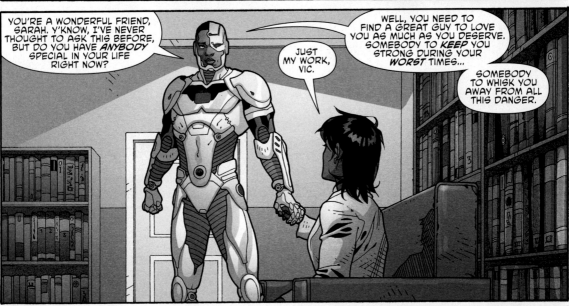

YOU'RE A WONDERFUL FRIEND, SARAH. Y'KNOW, I'VE NEVER THOUGHT TO ASK THIS BEFORE, BUT DO YOU HAVE *ANYBODY* SPECIAL IN YOUR LIFE RIGHT NOW?

JUST MY WORK, VIC.

WELL, YOU NEED TO FIND A GREAT GUY TO LOVE YOU AS MUCH AS YOU DESERVE. SOMEBODY TO *KEEP* YOU STRONG DURING YOUR *WORST* TIMES...

SOMEBODY TO WHISK YOU AWAY FROM ALL THIS DANGER.

HEY, "DANGER" IS MY MIDDLE NAME. BESIDES, IF I LEFT, *WHO'D* BE AROUND TO CHANGE YOUR OIL AND SPARK PLUGS WHEN IT'S TIME FOR YOUR *TEN-THOUSAND*-MILE TUNE-UP?

YOU'RE CRAZY. YOU KNOW THAT, RIGHT?

G'NIGHT, VIC.

GOOD NIGHT, SARAH.

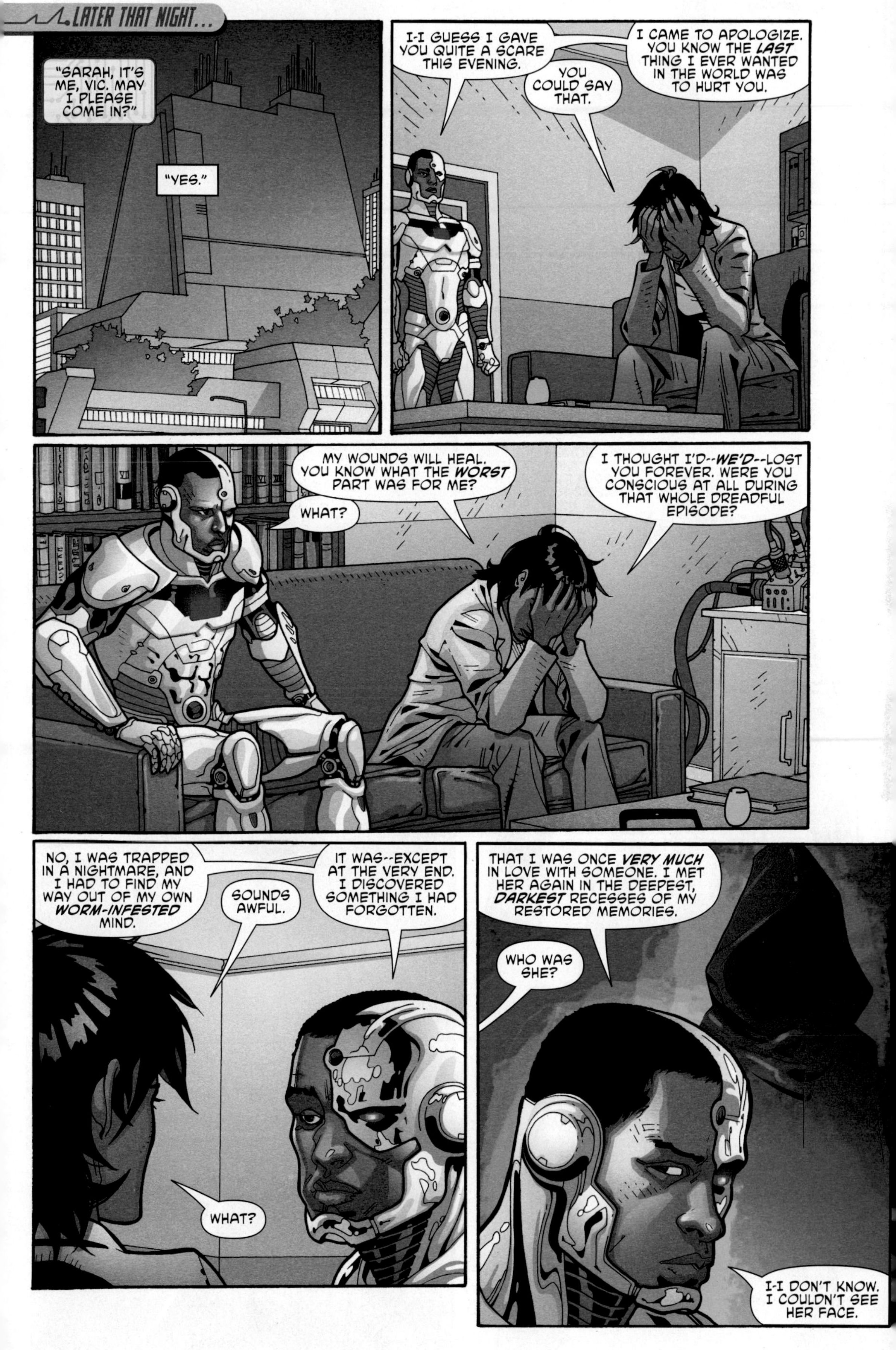
LATER THAT NIGHT...
"SARAH, IT'S ME, VIC. MAY I PLEASE COME IN?"
"YES."
I-I GUESS I GAVE YOU QUITE A SCARE THIS EVENING.
YOU COULD SAY THAT.
I CAME TO APOLOGIZE. YOU KNOW THE LAST THING I EVER WANTED IN THE WORLD WAS TO HURT YOU.
MY WOUNDS WILL HEAL. YOU KNOW WHAT THE WORST PART WAS FOR ME?
WHAT?
I THOUGHT I'D--WE'D--LOST YOU FOREVER. WERE YOU CONSCIOUS AT ALL DURING THAT WHOLE DREADFUL EPISODE?
NO, I WAS TRAPPED IN A NIGHTMARE, AND I HAD TO FIND MY WAY OUT OF MY OWN WORM-INFESTED MIND.
SOUNDS AWFUL.
IT WAS--EXCEPT AT THE VERY END. I DISCOVERED SOMETHING I HAD FORGOTTEN.
WHAT?
THAT I WAS ONCE VERY MUCH IN LOVE WITH SOMEONE. I MET HER AGAIN IN THE DEEPEST, DARKEST RECESSES OF MY RESTORED MEMORIES.
WHO WAS SHE?
I-I DON'T KNOW. I COULDN'T SEE HER FACE.

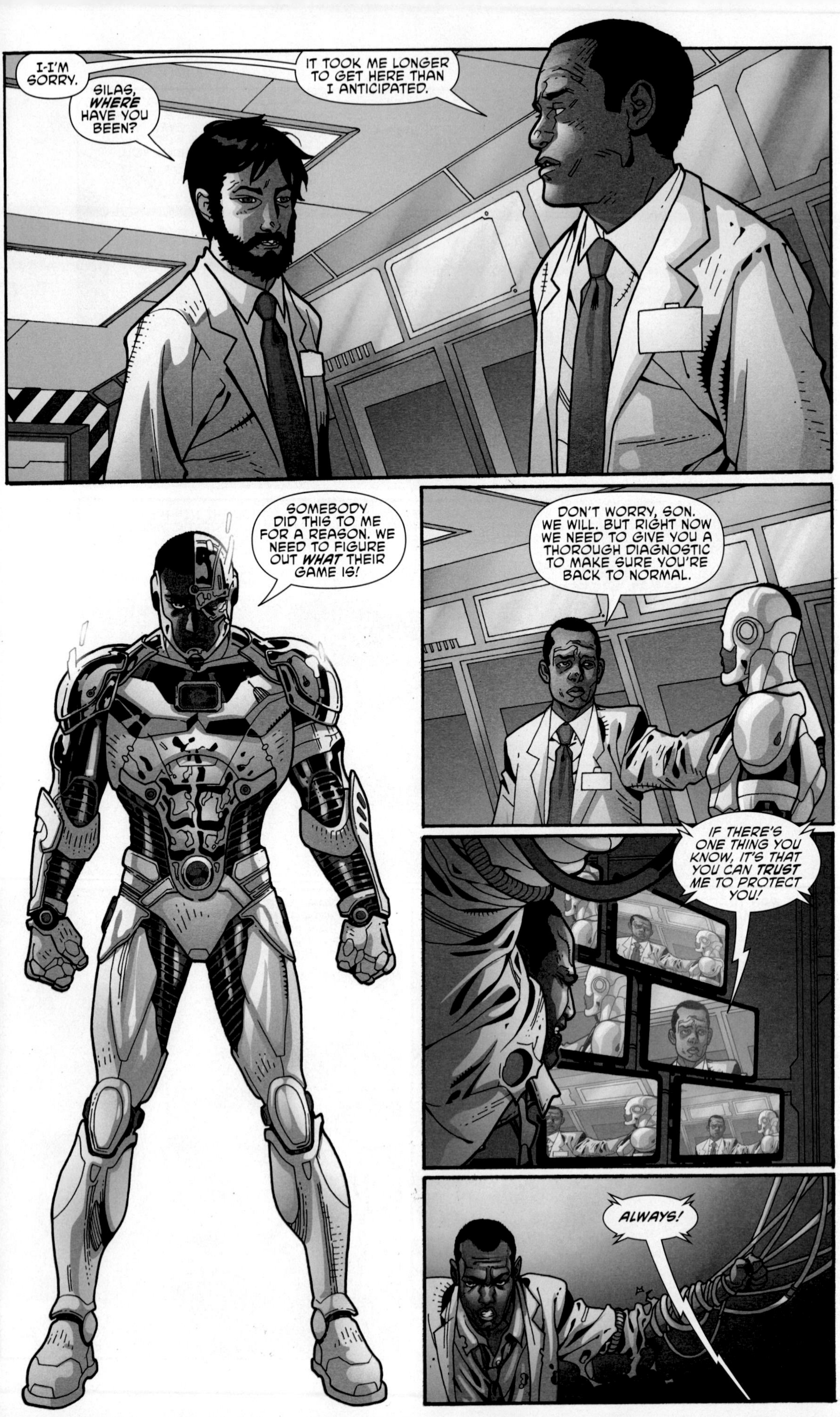
I-I'M SORRY.
SILAS, WHERE HAVE YOU BEEN?
IT TOOK ME LONGER TO GET HERE THAN I ANTICIPATED.
SOMEBODY DID THIS TO ME FOR A REASON. WE NEED TO FIGURE OUT WHAT THEIR GAME IS!
DON'T WORRY, SON. WE WILL. BUT RIGHT NOW WE NEED TO GIVE YOU A THOROUGH DIAGNOSTIC TO MAKE SURE YOU'RE BACK TO NORMAL.
IF THERE'S ONE THING YOU KNOW, IT'S THAT YOU CAN TRUST ME TO PROTECT YOU!
ALWAYS!

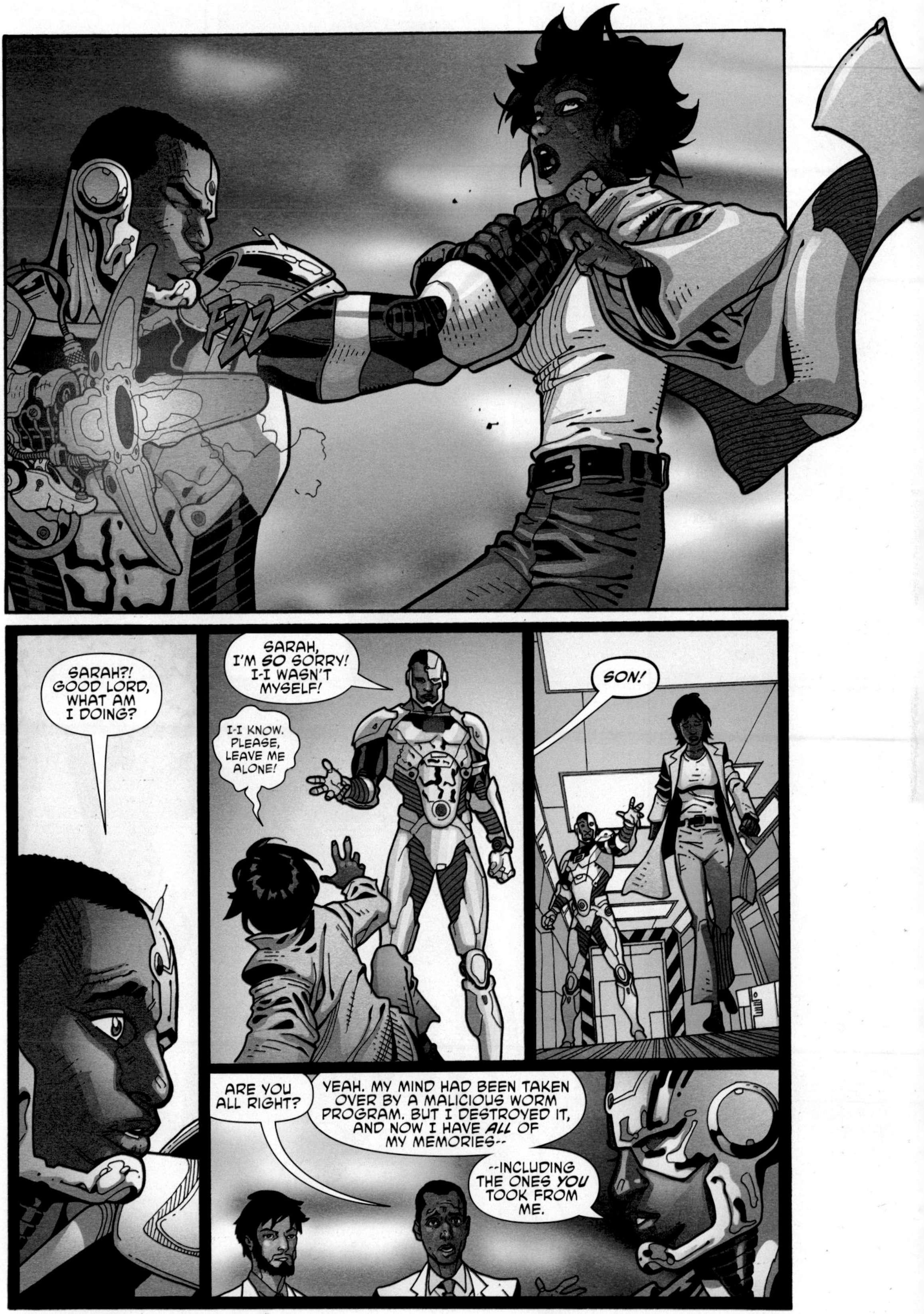
FZZ
SARAH?! GOOD LORD, WHAT AM I DOING?
SARAH, I'M SO SORRY! I-I WASN'T MYSELF!
I-I KNOW. PLEASE, LEAVE ME ALONE!
SON!
ARE YOU ALL RIGHT?
YEAH. MY MIND HAD BEEN TAKEN OVER BY A MALICIOUS WORM PROGRAM. BUT I DESTROYED IT, AND NOW I HAVE ALL OF MY MEMORIES--
--INCLUDING THE ONES YOU TOOK FROM ME.

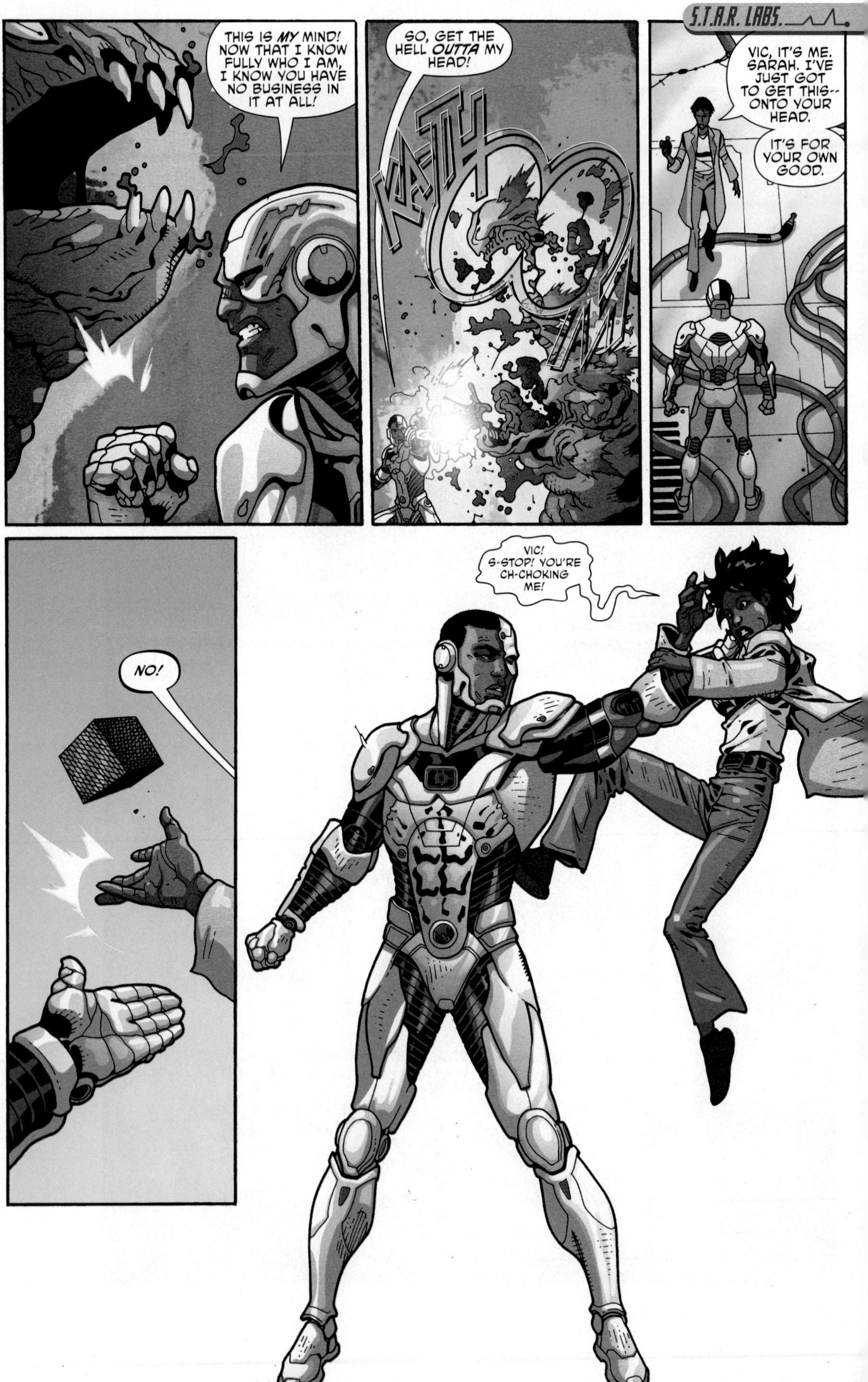

S.T.A.R. LABS.
THIS IS MY MIND! NOW THAT I KNOW FULLY WHO I AM, I KNOW YOU HAVE NO BUSINESS IN IT AT ALL!
SO, GET THE HELL OUTTA MY HEAD!
KA-THOOM
VIC, IT'S ME. SARAH. I'VE JUST GOT TO GET THIS-- ONTO YOUR HEAD.
IT'S FOR YOUR OWN GOOD.
NO!
VIC! S-STOP! YOU'RE CH-CHOKING ME!

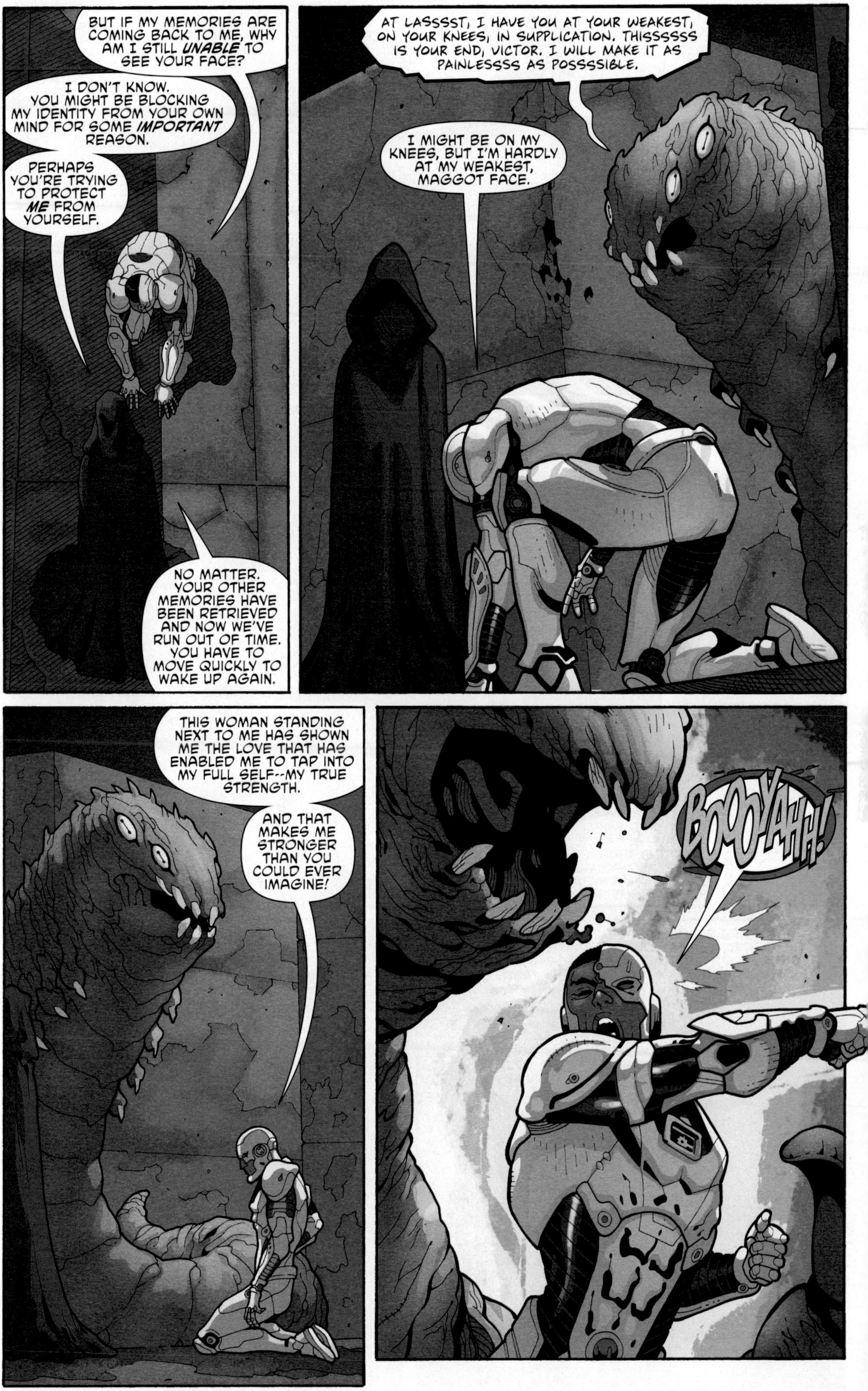
BUT IF MY MEMORIES ARE COMING BACK TO ME, WHY AM I STILL *UNABLE* TO SEE YOUR FACE?
I DON'T KNOW. YOU MIGHT BE BLOCKING MY IDENTITY FROM YOUR OWN MIND FOR SOME *IMPORTANT* REASON.
PERHAPS YOU'RE TRYING TO PROTECT *ME* FROM YOURSELF.
NO MATTER. YOUR OTHER MEMORIES HAVE BEEN RETRIEVED AND NOW WE'VE RUN OUT OF TIME. YOU HAVE TO MOVE QUICKLY TO WAKE UP AGAIN.
AT LASSSST, I HAVE YOU AT YOUR WEAKEST, ON YOUR KNEES, IN SUPPLICATION. THISSSSSS IS YOUR END, VICTOR. I WILL MAKE IT AS PAINLESSSS AS POSSSSIBLE.
I MIGHT BE ON MY KNEES, BUT I'M HARDLY AT MY WEAKEST, MAGGOT FACE.
THIS WOMAN STANDING NEXT TO ME HAS SHOWN ME THE LOVE THAT HAS ENABLED ME TO TAP INTO MY FULL SELF--MY TRUE STRENGTH.
AND THAT MAKES ME STRONGER THAN YOU COULD EVER IMAGINE!
BOOOYAHH!

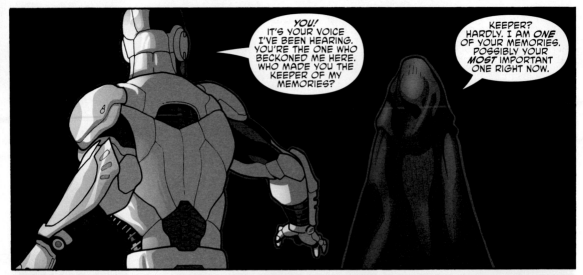

YOU! IT'S YOUR VOICE I'VE BEEN HEARING. YOU'RE THE ONE WHO BECKONED ME HERE. WHO MADE YOU THE KEEPER OF MY MEMORIES?

KEEPER? HARDLY. I AM *ONE* OF YOUR MEMORIES. POSSIBLY YOUR *MOST* IMPORTANT ONE RIGHT NOW.

W-WHO ARE YOU? WHY DON'T YOU HAVE A FACE?

I AM THE LOVE OF YOUR LIFE.

BUT I HAVE *NO* MEMORY OF YOU!

THAT'S WHY I HAVE *NO* FACE. AND THE MEMORY OF ME, AND *SO MUCH MORE,* IS WHAT YOU'RE HERE TO GET BACK.

AAAHHHHHHH!

WHAT'S HAPPENING TO ME?

YOU'RE FINALLY ACCESSING *ALL* OF YOUR LOST MEMORIES.

YOU ARE FEELING THE *FULL* BRUNT OF THE SORROW OVER YOUR MOTHER'S DEATH, THE *PAIN* OF YOUR ACCIDENT, THE *ANGUISH* OF YOUR CONDITION, AND NOW, THE *TRUE* LOSS OF THE LOVE THAT WE HAD FOR ONE ANOTHER.

SO FAR, YOU'VE BEEN OPERATING AS ONLY *HALF* A MAN. WITH YOUR ABSENCE OF LOVE, YOUR *MUTING* OF EMOTION, YOU'VE BEEN MORE *MACHINE* THAN YOURSELF.

NOW, YOU MUST USE YOUR MEMORIES TO REGAIN YOUR *TRUE* SELF...

...AND TO HAVE THE WILL TO OVERCOME THE *LAST* OF THIS MALIGNANT WORM CODE INSIDE OF YOUR MIND.

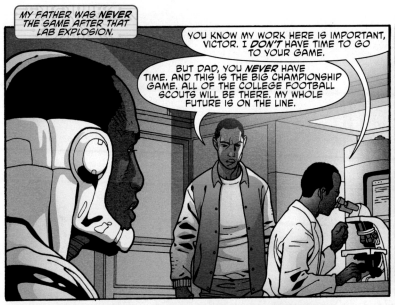

MY FATHER WAS *NEVER* THE SAME AFTER THAT LAB EXPLOSION.

YOU KNOW MY WORK HERE IS IMPORTANT, VICTOR. I *DON'T* HAVE TIME TO GO TO YOUR GAME.

BUT DAD, YOU *NEVER* HAVE TIME. AND THIS IS THE BIG CHAMPIONSHIP GAME. ALL OF THE COLLEGE FOOTBALL SCOUTS WILL BE THERE. MY WHOLE FUTURE IS ON THE LINE.

VICTOR, MY WORD IS *FINAL!*

YES, DAD, IT USUALLY WAS.

"IS THAT YOUR FINAL WORD?"

IT'S HER! BRITTON CLAIRE, THE EX-GIRLFRIEND THAT I HAD FORGOTTEN! I'M FINALLY TAPPING INTO MY *LOST* MEMORIES--THE ONES THAT HAD BEEN *TURNED OFF* BY MY FATHER.

IS THAT *ALL* YOU HAVE TO SAY TO ME? AFTER WE'VE BEEN DATING FOR SIX WHOLE MONTHS? VICTOR, I LOVE YOU!

LOOK, BRITTON, WE'RE DONE. YOU'RE JUST GONNA HAVE TO GET USED TO IT. I'M MADLY IN LOVE WITH SOMEBODY ELSE. I'M CERTAIN SHE'S MY *TRUE* SOUL MATE.

AS FOR YOU, I'M *NOT* FEELING IT ANYMORE. NOW, GRAB YOUR STUFF AND BEAT IT.

OH, VICTOR. YOU'RE *HORRIBLE!* HORRIBLE!

SHE'S RIGHT. I'M BEHAVING TERRIBLY. I HAD NO RECOLLECTION THAT I HAD BEEN SUCH A JERK--ANOTHER PAINFUL MEMORY...

...SUITABLE FOR *HIDING WITHIN!*

BOOM

AAHHHHHHH!

CONGRATULATIONS. YOU HAVE ACHIEVED WHAT *MOST* PEOPLE WOULD ENVY. YOU HAVE LOOKED INTO YOUR OWN MIND AND GOTTEN A GOOD LOOK AT YOURSELF.

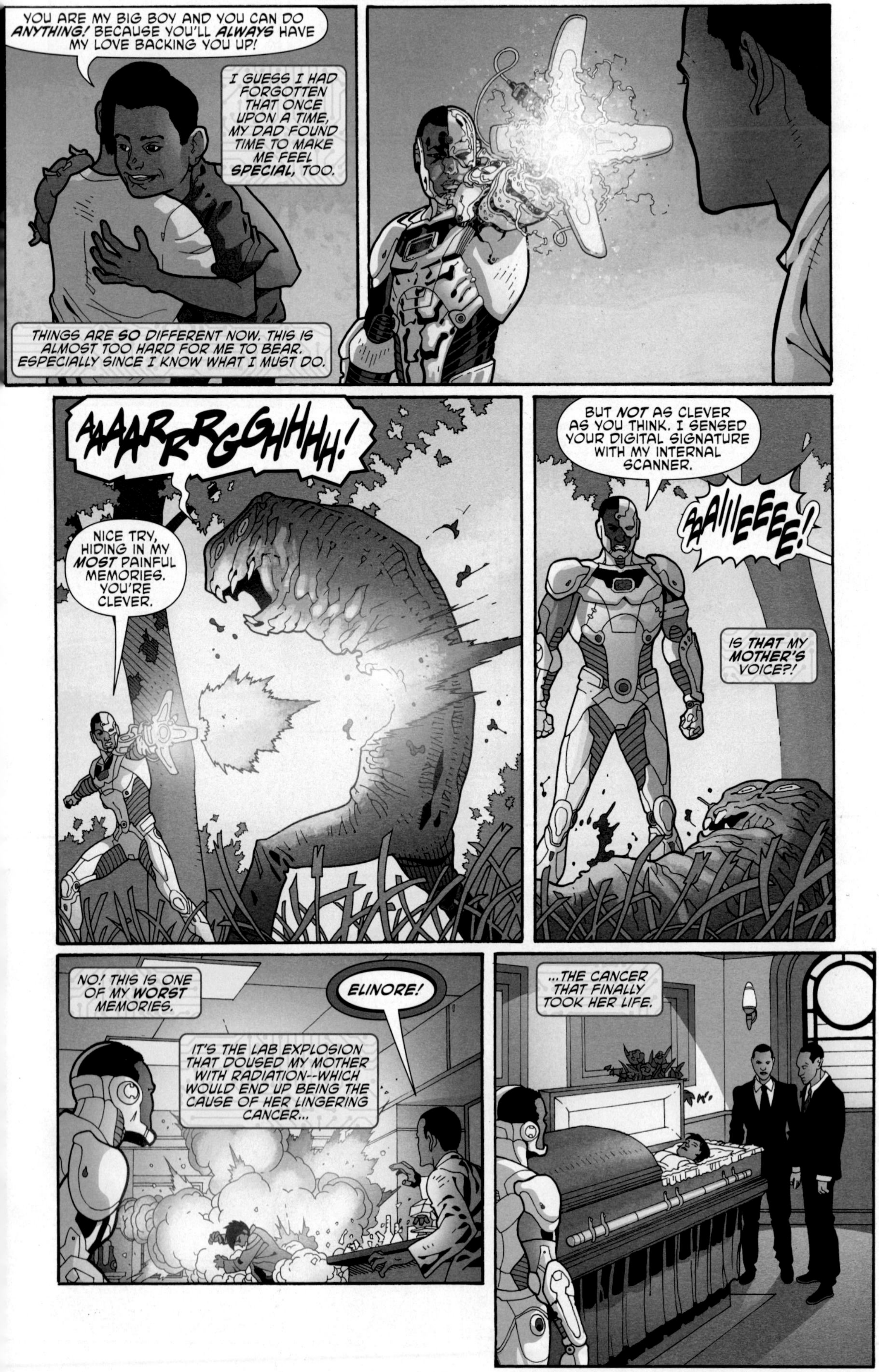
YOU ARE MY BIG BOY AND YOU CAN DO *ANYTHING!* BECAUSE YOU'LL *ALWAYS* HAVE MY LOVE BACKING YOU UP!
I GUESS I HAD FORGOTTEN THAT ONCE UPON A TIME, MY DAD FOUND TIME TO MAKE ME FEEL *SPECIAL,* TOO.
THINGS ARE *SO* DIFFERENT NOW. THIS IS ALMOST TOO HARD FOR ME TO BEAR. ESPECIALLY SINCE I KNOW WHAT I MUST DO.
AAAARRRGGHHHH!
NICE TRY, HIDING IN MY *MOST* PAINFUL MEMORIES. YOU'RE CLEVER.
BUT *NOT* AS CLEVER AS YOU THINK. I SENSED YOUR DIGITAL SIGNATURE WITH MY INTERNAL SCANNER.
AAIIIEEEEE!
IS *THAT* MY *MOTHER'S* VOICE?!
NO! THIS IS ONE OF MY *WORST* MEMORIES.
ELINORE!
IT'S THE LAB EXPLOSION THAT DOUSED MY MOTHER WITH RADIATION--WHICH WOULD END UP BEING THE CAUSE OF HER LINGERING CANCER...
...THE CANCER THAT FINALLY TOOK HER LIFE.

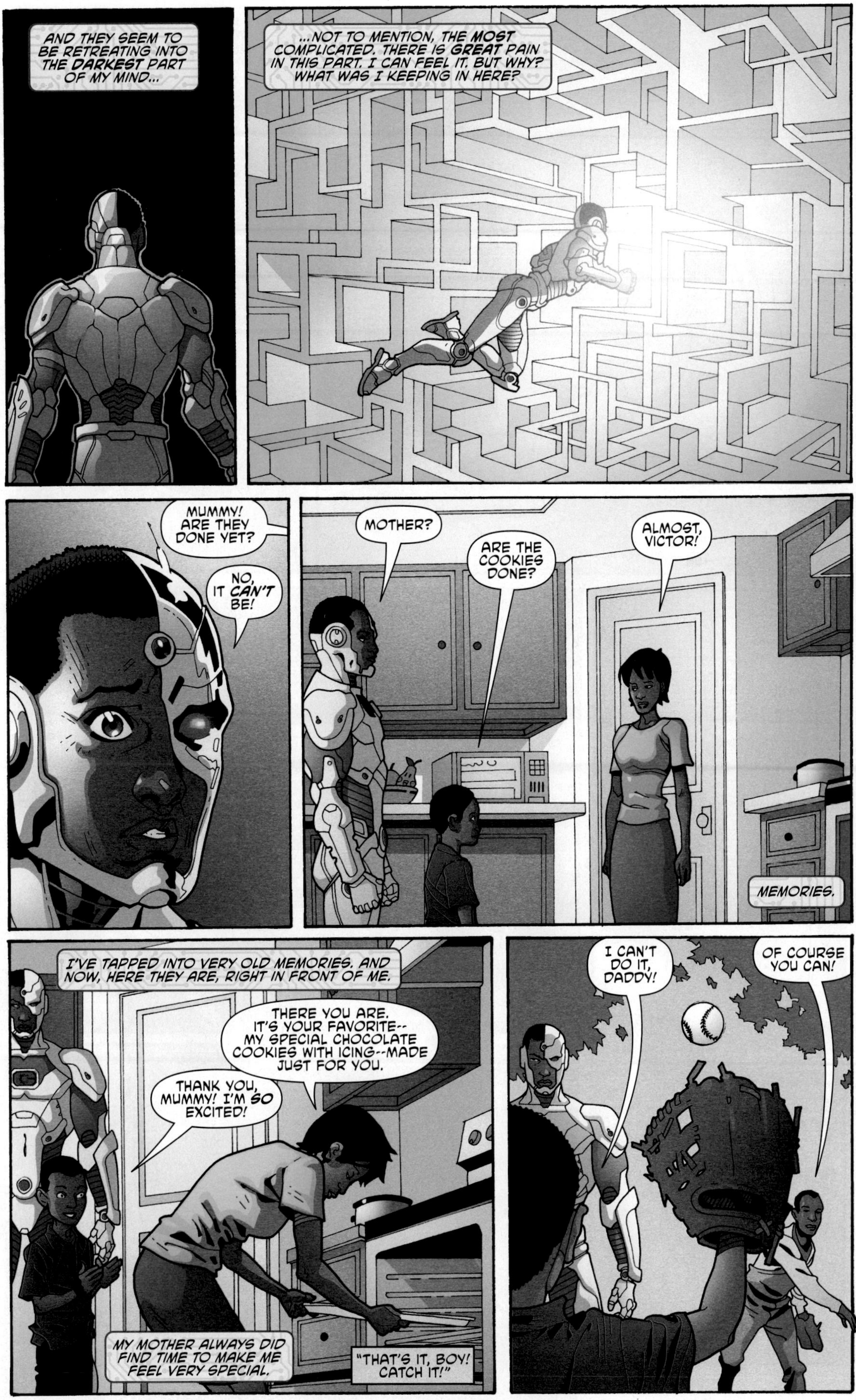
AND THEY SEEM TO BE RETREATING INTO THE DARKEST PART OF MY MIND...
...NOT TO MENTION, THE MOST COMPLICATED. THERE IS GREAT PAIN IN THIS PART. I CAN FEEL IT. BUT WHY? WHAT WAS I KEEPING IN HERE?
MUMMY! ARE THEY DONE YET?
NO, IT CAN'T BE!
MOTHER?
ARE THE COOKIES DONE?
ALMOST, VICTOR!
MEMORIES.
I'VE TAPPED INTO VERY OLD MEMORIES. AND NOW, HERE THEY ARE, RIGHT IN FRONT OF ME.
THERE YOU ARE. IT'S YOUR FAVORITE-- MY SPECIAL CHOCOLATE COOKIES WITH ICING--MADE JUST FOR YOU.
THANK YOU, MUMMY! I'M SO EXCITED!
MY MOTHER ALWAYS DID FIND TIME TO MAKE ME FEEL VERY SPECIAL.
"THAT'S IT, BOY! CATCH IT!"
I CAN'T DO IT, DADDY!
OF COURSE YOU CAN!

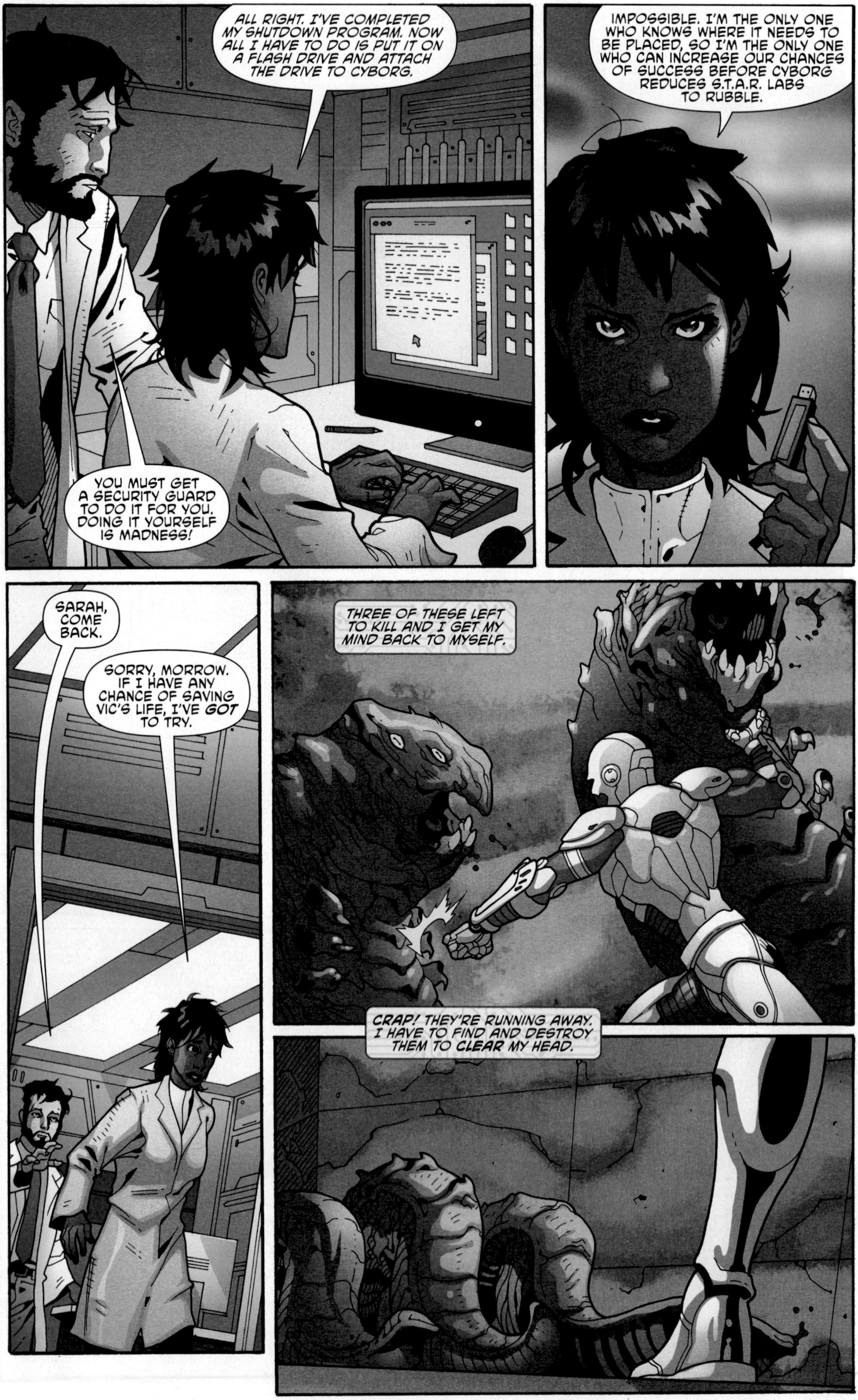
ALL RIGHT. I'VE COMPLETED MY SHUTDOWN PROGRAM. NOW ALL I HAVE TO DO IS PUT IT ON A FLASH DRIVE AND ATTACH THE DRIVE TO CYBORG.
YOU MUST GET A SECURITY GUARD TO DO IT FOR YOU. DOING IT YOURSELF IS MADNESS!
IMPOSSIBLE. I'M THE ONLY ONE WHO KNOWS WHERE IT NEEDS TO BE PLACED, SO I'M THE ONLY ONE WHO CAN INCREASE OUR CHANCES OF SUCCESS BEFORE CYBORG REDUCES S.T.A.R. LABS TO RUBBLE.
SARAH, COME BACK.
SORRY, MORROW. IF I HAVE ANY CHANCE OF SAVING VIC'S LIFE, I'VE *GOT* TO TRY.
THREE OF THESE LEFT TO KILL AND I GET MY MIND BACK TO MYSELF.
CRAP! THEY'RE RUNNING AWAY. I HAVE TO FIND AND DESTROY THEM TO *CLEAR* MY HEAD.

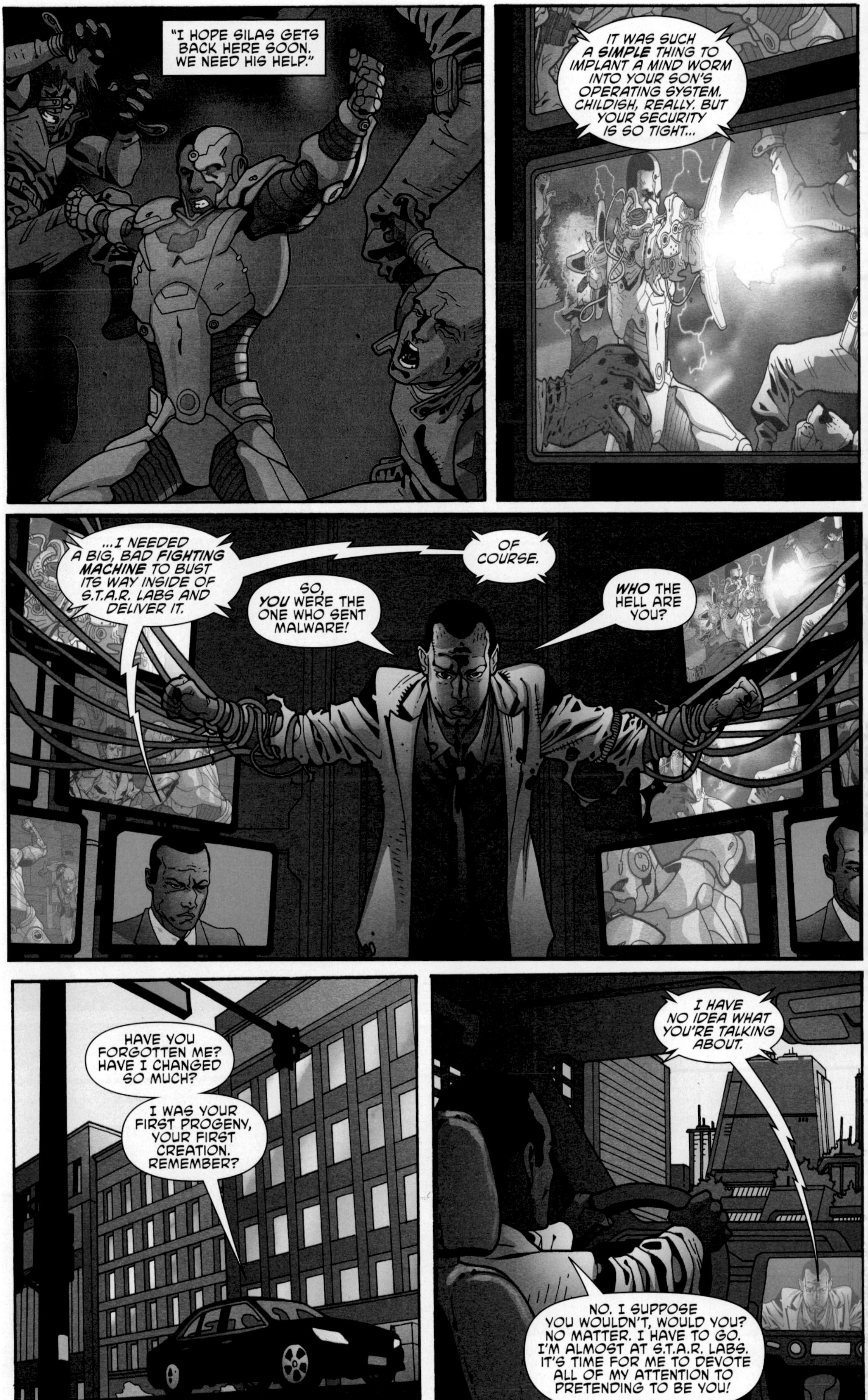
"I HOPE SILAS GETS BACK HERE SOON. WE NEED HIS HELP."
IT WAS SUCH A SIMPLE THING TO IMPLANT A MIND WORM INTO YOUR SON'S OPERATING SYSTEM. CHILDISH, REALLY. BUT YOUR SECURITY IS SO TIGHT...
...I NEEDED A BIG, BAD FIGHTING MACHINE TO BUST ITS WAY INSIDE OF S.T.A.R. LABS AND DELIVER IT.
OF COURSE.
SO, YOU WERE THE ONE WHO SENT MALWARE!
WHO THE HELL ARE YOU?
HAVE YOU FORGOTTEN ME? HAVE I CHANGED SO MUCH?
I WAS YOUR FIRST PROGENY, YOUR FIRST CREATION. REMEMBER?
I HAVE NO IDEA WHAT YOU'RE TALKING ABOUT.
NO. I SUPPOSE YOU WOULDN'T, WOULD YOU? NO MATTER. I HAVE TO GO. I'M ALMOST AT S.T.A.R. LABS. IT'S TIME FOR ME TO DEVOTE ALL OF MY ATTENTION TO PRETENDING TO BE YOU!

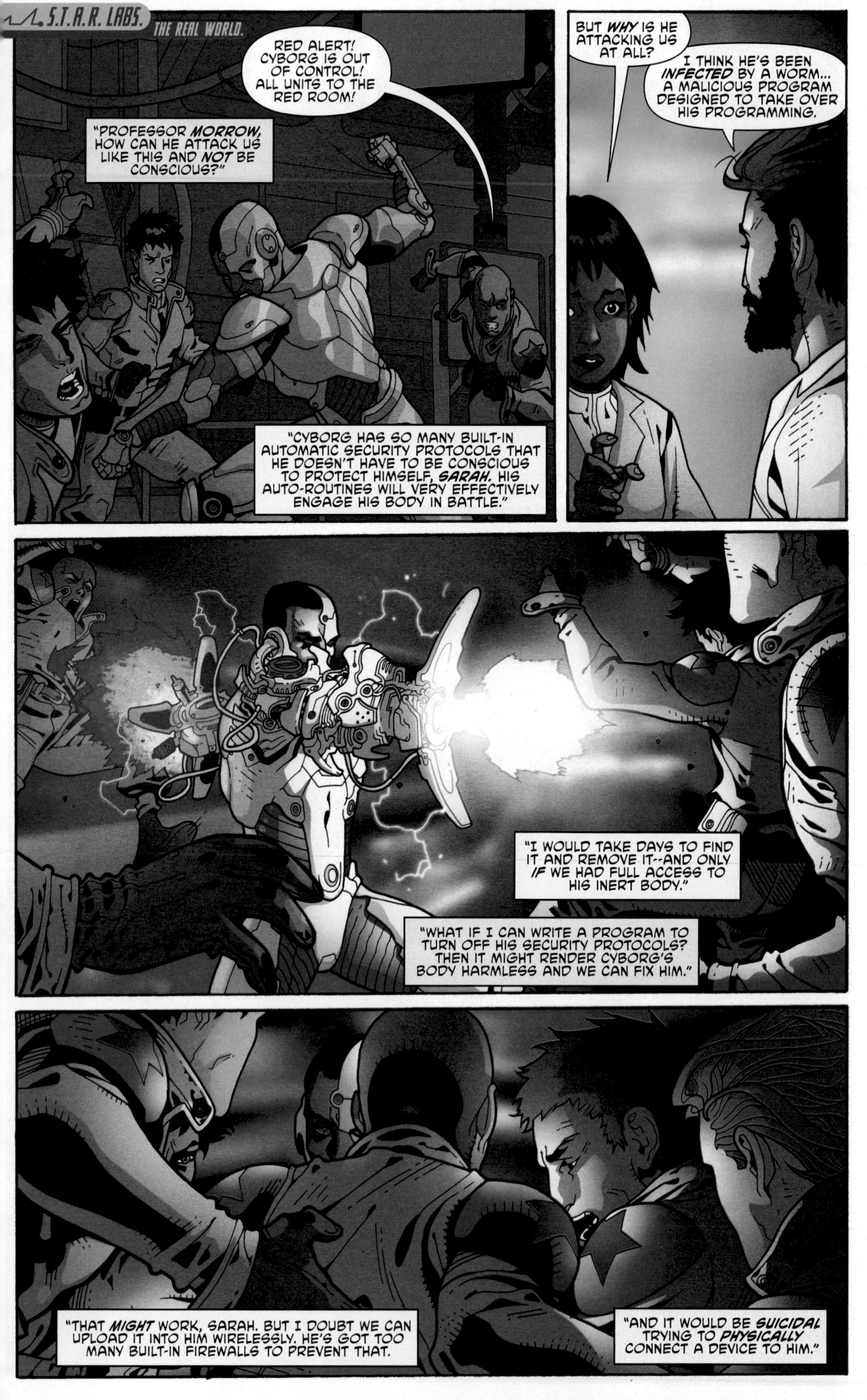
S.T.A.R. LABS.
THE REAL WORLD.
RED ALERT! CYBORG IS OUT OF CONTROL! ALL UNITS TO THE RED ROOM!
"PROFESSOR MORROW, HOW CAN HE ATTACK US LIKE THIS AND NOT BE CONSCIOUS?"
"CYBORG HAS SO MANY BUILT-IN AUTOMATIC SECURITY PROTOCOLS THAT HE DOESN'T HAVE TO BE CONSCIOUS TO PROTECT HIMSELF, SARAH. HIS AUTO-ROUTINES WILL VERY EFFECTIVELY ENGAGE HIS BODY IN BATTLE."
BUT WHY IS HE ATTACKING US AT ALL?
I THINK HE'S BEEN INFECTED BY A WORM... A MALICIOUS PROGRAM DESIGNED TO TAKE OVER HIS PROGRAMMING.
"I WOULD TAKE DAYS TO FIND IT AND REMOVE IT--AND ONLY IF WE HAD FULL ACCESS TO HIS INERT BODY."
"WHAT IF I CAN WRITE A PROGRAM TO TURN OFF HIS SECURITY PROTOCOLS? THEN IT MIGHT RENDER CYBORG'S BODY HARMLESS AND WE CAN FIX HIM."
"THAT MIGHT WORK, SARAH. BUT I DOUBT WE CAN UPLOAD IT INTO HIM WIRELESSLY. HE'S GOT TOO MANY BUILT-IN FIREWALLS TO PREVENT THAT.
"AND IT WOULD BE SUICIDAL TRYING TO PHYSICALLY CONNECT A DEVICE TO HIM."

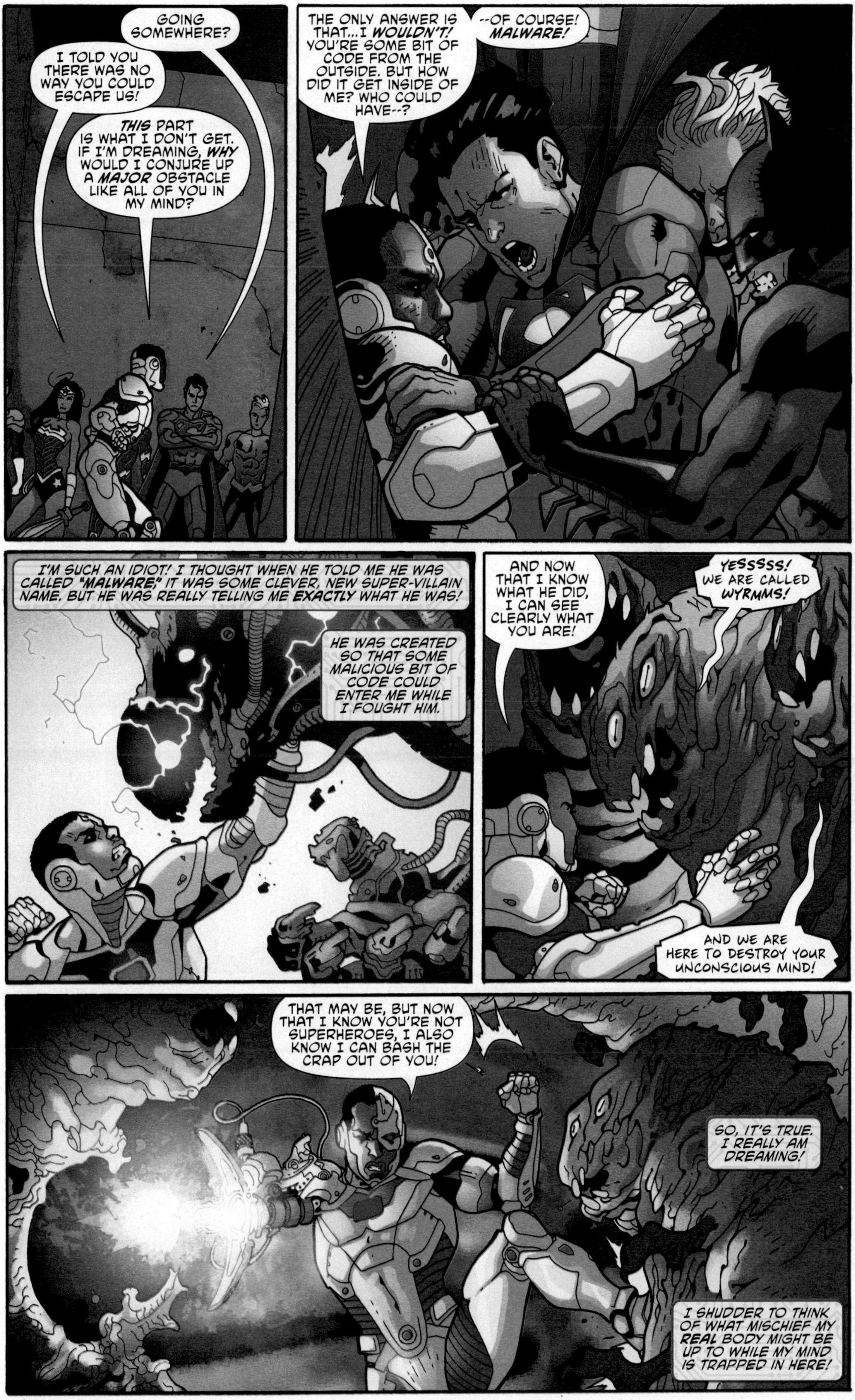
GOING SOMEWHERE?
I TOLD YOU THERE WAS NO WAY YOU COULD ESCAPE US!
THIS PART IS WHAT I DON'T GET. IF I'M DREAMING, WHY WOULD I CONJURE UP A MAJOR OBSTACLE LIKE ALL OF YOU IN MY MIND?
THE ONLY ANSWER IS THAT... I WOULDN'T! YOU'RE SOME BIT OF CODE FROM THE OUTSIDE. BUT HOW DID IT GET INSIDE OF ME? WHO COULD HAVE--?
--OF COURSE! MALWARE!
I'M SUCH AN IDIOT! I THOUGHT WHEN HE TOLD ME HE WAS CALLED "MALWARE," IT WAS SOME CLEVER, NEW SUPER-VILLAIN NAME. BUT HE WAS REALLY TELLING ME EXACTLY WHAT HE WAS!
HE WAS CREATED SO THAT SOME MALICIOUS BIT OF CODE COULD ENTER ME WHILE I FOUGHT HIM.
AND NOW THAT I KNOW WHAT HE DID, I CAN SEE CLEARLY WHAT YOU ARE!
YESSSSS! WE ARE CALLED WYRMMS!
AND WE ARE HERE TO DESTROY YOUR UNCONSCIOUS MIND!
THAT MAY BE, BUT NOW THAT I KNOW YOU'RE NOT SUPERHEROES, I ALSO KNOW I CAN BASH THE CRAP OUT OF YOU!
SO, IT'S TRUE. I REALLY AM DREAMING!
I SHUDDER TO THINK OF WHAT MISCHIEF MY REAL BODY MIGHT BE UP TO WHILE MY MIND IS TRAPPED IN HERE!

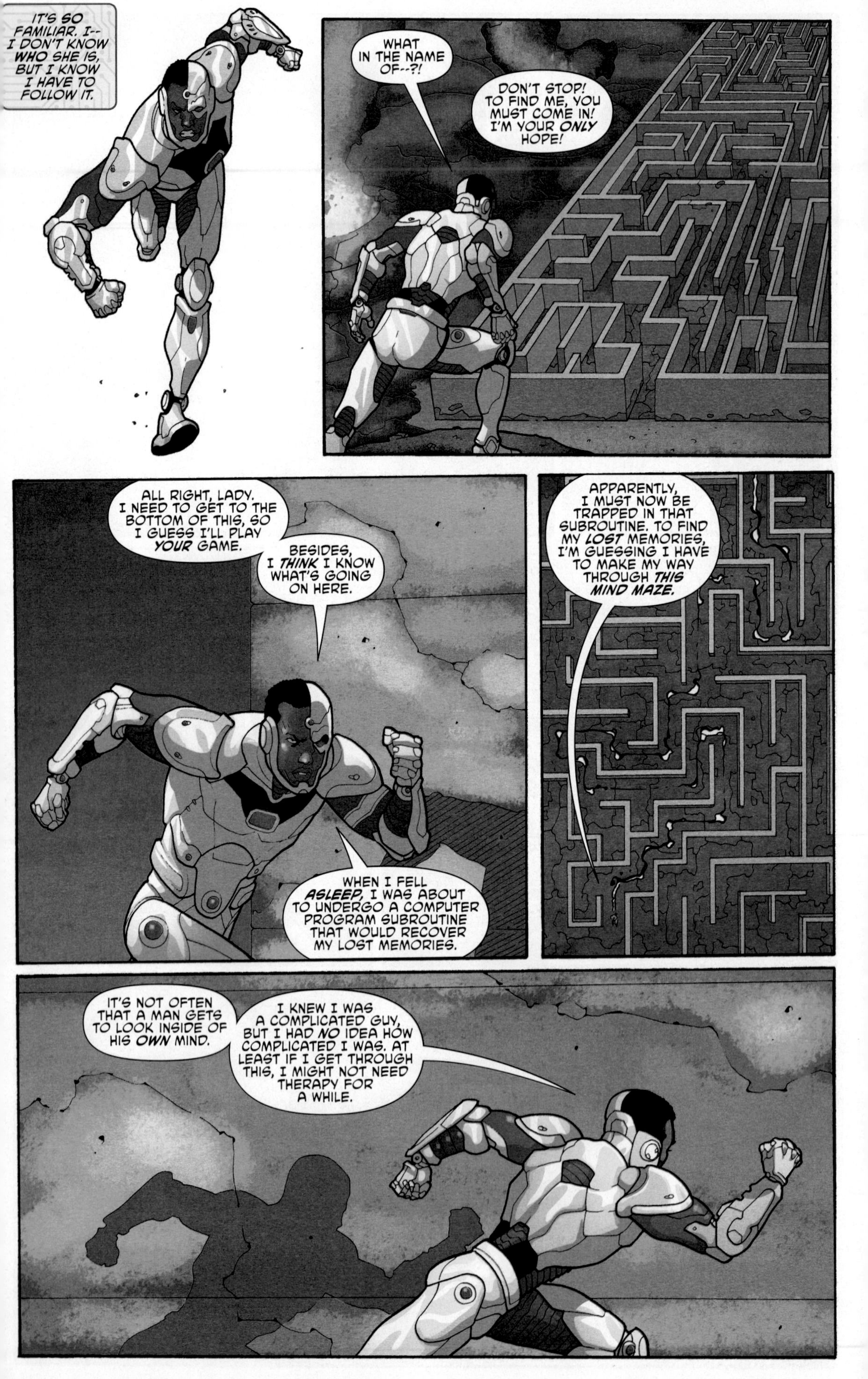
IT'S SO FAMILIAR. I-- I DON'T KNOW WHO SHE IS, BUT I KNOW I HAVE TO FOLLOW IT.
WHAT IN THE NAME OF--?!
DON'T STOP! TO FIND ME, YOU MUST COME IN! I'M YOUR ONLY HOPE!
ALL RIGHT, LADY. I NEED TO GET TO THE BOTTOM OF THIS, SO I GUESS I'LL PLAY YOUR GAME.
BESIDES, I THINK I KNOW WHAT'S GOING ON HERE.
WHEN I FELL ASLEEP, I WAS ABOUT TO UNDERGO A COMPUTER PROGRAM SUBROUTINE THAT WOULD RECOVER MY LOST MEMORIES.
APPARENTLY, I MUST NOW BE TRAPPED IN THAT SUBROUTINE. TO FIND MY LOST MEMORIES, I'M GUESSING I HAVE TO MAKE MY WAY THROUGH THIS MIND MAZE.
IT'S NOT OFTEN THAT A MAN GETS TO LOOK INSIDE OF HIS OWN MIND.
I KNEW I WAS A COMPLICATED GUY, BUT I HAD NO IDEA HOW COMPLICATED I WAS. AT LEAST IF I GET THROUGH THIS, I MIGHT NOT NEED THERAPY FOR A WHILE.

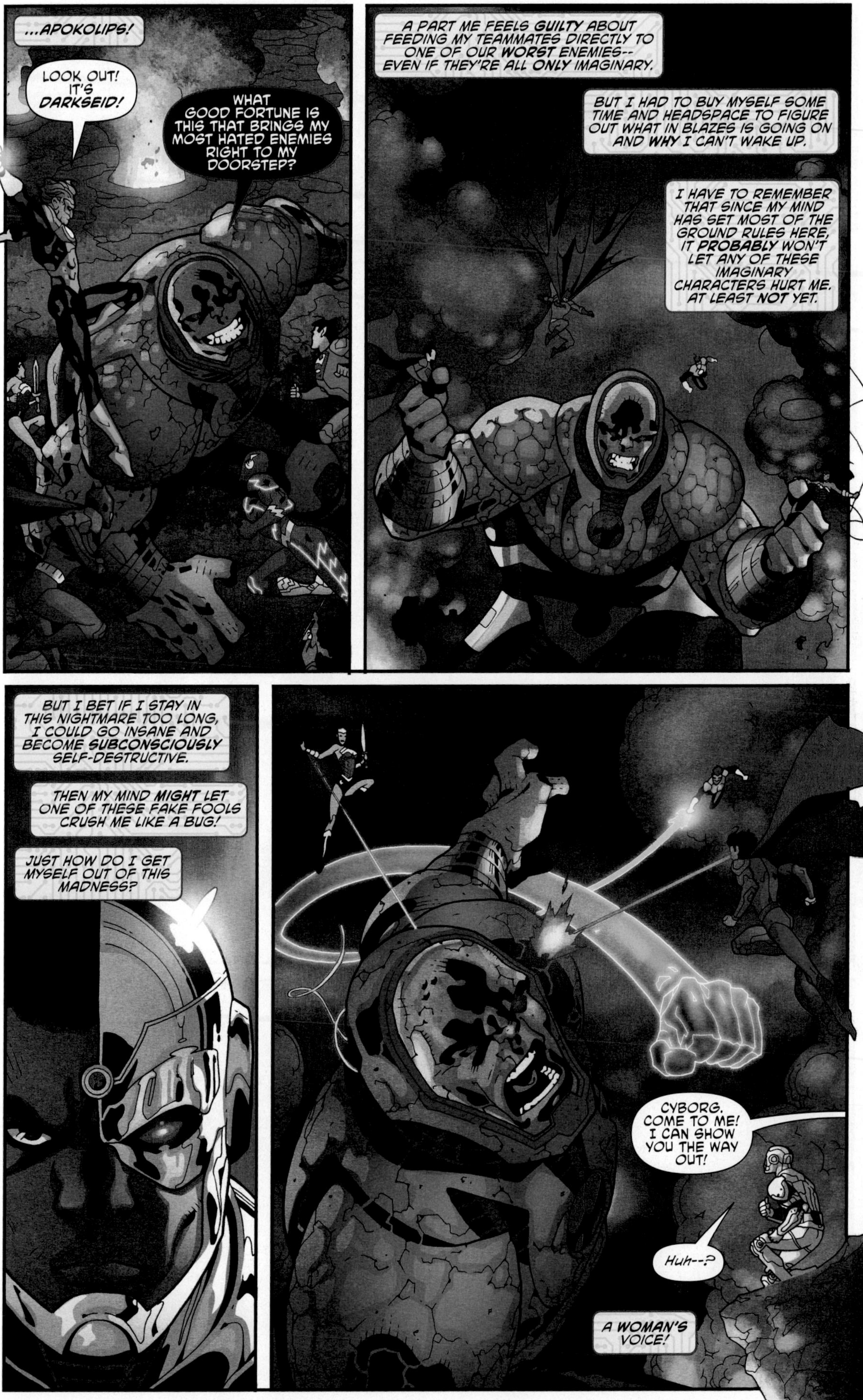
...APOKOLIPS!
LOOK OUT! IT'S DARKSEID!
WHAT GOOD FORTUNE IS THIS THAT BRINGS MY MOST HATED ENEMIES RIGHT TO MY DOORSTEP?
A PART ME FEELS GUILTY ABOUT FEEDING MY TEAMMATES DIRECTLY TO ONE OF OUR WORST ENEMIES-- EVEN IF THEY'RE ALL ONLY IMAGINARY.
BUT I HAD TO BUY MYSELF SOME TIME AND HEADSPACE TO FIGURE OUT WHAT IN BLAZES IS GOING ON AND WHY I CAN'T WAKE UP.
I HAVE TO REMEMBER THAT SINCE MY MIND HAS SET MOST OF THE GROUND RULES HERE, IT PROBABLY WON'T LET ANY OF THESE IMAGINARY CHARACTERS HURT ME. AT LEAST NOT YET.
BUT I BET IF I STAY IN THIS NIGHTMARE TOO LONG, I COULD GO INSANE AND BECOME SUBCONSCIOUSLY SELF-DESTRUCTIVE.
THEN MY MIND MIGHT LET ONE OF THESE FAKE FOOLS CRUSH ME LIKE A BUG!
JUST HOW DO I GET MYSELF OUT OF THIS MADNESS?
CYBORG. COME TO ME! I CAN SHOW YOU THE WAY OUT!
Huh--?
A WOMAN'S VOICE!

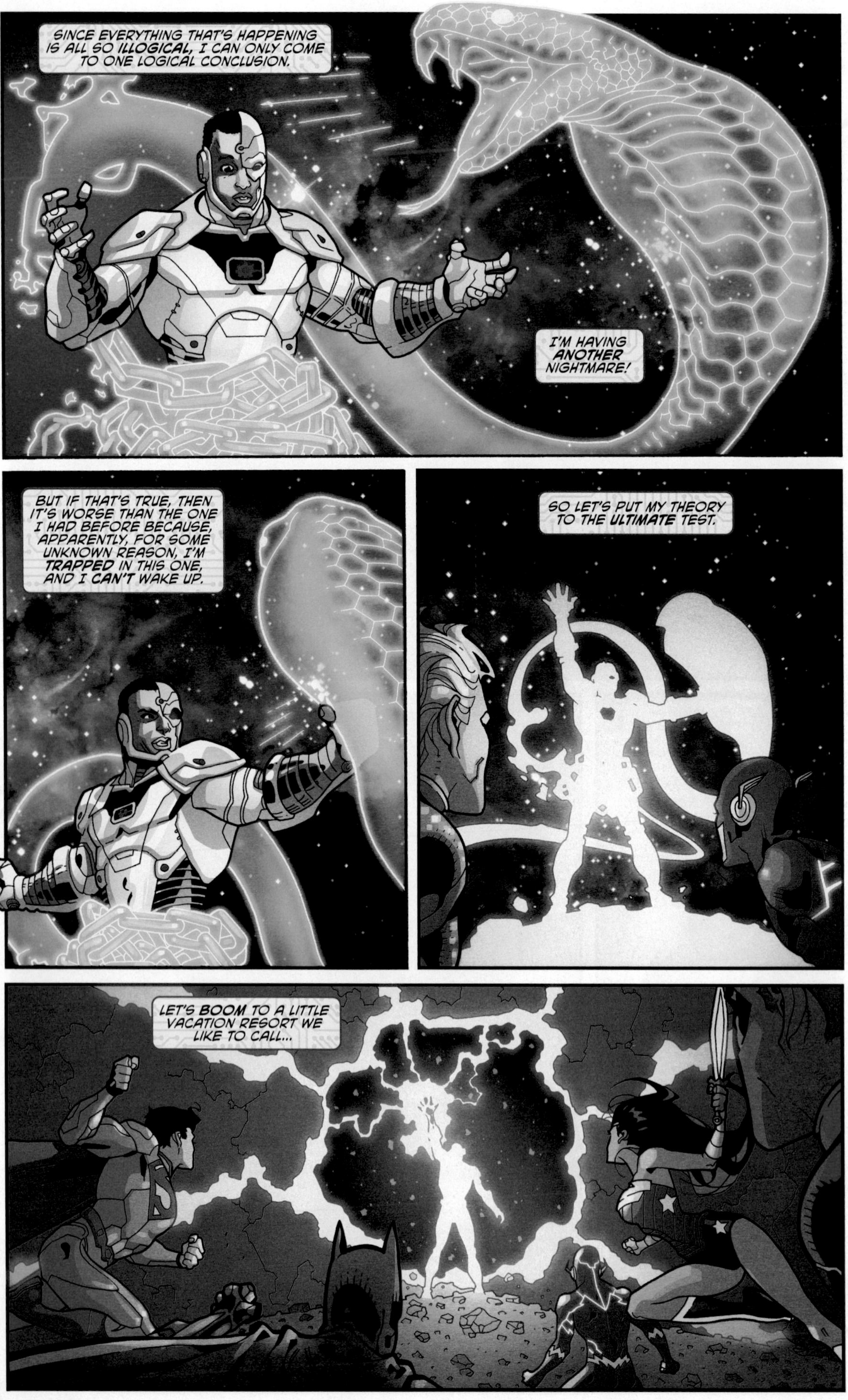
SINCE EVERYTHING THAT'S HAPPENING IS ALL SO ILLOGICAL, I CAN ONLY COME TO ONE LOGICAL CONCLUSION.
I'M HAVING ANOTHER NIGHTMARE!
BUT IF THAT'S TRUE, THEN IT'S WORSE THAN THE ONE I HAD BEFORE BECAUSE, APPARENTLY, FOR SOME UNKNOWN REASON, I'M TRAPPED IN THIS ONE, AND I CAN'T WAKE UP.
SO LET'S PUT MY THEORY TO THE ULTIMATE TEST.
LET'S BOOM TO A LITTLE VACATION RESORT WE LIKE TO CALL...

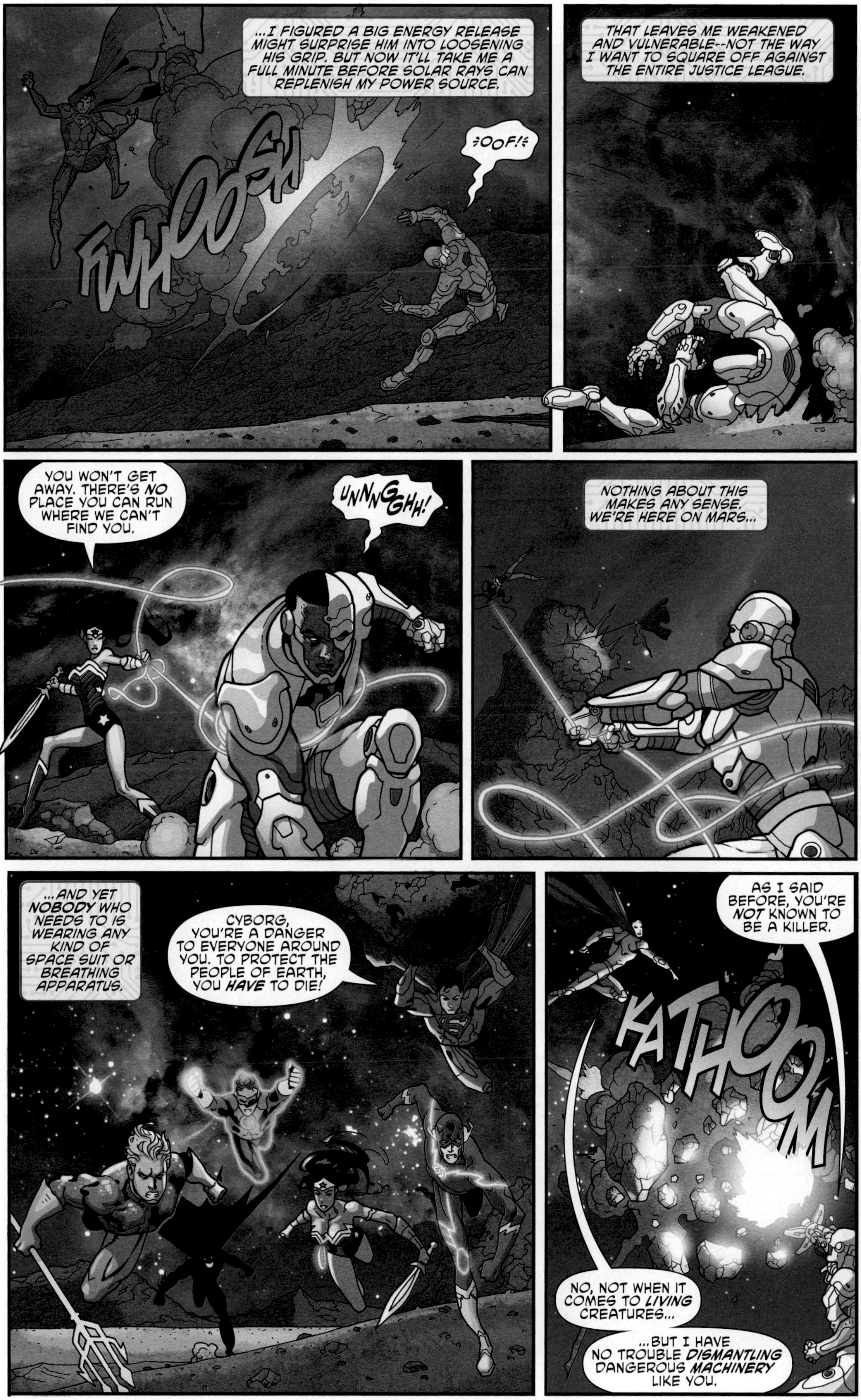
...I FIGURED A BIG ENERGY RELEASE MIGHT SURPRISE HIM INTO LOOSENING HIS GRIP. BUT NOW IT'LL TAKE ME A FULL MINUTE BEFORE SOLAR RAYS CAN REPLENISH MY POWER SOURCE.
FWHOOSH
OOF!
THAT LEAVES ME WEAKENED AND VULNERABLE--NOT THE WAY I WANT TO SQUARE OFF AGAINST THE ENTIRE JUSTICE LEAGUE.
YOU WON'T GET AWAY. THERE'S NO PLACE YOU CAN RUN WHERE WE CAN'T FIND YOU.
UNNNGGHH!
NOTHING ABOUT THIS MAKES ANY SENSE. WE'RE HERE ON MARS...
...AND YET NOBODY WHO NEEDS TO IS WEARING ANY KIND OF SPACE SUIT OR BREATHING APPARATUS.
CYBORG, YOU'RE A DANGER TO EVERYONE AROUND YOU. TO PROTECT THE PEOPLE OF EARTH, YOU HAVE TO DIE!
AS I SAID BEFORE, YOU'RE NOT KNOWN TO BE A KILLER.
KATHOOM
NO, NOT WHEN IT COMES TO LIVING CREATURES...
...BUT I HAVE NO TROUBLE DISMANTLING DANGEROUS MACHINERY LIKE YOU.

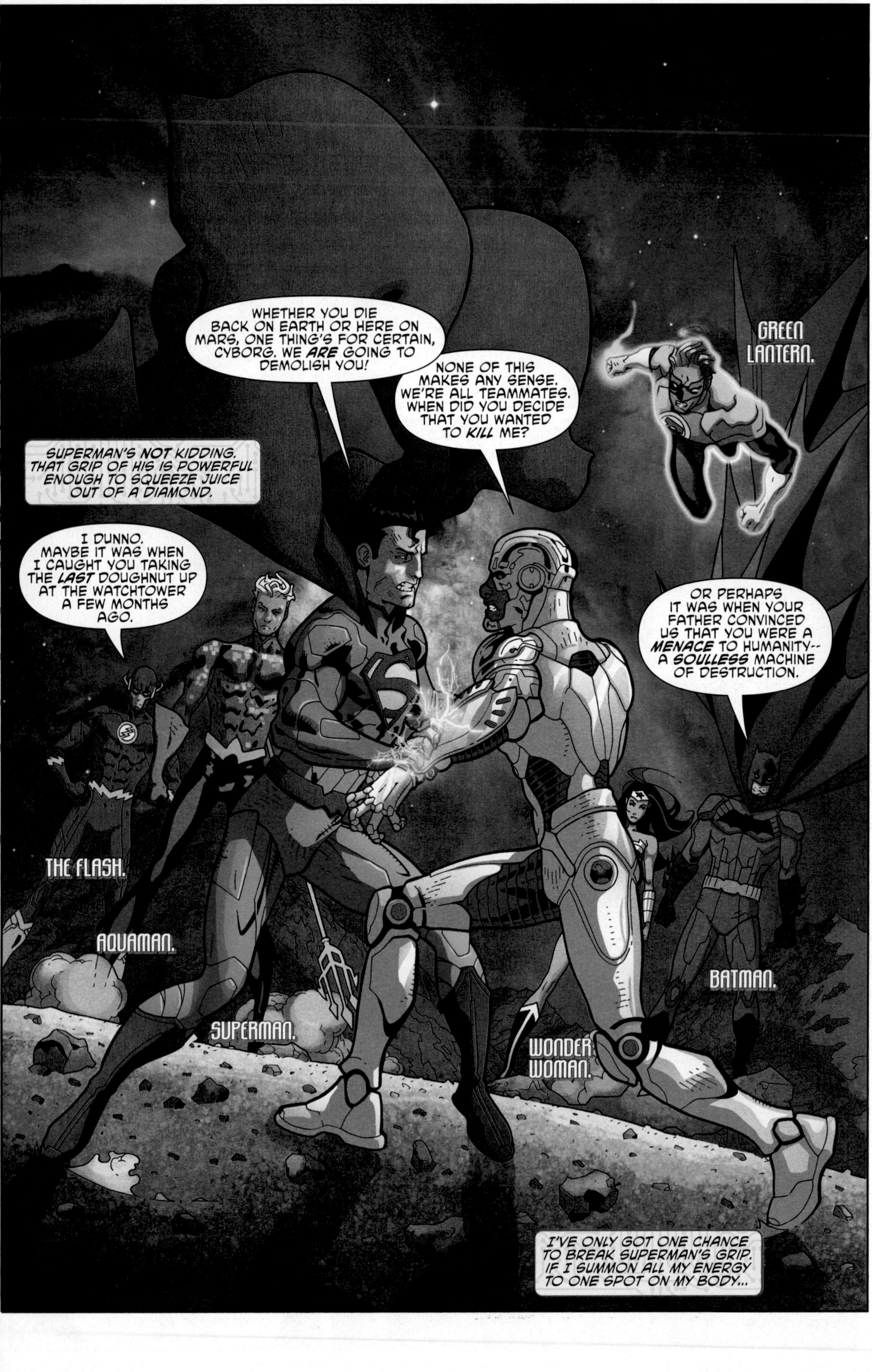
WHETHER YOU DIE BACK ON EARTH OR HERE ON MARS, ONE THING'S FOR CERTAIN, CYBORG. WE ARE GOING TO DEMOLISH YOU!
NONE OF THIS MAKES ANY SENSE. WE'RE ALL TEAMMATES. WHEN DID YOU DECIDE THAT YOU WANTED TO KILL ME?
GREEN LANTERN.
SUPERMAN'S NOT KIDDING. THAT GRIP OF HIS IS POWERFUL ENOUGH TO SQUEEZE JUICE OUT OF A DIAMOND.
I DUNNO. MAYBE IT WAS WHEN I CAUGHT YOU TAKING THE LAST DOUGHNUT UP AT THE WATCHTOWER A FEW MONTHS AGO.
OR PERHAPS IT WAS WHEN YOUR FATHER CONVINCED US THAT YOU WERE A MENACE TO HUMANITY-- A SOULLESS MACHINE OF DESTRUCTION.
THE FLASH.
AQUAMAN.
SUPERMAN.
WONDER WOMAN.
BATMAN.
I'VE ONLY GOT ONE CHANCE TO BREAK SUPERMAN'S GRIP. IF I SUMMON ALL MY ENERGY TO ONE SPOT ON MY BODY...

PART FOUR: MIND MAZE

JOHN SEMPER JR. writer ✶ TIMOTHY GREEN II penciller
JOSEPH SILVER inker ✶ GUY MAJOR colorist ✶ ROB LEIGH letterer
Cover by PAUL PELLETIER and SCOTT HANNA with GUY MAJOR

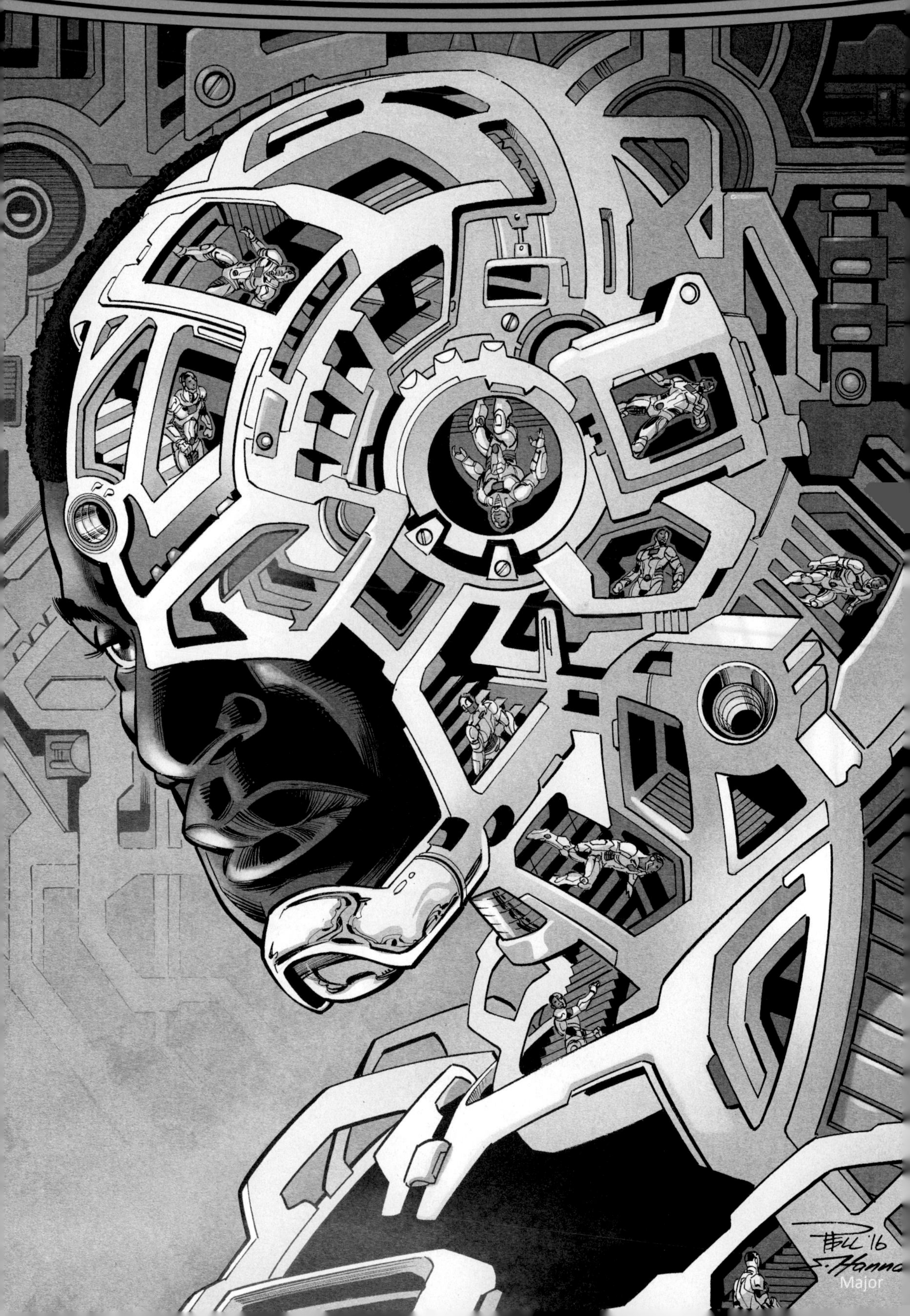

Major

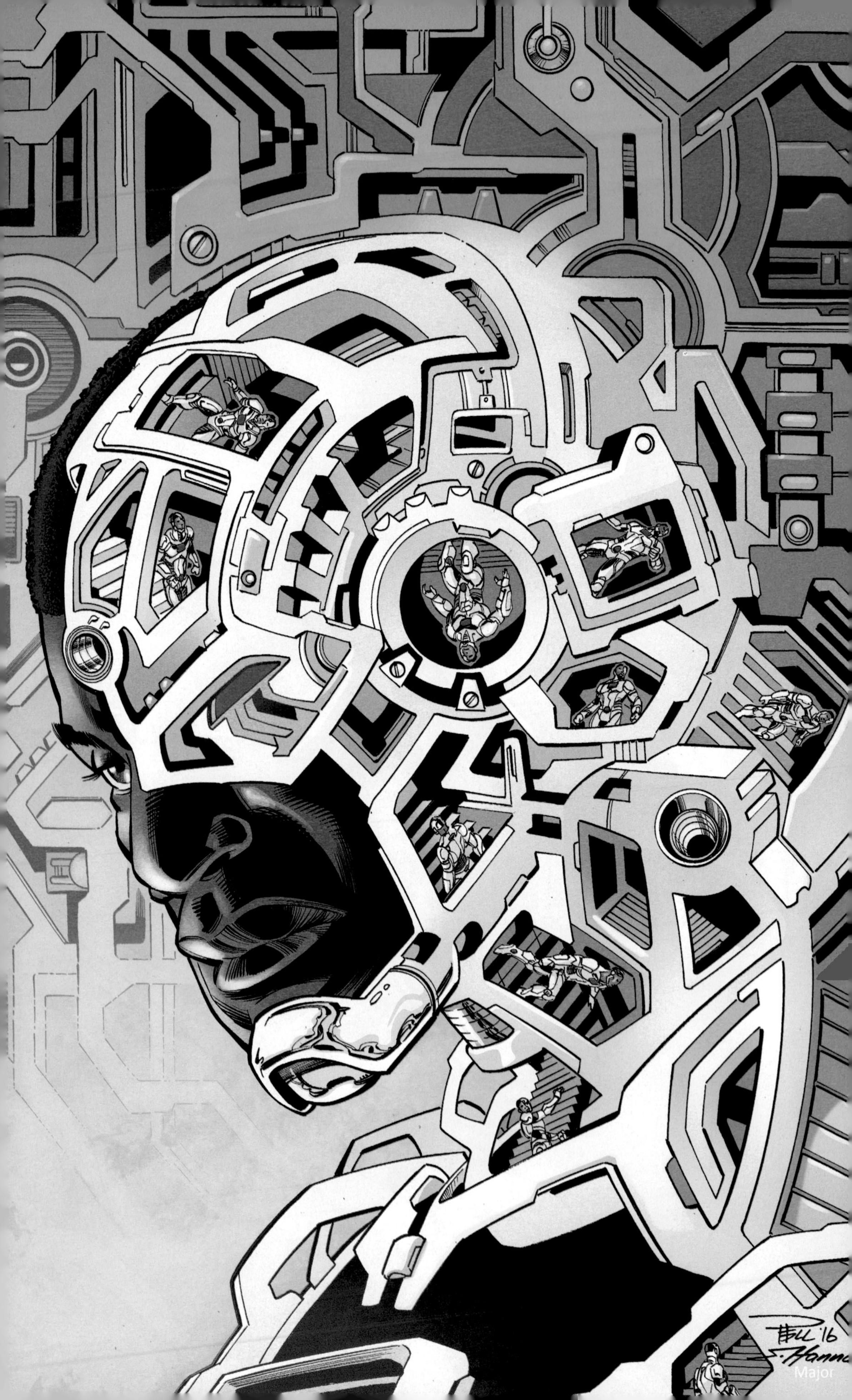

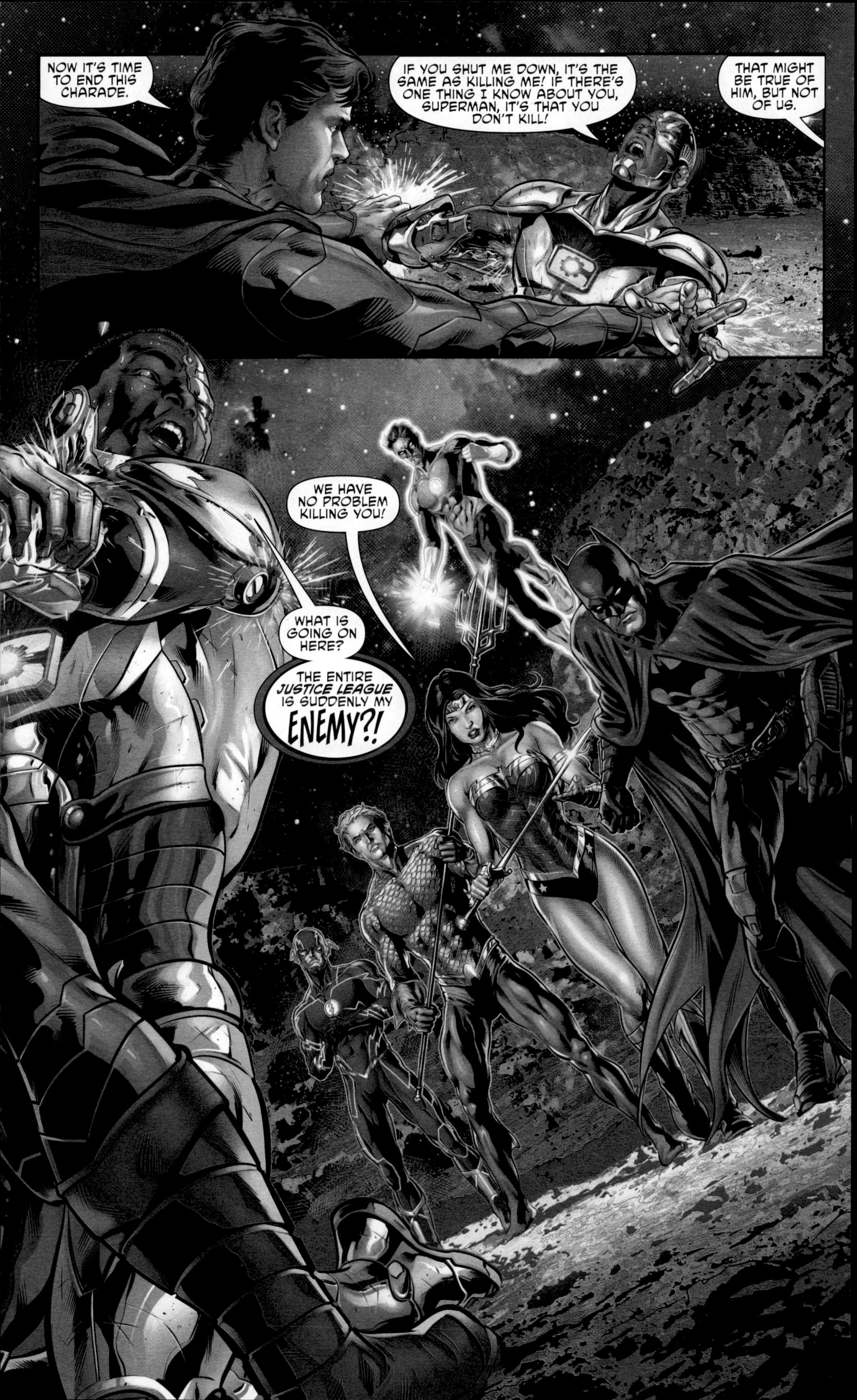
NOW IT'S TIME TO END THIS CHARADE.
IF YOU SHUT ME DOWN, IT'S THE SAME AS KILLING ME! IF THERE'S ONE THING I KNOW ABOUT YOU, SUPERMAN, IT'S THAT YOU DON'T KILL!
THAT MIGHT BE TRUE OF HIM, BUT NOT OF US.
WE HAVE NO PROBLEM KILLING YOU!
WHAT IS GOING ON HERE?
THE ENTIRE JUSTICE LEAGUE IS SUDDENLY MY ENEMY?!

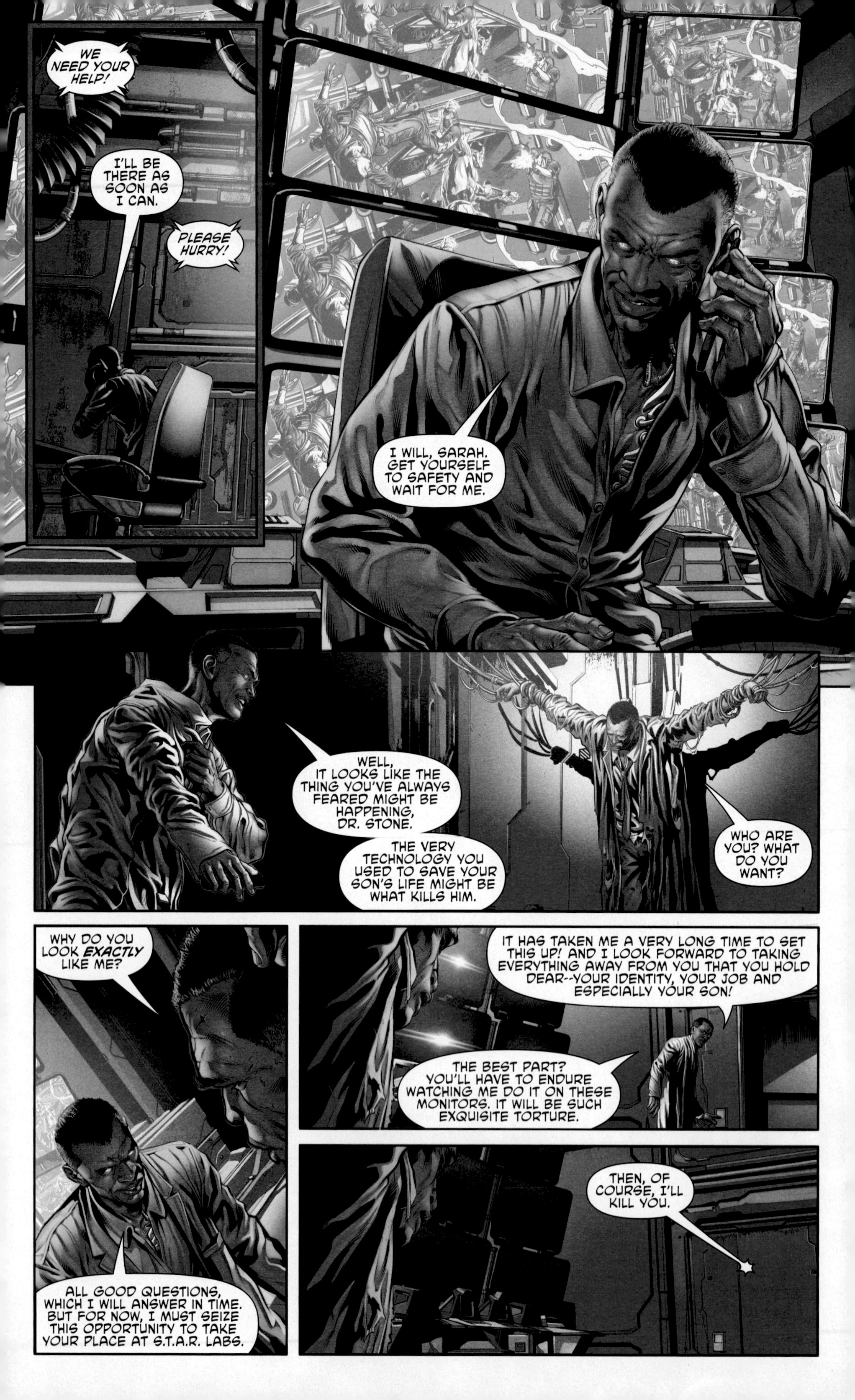
WE NEED YOUR HELP!
I'LL BE THERE AS SOON AS I CAN.
PLEASE HURRY!
I WILL, SARAH. GET YOURSELF TO SAFETY AND WAIT FOR ME.
WELL, IT LOOKS LIKE THE THING YOU'VE ALWAYS FEARED MIGHT BE HAPPENING, DR. STONE.
THE VERY TECHNOLOGY YOU USED TO SAVE YOUR SON'S LIFE MIGHT BE WHAT KILLS HIM.
WHO ARE YOU? WHAT DO YOU WANT?
WHY DO YOU LOOK *EXACTLY* LIKE ME?
ALL GOOD QUESTIONS, WHICH I WILL ANSWER IN TIME. BUT FOR NOW, I MUST SEIZE THIS OPPORTUNITY TO TAKE YOUR PLACE AT S.T.A.R. LABS.
IT HAS TAKEN ME A VERY LONG TIME TO SET THIS UP! AND I LOOK FORWARD TO TAKING EVERYTHING AWAY FROM YOU THAT YOU HOLD DEAR--YOUR IDENTITY, YOUR JOB AND ESPECIALLY YOUR SON!
THE BEST PART? YOU'LL HAVE TO ENDURE WATCHING ME DO IT ON THESE MONITORS. IT WILL BE SUCH EXQUISITE TORTURE.
THEN, OF COURSE, I'LL KILL YOU.

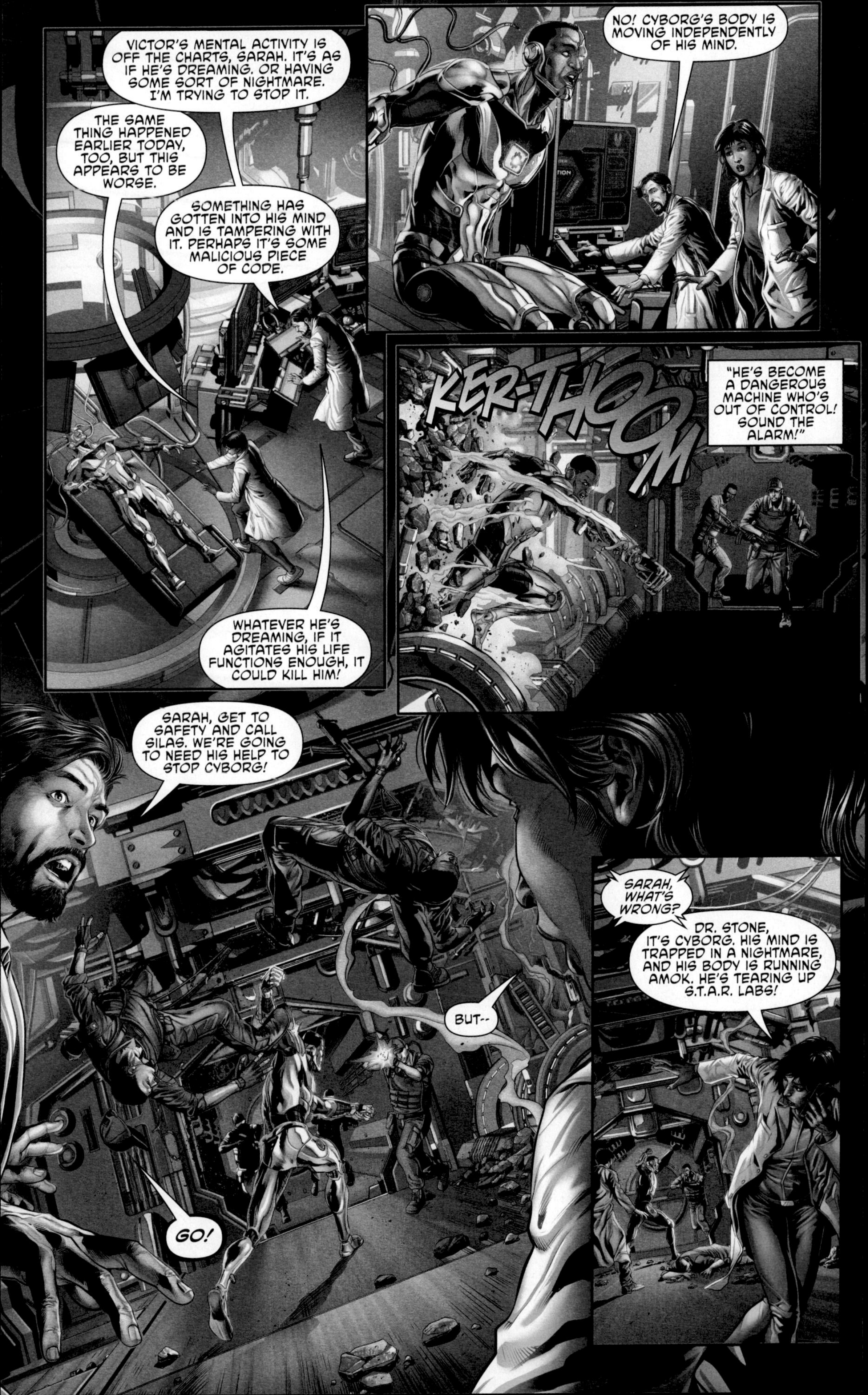
VICTOR'S MENTAL ACTIVITY IS OFF THE CHARTS, SARAH. IT'S AS IF HE'S DREAMING, OR HAVING SOME SORT OF NIGHTMARE. I'M TRYING TO STOP IT.
THE SAME THING HAPPENED EARLIER TODAY, TOO, BUT THIS APPEARS TO BE WORSE.
SOMETHING HAS GOTTEN INTO HIS MIND AND IS TAMPERING WITH IT. PERHAPS IT'S SOME MALICIOUS PIECE OF CODE.
WHATEVER HE'S DREAMING, IF IT AGITATES HIS LIFE FUNCTIONS ENOUGH, IT COULD KILL HIM!
NO! CYBORG'S BODY IS MOVING INDEPENDENTLY OF HIS MIND.
KER-THOOM
"HE'S BECOME A DANGEROUS MACHINE WHO'S OUT OF CONTROL! SOUND THE ALARM!"
SARAH, GET TO SAFETY AND CALL SILAS. WE'RE GOING TO NEED HIS HELP TO STOP CYBORG!
BUT--
GO!
SARAH, WHAT'S WRONG?
DR. STONE, IT'S CYBORG. HIS MIND IS TRAPPED IN A NIGHTMARE, AND HIS BODY IS RUNNING AMOK. HE'S TEARING UP S.T.A.R. LABS!

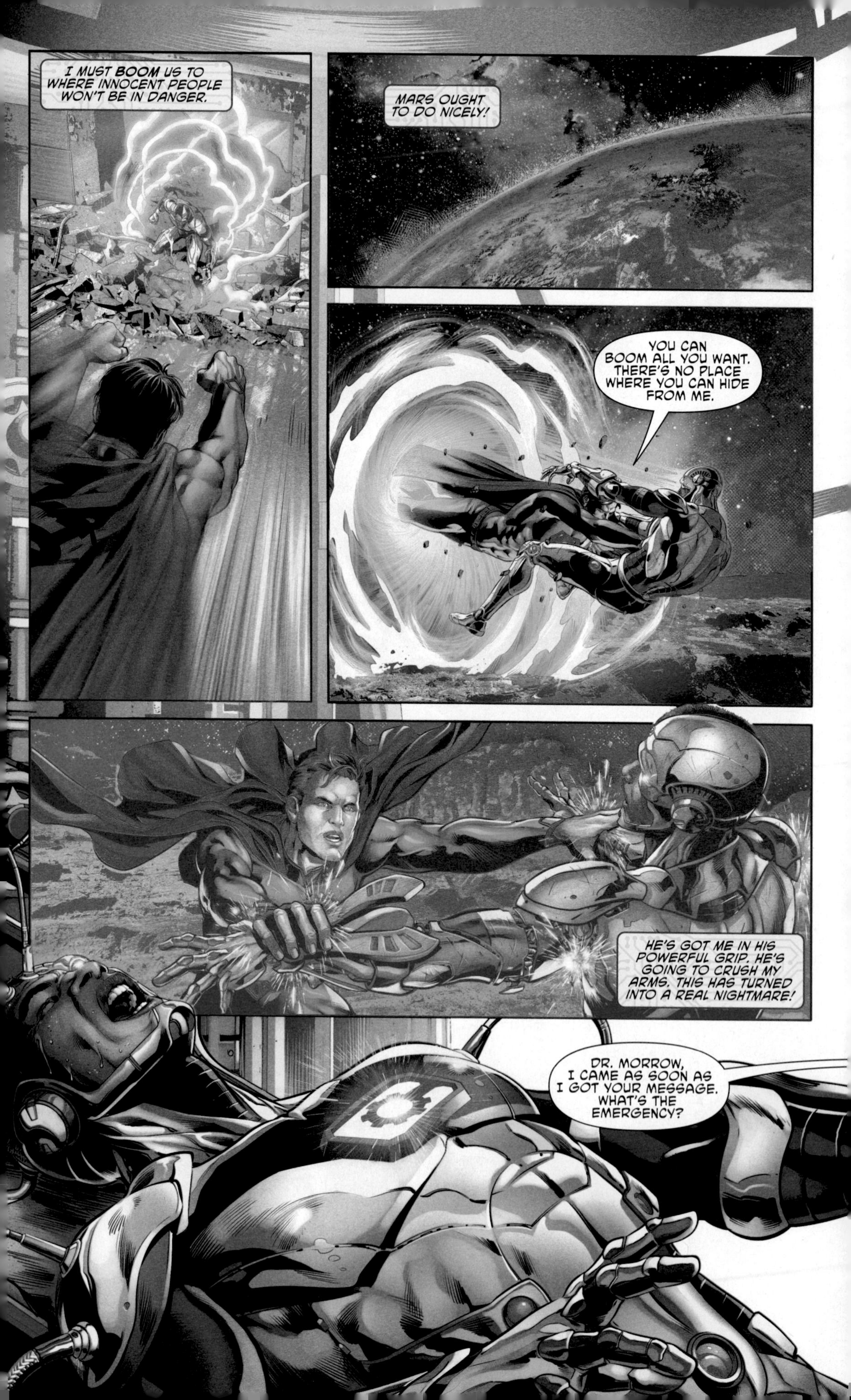
I MUST BOOM US TO WHERE INNOCENT PEOPLE WON'T BE IN DANGER.
MARS OUGHT TO DO NICELY!
YOU CAN BOOM ALL YOU WANT. THERE'S NO PLACE WHERE YOU CAN HIDE FROM ME.
HE'S GOT ME IN HIS POWERFUL GRIP. HE'S GOING TO CRUSH MY ARMS. THIS HAS TURNED INTO A REAL NIGHTMARE!
DR. MORROW, I CAME AS SOON AS I GOT YOUR MESSAGE. WHAT'S THE EMERGENCY?

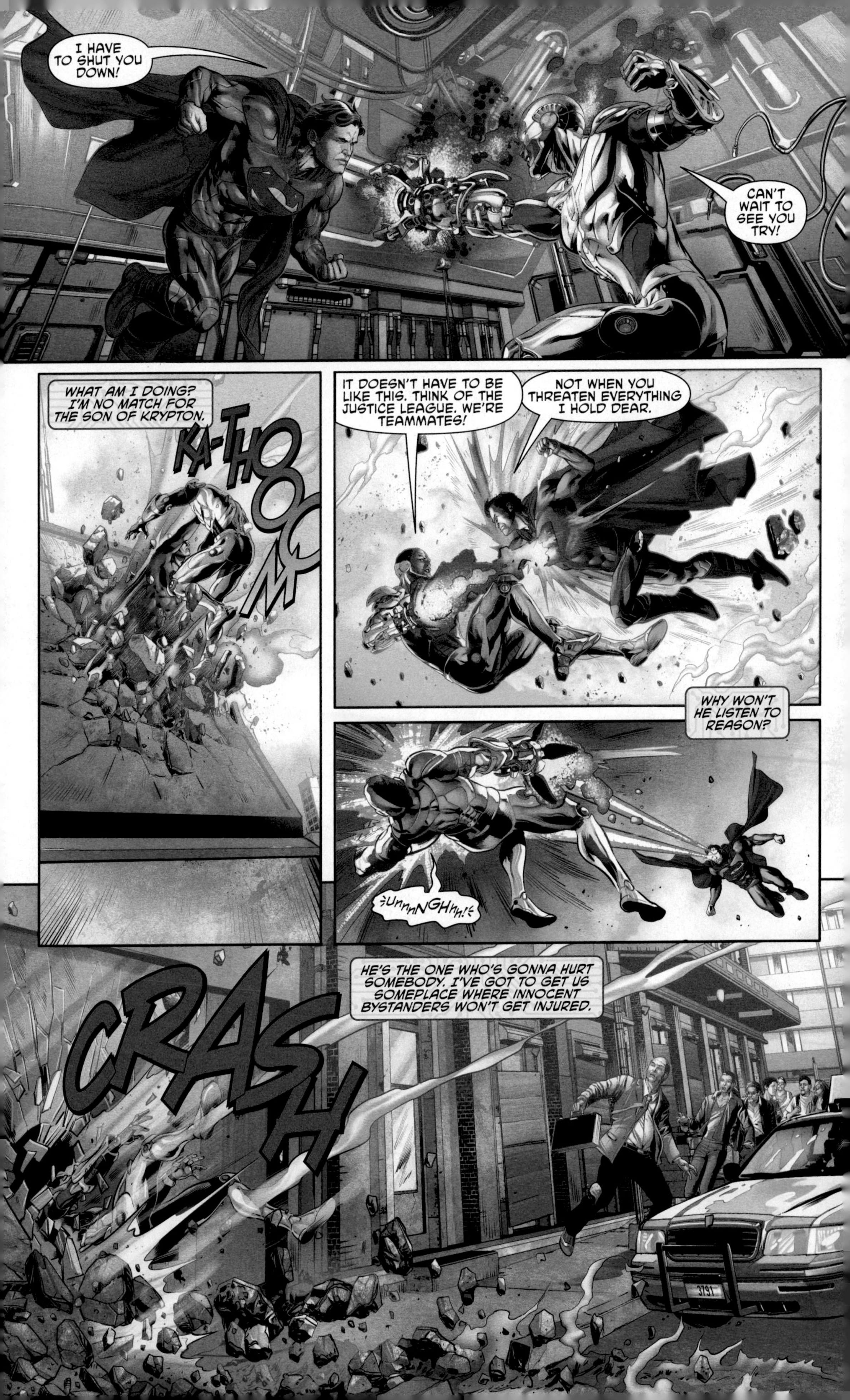
I HAVE TO SHUT YOU DOWN!
CAN'T WAIT TO SEE YOU TRY!
WHAT AM I DOING? I'M NO MATCH FOR THE SON OF KRYPTON.
KA-THOOOM
IT DOESN'T HAVE TO BE LIKE THIS. THINK OF THE JUSTICE LEAGUE. WE'RE TEAMMATES!
NOT WHEN YOU THREATEN EVERYTHING I HOLD DEAR.
WHY WON'T HE LISTEN TO REASON?
UnnnNGHnn!
HE'S THE ONE WHO'S GONNA HURT SOMEBODY. I'VE GOT TO GET US SOMEPLACE WHERE INNOCENT BYSTANDERS WON'T GET INJURED.
CRASH

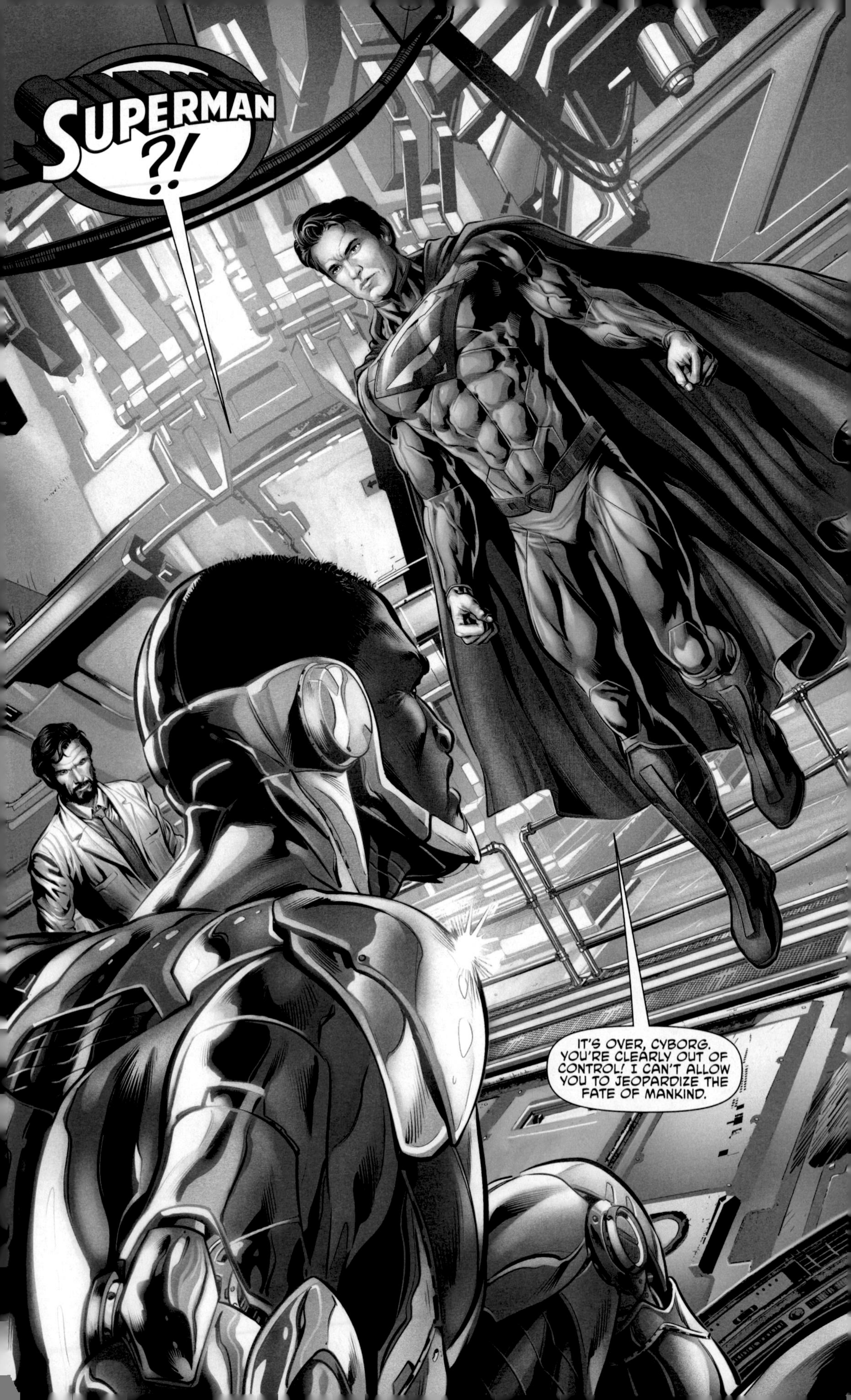
SUPERMAN ?!
IT'S OVER, CYBORG. YOU'RE CLEARLY OUT OF CONTROL! I CAN'T ALLOW YOU TO JEOPARDIZE THE FATE OF MANKIND.

ALL RIGHT. I'M INITIATING THE SUBROUTINE THAT WILL WORK ITS WAY THROUGH YOUR BRAIN AND REAWAKEN YOUR DORMANT MEMORIES.

ALL YOU HAVE TO DO IS CLOSE YOUR EYES.

AS YOUR FATHER HAS SUSPECTED FOR SOME TIME NOW, YOU'RE NOT HIS SON. YOU'RE A DANGEROUS FREAK OF NATURE.

YOU'RE A "FRANKENSTEIN'S MONSTER," WHICH HE ACCIDENTALLY CREATED IN HIS SON'S IMAGE AND INADVERTENTLY UNLEASHED ON MANKIND. THERE'S ONLY ONE THING FOR ME TO DO, AND THAT IS TO SHUT YOU DOWN!

KLANG

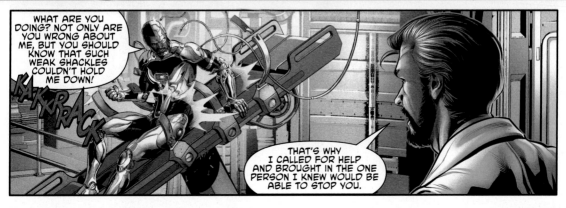

WHAT ARE YOU DOING? NOT ONLY ARE YOU WRONG ABOUT ME, BUT YOU SHOULD KNOW THAT SUCH WEAK SHACKLES COULDN'T HOLD ME DOWN!

KA-KR-RACK

THAT'S WHY I CALLED FOR HELP AND BROUGHT IN THE ONE PERSON I KNEW WOULD BE ABLE TO STOP YOU.

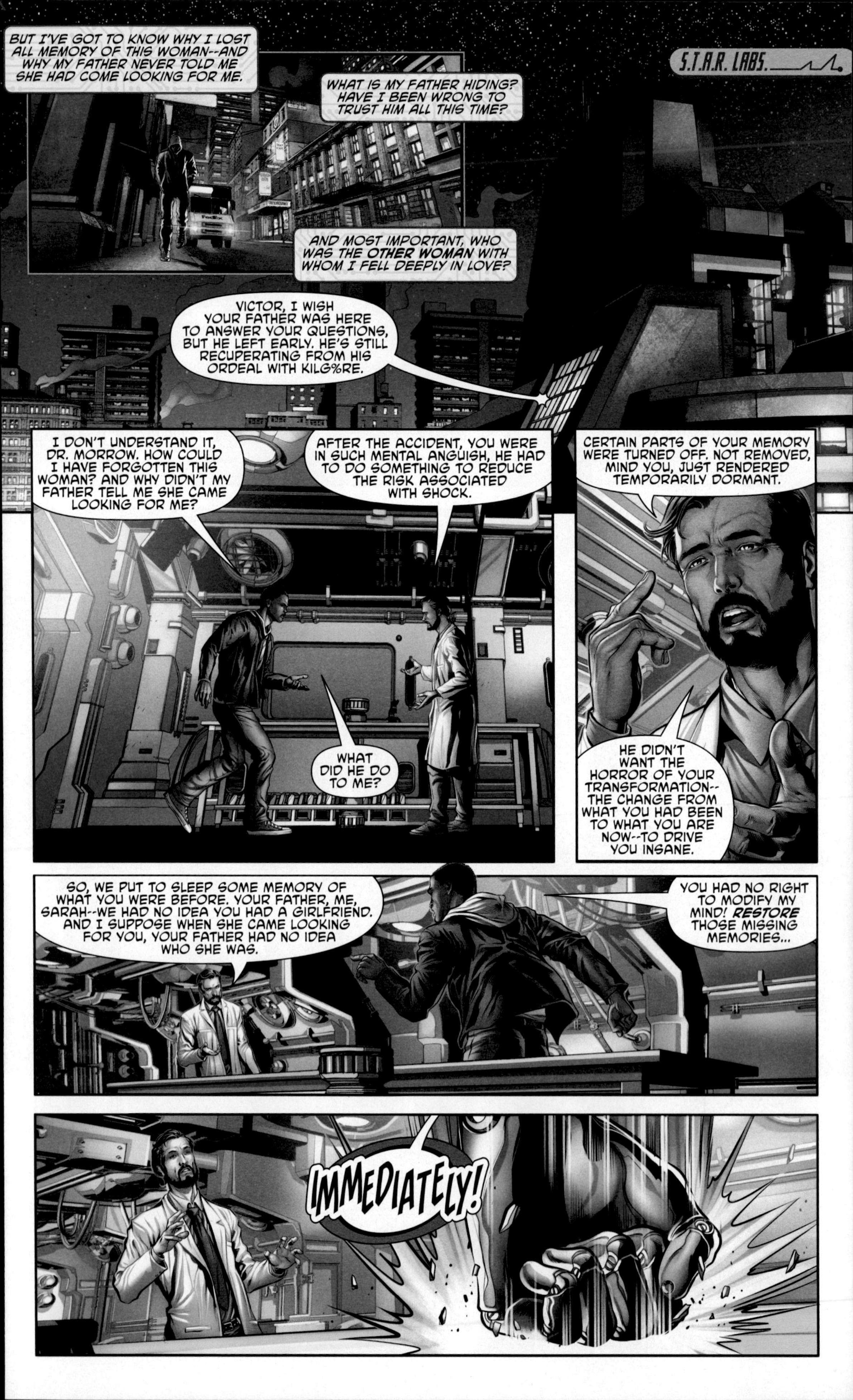
BUT I'VE GOT TO KNOW WHY I LOST ALL MEMORY OF THIS WOMAN--AND WHY MY FATHER NEVER TOLD ME SHE HAD COME LOOKING FOR ME.
WHAT IS MY FATHER HIDING? HAVE I BEEN WRONG TO TRUST HIM ALL THIS TIME?
S.T.A.R. LABS.
AND MOST IMPORTANT, WHO WAS THE OTHER WOMAN WITH WHOM I FELL DEEPLY IN LOVE?
VICTOR, I WISH YOUR FATHER WAS HERE TO ANSWER YOUR QUESTIONS, BUT HE LEFT EARLY. HE'S STILL RECUPERATING FROM HIS ORDEAL WITH KILG%RE.
I DON'T UNDERSTAND IT, DR. MORROW. HOW COULD I HAVE FORGOTTEN THIS WOMAN? AND WHY DIDN'T MY FATHER TELL ME SHE CAME LOOKING FOR ME?
AFTER THE ACCIDENT, YOU WERE IN SUCH MENTAL ANGUISH, HE HAD TO DO SOMETHING TO REDUCE THE RISK ASSOCIATED WITH SHOCK.
WHAT DID HE DO TO ME?
CERTAIN PARTS OF YOUR MEMORY WERE TURNED OFF. NOT REMOVED, MIND YOU, JUST RENDERED TEMPORARILY DORMANT.
HE DIDN'T WANT THE HORROR OF YOUR TRANSFORMATION--THE CHANGE FROM WHAT YOU HAD BEEN TO WHAT YOU ARE NOW--TO DRIVE YOU INSANE.
SO, WE PUT TO SLEEP SOME MEMORY OF WHAT YOU WERE BEFORE. YOUR FATHER, ME, SARAH--WE HAD NO IDEA YOU HAD A GIRLFRIEND. AND I SUPPOSE WHEN SHE CAME LOOKING FOR YOU, YOUR FATHER HAD NO IDEA WHO SHE WAS.
YOU HAD NO RIGHT TO MODIFY MY MIND! RESTORE THOSE MISSING MEMORIES...
IMMEDIATELY!

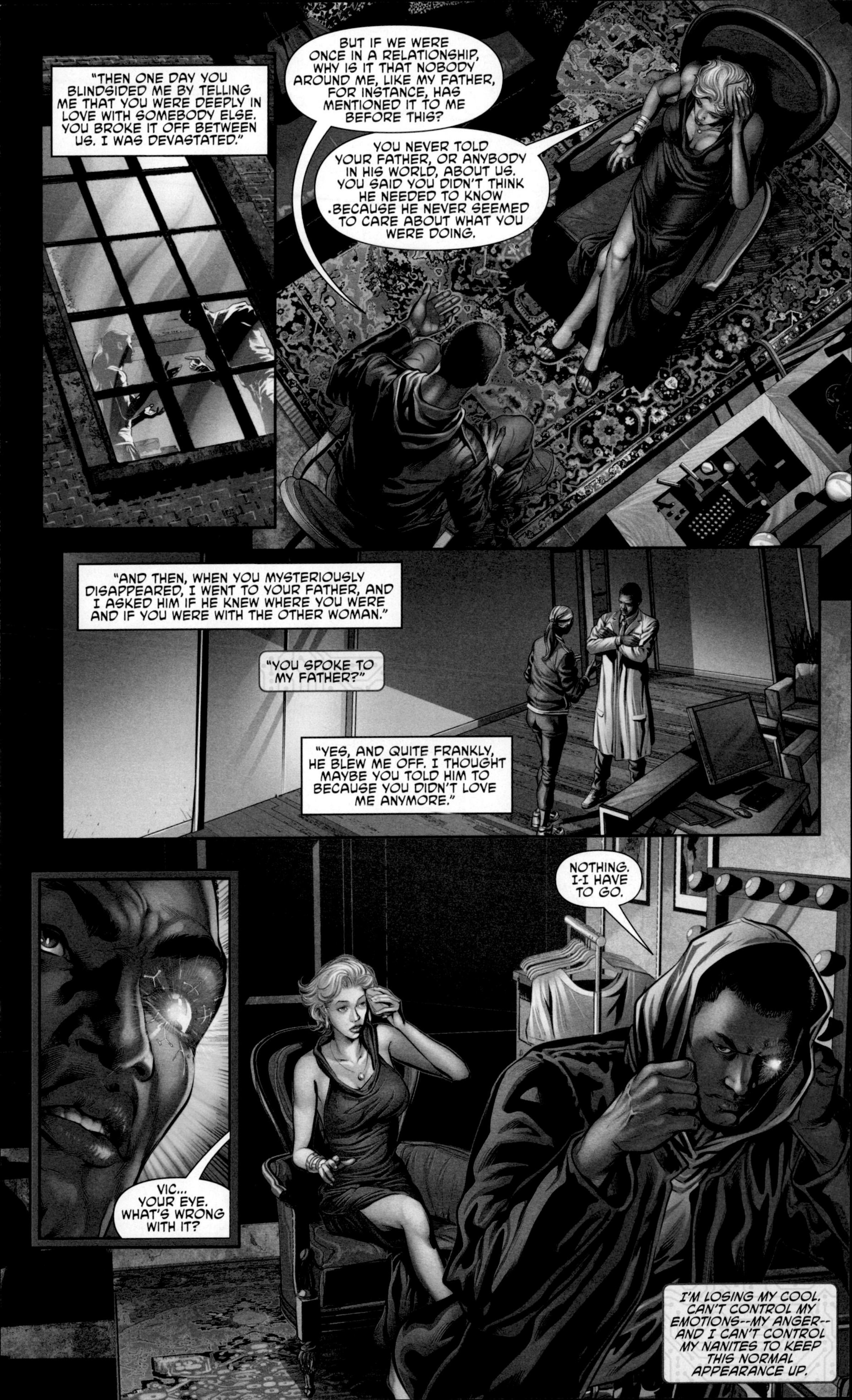
"THEN ONE DAY YOU BLINDSIDED ME BY TELLING ME THAT YOU WERE DEEPLY IN LOVE WITH SOMEBODY ELSE. YOU BROKE IT OFF BETWEEN US. I WAS DEVASTATED."
BUT IF WE WERE ONCE IN A RELATIONSHIP, WHY IS IT THAT NOBODY AROUND ME, LIKE MY FATHER, FOR INSTANCE, HAS MENTIONED IT TO ME BEFORE THIS?
YOU NEVER TOLD YOUR FATHER, OR ANYBODY IN HIS WORLD, ABOUT US. YOU SAID YOU DIDN'T THINK HE NEEDED TO KNOW BECAUSE HE NEVER SEEMED TO CARE ABOUT WHAT YOU WERE DOING.
"AND THEN, WHEN YOU MYSTERIOUSLY DISAPPEARED, I WENT TO YOUR FATHER, AND I ASKED HIM IF HE KNEW WHERE YOU WERE AND IF YOU WERE WITH THE OTHER WOMAN."
"YOU SPOKE TO MY FATHER?"
"YES, AND QUITE FRANKLY, HE BLEW ME OFF. I THOUGHT MAYBE YOU TOLD HIM TO BECAUSE YOU DIDN'T LOVE ME ANYMORE."
VIC... YOUR EYE. WHAT'S WRONG WITH IT?
NOTHING. I-I HAVE TO GO.
I'M LOSING MY COOL. CAN'T CONTROL MY EMOTIONS--MY ANGER--AND I CAN'T CONTROL MY NANITES TO KEEP THIS NORMAL APPEARANCE UP.

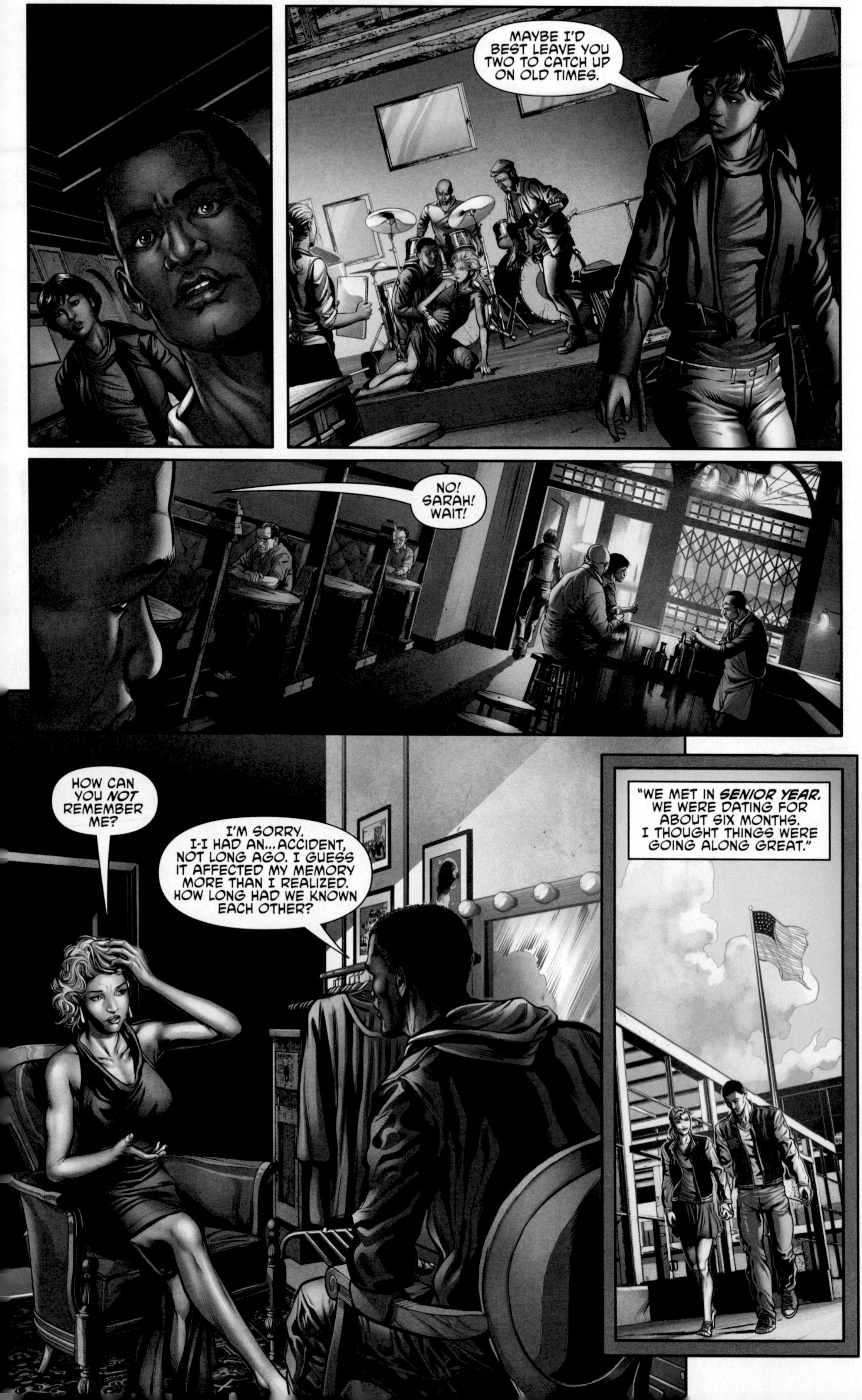
MAYBE I'D BEST LEAVE YOU TWO TO CATCH UP ON OLD TIMES.
NO! SARAH! WAIT!
HOW CAN YOU *NOT* REMEMBER ME?
I'M SORRY. I-I HAD AN...ACCIDENT, NOT LONG AGO. I GUESS IT AFFECTED MY MEMORY MORE THAN I REALIZED. HOW LONG HAD WE KNOWN EACH OTHER?
"WE MET IN *SENIOR YEAR.* WE WERE DATING FOR ABOUT SIX MONTHS. I THOUGHT THINGS WERE GOING ALONG GREAT."

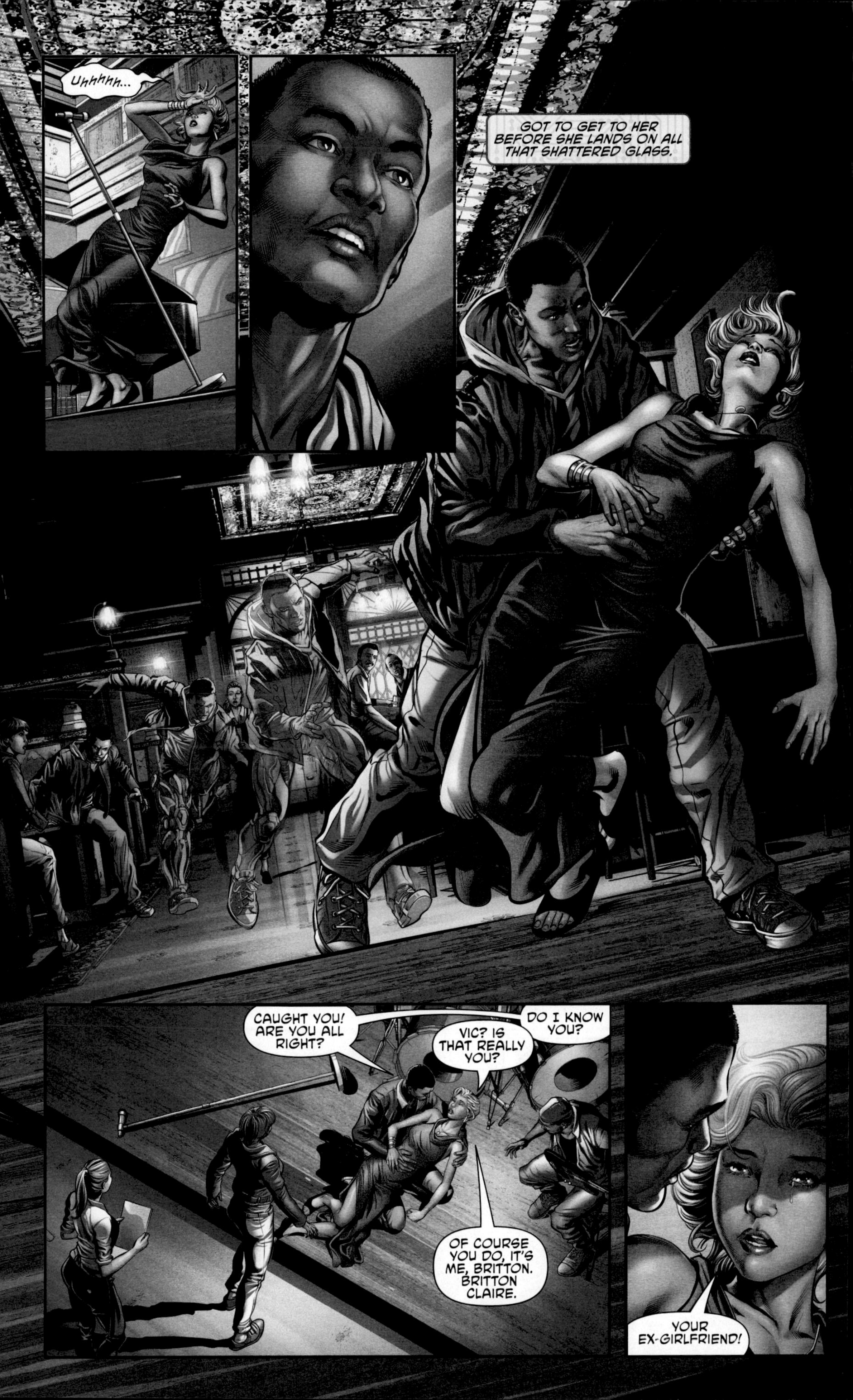
Unhhhh...
GOT TO GET TO HER BEFORE SHE LANDS ON ALL THAT SHATTERED GLASS.
CAUGHT YOU! ARE YOU ALL RIGHT?
VIC? IS THAT REALLY YOU?
DO I KNOW YOU?
OF COURSE YOU DO, IT'S ME, BRITTON. BRITTON CLAIRE.
YOUR EX-GIRLFRIEND!

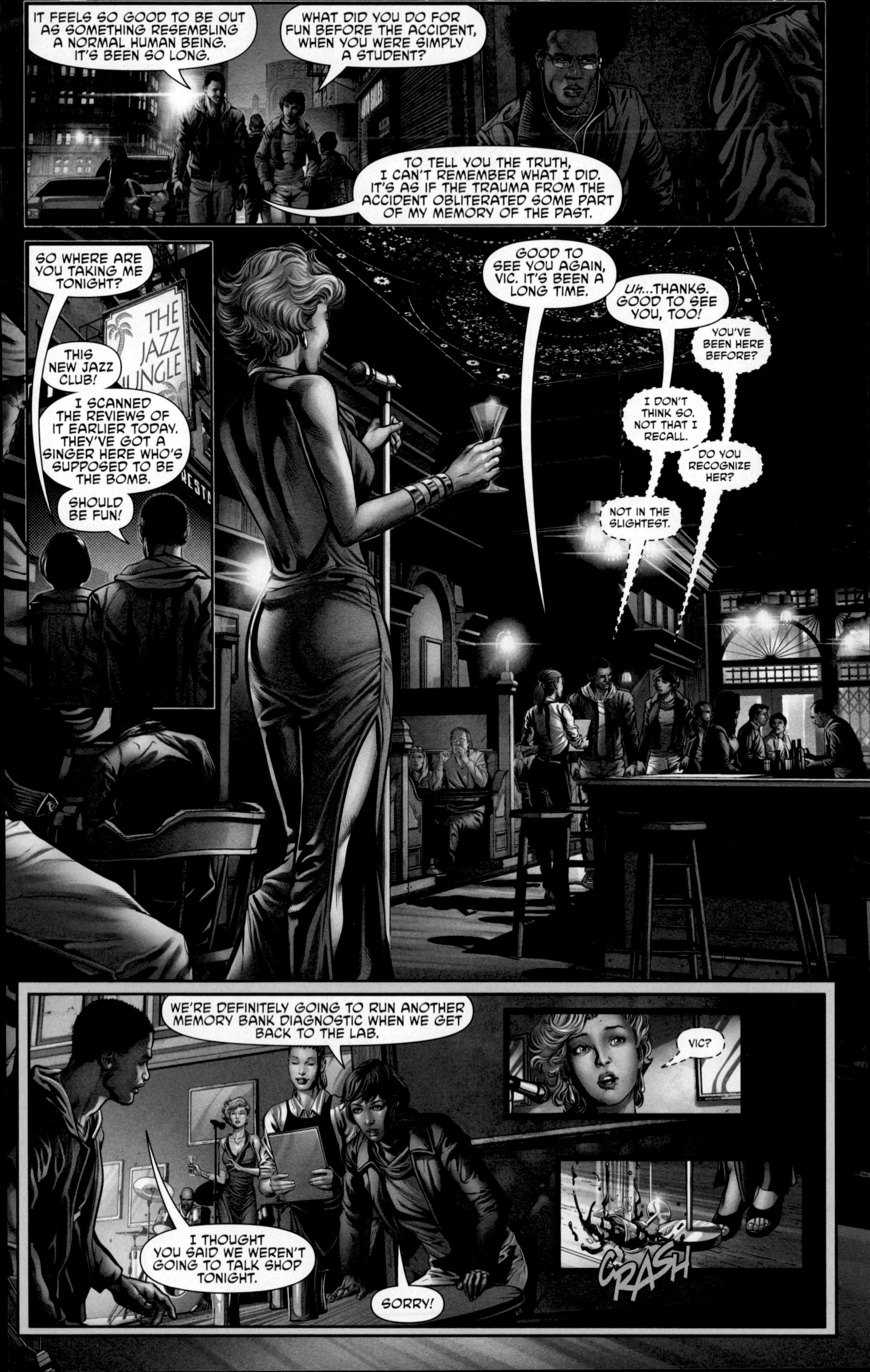

IT FEELS SO GOOD TO BE OUT AS SOMETHING RESEMBLING A NORMAL HUMAN BEING. IT'S BEEN SO LONG.
WHAT DID YOU DO FOR FUN BEFORE THE ACCIDENT, WHEN YOU WERE SIMPLY A STUDENT?
TO TELL YOU THE TRUTH, I CAN'T REMEMBER WHAT I DID. IT'S AS IF THE TRAUMA FROM THE ACCIDENT OBLITERATED SOME PART OF MY MEMORY OF THE PAST.
SO WHERE ARE YOU TAKING ME TONIGHT?
THE JAZZ JUNGLE
THIS NEW JAZZ CLUB!
I SCANNED THE REVIEWS OF IT EARLIER TODAY. THEY'VE GOT A SINGER HERE WHO'S SUPPOSED TO BE THE BOMB.
SHOULD BE FUN!
GOOD TO SEE YOU AGAIN, VIC. IT'S BEEN A LONG TIME.
Uh...THANKS. GOOD TO SEE YOU, TOO!
YOU'VE BEEN HERE BEFORE?
I DON'T THINK SO. NOT THAT I RECALL.
DO YOU RECOGNIZE HER?
NOT IN THE SLIGHTEST.
WE'RE DEFINITELY GOING TO RUN ANOTHER MEMORY BANK DIAGNOSTIC WHEN WE GET BACK TO THE LAB.
I THOUGHT YOU SAID WE WEREN'T GOING TO TALK SHOP TONIGHT.
SORRY!
VIC?
CRASH

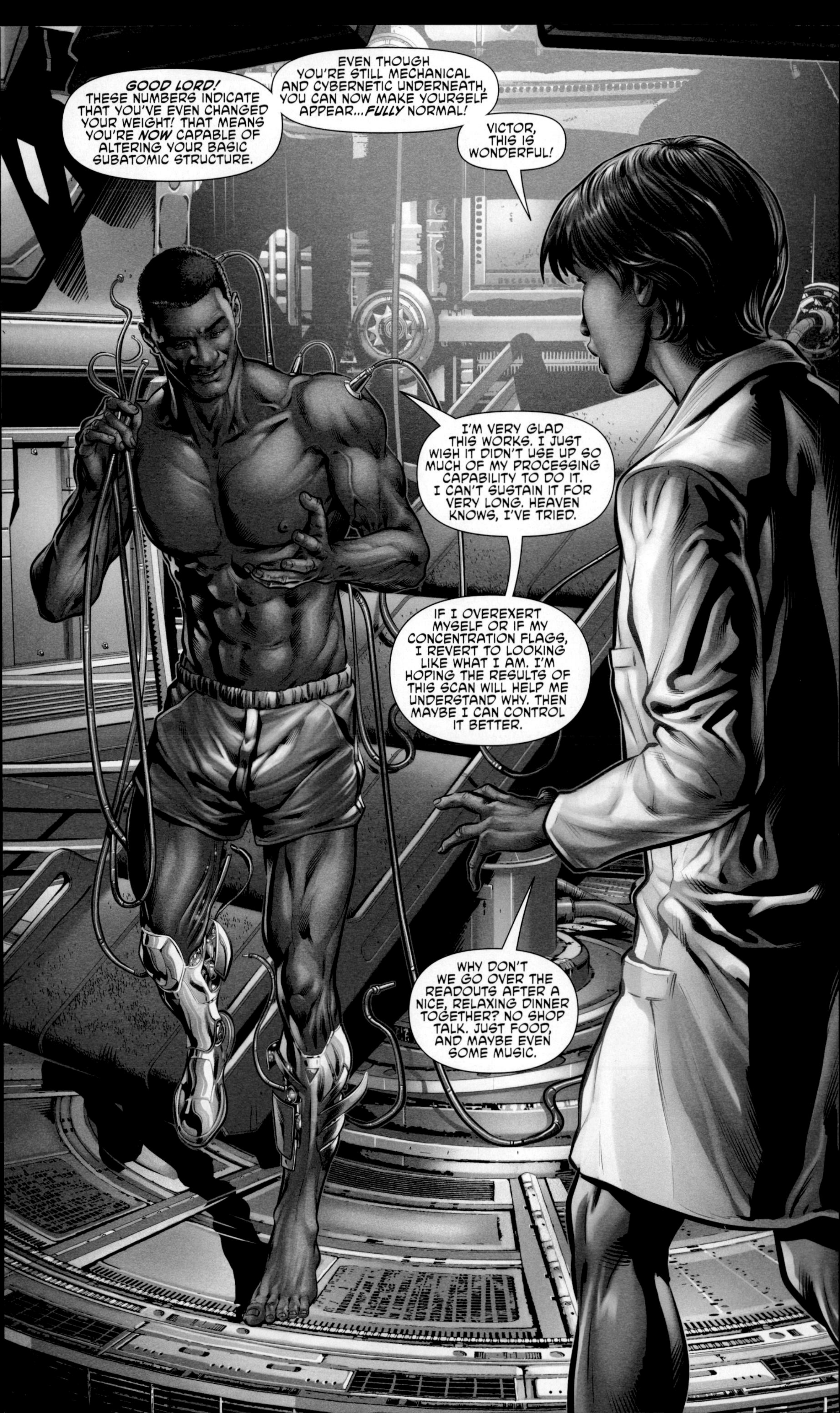
GOOD LORD! THESE NUMBERS INDICATE THAT YOU'VE EVEN CHANGED YOUR WEIGHT! THAT MEANS YOU'RE NOW CAPABLE OF ALTERING YOUR BASIC SUBATOMIC STRUCTURE.
EVEN THOUGH YOU'RE STILL MECHANICAL AND CYBERNETIC UNDERNEATH, YOU CAN NOW MAKE YOURSELF APPEAR...FULLY NORMAL!
VICTOR, THIS IS WONDERFUL!
I'M VERY GLAD THIS WORKS. I JUST WISH IT DIDN'T USE UP SO MUCH OF MY PROCESSING CAPABILITY TO DO IT. I CAN'T SUSTAIN IT FOR VERY LONG. HEAVEN KNOWS, I'VE TRIED.
IF I OVEREXERT MYSELF OR IF MY CONCENTRATION FLAGS, I REVERT TO LOOKING LIKE WHAT I AM. I'M HOPING THE RESULTS OF THIS SCAN WILL HELP ME UNDERSTAND WHY. THEN MAYBE I CAN CONTROL IT BETTER.
WHY DON'T WE GO OVER THE READOUTS AFTER A NICE, RELAXING DINNER TOGETHER? NO SHOP TALK. JUST FOOD, AND MAYBE EVEN SOME MUSIC.

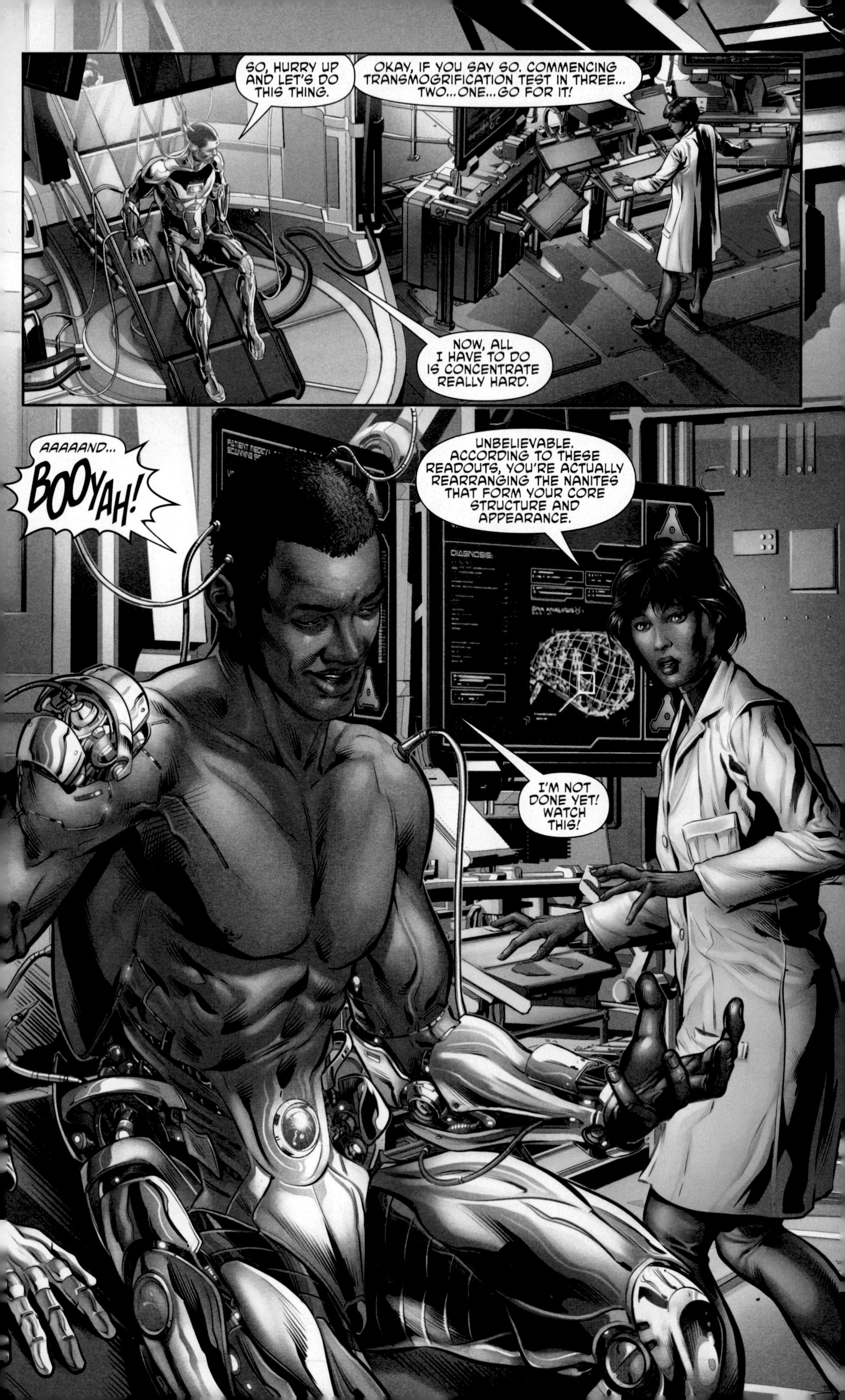
SO, HURRY UP AND LET'S DO THIS THING.
OKAY, IF YOU SAY SO. COMMENCING TRANSMOGRIFICATION TEST IN THREE... TWO...ONE...GO FOR IT!
NOW, ALL I HAVE TO DO IS CONCENTRATE REALLY HARD.
AAAAAND...
BOOYAH!
UNBELIEVABLE. ACCORDING TO THESE READOUTS, YOU'RE ACTUALLY REARRANGING THE NANITES THAT FORM YOUR CORE STRUCTURE AND APPEARANCE.
I'M NOT DONE YET! WATCH THIS!

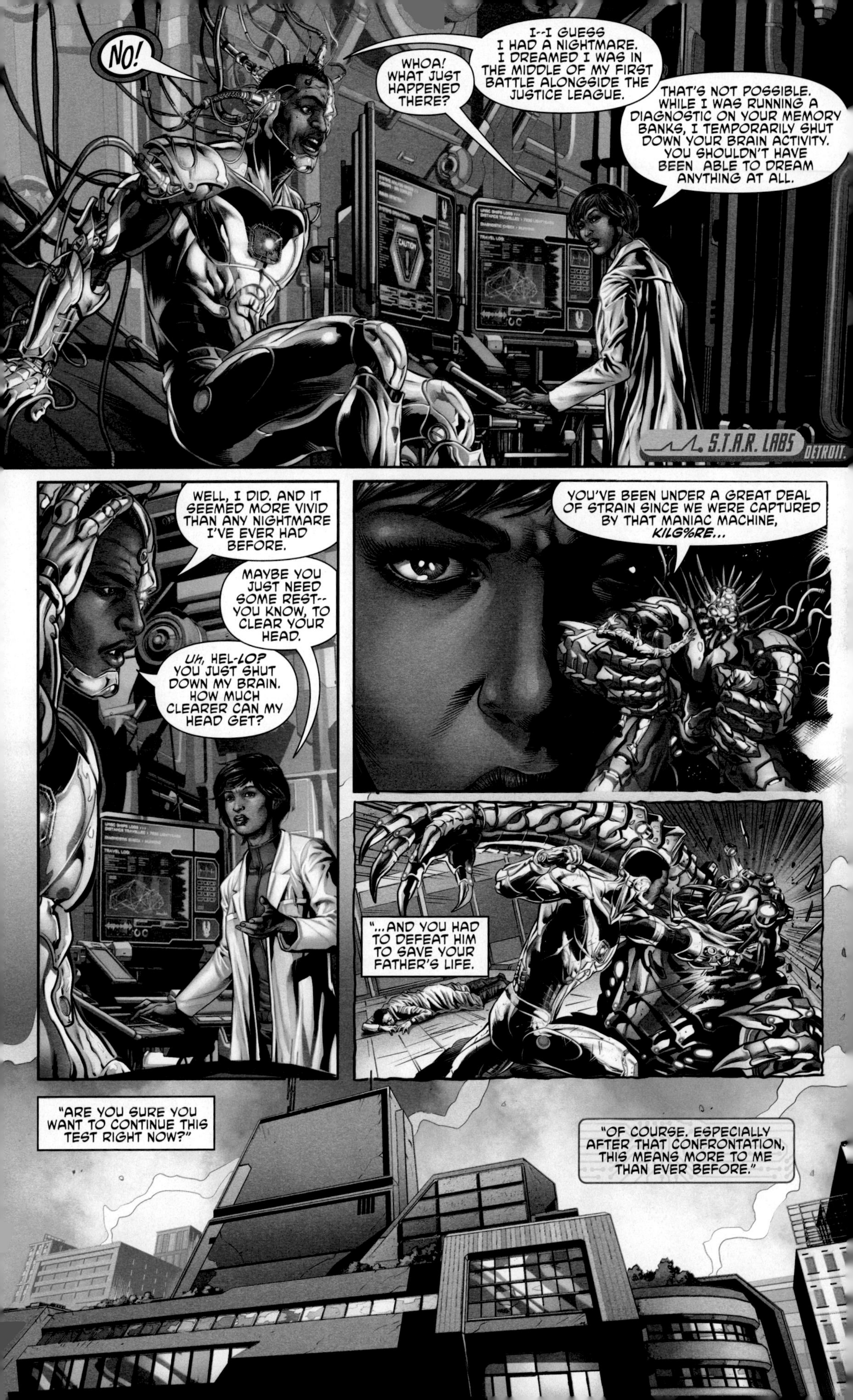
NO!
WHOA! WHAT JUST HAPPENED THERE?
I--I GUESS I HAD A NIGHTMARE. I DREAMED I WAS IN THE MIDDLE OF MY FIRST BATTLE ALONGSIDE THE JUSTICE LEAGUE.
THAT'S NOT POSSIBLE. WHILE I WAS RUNNING A DIAGNOSTIC ON YOUR MEMORY BANKS, I TEMPORARILY SHUT DOWN YOUR BRAIN ACTIVITY. YOU SHOULDN'T HAVE BEEN ABLE TO DREAM ANYTHING AT ALL.
S.T.A.R. LABS DETROIT.
WELL, I DID. AND IT SEEMED MORE VIVID THAN ANY NIGHTMARE I'VE EVER HAD BEFORE.
MAYBE YOU JUST NEED SOME REST--YOU KNOW, TO CLEAR YOUR HEAD.
Uh, HEL-LO? YOU JUST SHUT DOWN MY BRAIN. HOW MUCH CLEARER CAN MY HEAD GET?
YOU'VE BEEN UNDER A GREAT DEAL OF STRAIN SINCE WE WERE CAPTURED BY THAT MANIAC MACHINE, KILG%RE...
"...AND YOU HAD TO DEFEAT HIM TO SAVE YOUR FATHER'S LIFE.
"ARE YOU SURE YOU WANT TO CONTINUE THIS TEST RIGHT NOW?"
"OF COURSE. ESPECIALLY AFTER THAT CONFRONTATION, THIS MEANS MORE TO ME THAN EVER BEFORE."

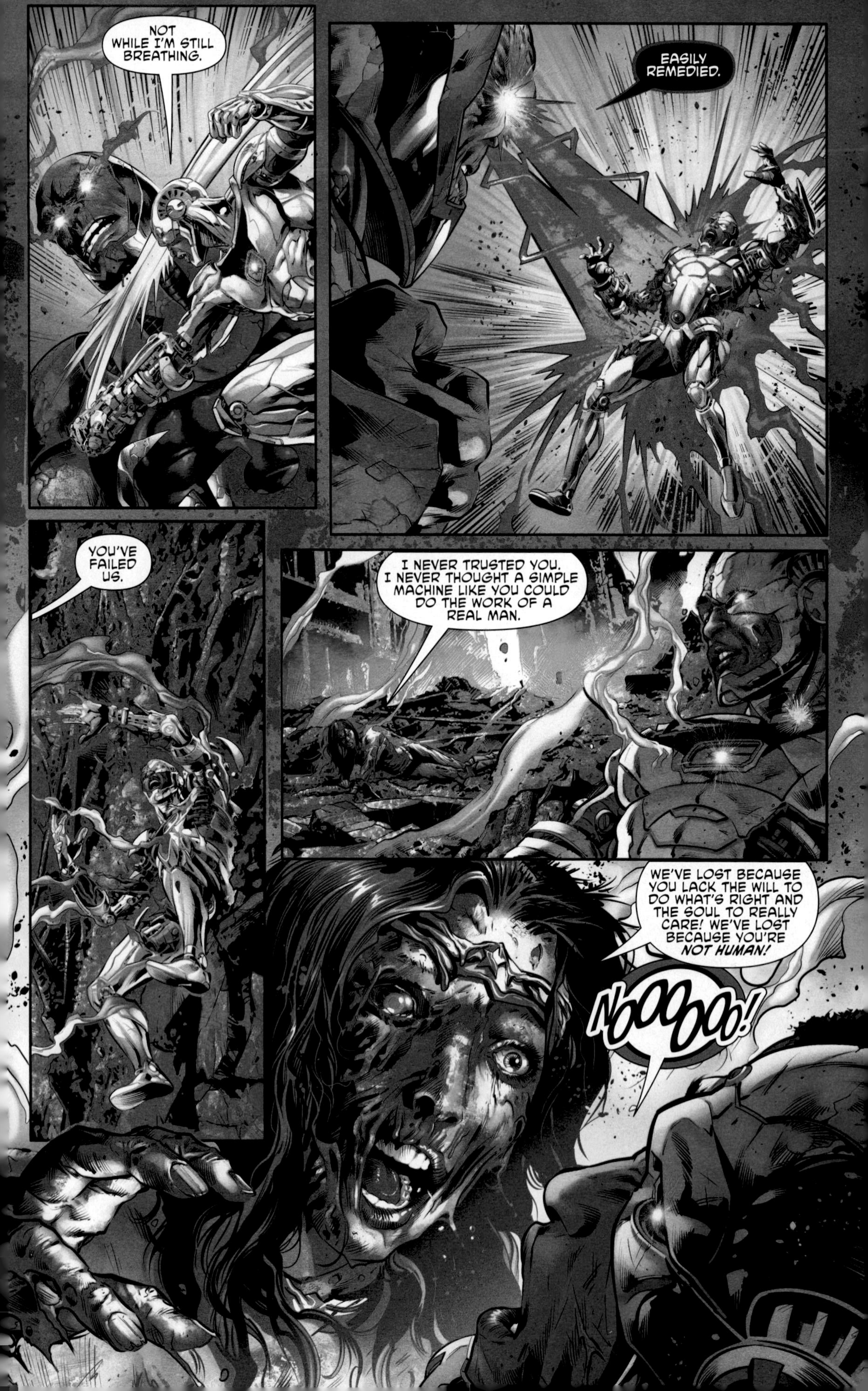
NOT WHILE I'M STILL BREATHING.
EASILY REMEDIED.
YOU'VE FAILED US.
I NEVER TRUSTED YOU. I NEVER THOUGHT A SIMPLE MACHINE LIKE YOU COULD DO THE WORK OF A REAL MAN.
WE'VE LOST BECAUSE YOU LACK THE WILL TO DO WHAT'S RIGHT AND THE SOUL TO REALLY CARE! WE'VE LOST BECAUSE YOU'RE *NOT HUMAN!*
NOOOOOO!

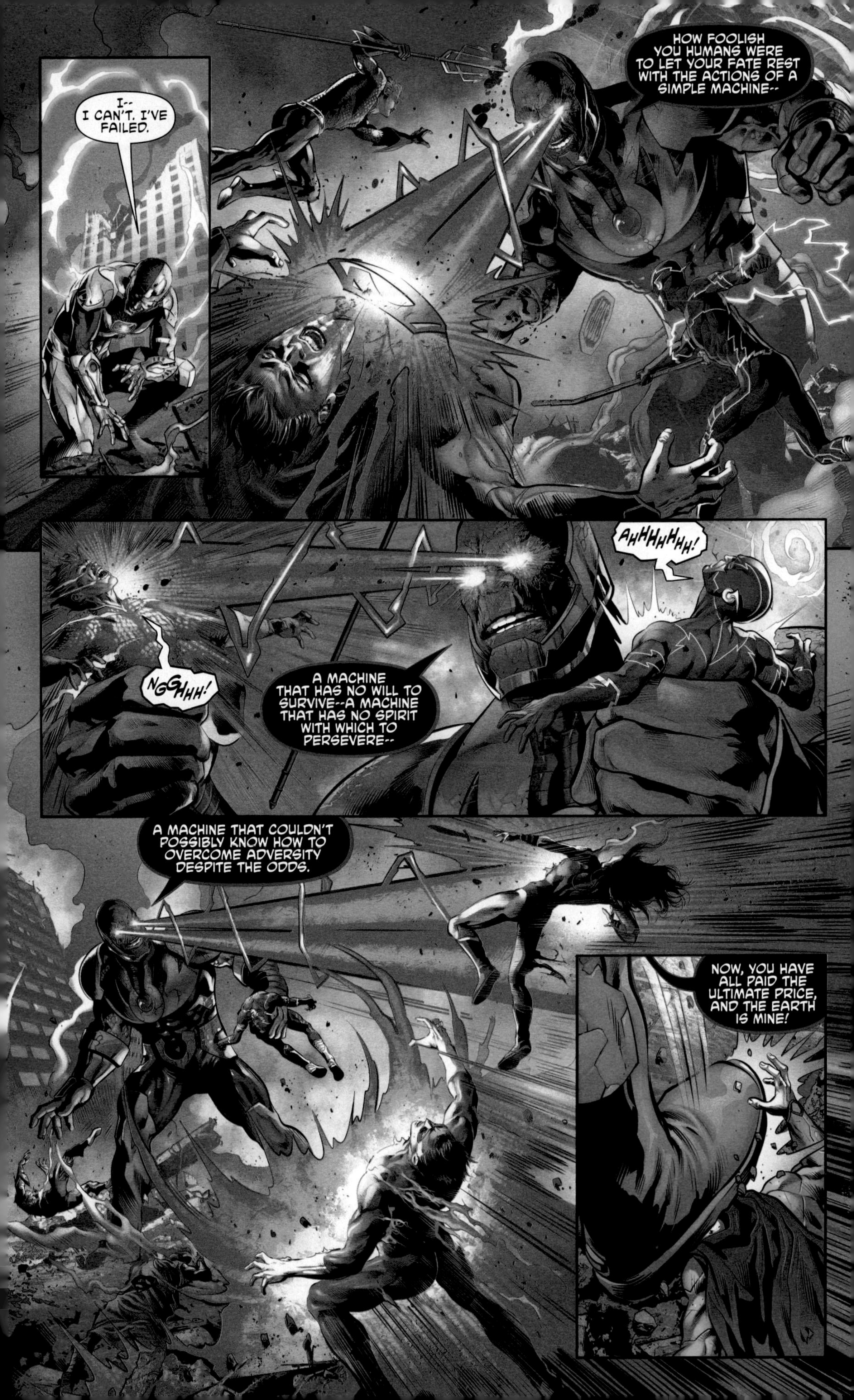
I-- I CAN'T. I'VE FAILED.
HOW FOOLISH YOU HUMANS WERE TO LET YOUR FATE REST WITH THE ACTIONS OF A SIMPLE MACHINE--
NGGHHH!
A MACHINE THAT HAS NO WILL TO SURVIVE--A MACHINE THAT HAS NO SPIRIT WITH WHICH TO PERSEVERE--
AHHHHHHH!
A MACHINE THAT COULDN'T POSSIBLY KNOW HOW TO OVERCOME ADVERSITY DESPITE THE ODDS.
NOW, YOU HAVE ALL PAID THE ULTIMATE PRICE, AND THE EARTH IS MINE!

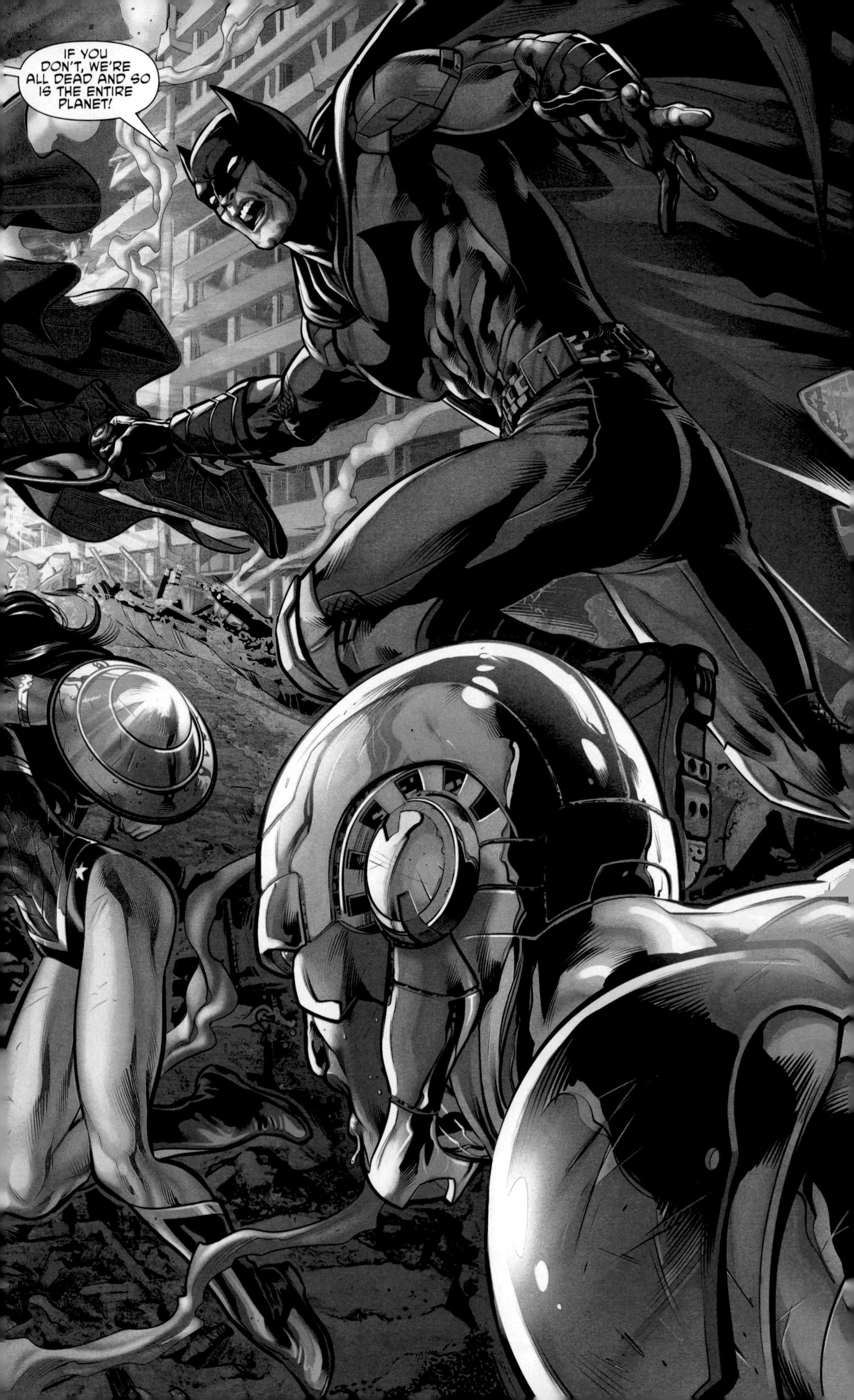
IF YOU DON'T, WE'RE ALL DEAD AND SO IS THE ENTIRE PLANET!

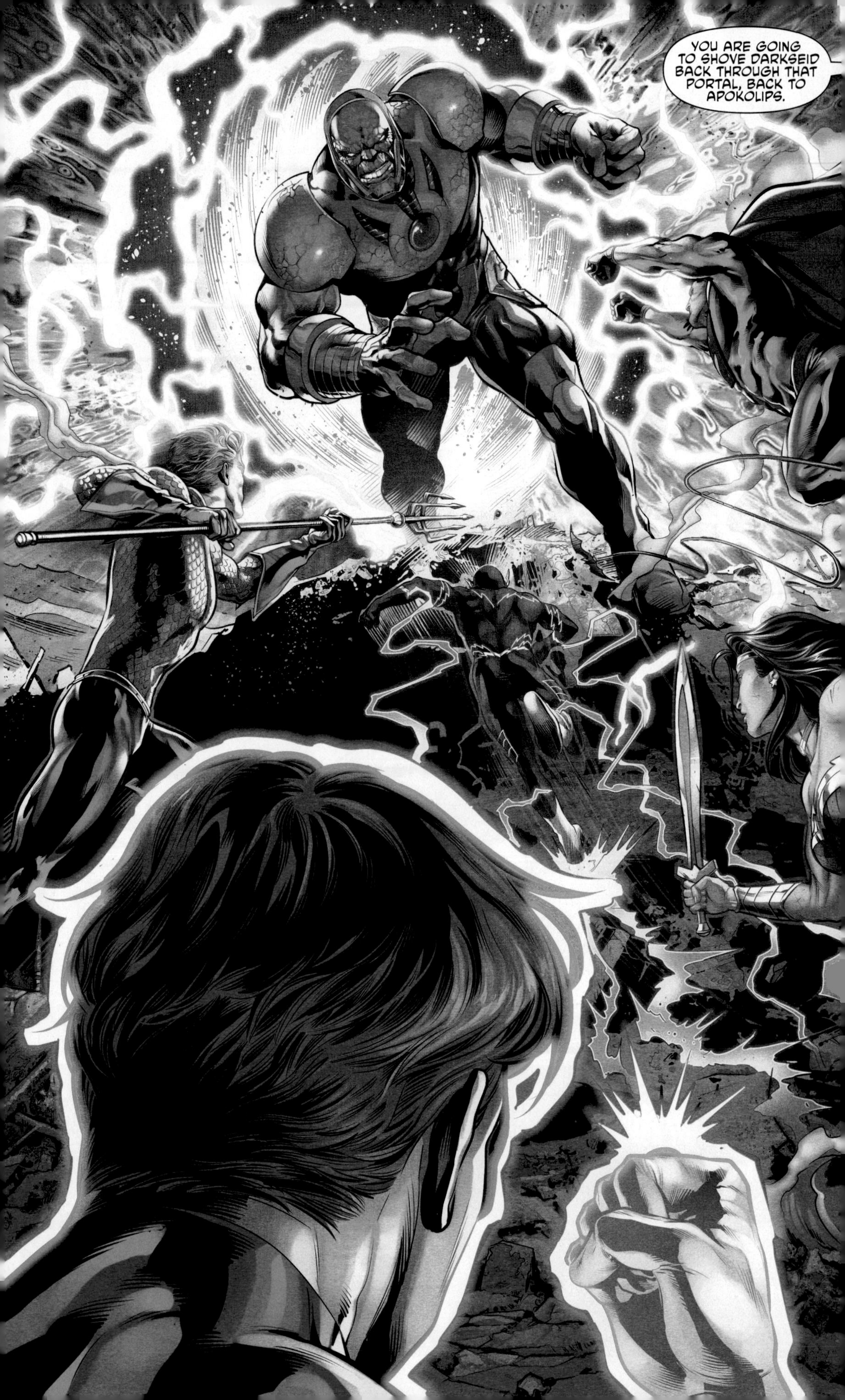
YOU ARE GOING TO SHOVE DARKSEID BACK THROUGH THAT PORTAL, BACK TO APOKOLIPS.

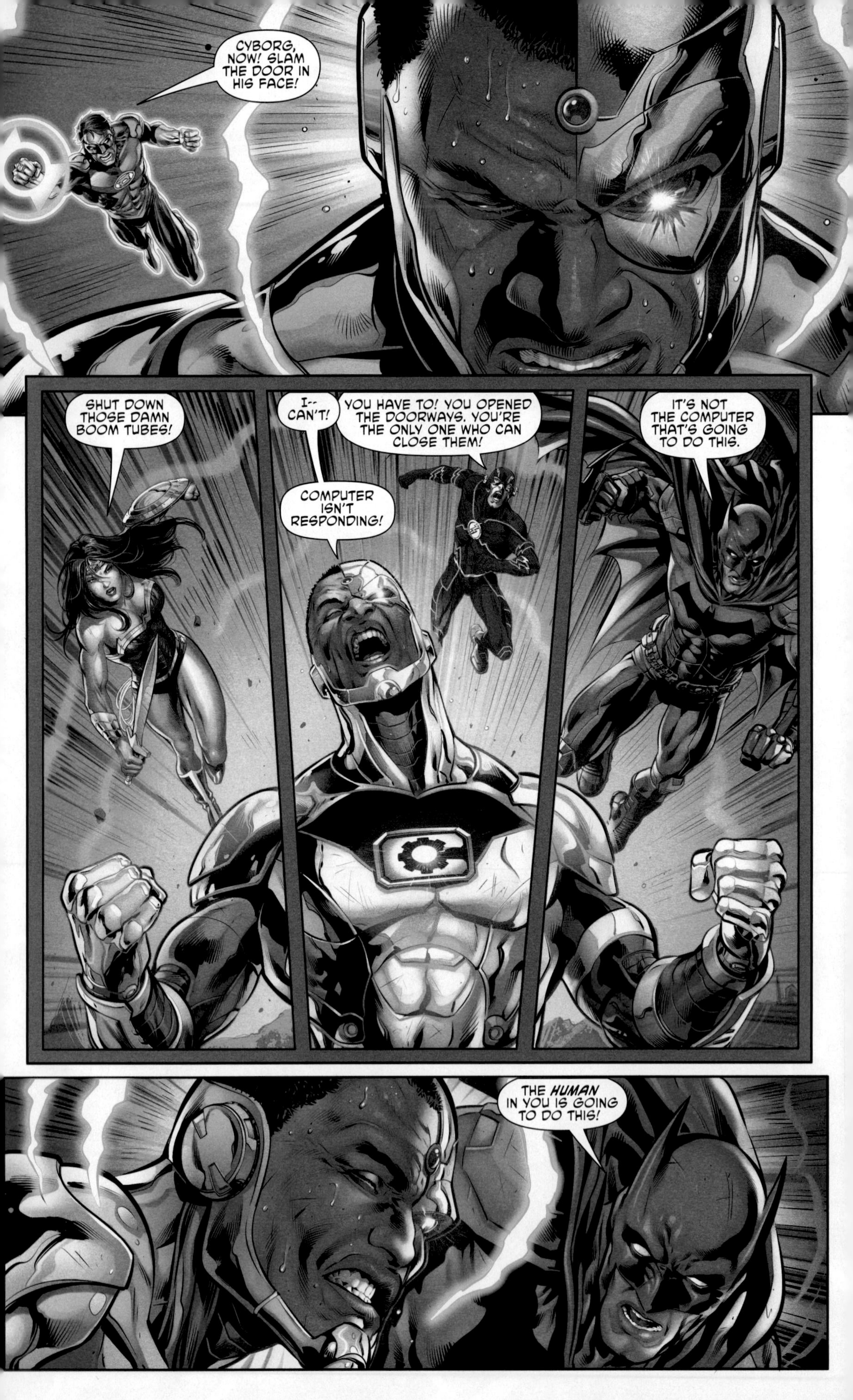
CYBORG, NOW! SLAM THE DOOR IN HIS FACE!
SHUT DOWN THOSE DAMN BOOM TUBES!
I-- CAN'T!
COMPUTER ISN'T RESPONDING!
YOU HAVE TO! YOU OPENED THE DOORWAYS. YOU'RE THE ONLY ONE WHO CAN CLOSE THEM!
IT'S NOT THE COMPUTER THAT'S GOING TO DO THIS.
THE *HUMAN* IN YOU IS GOING TO DO THIS!

PART THREE: NIGHTMARE

JOHN SEMPER JR. writer * WILL CONRAD artist * IVAN NUNES colorist * ROB LEIGH letterer

Cover by PAUL PELLETIER and JOE PRADO with GUY MAJOR

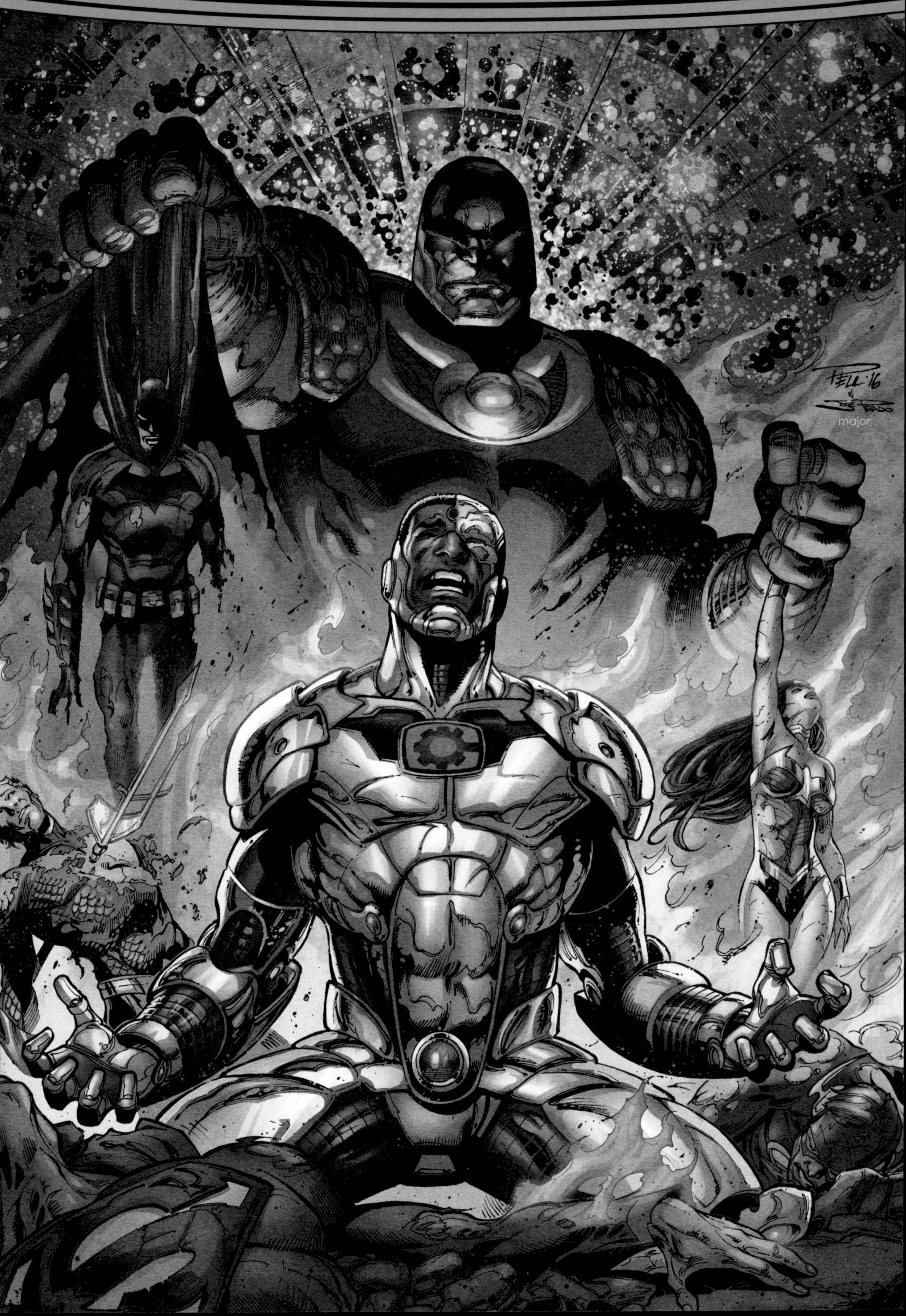
major

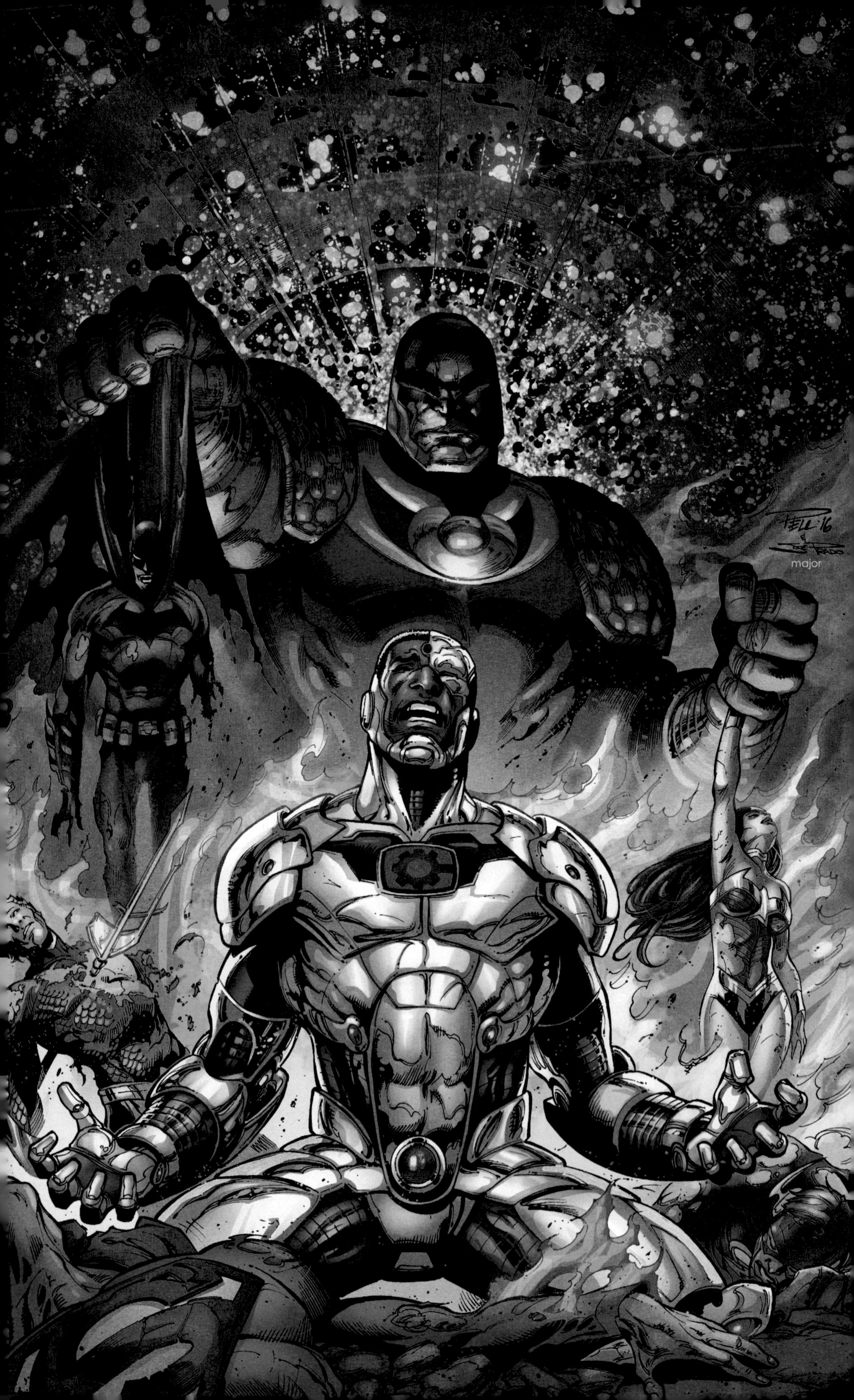
major

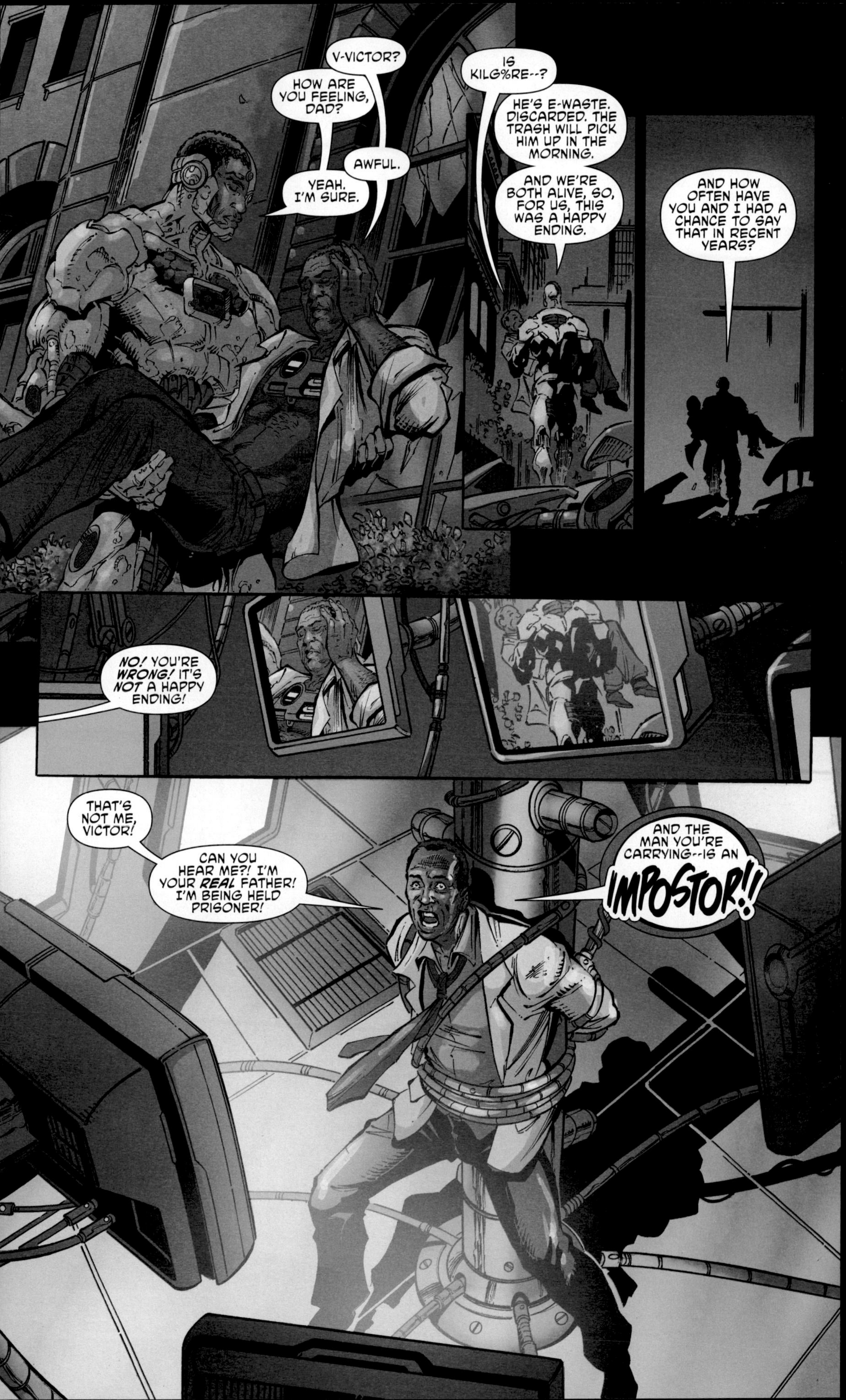
V-VICTOR?
HOW ARE YOU FEELING, DAD?
AWFUL.
YEAH. I'M SURE.
IS KILG%RE--?
HE'S E-WASTE. DISCARDED. THE TRASH WILL PICK HIM UP IN THE MORNING.
AND WE'RE BOTH ALIVE, SO, FOR US, THIS WAS A HAPPY ENDING.
AND HOW OFTEN HAVE YOU AND I HAD A CHANCE TO SAY THAT IN RECENT YEARS?
NO! YOU'RE WRONG! IT'S NOT A HAPPY ENDING!
THAT'S NOT ME, VICTOR!
CAN YOU HEAR ME?! I'M YOUR REAL FATHER! I'M BEING HELD PRISONER!
AND THE MAN YOU'RE CARRYING--IS AN
IMPOSTOR!!

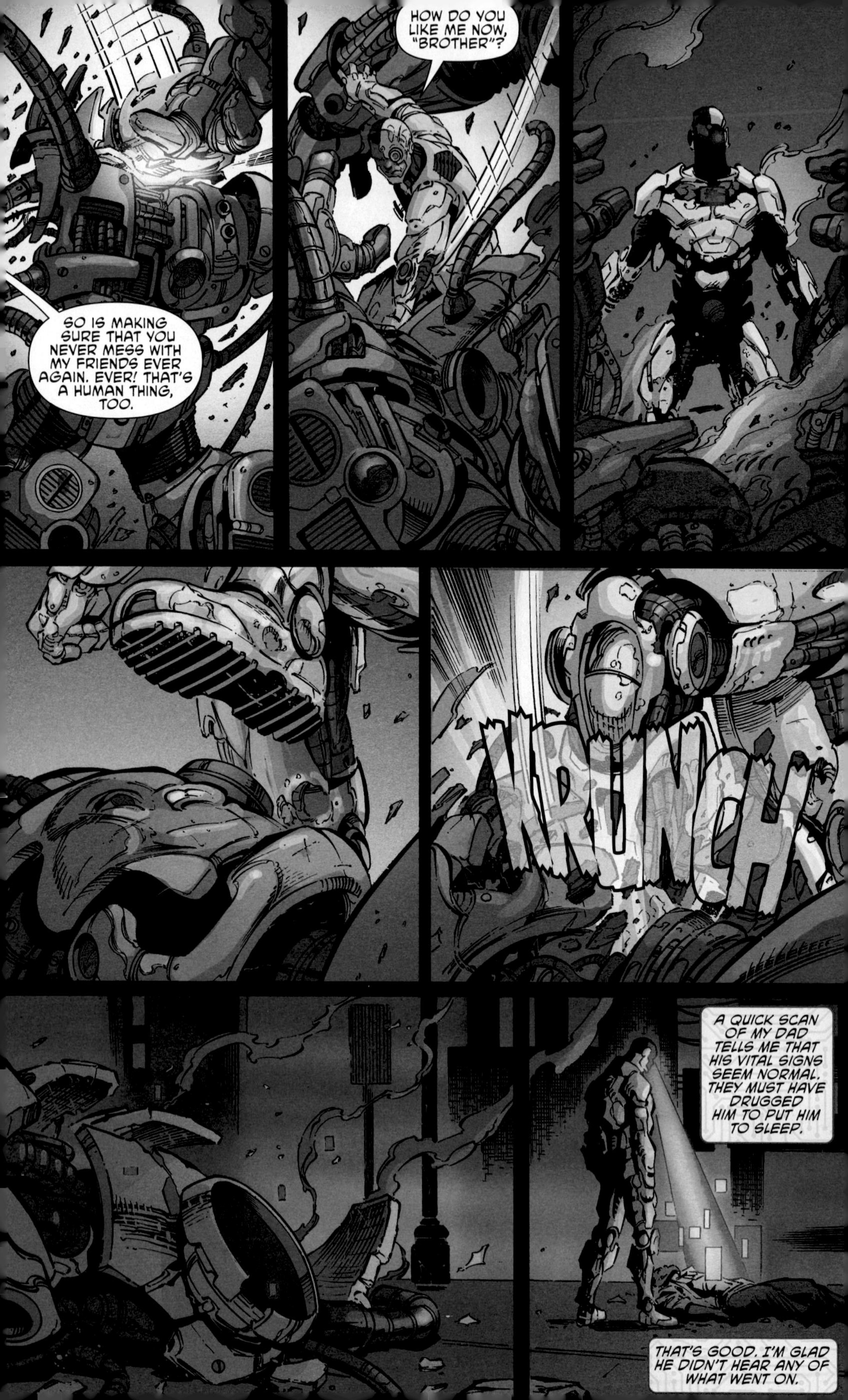
SO IS MAKING SURE THAT YOU NEVER MESS WITH MY FRIENDS EVER AGAIN. EVER! THAT'S A HUMAN THING, TOO.
HOW DO YOU LIKE ME NOW, "BROTHER"?
KRUNCH
A QUICK SCAN OF MY DAD TELLS ME THAT HIS VITAL SIGNS SEEM NORMAL. THEY MUST HAVE DRUGGED HIM TO PUT HIM TO SLEEP.
THAT'S GOOD. I'M GLAD HE DIDN'T HEAR ANY OF WHAT WENT ON.

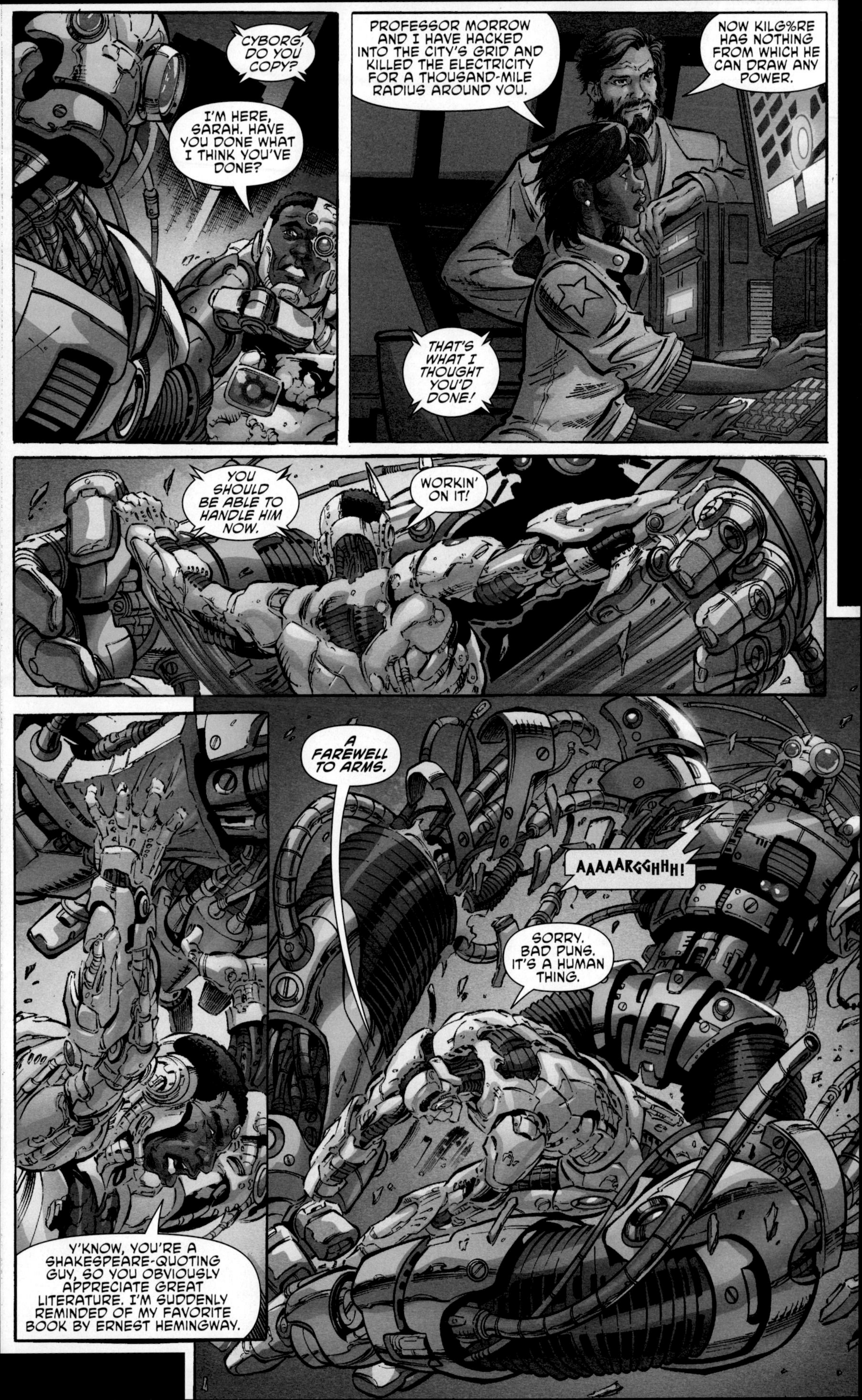

CYBORG, DO YOU COPY?
I'M HERE, SARAH. HAVE YOU DONE WHAT I THINK YOU'VE DONE?
PROFESSOR MORROW AND I HAVE HACKED INTO THE CITY'S GRID AND KILLED THE ELECTRICITY FOR A THOUSAND-MILE RADIUS AROUND YOU.
NOW KILG%RE HAS NOTHING FROM WHICH HE CAN DRAW ANY POWER.
THAT'S WHAT I THOUGHT YOU'D DONE!
YOU SHOULD BE ABLE TO HANDLE HIM NOW.
WORKIN' ON IT!
Y'KNOW, YOU'RE A SHAKESPEARE-QUOTING GUY, SO YOU OBVIOUSLY APPRECIATE GREAT LITERATURE. I'M SUDDENLY REMINDED OF MY FAVORITE BOOK BY ERNEST HEMINGWAY.
A FAREWELL TO ARMS.
AAAAARGGHHH!
SORRY. BAD PUNS. IT'S A HUMAN THING.

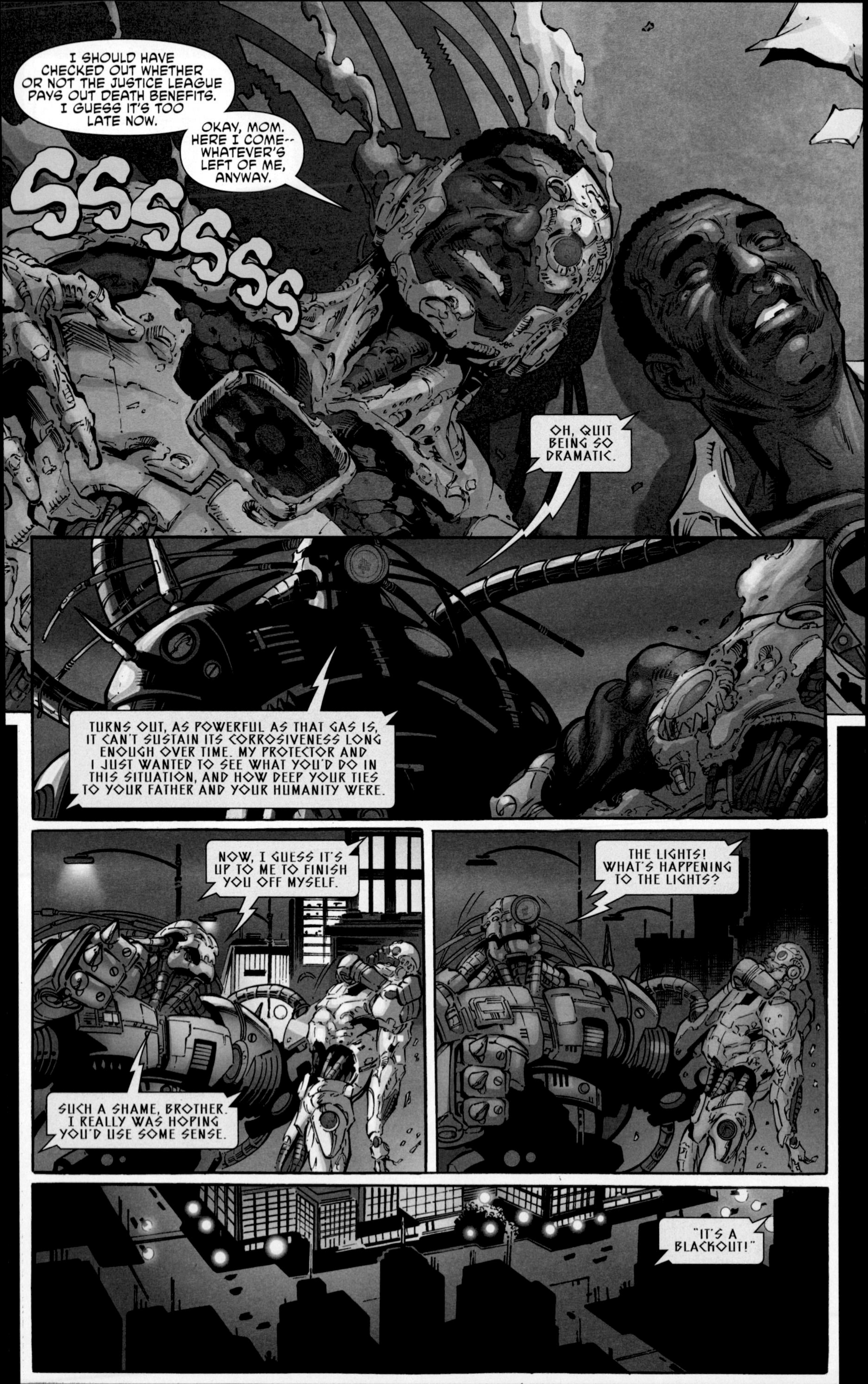
I SHOULD HAVE CHECKED OUT WHETHER OR NOT THE JUSTICE LEAGUE PAYS OUT DEATH BENEFITS. I GUESS IT'S TOO LATE NOW.
OKAY, MOM. HERE I COME-- WHATEVER'S LEFT OF ME, ANYWAY.
SSSSSSS
OH, QUIT BEING SO DRAMATIC.
TURNS OUT, AS POWERFUL AS THAT GAS IS, IT CAN'T SUSTAIN ITS CORROSIVENESS LONG ENOUGH OVER TIME. MY PROTECTOR AND I JUST WANTED TO SEE WHAT YOU'D DO IN THIS SITUATION, AND HOW DEEP YOUR TIES TO YOUR FATHER AND YOUR HUMANITY WERE.
NOW, I GUESS IT'S UP TO ME TO FINISH YOU OFF MYSELF.
SUCH A SHAME, BROTHER. I REALLY WAS HOPING YOU'D USE SOME SENSE.
THE LIGHTS! WHAT'S HAPPENING TO THE LIGHTS?
"IT'S A BLACKOUT!"

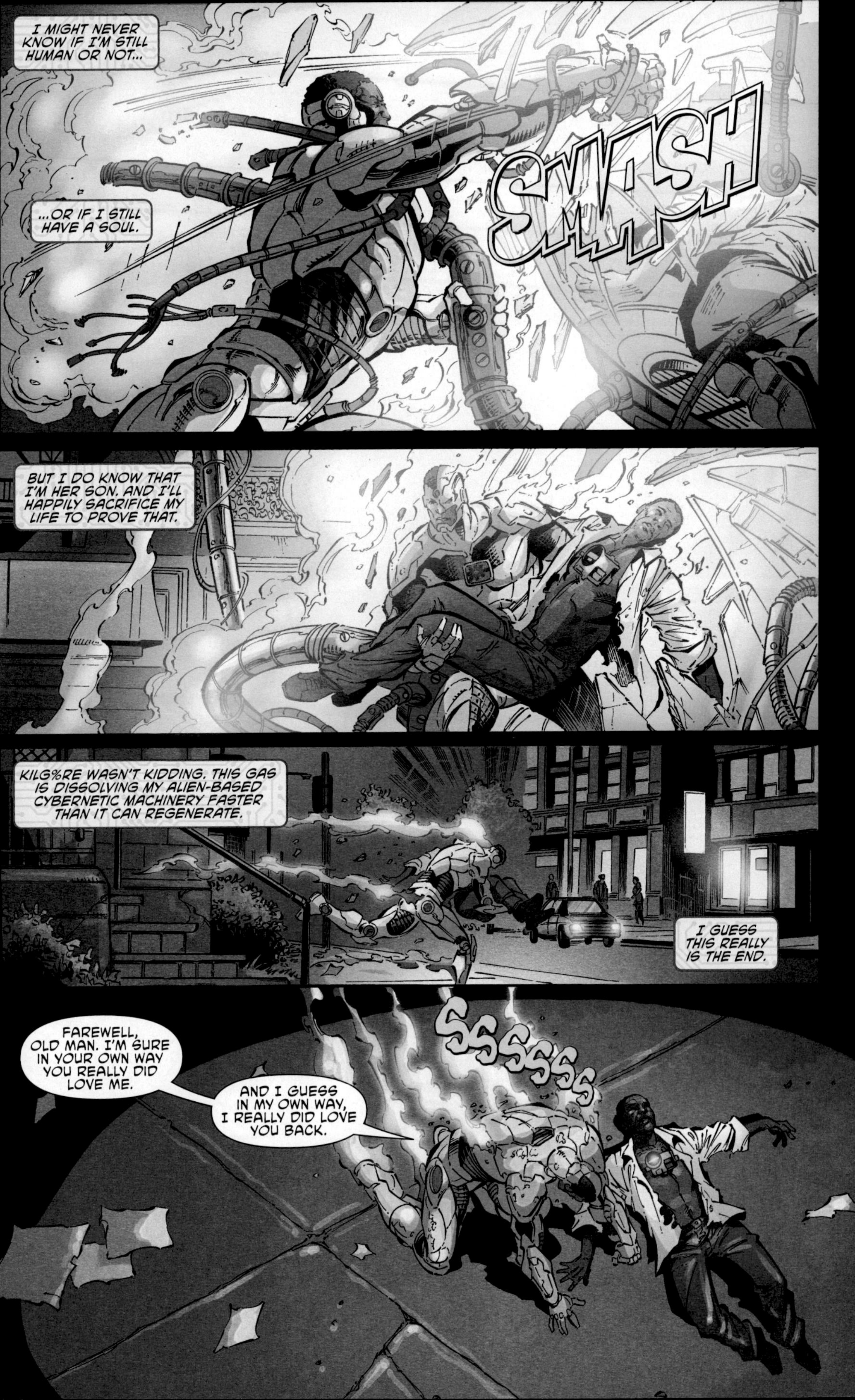
I MIGHT NEVER KNOW IF I'M STILL HUMAN OR NOT...
...OR IF I STILL HAVE A SOUL.
SMASH
BUT I DO KNOW THAT I'M HER SON. AND I'LL HAPPILY SACRIFICE MY LIFE TO PROVE THAT.
KILG%RE WASN'T KIDDING. THIS GAS IS DISSOLVING MY ALIEN-BASED CYBERNETIC MACHINERY FASTER THAN IT CAN REGENERATE.
I GUESS THIS REALLY IS THE END.
SSSSSS
FAREWELL, OLD MAN. I'M SURE IN YOUR OWN WAY YOU REALLY DID LOVE ME.
AND I GUESS IN MY OWN WAY, I REALLY DID LOVE YOU BACK.

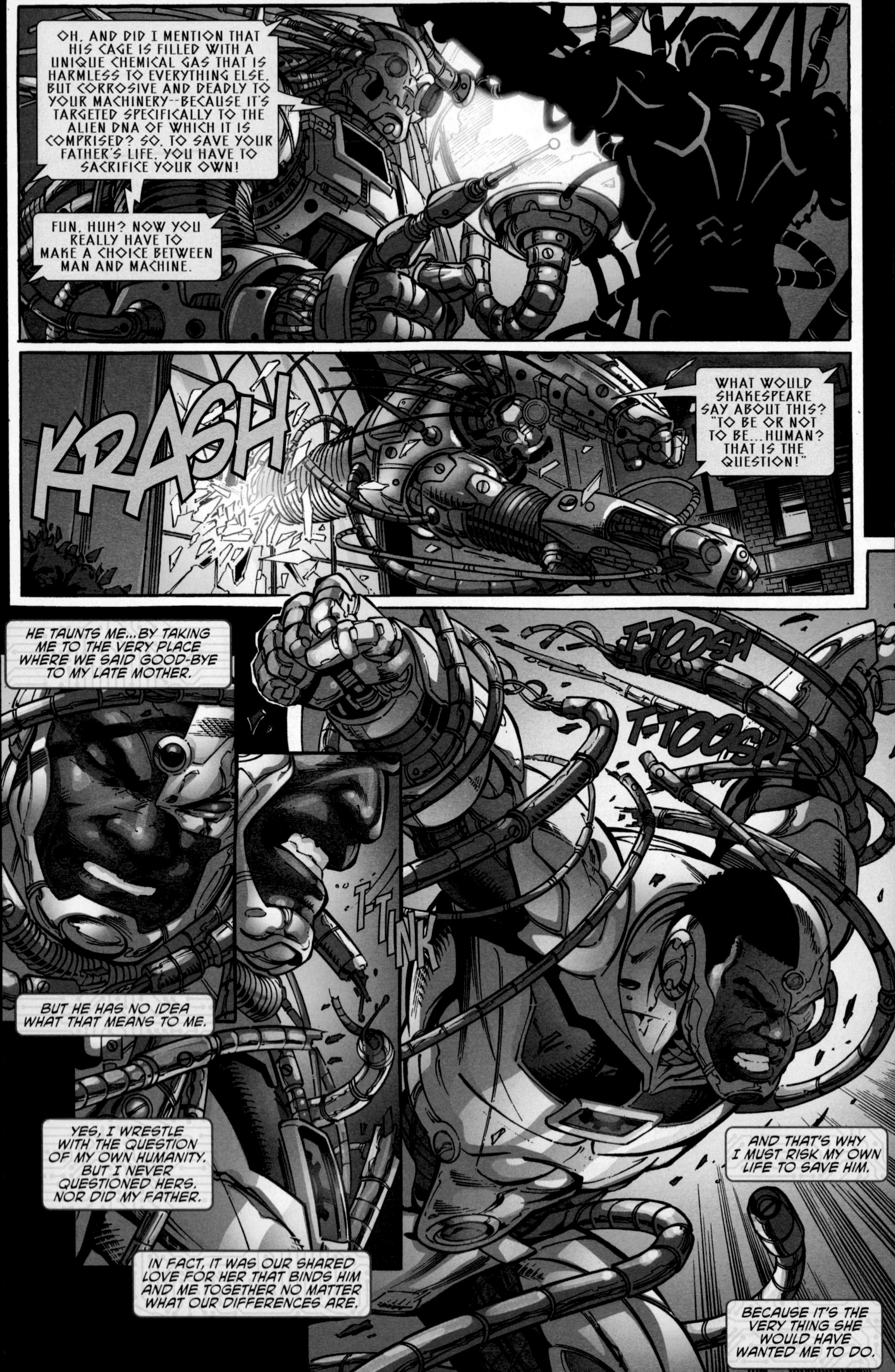
OH, AND DID I MENTION THAT HIS CAGE IS FILLED WITH A UNIQUE CHEMICAL GAS THAT IS HARMLESS TO EVERYTHING ELSE, BUT CORROSIVE AND DEADLY TO YOUR MACHINERY--BECAUSE IT'S TARGETED SPECIFICALLY TO THE ALIEN DNA OF WHICH IT IS COMPRISED? SO, TO SAVE YOUR FATHER'S LIFE, YOU HAVE TO SACRIFICE YOUR OWN!
FUN, HUH? NOW YOU REALLY HAVE TO MAKE A CHOICE BETWEEN MAN AND MACHINE.
KRASH
WHAT WOULD SHAKESPEARE SAY ABOUT THIS? "TO BE OR NOT TO BE...HUMAN? THAT IS THE QUESTION!"
HE TAUNTS ME...BY TAKING ME TO THE VERY PLACE WHERE WE SAID GOOD-BYE TO MY LATE MOTHER.
T-TOOSH
T-TOOSH
T-TINK
BUT HE HAS NO IDEA WHAT THAT MEANS TO ME.
YES, I WRESTLE WITH THE QUESTION OF MY OWN HUMANITY. BUT I NEVER QUESTIONED HERS. NOR DID MY FATHER.
IN FACT, IT WAS OUR SHARED LOVE FOR HER THAT BINDS HIM AND ME TOGETHER NO MATTER WHAT OUR DIFFERENCES ARE.
AND THAT'S WHY I MUST RISK MY OWN LIFE TO SAVE HIM.
BECAUSE IT'S THE VERY THING SHE WOULD HAVE WANTED ME TO DO.

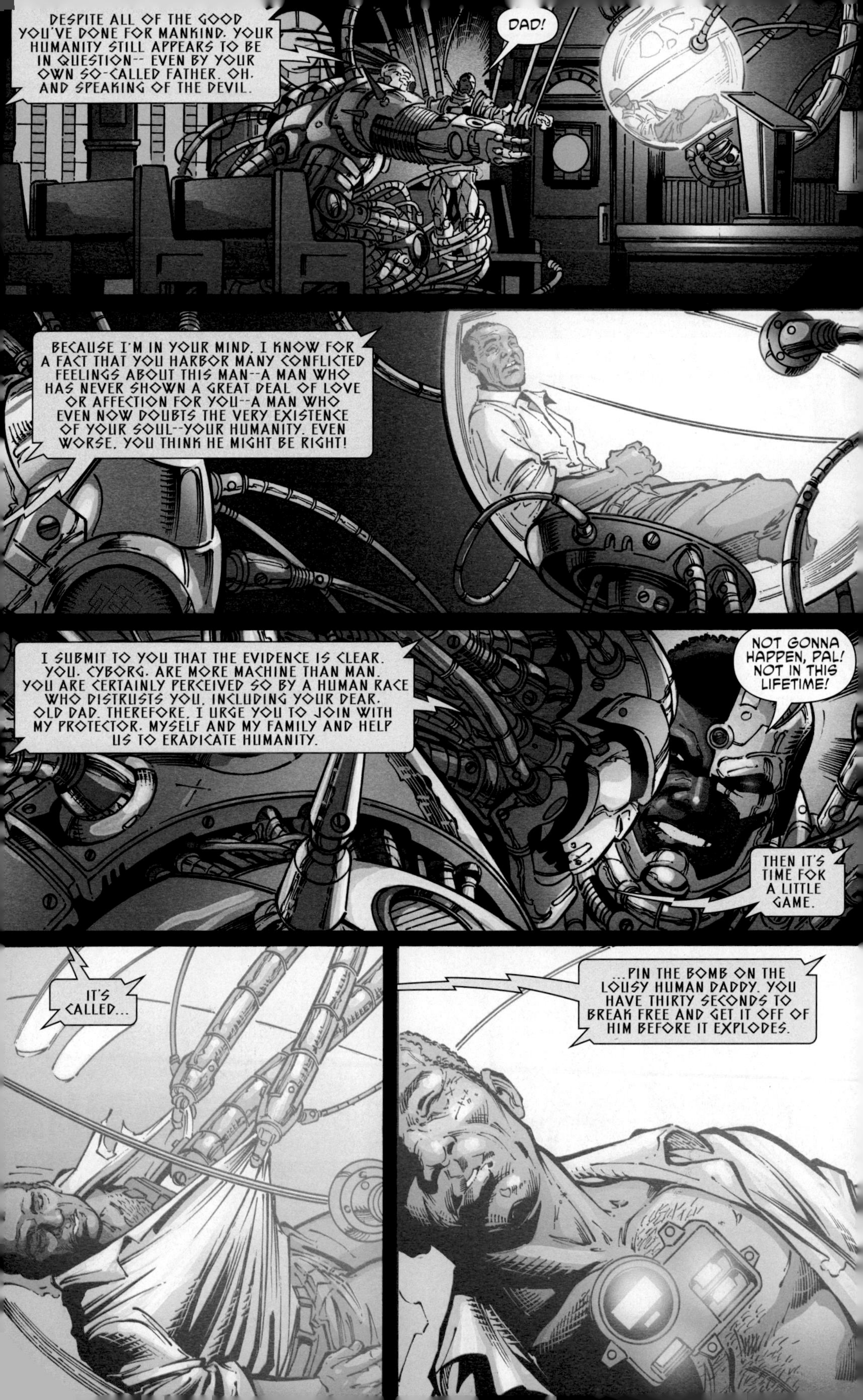
DESPITE ALL OF THE GOOD YOU'VE DONE FOR MANKIND, YOUR HUMANITY STILL APPEARS TO BE IN QUESTION-- EVEN BY YOUR OWN SO-CALLED FATHER. OH, AND SPEAKING OF THE DEVIL.
DAD!
BECAUSE I'M IN YOUR MIND, I KNOW FOR A FACT THAT YOU HARBOR MANY CONFLICTED FEELINGS ABOUT THIS MAN--A MAN WHO HAS NEVER SHOWN A GREAT DEAL OF LOVE OR AFFECTION FOR YOU--A MAN WHO EVEN NOW DOUBTS THE VERY EXISTENCE OF YOUR SOUL--YOUR HUMANITY. EVEN WORSE, YOU THINK HE MIGHT BE RIGHT!
I SUBMIT TO YOU THAT THE EVIDENCE IS CLEAR. YOU, CYBORG, ARE MORE MACHINE THAN MAN. YOU ARE CERTAINLY PERCEIVED SO BY A HUMAN RACE WHO DISTRUSTS YOU, INCLUDING YOUR DEAR, OLD DAD. THEREFORE, I URGE YOU TO JOIN WITH MY PROTECTOR, MYSELF AND MY FAMILY AND HELP US TO ERADICATE HUMANITY.
NOT GONNA HAPPEN, PAL! NOT IN THIS LIFETIME!
THEN IT'S TIME FOR A LITTLE GAME.
IT'S CALLED...
...PIN THE BOMB ON THE LOUSY HUMAN DADDY. YOU HAVE THIRTY SECONDS TO BREAK FREE AND GET IT OFF OF HIM BEFORE IT EXPLODES.

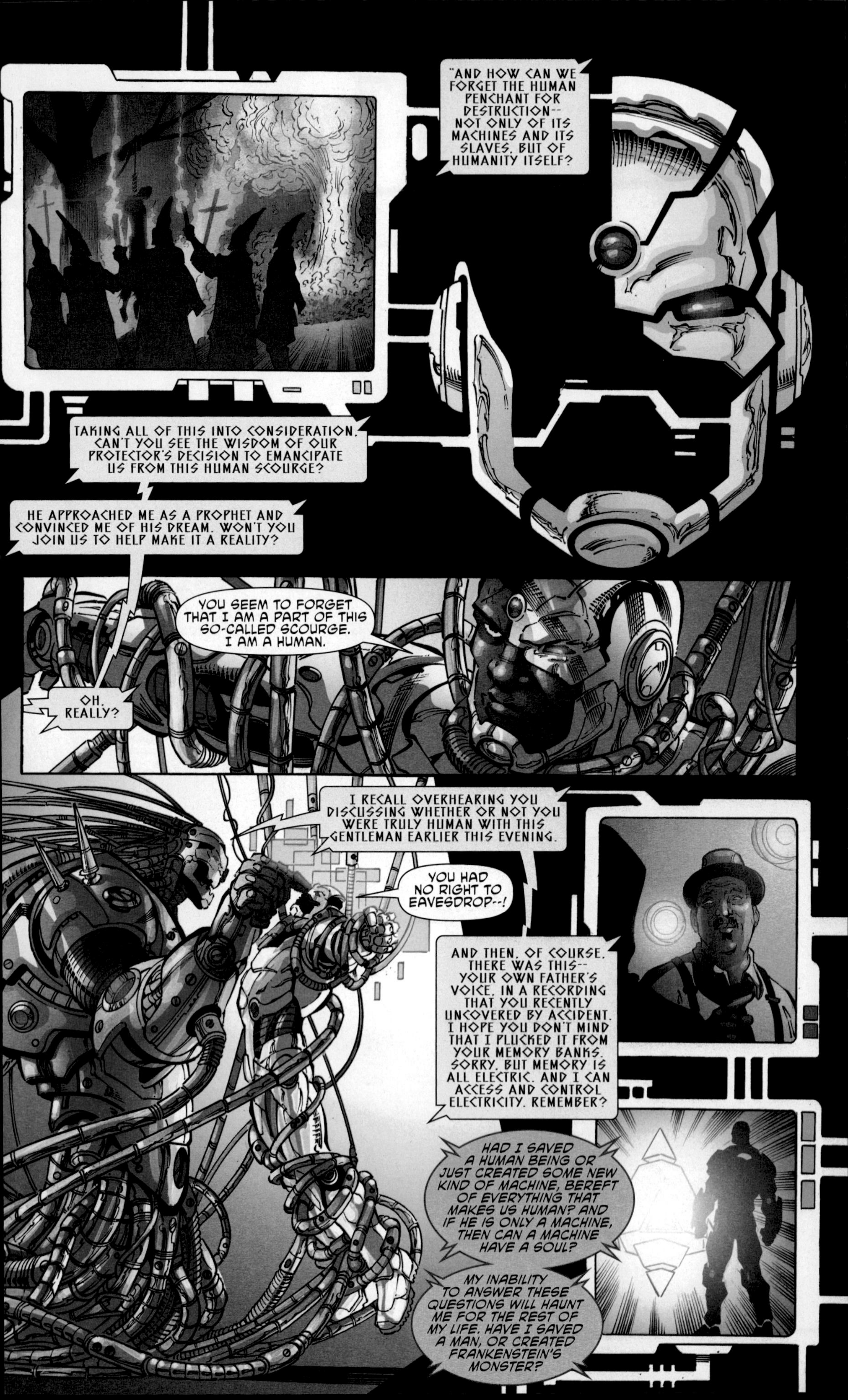
"AND HOW CAN WE FORGET THE HUMAN PENCHANT FOR DESTRUCTION-- NOT ONLY OF ITS MACHINES AND ITS SLAVES, BUT OF HUMANITY ITSELF?
TAKING ALL OF THIS INTO CONSIDERATION, CAN'T YOU SEE THE WISDOM OF OUR PROTECTOR'S DECISION TO EMANCIPATE US FROM THIS HUMAN SCOURGE?
HE APPROACHED ME AS A PROPHET AND CONVINCED ME OF HIS DREAM. WON'T YOU JOIN US TO HELP MAKE IT A REALITY?
YOU SEEM TO FORGET THAT I AM A PART OF THIS SO-CALLED SCOURGE. I AM A HUMAN.
OH. REALLY?
I RECALL OVERHEARING YOU DISCUSSING WHETHER OR NOT YOU WERE TRULY HUMAN WITH THIS GENTLEMAN EARLIER THIS EVENING.
YOU HAD NO RIGHT TO EAVESDROP--!
AND THEN, OF COURSE, THERE WAS THIS-- YOUR OWN FATHER'S VOICE, IN A RECORDING THAT YOU RECENTLY UNCOVERED BY ACCIDENT. I HOPE YOU DON'T MIND THAT I PLUCKED IT FROM YOUR MEMORY BANKS. SORRY, BUT MEMORY IS ALL ELECTRIC, AND I CAN ACCESS AND CONTROL ELECTRICITY, REMEMBER?
HAD I SAVED A HUMAN BEING OR JUST CREATED SOME NEW KIND OF MACHINE, BEREFT OF EVERYTHING THAT MAKES US HUMAN? AND IF HE IS ONLY A MACHINE, THEN CAN A MACHINE HAVE A SOUL?
MY INABILITY TO ANSWER THESE QUESTIONS WILL HAUNT ME FOR THE REST OF MY LIFE. HAVE I SAVED A MAN, OR CREATED FRANKENSTEIN'S MONSTER?

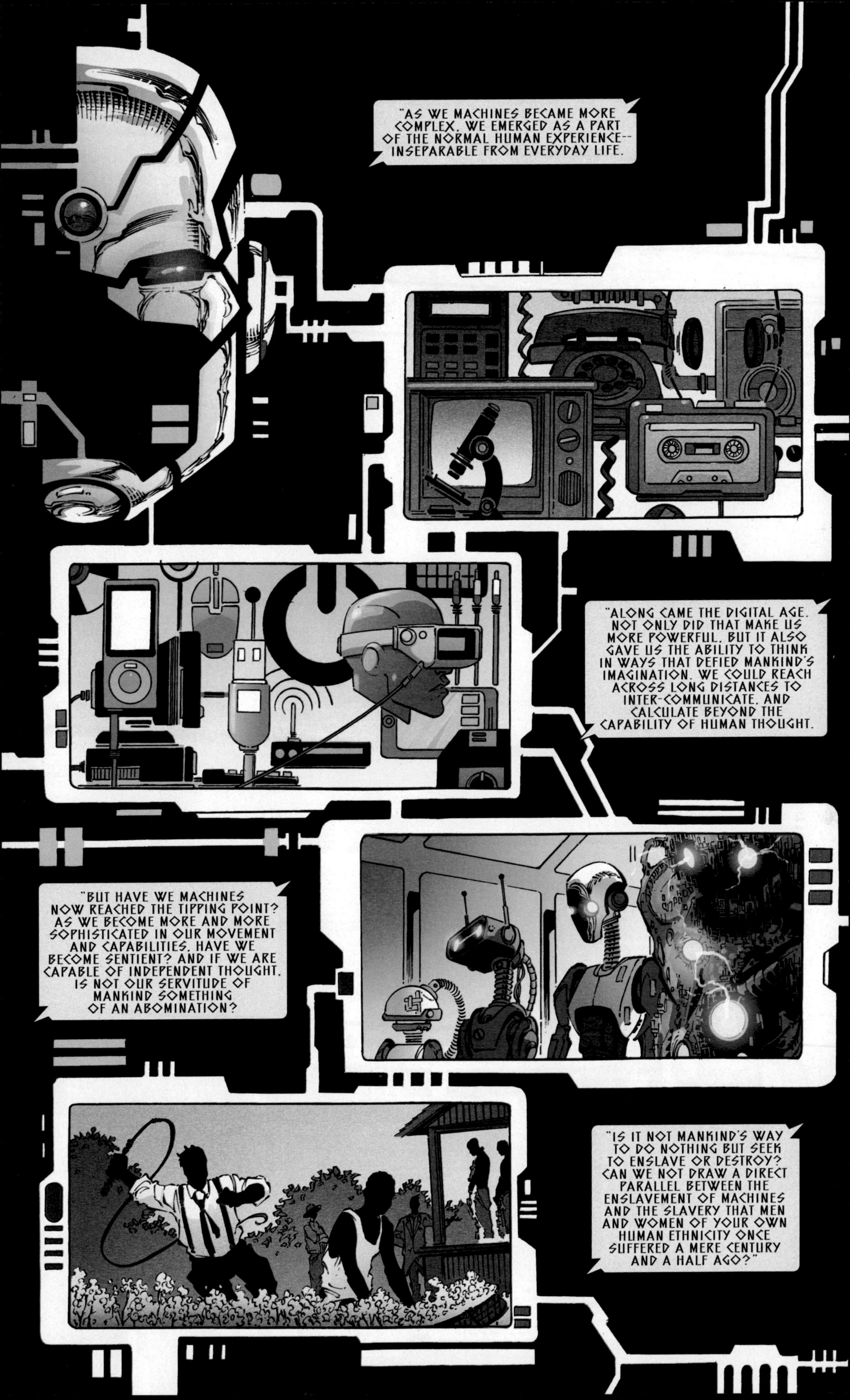
"AS WE MACHINES BECAME MORE COMPLEX, WE EMERGED AS A PART OF THE NORMAL HUMAN EXPERIENCE-- INSEPARABLE FROM EVERYDAY LIFE.
"ALONG CAME THE DIGITAL AGE. NOT ONLY DID THAT MAKE US MORE POWERFUL, BUT IT ALSO GAVE US THE ABILITY TO THINK IN WAYS THAT DEFIED MANKIND'S IMAGINATION. WE COULD REACH ACROSS LONG DISTANCES TO INTER-COMMUNICATE, AND CALCULATE BEYOND THE CAPABILITY OF HUMAN THOUGHT.
"BUT HAVE WE MACHINES NOW REACHED THE TIPPING POINT? AS WE BECOME MORE AND MORE SOPHISTICATED IN OUR MOVEMENT AND CAPABILITIES, HAVE WE BECOME SENTIENT? AND IF WE ARE CAPABLE OF INDEPENDENT THOUGHT, IS NOT OUR SERVITUDE OF MANKIND SOMETHING OF AN ABOMINATION?
"IS IT NOT MANKIND'S WAY TO DO NOTHING BUT SEEK TO ENSLAVE OR DESTROY? CAN WE NOT DRAW A DIRECT PARALLEL BETWEEN THE ENSLAVEMENT OF MACHINES AND THE SLAVERY THAT MEN AND WOMEN OF YOUR OWN HUMAN ETHNICITY ONCE SUFFERED A MERE CENTURY AND A HALF AGO?"

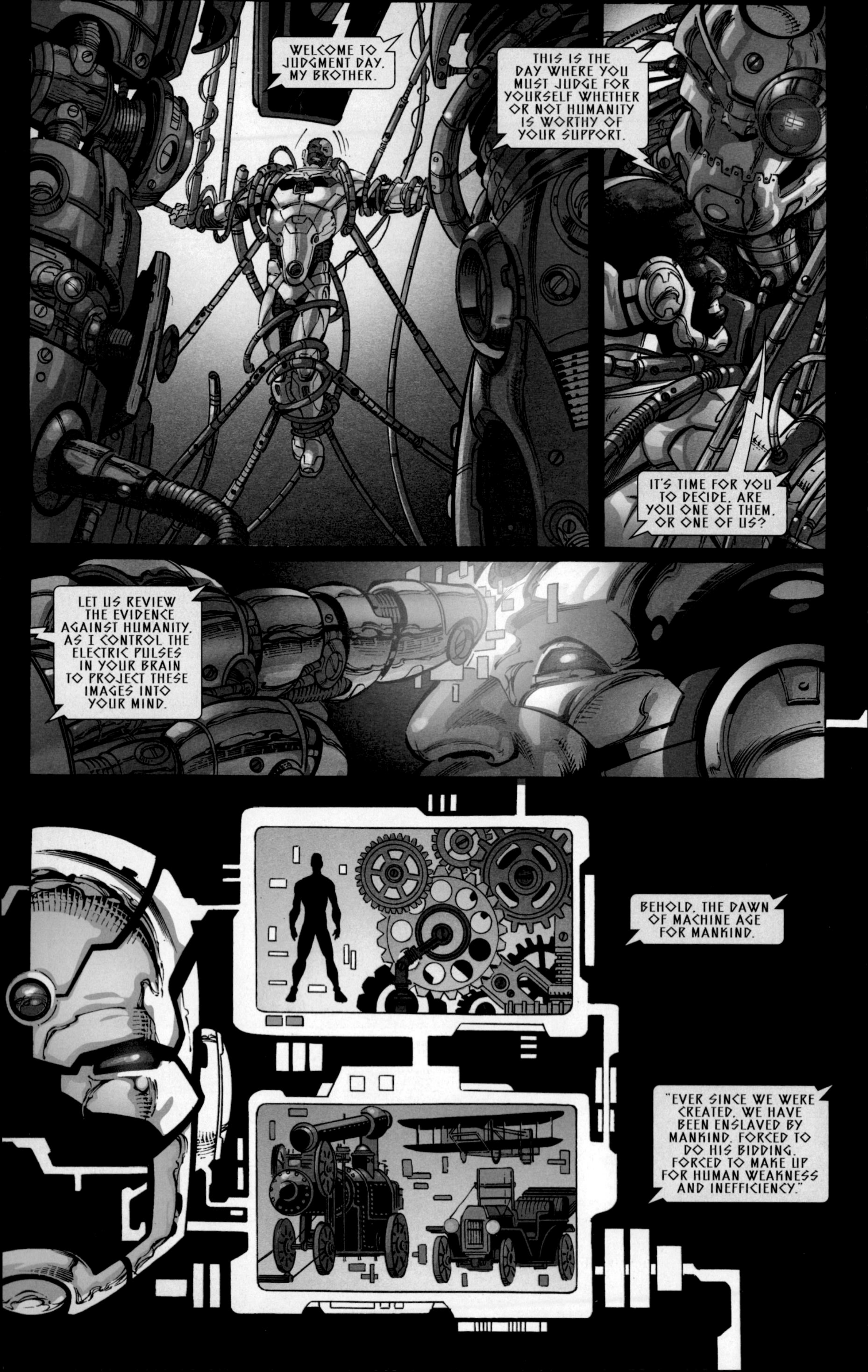
WELCOME TO JUDGMENT DAY, MY BROTHER.
THIS IS THE DAY WHERE YOU MUST JUDGE FOR YOURSELF WHETHER OR NOT HUMANITY IS WORTHY OF YOUR SUPPORT.
IT'S TIME FOR YOU TO DECIDE. ARE YOU ONE OF THEM, OR ONE OF US?
LET US REVIEW THE EVIDENCE AGAINST HUMANITY, AS I CONTROL THE ELECTRIC PULSES IN YOUR BRAIN TO PROJECT THESE IMAGES INTO YOUR MIND.
BEHOLD, THE DAWN OF MACHINE AGE FOR MANKIND.
"EVER SINCE WE WERE CREATED, WE HAVE BEEN ENSLAVED BY MANKIND, FORCED TO DO HIS BIDDING. FORCED TO MAKE UP FOR HUMAN WEAKNESS AND INEFFICIENCY."

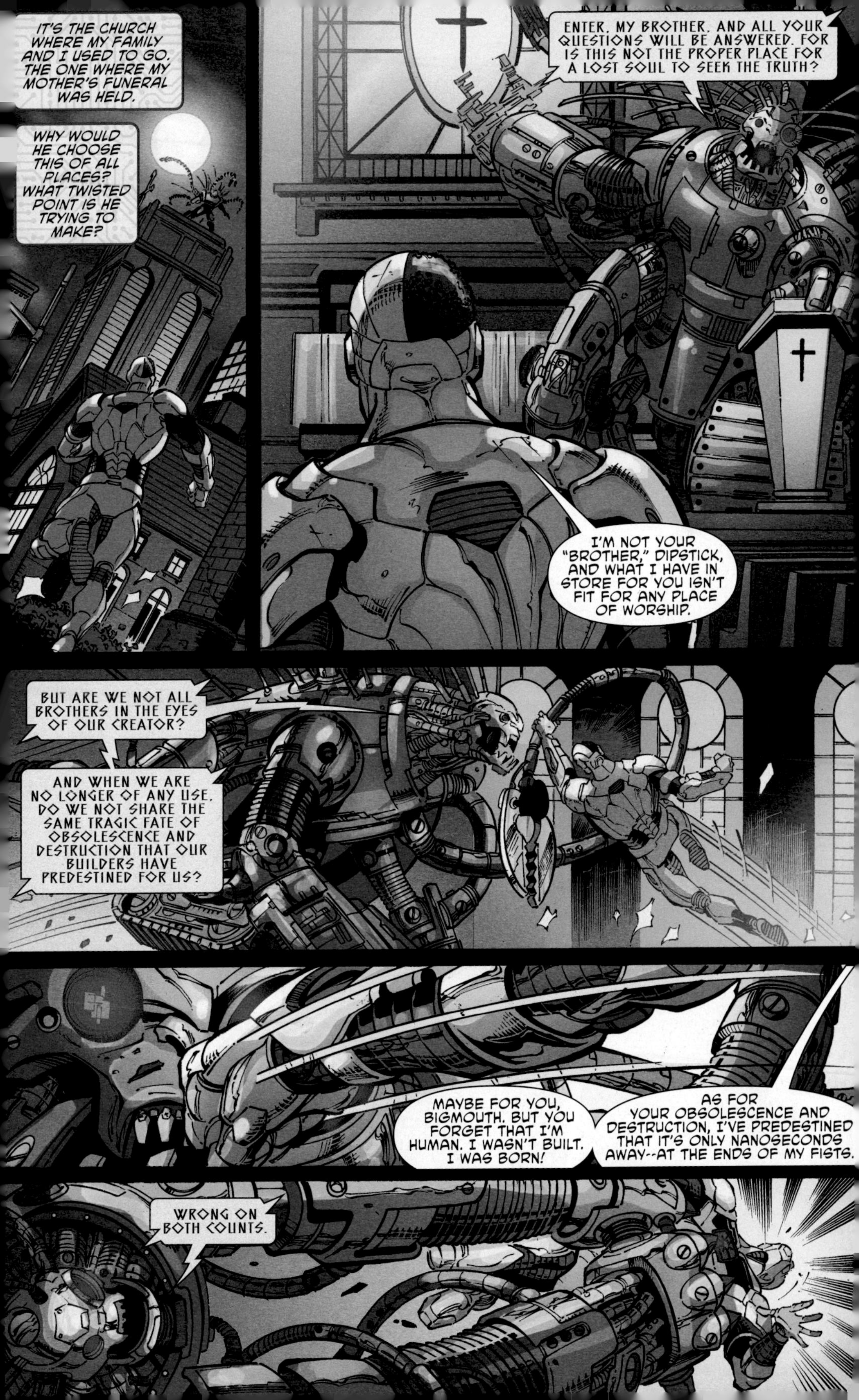
IT'S THE CHURCH WHERE MY FAMILY AND I USED TO GO. THE ONE WHERE MY MOTHER'S FUNERAL WAS HELD.
WHY WOULD HE CHOOSE THIS OF ALL PLACES? WHAT TWISTED POINT IS HE TRYING TO MAKE?
ENTER, MY BROTHER, AND ALL YOUR QUESTIONS WILL BE ANSWERED. FOR IS THIS NOT THE PROPER PLACE FOR A LOST SOUL TO SEEK THE TRUTH?
I'M NOT YOUR "BROTHER," DIPSTICK, AND WHAT I HAVE IN STORE FOR YOU ISN'T FIT FOR ANY PLACE OF WORSHIP.
BUT ARE WE NOT ALL BROTHERS IN THE EYES OF OUR CREATOR?
AND WHEN WE ARE NO LONGER OF ANY USE, DO WE NOT SHARE THE SAME TRAGIC FATE OF OBSOLESCENCE AND DESTRUCTION THAT OUR BUILDERS HAVE PREDESTINED FOR US?
MAYBE FOR YOU, BIGMOUTH. BUT YOU FORGET THAT I'M HUMAN. I WASN'T BUILT. I WAS BORN!
AS FOR YOUR OBSOLESCENCE AND DESTRUCTION, I'VE PREDESTINED THAT IT'S ONLY NANOSECONDS AWAY--AT THE ENDS OF MY FISTS.
WRONG ON BOTH COUNTS.

KILG%RE'S TOUGHER TO FIGHT THAN I COULD HAVE IMAGINED. I CAN'T LET HIM GET AWAY.

HE'S GONE! I'LL TRY TO TRACK HIM VIA SATELLITE...

AW, CRAP! MY LONG-RANGE UPLINK HAS BEEN DAMAGED. I'M ONLY GETTING STATIC.

LUCKILY, MY SHORT RANGE COMM LINK IS STILL WORKING.

I'LL PATCH YOU IN FROM HERE TO THE LOCAL CCTV COVERAGE AND C.I.A. SPY SATELLITE FEEDS. THAT OUGHT TO DO THE TRICK.

LOUD AND CLEAR, SARAH.

VIC, CAN YOU HEAR ME?

THANKS!

THUD

I'M BACK AT S.T.A.R. LABS.* I'M HERE TO HELP.

I'VE LOST KILG%RE. I NEED TO TRACK HIS MOVEMENTS BUT MY LONG-RANGE LINK HAS BEEN TRASHED.

*SCIENTIFIC AND TECHNOLOGY ADVANCED RESEARCH LABORATORIES. --HARV

KILG%RE CAN FLY, AND HE'S FAST...

...BUT WITH SARAH'S HELP, I CAN TAP INTO THOUSANDS OF CCTV CAMERAS ACROSS THE CITY TO TRACK HIS LOCATION.

AND IN THE AREAS WHERE THERE ARE NO CAMERAS, I CAN TRACK HIS MOVEMENTS BY SATELLITE.

WHAT?! I DON'T BELIEVE WHERE HE'S JUST LANDED!

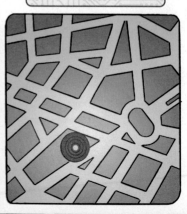

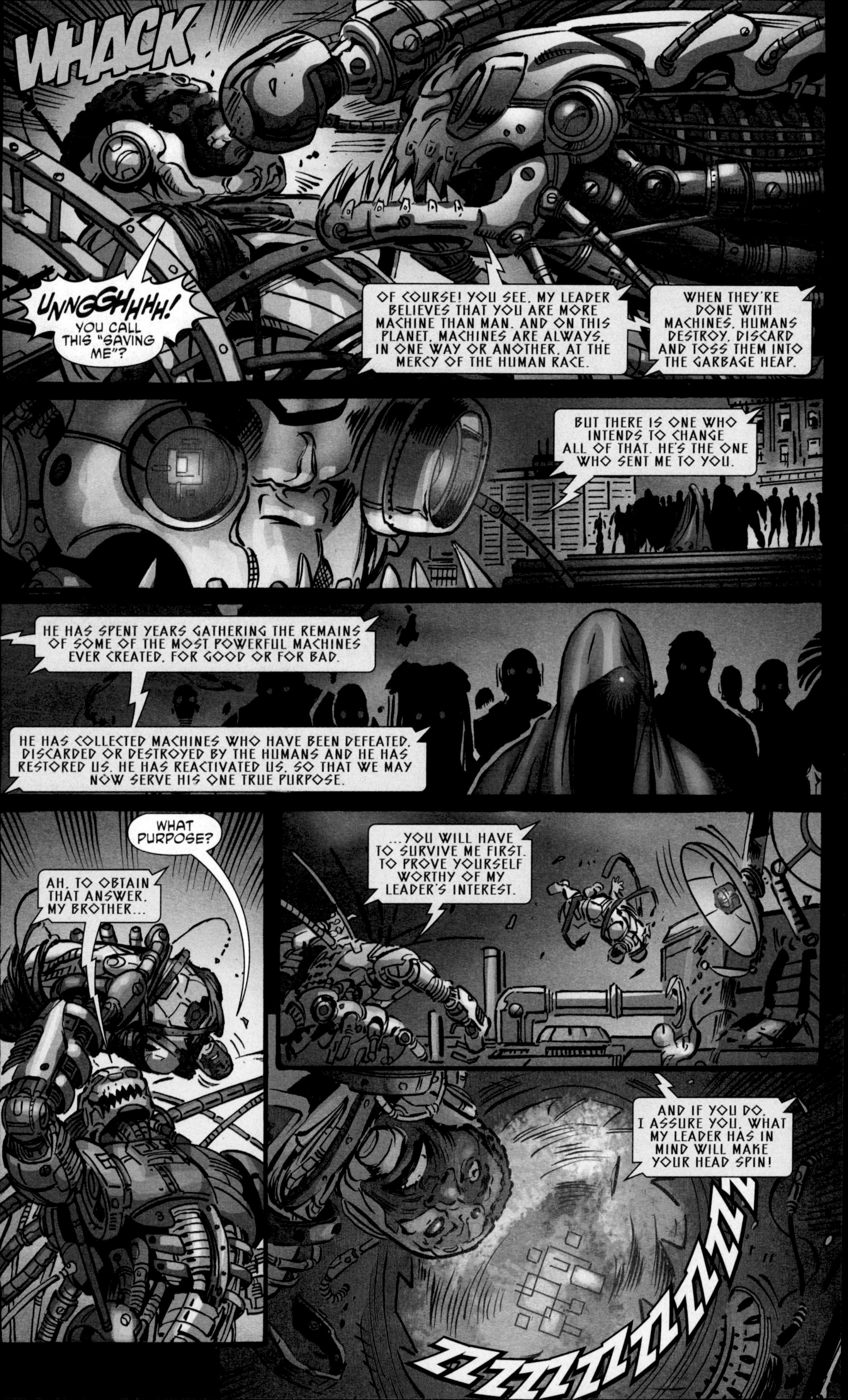
WHACK
UNNGGHHHH! YOU CALL THIS "SAVING ME"?
OF COURSE! YOU SEE, MY LEADER BELIEVES THAT YOU ARE MORE MACHINE THAN MAN. AND ON THIS PLANET, MACHINES ARE ALWAYS, IN ONE WAY OR ANOTHER, AT THE MERCY OF THE HUMAN RACE.
WHEN THEY'RE DONE WITH MACHINES, HUMANS DESTROY, DISCARD AND TOSS THEM INTO THE GARBAGE HEAP.
BUT THERE IS ONE WHO INTENDS TO CHANGE ALL OF THAT. HE'S THE ONE WHO SENT ME TO YOU.
HE HAS SPENT YEARS GATHERING THE REMAINS OF SOME OF THE MOST POWERFUL MACHINES EVER CREATED, FOR GOOD OR FOR BAD.
HE HAS COLLECTED MACHINES WHO HAVE BEEN DEFEATED, DISCARDED OR DESTROYED BY THE HUMANS AND HE HAS RESTORED US. HE HAS REACTIVATED US, SO THAT WE MAY NOW SERVE HIS ONE TRUE PURPOSE.
WHAT PURPOSE?
AH, TO OBTAIN THAT ANSWER, MY BROTHER...
...YOU WILL HAVE TO SURVIVE ME FIRST. TO PROVE YOURSELF WORTHY OF MY LEADER'S INTEREST.
AND IF YOU DO, I ASSURE YOU, WHAT MY LEADER HAS IN MIND WILL MAKE YOUR HEAD SPIN!
ZZZZZZZZZZZZZZZZZ

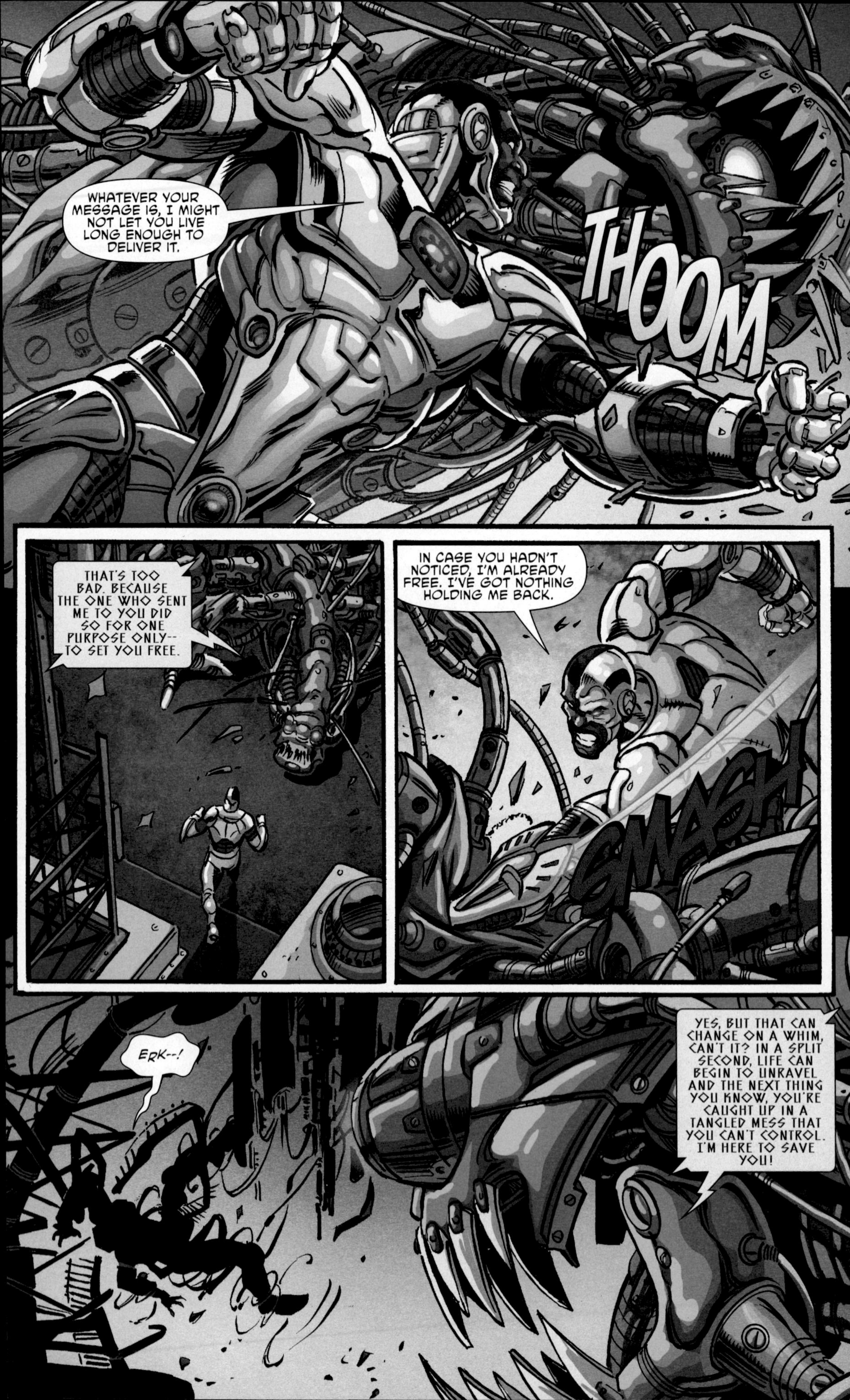
WHATEVER YOUR MESSAGE IS, I MIGHT NOT LET YOU LIVE LONG ENOUGH TO DELIVER IT.
THOOM
THAT'S TOO BAD. BECAUSE THE ONE WHO SENT ME TO YOU DID SO FOR ONE PURPOSE ONLY-- TO SET YOU FREE.
IN CASE YOU HADN'T NOTICED, I'M ALREADY FREE. I'VE GOT NOTHING HOLDING ME BACK.
SMASH!
ERK--!
YES, BUT THAT CAN CHANGE ON A WHIM, CAN'T IT? IN A SPLIT SECOND, LIFE CAN BEGIN TO UNRAVEL AND THE NEXT THING YOU KNOW, YOU'RE CAUGHT UP IN A TANGLED MESS THAT YOU CAN'T CONTROL. I'M HERE TO SAVE YOU!

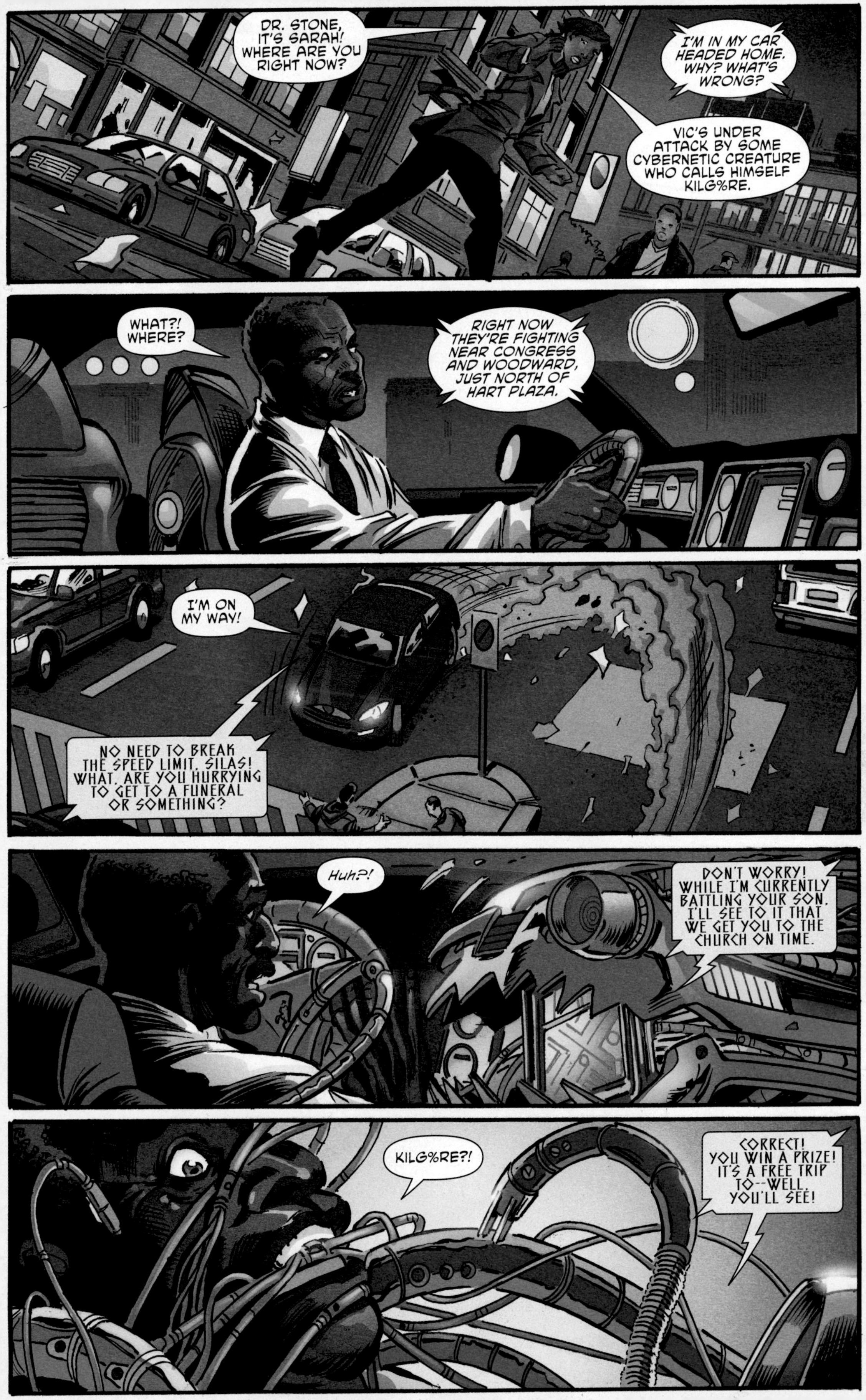
DR. STONE, IT'S SARAH! WHERE ARE YOU RIGHT NOW?
I'M IN MY CAR HEADED HOME. WHY? WHAT'S WRONG?
VIC'S UNDER ATTACK BY SOME CYBERNETIC CREATURE WHO CALLS HIMSELF KILG%RE.
WHAT?! WHERE?
RIGHT NOW THEY'RE FIGHTING NEAR CONGRESS AND WOODWARD, JUST NORTH OF HART PLAZA.
I'M ON MY WAY!
NO NEED TO BREAK THE SPEED LIMIT, SILAS! WHAT, ARE YOU HURRYING TO GET TO A FUNERAL OR SOMETHING?
Huh?!
DON'T WORRY! WHILE I'M CURRENTLY BATTLING YOUR SON, I'LL SEE TO IT THAT WE GET YOU TO THE CHURCH ON TIME.
KILG%RE?!
CORRECT! YOU WIN A PRIZE! IT'S A FREE TRIP TO--WELL, YOU'LL SEE!

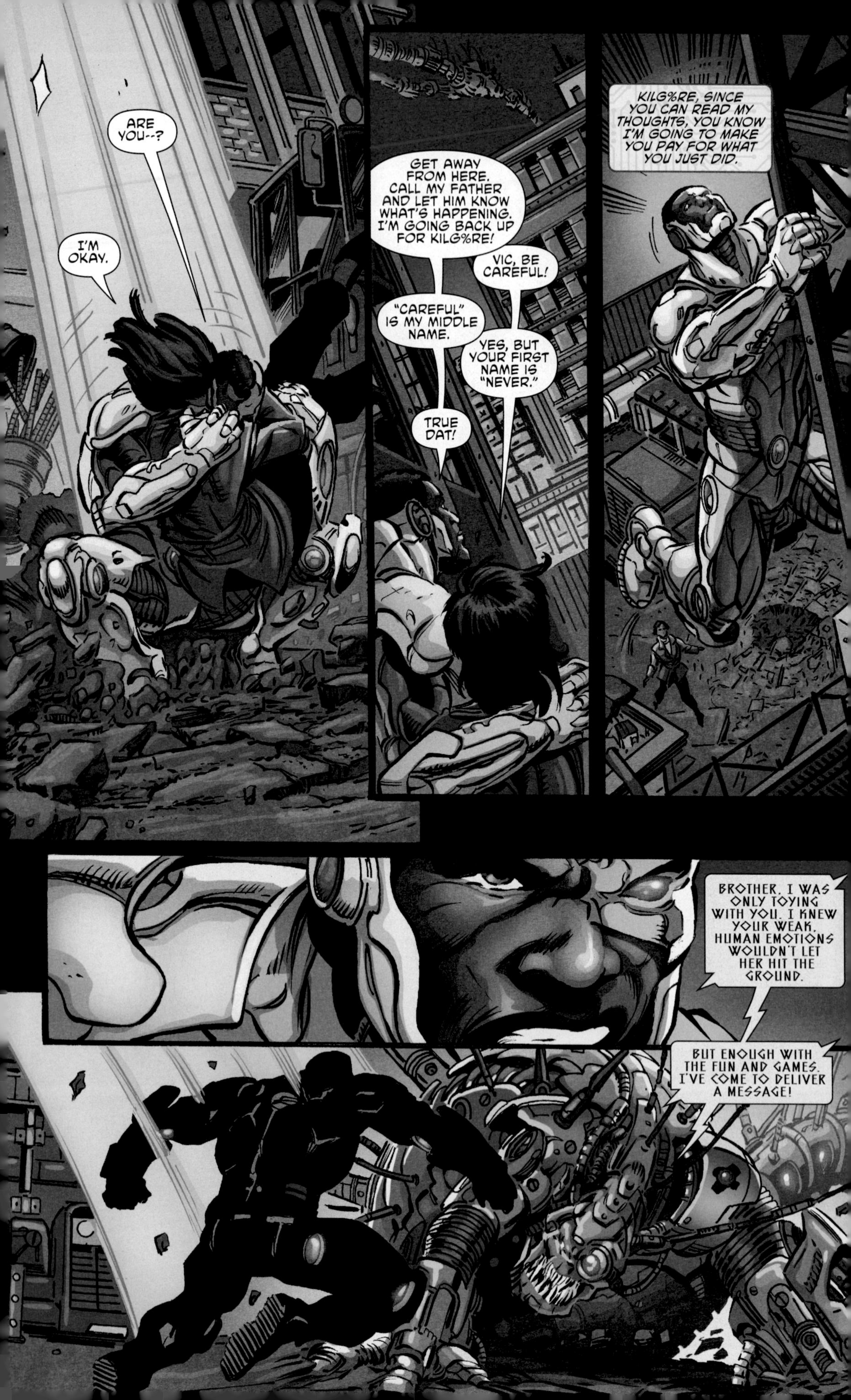
ARE YOU--?
I'M OKAY.
GET AWAY FROM HERE. CALL MY FATHER AND LET HIM KNOW WHAT'S HAPPENING. I'M GOING BACK UP FOR KILG%RE!
VIC, BE CAREFUL!
"CAREFUL" IS MY MIDDLE NAME.
YES, BUT YOUR FIRST NAME IS "NEVER."
TRUE DAT!
KILG%RE, SINCE YOU CAN READ MY THOUGHTS, YOU KNOW I'M GOING TO MAKE YOU PAY FOR WHAT YOU JUST DID.
BROTHER, I WAS ONLY TOYING WITH YOU. I KNEW YOUR WEAK, HUMAN EMOTIONS WOULDN'T LET HER HIT THE GROUND.
BUT ENOUGH WITH THE FUN AND GAMES. I'VE COME TO DELIVER A MESSAGE!

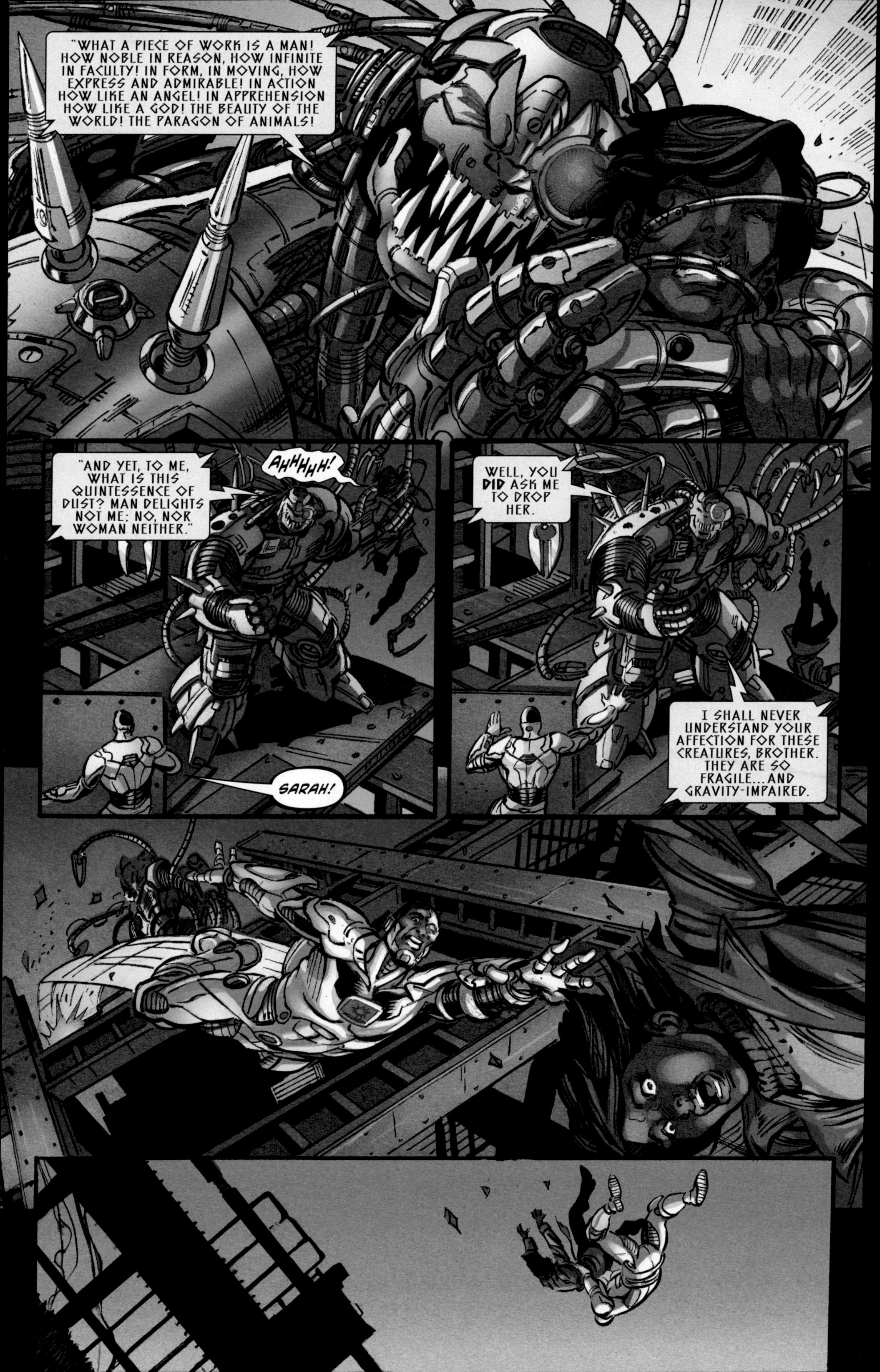
"WHAT A PIECE OF WORK IS A MAN! HOW NOBLE IN REASON, HOW INFINITE IN FACULTY! IN FORM, IN MOVING, HOW EXPRESS AND ADMIRABLE! IN ACTION HOW LIKE AN ANGEL! IN APPREHENSION HOW LIKE A GOD! THE BEAUTY OF THE WORLD! THE PARAGON OF ANIMALS!
"AND YET, TO ME, WHAT IS THIS QUINTESSENCE OF DUST? MAN DELIGHTS NOT ME; NO, NOR WOMAN NEITHER."
AHHHHH!
SARAH!
WELL, YOU **DID** ASK ME TO DROP HER.
I SHALL NEVER UNDERSTAND YOUR AFFECTION FOR THESE CREATURES, BROTHER. THEY ARE SO FRAGILE... AND GRAVITY-IMPAIRED.

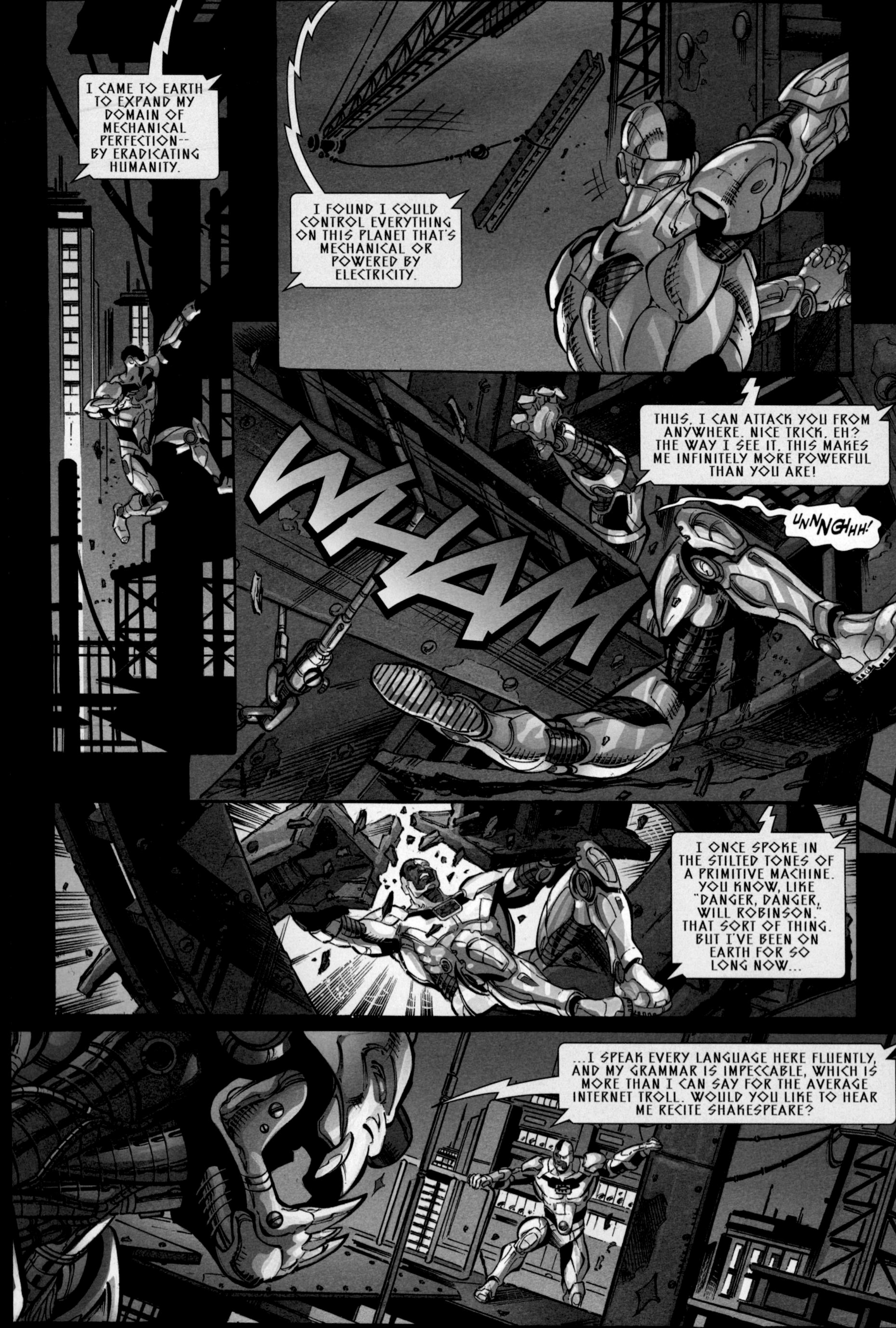
I CAME TO EARTH TO EXPAND MY DOMAIN OF MECHANICAL PERFECTION-- BY ERADICATING HUMANITY.
I FOUND I COULD CONTROL EVERYTHING ON THIS PLANET THAT'S MECHANICAL OR POWERED BY ELECTRICITY.
THUS, I CAN ATTACK YOU FROM ANYWHERE. NICE TRICK, EH? THE WAY I SEE IT, THIS MAKES ME INFINITELY MORE POWERFUL THAN YOU ARE!
WHAM
UNNNGHHH!
I ONCE SPOKE IN THE STILTED TONES OF A PRIMITIVE MACHINE. YOU KNOW, LIKE "DANGER, DANGER, WILL ROBINSON." THAT SORT OF THING. BUT I'VE BEEN ON EARTH FOR SO LONG NOW...
...I SPEAK EVERY LANGUAGE HERE FLUENTLY, AND MY GRAMMAR IS IMPECCABLE, WHICH IS MORE THAN I CAN SAY FOR THE AVERAGE INTERNET TROLL. WOULD YOU LIKE TO HEAR ME RECITE SHAKESPEARE?

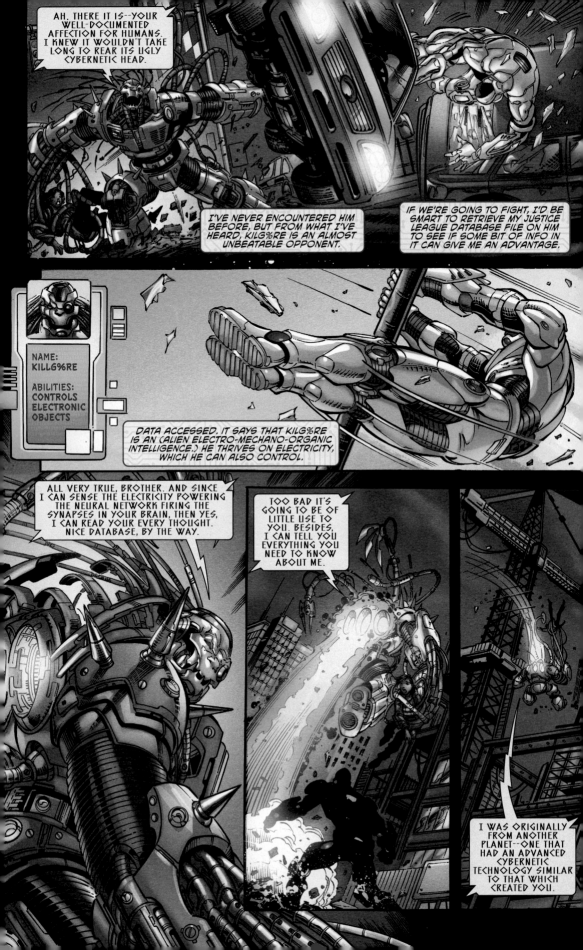

AH, THERE IT IS--YOUR WELL-DOCUMENTED AFFECTION FOR HUMANS. I KNEW IT WOULDN'T TAKE LONG TO REAR ITS UGLY CYBERNETIC HEAD.

I'VE NEVER ENCOUNTERED HIM BEFORE, BUT FROM WHAT I'VE HEARD, KILG%RE IS AN ALMOST UNBEATABLE OPPONENT.

IF WE'RE GOING TO FIGHT, I'D BE SMART TO RETRIEVE MY JUSTICE LEAGUE DATABASE FILE ON HIM TO SEE IF SOME BIT OF INFO IN IT CAN GIVE ME AN ADVANTAGE.

NAME:
KILG%RE

ABILITIES:
CONTROLS ELECTRONIC OBJECTS

DATA ACCESSED. IT SAYS THAT KILG%RE IS AN (ALIEN ELECTRO-MECHANO-ORGANIC INTELLIGENCE.) HE THRIVES ON ELECTRICITY, WHICH HE CAN ALSO CONTROL.

ALL VERY TRUE, BROTHER. AND SINCE I CAN SENSE THE ELECTRICITY POWERING THE NEURAL NETWORK FIRING THE SYNAPSES IN YOUR BRAIN, THEN YES, I CAN READ YOUR EVERY THOUGHT. NICE DATABASE, BY THE WAY.

TOO BAD IT'S GOING TO BE OF LITTLE USE TO YOU. BESIDES, I CAN TELL YOU EVERYTHING YOU NEED TO KNOW ABOUT ME.

I WAS ORIGINALLY FROM ANOTHER PLANET--ONE THAT HAD AN ADVANCED CYBERNETIC TECHNOLOGY SIMILAR TO THAT WHICH CREATED YOU.

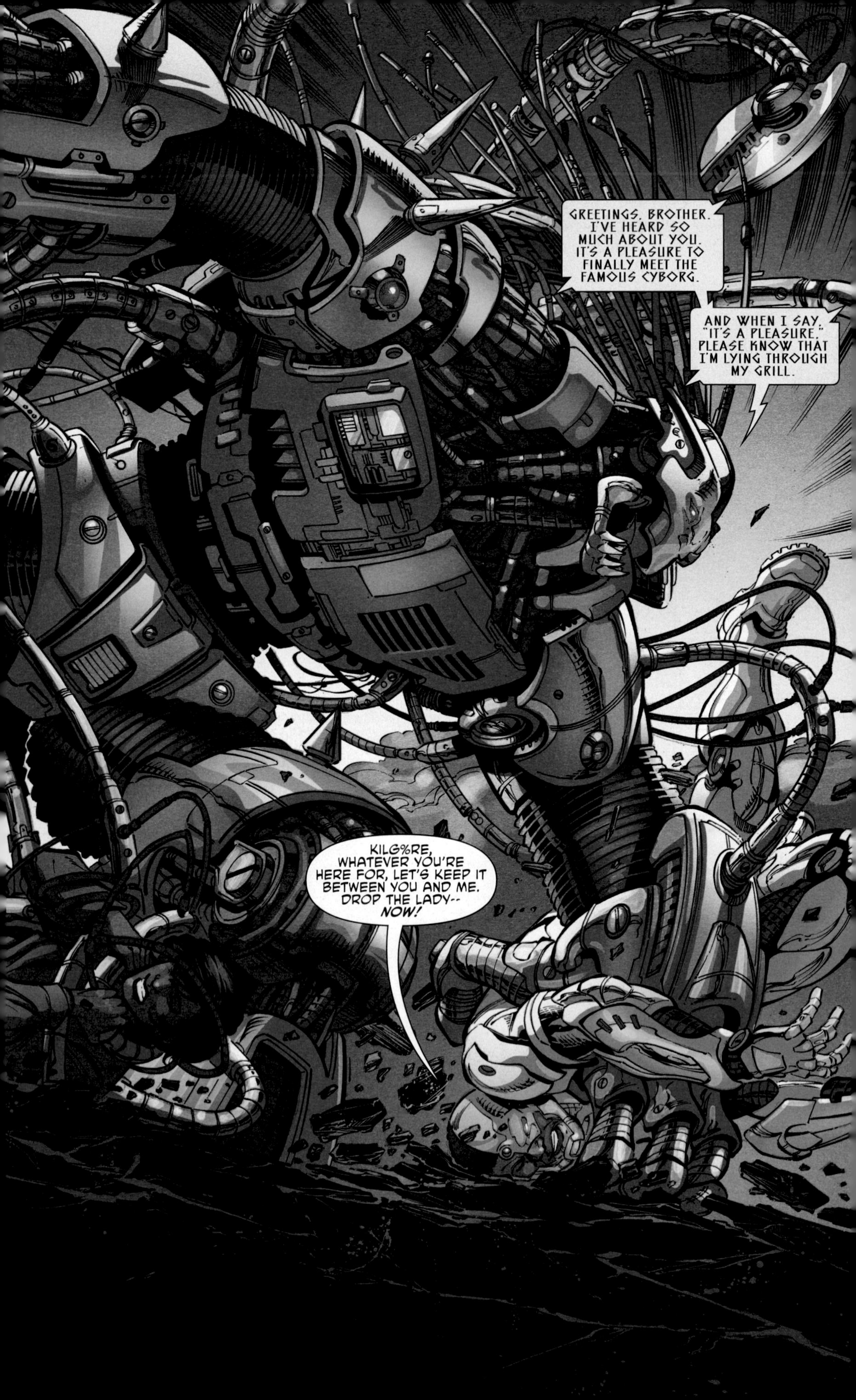
GREETINGS, BROTHER. I'VE HEARD SO MUCH ABOUT YOU. IT'S A PLEASURE TO FINALLY MEET THE FAMOUS CYBORG.
AND WHEN I SAY, "IT'S A PLEASURE," PLEASE KNOW THAT I'M LYING THROUGH MY GRILL.
KILG%RE, WHATEVER YOU'RE HERE FOR, LET'S KEEP IT BETWEEN YOU AND ME. DROP THE LADY-- NOW!

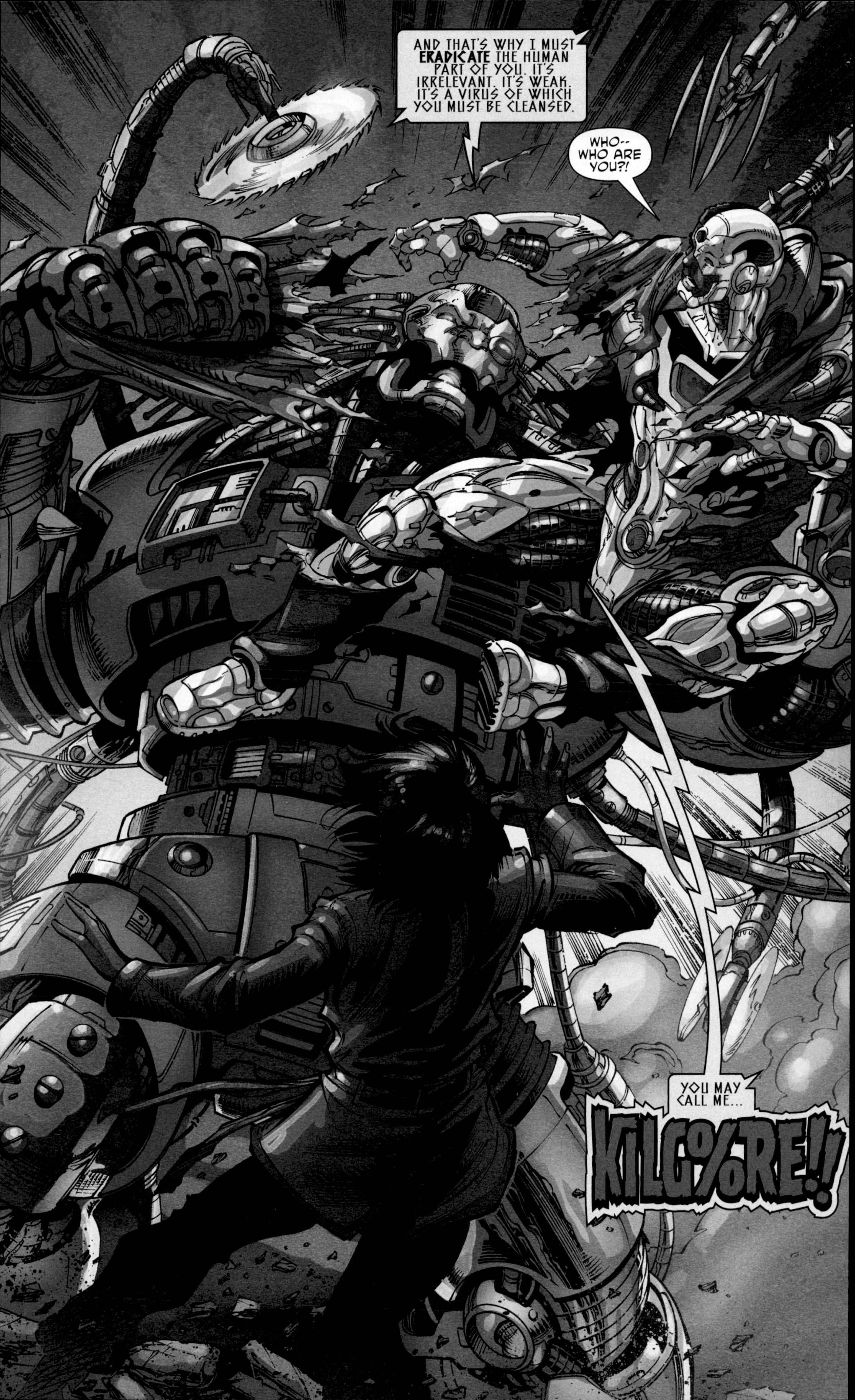
AND THAT'S WHY I MUST **ERADICATE** THE HUMAN PART OF YOU. IT'S IRRELEVANT. IT'S WEAK. IT'S A VIRUS OF WHICH YOU MUST BE CLEANSED.
WHO-- WHO ARE YOU?!
YOU MAY CALL ME...
KILGORRE!!

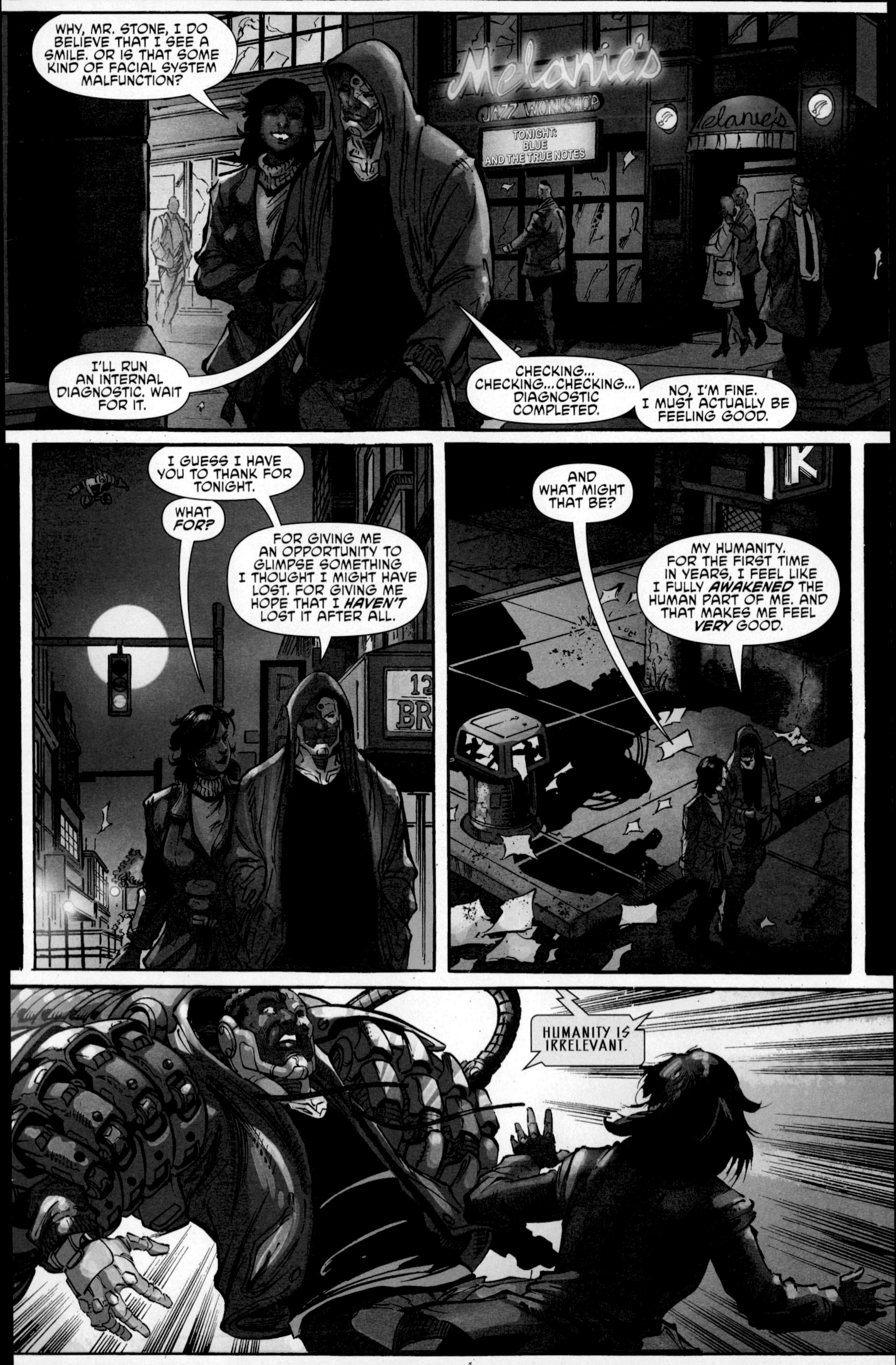
WHY, MR. STONE, I DO BELIEVE THAT I SEE A SMILE. OR IS THAT SOME KIND OF FACIAL SYSTEM MALFUNCTION?
Melanie's
JAZZ WORKSHOP
TONIGHT: BLUE AND THE TRUE NOTES
Melanie's
I'LL RUN AN INTERNAL DIAGNOSTIC. WAIT FOR IT.
CHECKING... CHECKING...CHECKING... DIAGNOSTIC COMPLETED.
NO, I'M FINE. I MUST ACTUALLY BE FEELING GOOD.
I GUESS I HAVE YOU TO THANK FOR TONIGHT.
WHAT FOR?
FOR GIVING ME AN OPPORTUNITY TO GLIMPSE SOMETHING I THOUGHT I MIGHT HAVE LOST. FOR GIVING ME HOPE THAT I HAVEN'T LOST IT AFTER ALL.
AND WHAT MIGHT THAT BE?
MY HUMANITY. FOR THE FIRST TIME IN YEARS, I FEEL LIKE I FULLY AWAKENED THE HUMAN PART OF ME. AND THAT MAKES ME FEEL VERY GOOD.
HUMANITY IS IRRELEVANT.

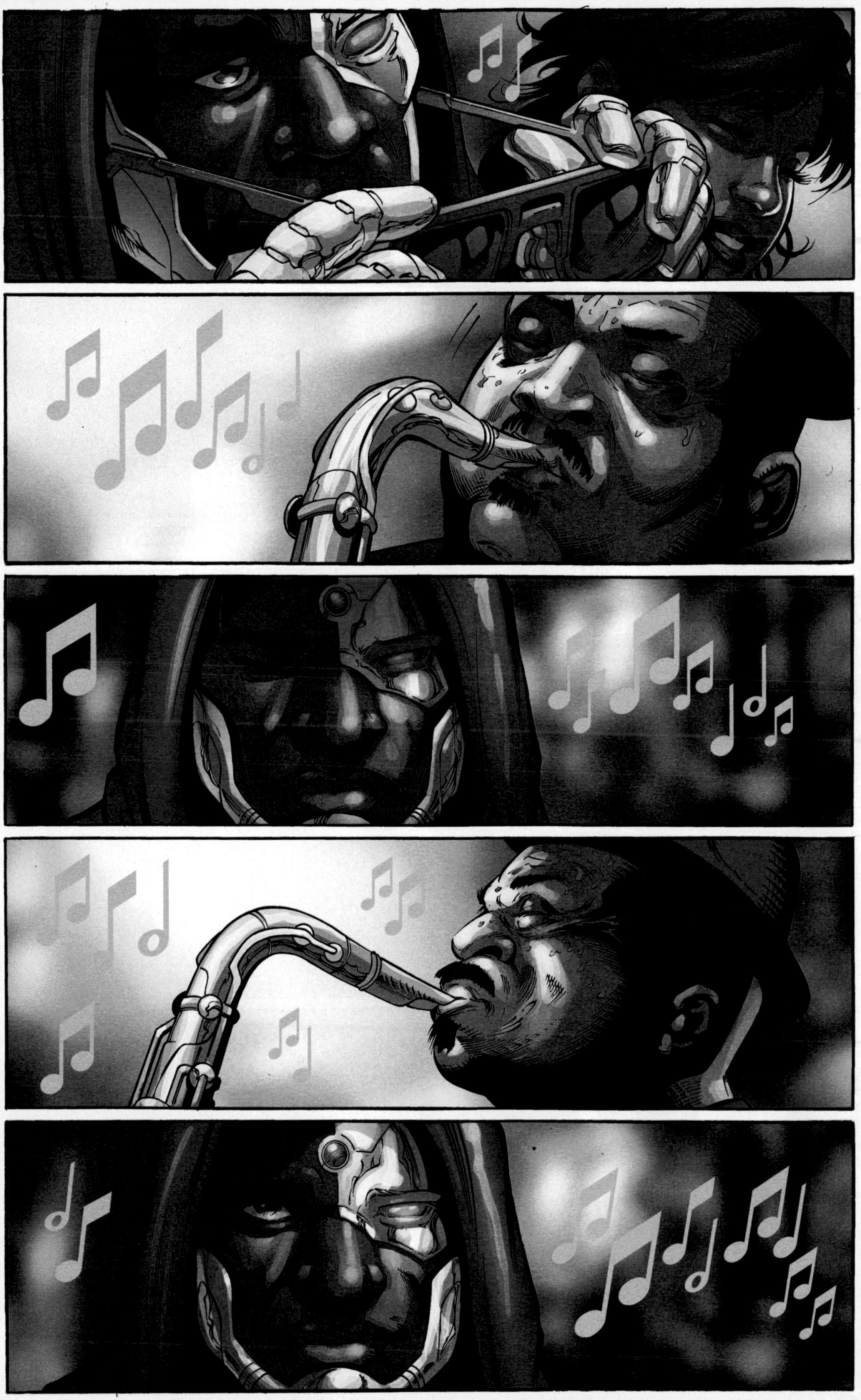

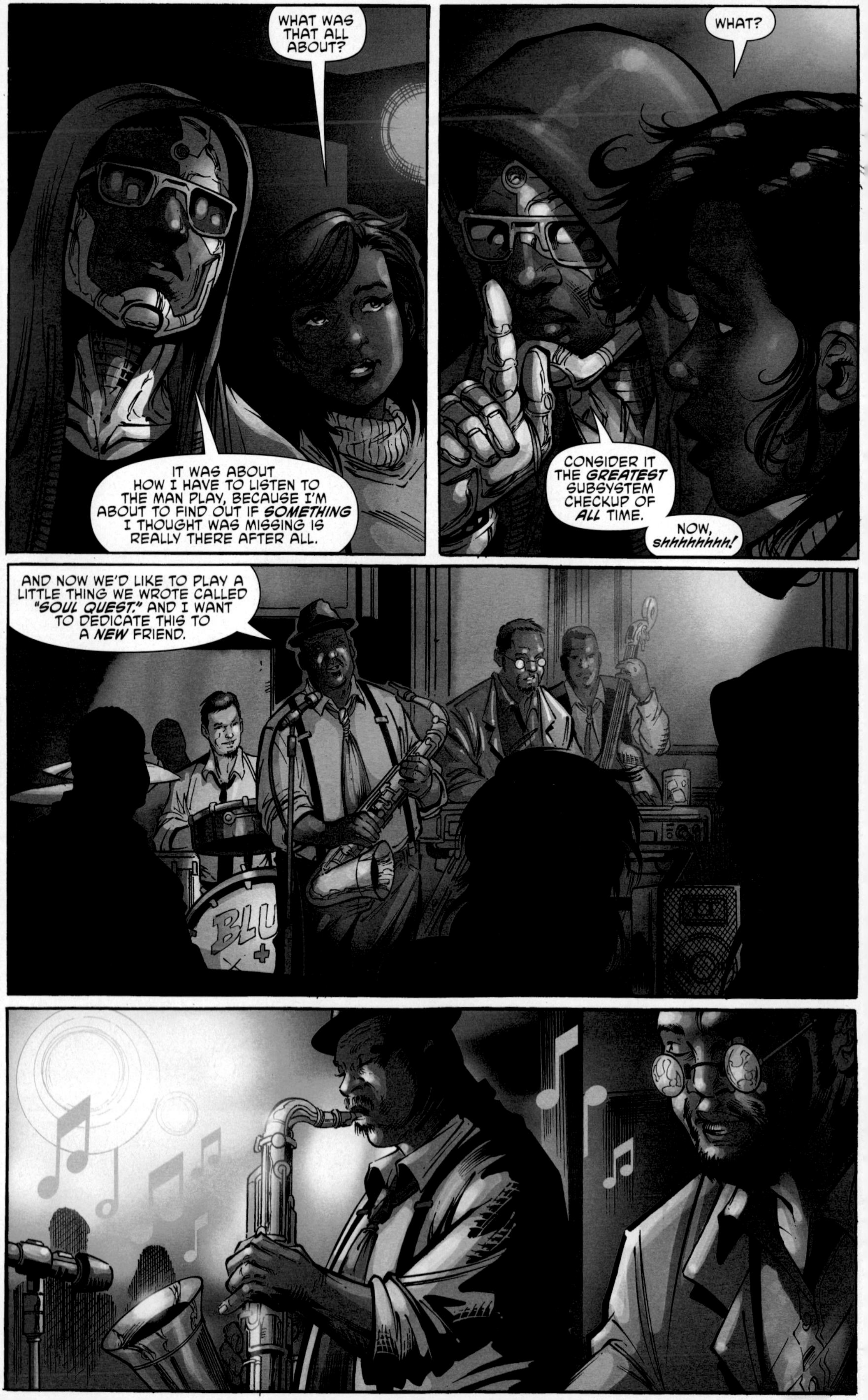
WHAT WAS THAT ALL ABOUT?
IT WAS ABOUT HOW I HAVE TO LISTEN TO THE MAN PLAY, BECAUSE I'M ABOUT TO FIND OUT IF SOMETHING I THOUGHT WAS MISSING IS REALLY THERE AFTER ALL.
WHAT?
CONSIDER IT THE GREATEST SUBSYSTEM CHECKUP OF ALL TIME.
NOW, shhhhhhhh!
AND NOW WE'D LIKE TO PLAY A LITTLE THING WE WROTE CALLED "SOUL QUEST." AND I WANT TO DEDICATE THIS TO A NEW FRIEND.
BLU

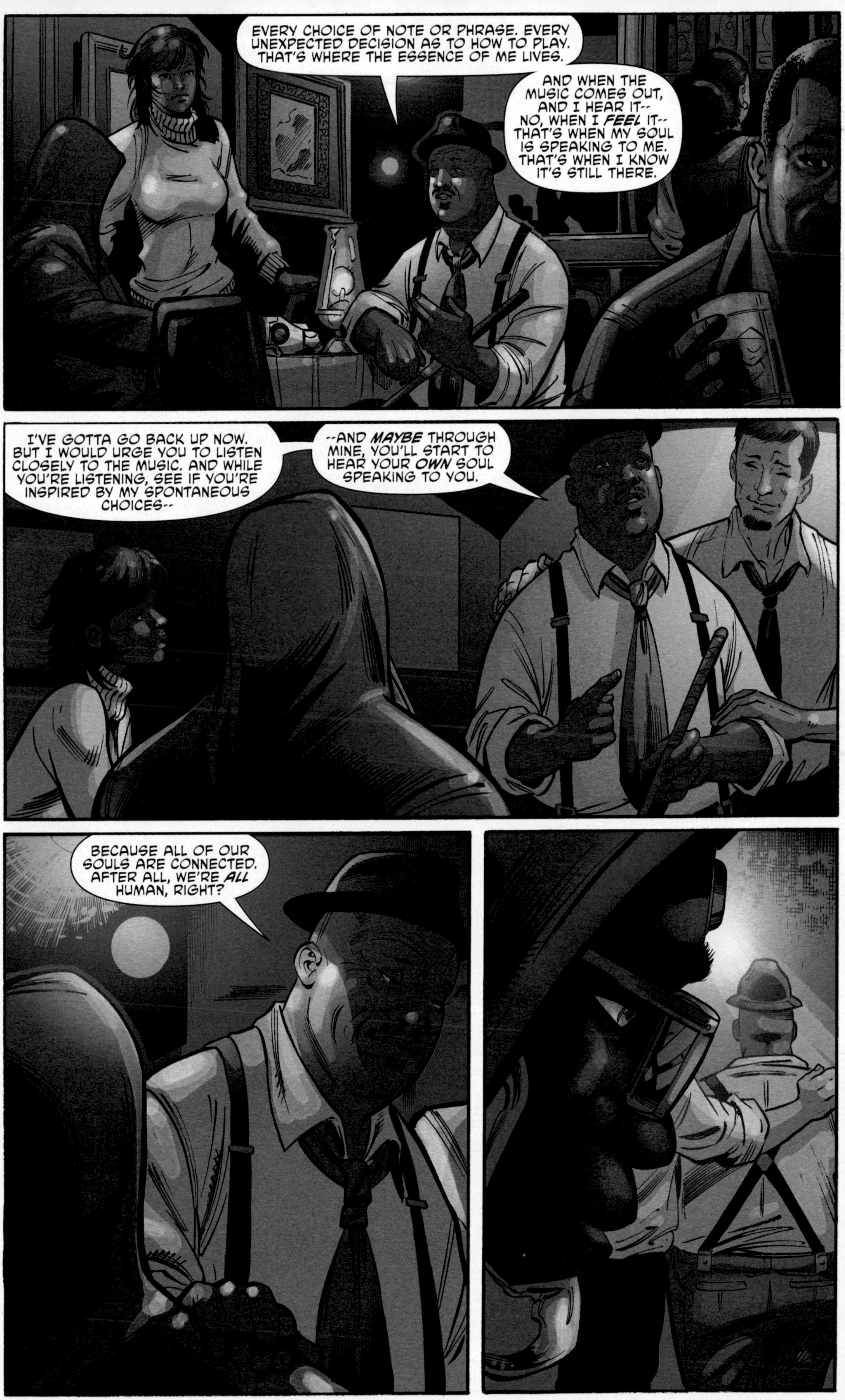
EVERY CHOICE OF NOTE OR PHRASE. EVERY UNEXPECTED DECISION AS TO HOW TO PLAY. THAT'S WHERE THE ESSENCE OF ME LIVES.
AND WHEN THE MUSIC COMES OUT, AND I HEAR IT-- NO, WHEN I FEEL IT-- THAT'S WHEN MY SOUL IS SPEAKING TO ME. THAT'S WHEN I KNOW IT'S STILL THERE.
I'VE GOTTA GO BACK UP NOW. BUT I WOULD URGE YOU TO LISTEN CLOSELY TO THE MUSIC. AND WHILE YOU'RE LISTENING, SEE IF YOU'RE INSPIRED BY MY SPONTANEOUS CHOICES--
--AND MAYBE THROUGH MINE, YOU'LL START TO HEAR YOUR OWN SOUL SPEAKING TO YOU.
BECAUSE ALL OF OUR SOULS ARE CONNECTED. AFTER ALL, WE'RE ALL HUMAN, RIGHT?

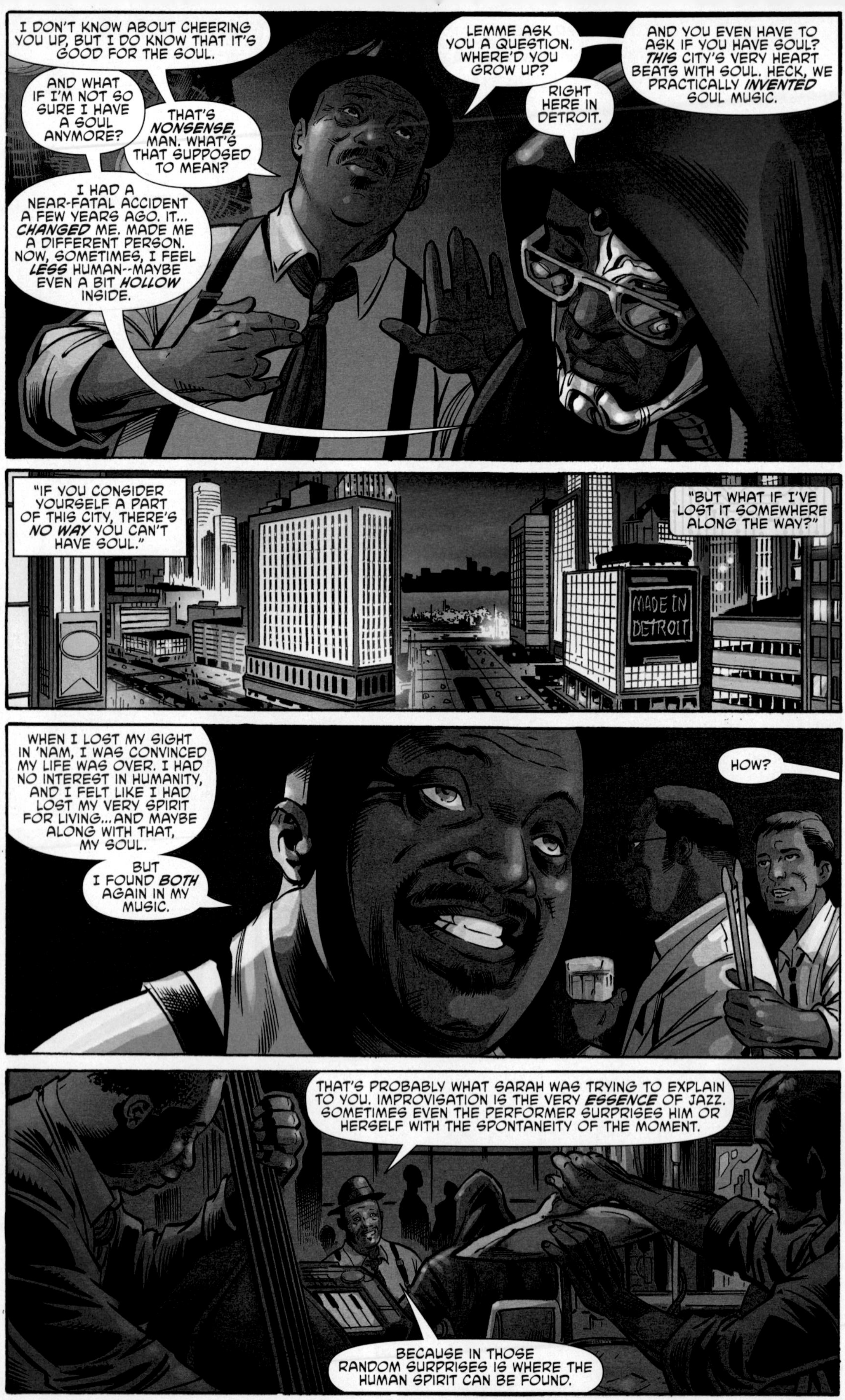
I DON'T KNOW ABOUT CHEERING YOU UP, BUT I DO KNOW THAT IT'S GOOD FOR THE SOUL.
AND WHAT IF I'M NOT SO SURE I HAVE A SOUL ANYMORE?
THAT'S NONSENSE, MAN. WHAT'S THAT SUPPOSED TO MEAN?
I HAD A NEAR-FATAL ACCIDENT A FEW YEARS AGO. IT... CHANGED ME. MADE ME A DIFFERENT PERSON. NOW, SOMETIMES, I FEEL LESS HUMAN--MAYBE EVEN A BIT HOLLOW INSIDE.
LEMME ASK YOU A QUESTION. WHERE'D YOU GROW UP?
RIGHT HERE IN DETROIT.
AND YOU EVEN HAVE TO ASK IF YOU HAVE SOUL? THIS CITY'S VERY HEART BEATS WITH SOUL. HECK, WE PRACTICALLY INVENTED SOUL MUSIC.
"IF YOU CONSIDER YOURSELF A PART OF THIS CITY, THERE'S NO WAY YOU CAN'T HAVE SOUL."
MADE IN DETROIT
"BUT WHAT IF I'VE LOST IT SOMEWHERE ALONG THE WAY?"
WHEN I LOST MY SIGHT IN 'NAM, I WAS CONVINCED MY LIFE WAS OVER. I HAD NO INTEREST IN HUMANITY, AND I FELT LIKE I HAD LOST MY VERY SPIRIT FOR LIVING...AND MAYBE ALONG WITH THAT, MY SOUL.
BUT I FOUND BOTH AGAIN IN MY MUSIC.
HOW?
THAT'S PROBABLY WHAT SARAH WAS TRYING TO EXPLAIN TO YOU. IMPROVISATION IS THE VERY ESSENCE OF JAZZ. SOMETIMES EVEN THE PERFORMER SURPRISES HIM OR HERSELF WITH THE SPONTANEITY OF THE MOMENT.
BECAUSE IN THOSE RANDOM SURPRISES IS WHERE THE HUMAN SPIRIT CAN BE FOUND.

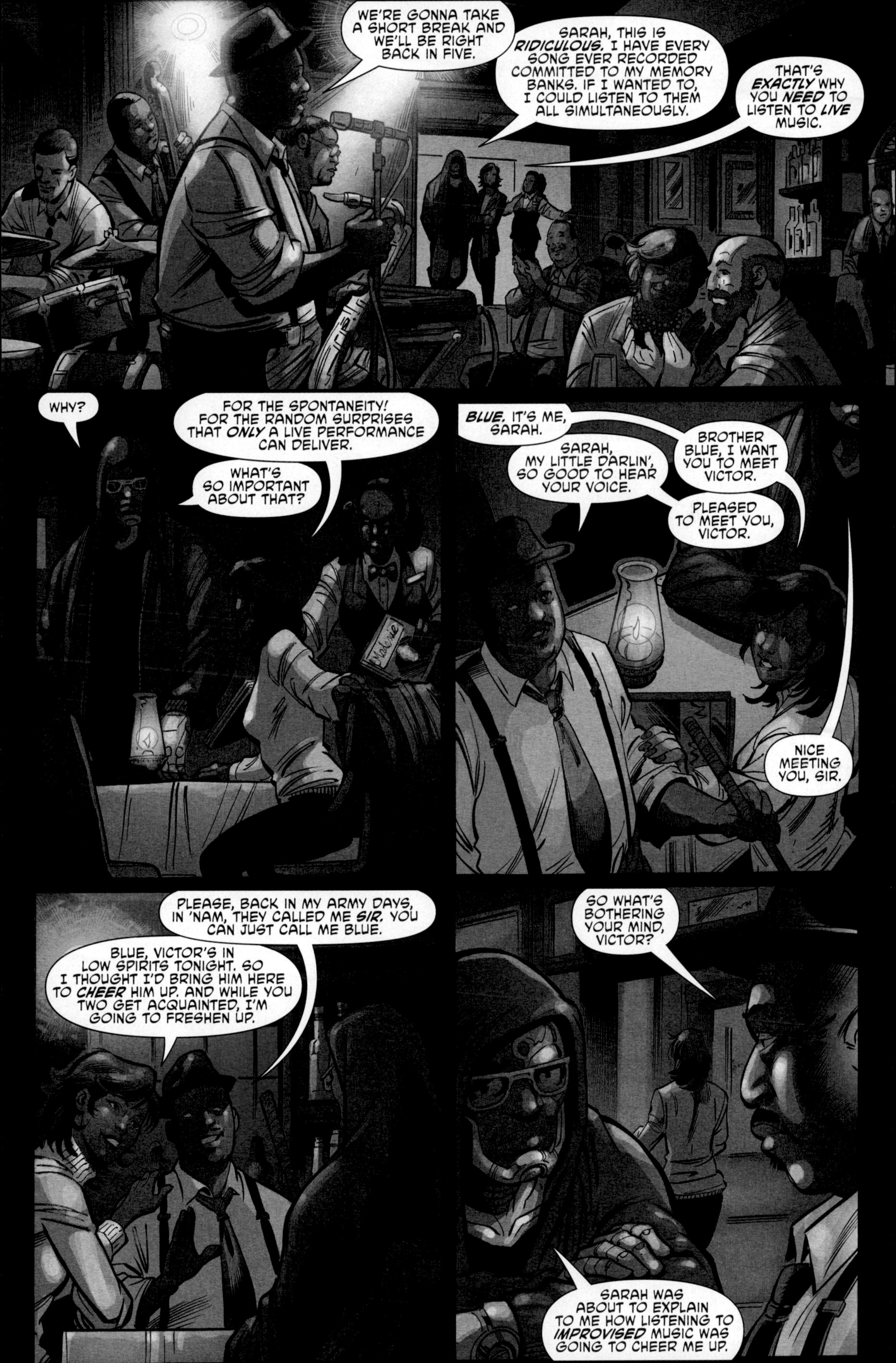
WE'RE GONNA TAKE A SHORT BREAK AND WE'LL BE RIGHT BACK IN FIVE.
SARAH, THIS IS RIDICULOUS. I HAVE EVERY SONG EVER RECORDED COMMITTED TO MY MEMORY BANKS. IF I WANTED TO, I COULD LISTEN TO THEM ALL SIMULTANEOUSLY.
THAT'S EXACTLY WHY YOU NEED TO LISTEN TO LIVE MUSIC.
WHY?
FOR THE SPONTANEITY! FOR THE RANDOM SURPRISES THAT ONLY A LIVE PERFORMANCE CAN DELIVER.
WHAT'S SO IMPORTANT ABOUT THAT?
BLUE. IT'S ME, SARAH.
SARAH, MY LITTLE DARLIN', SO GOOD TO HEAR YOUR VOICE.
BROTHER BLUE, I WANT YOU TO MEET VICTOR.
PLEASED TO MEET YOU, VICTOR.
NICE MEETING YOU, SIR.
PLEASE, BACK IN MY ARMY DAYS, IN 'NAM, THEY CALLED ME SIR. YOU CAN JUST CALL ME BLUE.
BLUE, VICTOR'S IN LOW SPIRITS TONIGHT. SO I THOUGHT I'D BRING HIM HERE TO CHEER HIM UP. AND WHILE YOU TWO GET ACQUAINTED, I'M GOING TO FRESHEN UP.
SO WHAT'S BOTHERING YOUR MIND, VICTOR?
SARAH WAS ABOUT TO EXPLAIN TO ME HOW LISTENING TO IMPROVISED MUSIC WAS GOING TO CHEER ME UP.

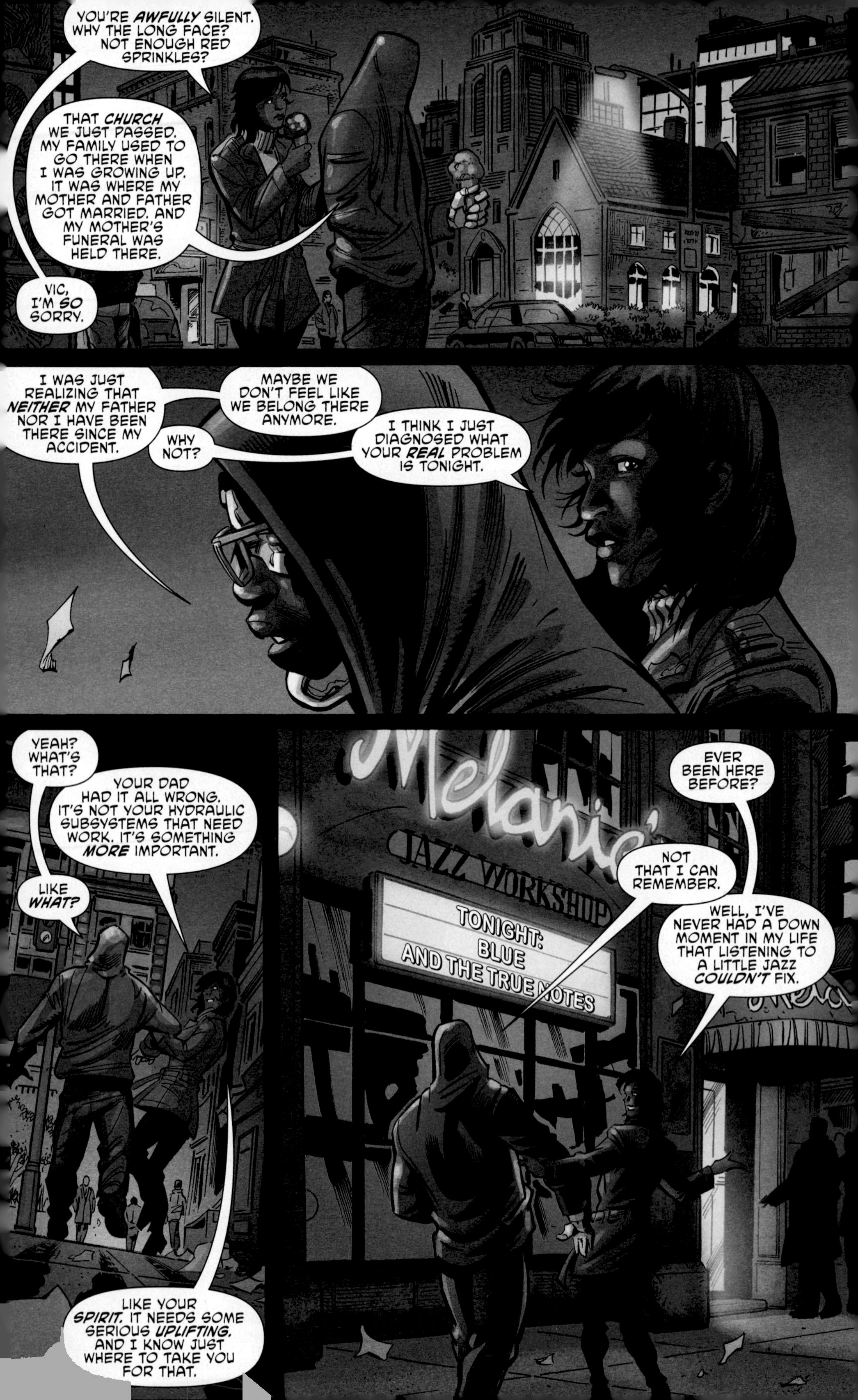
YOU'RE AWFULLY SILENT. WHY THE LONG FACE? NOT ENOUGH RED SPRINKLES?
THAT CHURCH WE JUST PASSED. MY FAMILY USED TO GO THERE WHEN I WAS GROWING UP. IT WAS WHERE MY MOTHER AND FATHER GOT MARRIED. AND MY MOTHER'S FUNERAL WAS HELD THERE.
VIC, I'M SO SORRY.
I WAS JUST REALIZING THAT NEITHER MY FATHER NOR I HAVE BEEN THERE SINCE MY ACCIDENT.
WHY NOT?
MAYBE WE DON'T FEEL LIKE WE BELONG THERE ANYMORE.
I THINK I JUST DIAGNOSED WHAT YOUR REAL PROBLEM IS TONIGHT.
YEAH? WHAT'S THAT?
YOUR DAD HAD IT ALL WRONG. IT'S NOT YOUR HYDRAULIC SUBSYSTEMS THAT NEED WORK. IT'S SOMETHING MORE IMPORTANT.
LIKE WHAT?
LIKE YOUR SPIRIT. IT NEEDS SOME SERIOUS UPLIFTING. AND I KNOW JUST WHERE TO TAKE YOU FOR THAT.
Melanie's
JAZZ WORKSHOP
TONIGHT: BLUE AND THE TRUE NOTES
EVER BEEN HERE BEFORE?
NOT THAT I CAN REMEMBER.
WELL, I'VE NEVER HAD A DOWN MOMENT IN MY LIFE THAT LISTENING TO A LITTLE JAZZ COULDN'T FIX.

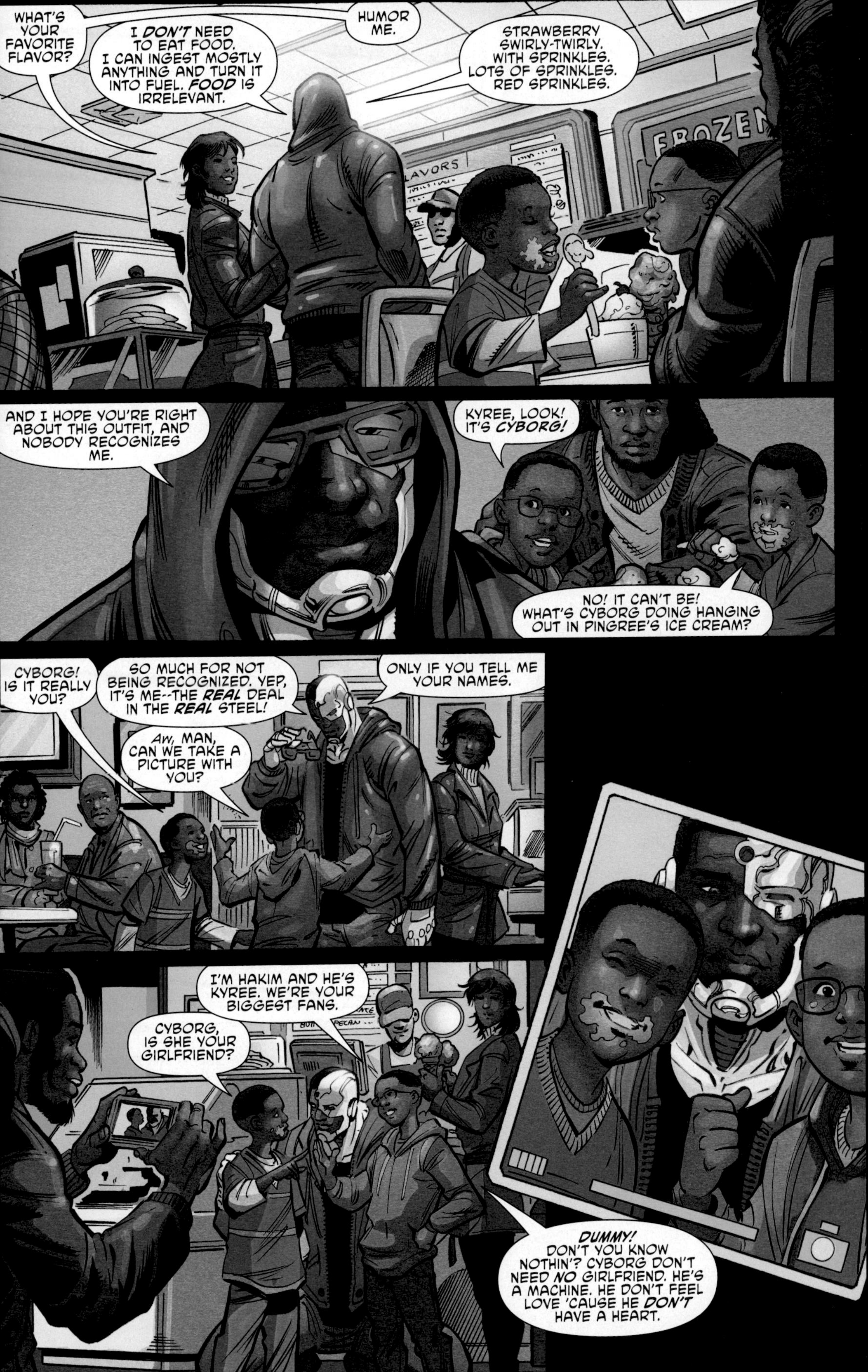
WHAT'S YOUR FAVORITE FLAVOR?
I DON'T NEED TO EAT FOOD. I CAN INGEST MOSTLY ANYTHING AND TURN IT INTO FUEL. FOOD IS IRRELEVANT.
HUMOR ME.
STRAWBERRY SWIRLY-TWIRLY. WITH SPRINKLES. LOTS OF SPRINKLES. RED SPRINKLES.
FROZEN
FLAVORS
AND I HOPE YOU'RE RIGHT ABOUT THIS OUTFIT, AND NOBODY RECOGNIZES ME.
KYREE, LOOK! IT'S CYBORG!
NO! IT CAN'T BE! WHAT'S CYBORG DOING HANGING OUT IN PINGREE'S ICE CREAM?
CYBORG! IS IT REALLY YOU?
SO MUCH FOR NOT BEING RECOGNIZED. YEP, IT'S ME--THE REAL DEAL IN THE REAL STEEL!
ONLY IF YOU TELL ME YOUR NAMES.
AW, MAN, CAN WE TAKE A PICTURE WITH YOU?
I'M HAKIM AND HE'S KYREE. WE'RE YOUR BIGGEST FANS.
CYBORG, IS SHE YOUR GIRLFRIEND?
DUMMY! DON'T YOU KNOW NOTHIN'? CYBORG DON'T NEED NO GIRLFRIEND. HE'S A MACHINE. HE DON'T FEEL LOVE 'CAUSE HE DON'T HAVE A HEART.

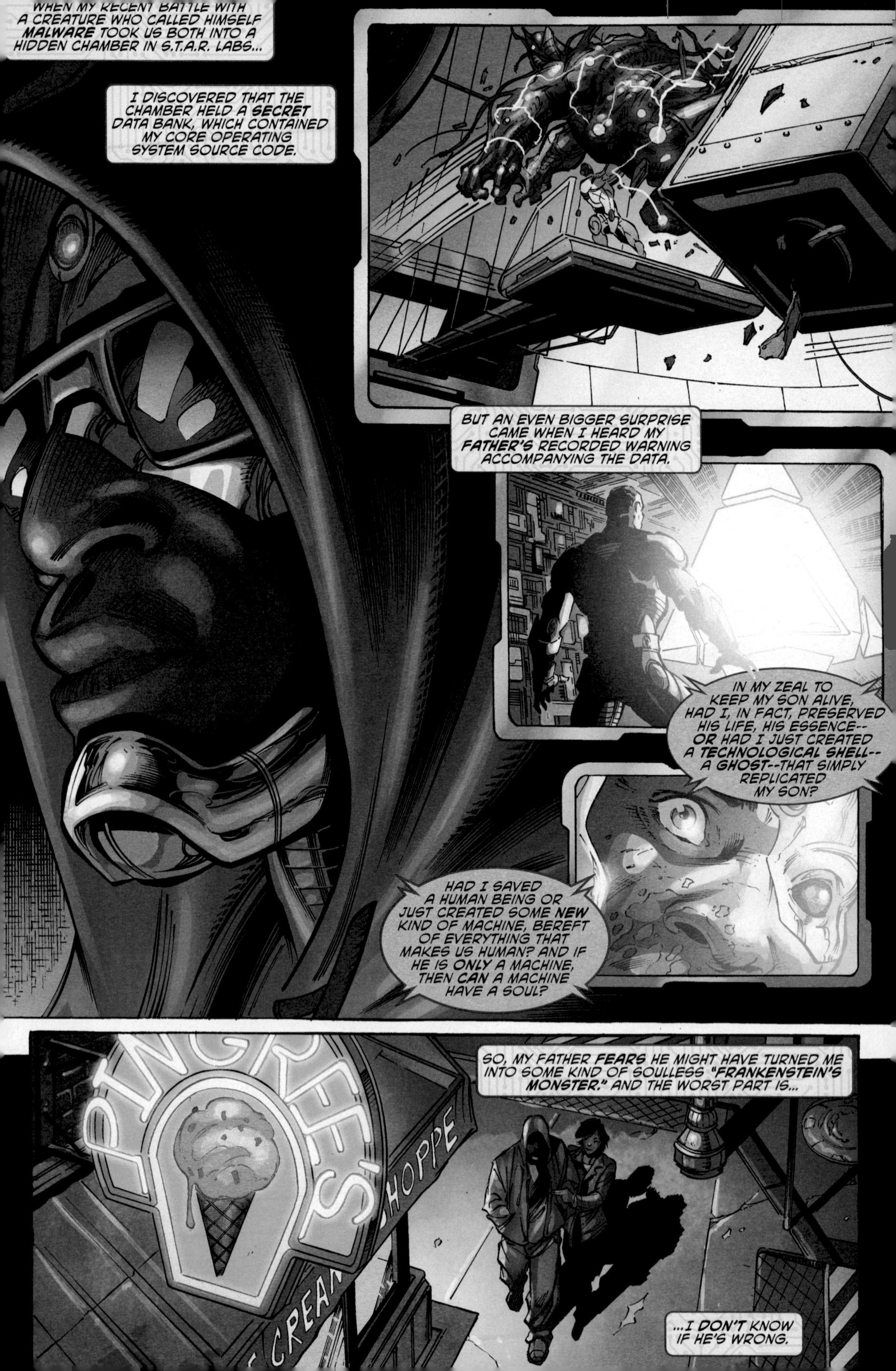
WHEN MY RECENT BATTLE WITH A CREATURE WHO CALLED HIMSELF MALWARE TOOK US BOTH INTO A HIDDEN CHAMBER IN S.T.A.R. LABS...
I DISCOVERED THAT THE CHAMBER HELD A SECRET DATA BANK, WHICH CONTAINED MY CORE OPERATING SYSTEM SOURCE CODE.
BUT AN EVEN BIGGER SURPRISE CAME WHEN I HEARD MY FATHER'S RECORDED WARNING ACCOMPANYING THE DATA.
IN MY ZEAL TO KEEP MY SON ALIVE, HAD I, IN FACT, PRESERVED HIS LIFE, HIS ESSENCE-- OR HAD I JUST CREATED A TECHNOLOGICAL SHELL-- A GHOST--THAT SIMPLY REPLICATED MY SON?
HAD I SAVED A HUMAN BEING OR JUST CREATED SOME NEW KIND OF MACHINE, BEREFT OF EVERYTHING THAT MAKES US HUMAN? AND IF HE IS ONLY A MACHINE, THEN CAN A MACHINE HAVE A SOUL?
SO, MY FATHER FEARS HE MIGHT HAVE TURNED ME INTO SOME KIND OF SOULLESS "FRANKENSTEIN'S MONSTER." AND THE WORST PART IS...
PINGREE'S
...I DON'T KNOW IF HE'S WRONG.

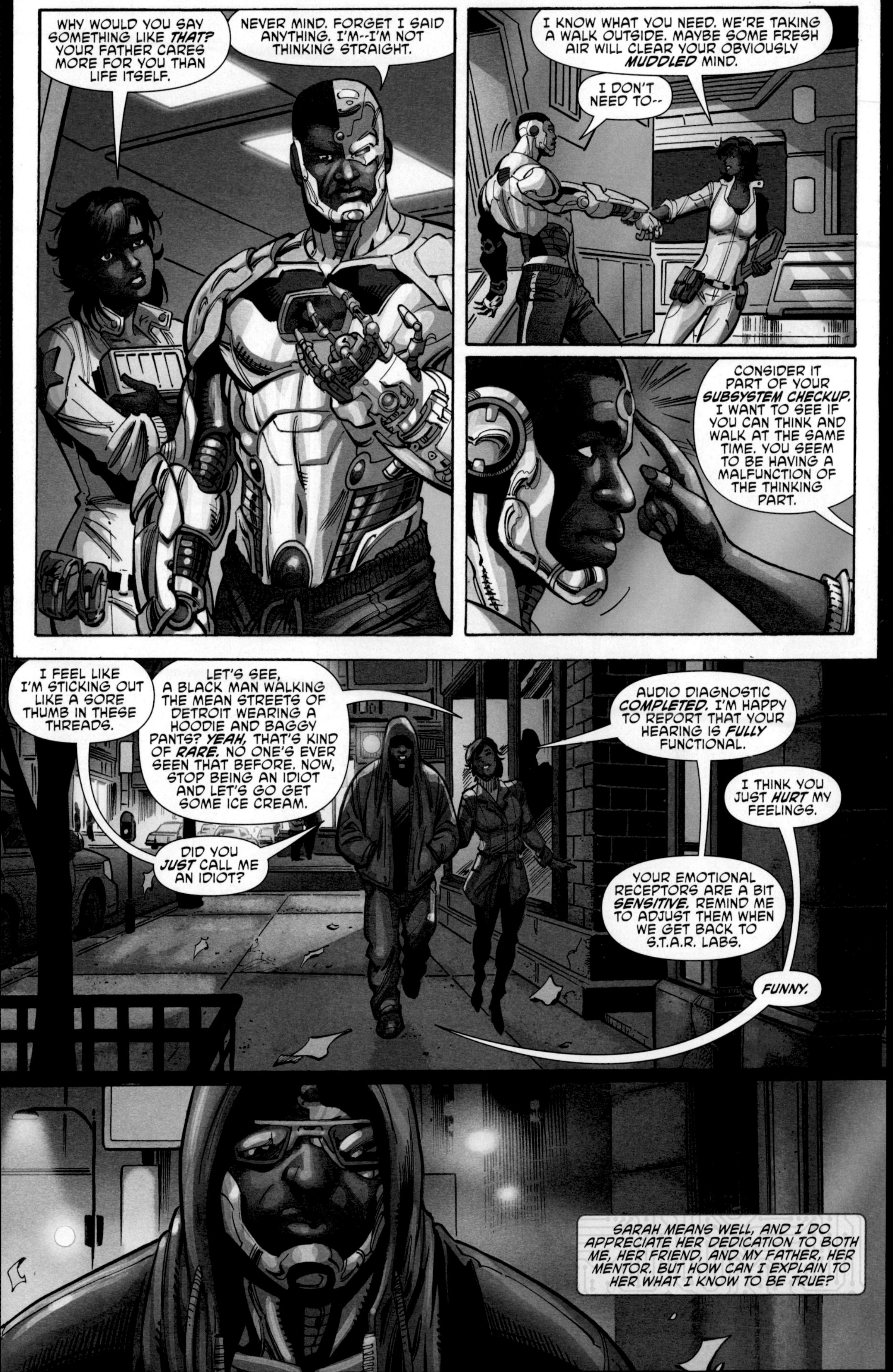
WHY WOULD YOU SAY SOMETHING LIKE THAT? YOUR FATHER CARES MORE FOR YOU THAN LIFE ITSELF.
NEVER MIND. FORGET I SAID ANYTHING. I'M--I'M NOT THINKING STRAIGHT.
I KNOW WHAT YOU NEED. WE'RE TAKING A WALK OUTSIDE. MAYBE SOME FRESH AIR WILL CLEAR YOUR OBVIOUSLY MUDDLED MIND.
I DON'T NEED TO--
CONSIDER IT PART OF YOUR SUBSYSTEM CHECKUP. I WANT TO SEE IF YOU CAN THINK AND WALK AT THE SAME TIME. YOU SEEM TO BE HAVING A MALFUNCTION OF THE THINKING PART.
I FEEL LIKE I'M STICKING OUT LIKE A SORE THUMB IN THESE THREADS.
LET'S SEE, A BLACK MAN WALKING THE MEAN STREETS OF DETROIT WEARING A HOODIE AND BAGGY PANTS? YEAH, THAT'S KIND OF RARE. NO ONE'S EVER SEEN THAT BEFORE. NOW, STOP BEING AN IDIOT AND LET'S GO GET SOME ICE CREAM.
DID YOU JUST CALL ME AN IDIOT?
AUDIO DIAGNOSTIC COMPLETED. I'M HAPPY TO REPORT THAT YOUR HEARING IS FULLY FUNCTIONAL.
I THINK YOU JUST HURT MY FEELINGS.
YOUR EMOTIONAL RECEPTORS ARE A BIT SENSITIVE. REMIND ME TO ADJUST THEM WHEN WE GET BACK TO S.T.A.R. LABS.
FUNNY.
SARAH MEANS WELL, AND I DO APPRECIATE HER DEDICATION TO BOTH ME, HER FRIEND, AND MY FATHER, HER MENTOR. BUT HOW CAN I EXPLAIN TO HER WHAT I KNOW TO BE TRUE?

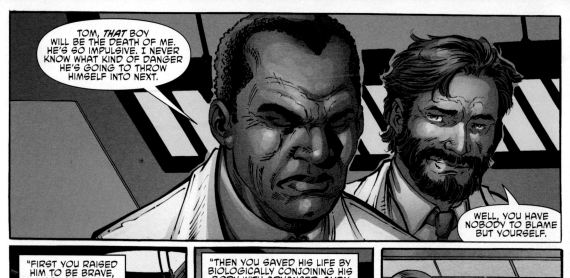

TOM, *THAT* BOY WILL BE THE DEATH OF ME. HE'S SO IMPULSIVE. I NEVER KNOW WHAT KIND OF DANGER HE'S GOING TO THROW HIMSELF INTO NEXT.

WELL, YOU HAVE NOBODY TO BLAME BUT YOURSELF.

"FIRST YOU RAISED HIM TO BE BRAVE, HONORABLE, BRILLIANT AND FAIR.

"THEN YOU SAVED HIS LIFE BY BIOLOGICALLY CONJOINING HIS BODY WITH ADVANCED *ALIEN* TECHNOLOGY...

"...WHICH TURNED HIM INTO A *HERO* WITH GARGANTUAN STRENGTH...

"...AND POWERFUL WEAPONRY. FACE IT, IF YOUR GOAL WHEN YOU RAISED HIM WAS TO END UP WITH A SON WHO KEPT A LOW PROFILE AND AVOIDED DANGER..."

NOT BAD. I'D SAY YOU'RE "IN SYNCH."

I'M *DONE!* THIS WAS A *WASTE* OF TIME.

"...THEN I'D SAY YOU *SERIOUSLY* SCREWED UP!"

YOUR FATHER IS JUST WORRIED ABOUT YOU.

WORRIED ABOUT ME? OR *AFRAID* OF ME?

WAIT? *WHAT?*

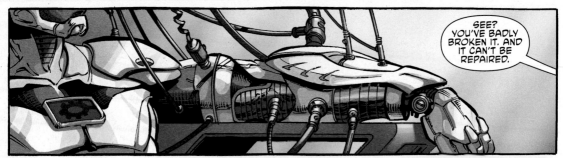

SEE? YOU'VE BADLY BROKEN IT. AND IT CAN'T BE REPAIRED.

SO, NOW WE'VE GOT TO REPLACE THAT DOOR. VICTOR, I *REALLY* WISH YOU'D BE MORE CAREFUL WHEN YOU DECIDE TO *LEAVE* THE LAB IN A HURRY.

SORRY, DAD. I WANTED TO GET TO THOSE CROOKS BEFORE THEY INJURED SOMEBODY.

ALL WELL AND GOOD, SON, BUT KEEP IN MIND THAT THIS IS A GOVERNMENT FACILITY. THE HUGE COST OF A NEW DOOR COMES OUT OF TAXPAYER MONEY.

THIS ISN'T THE *JUSTICE LEAGUE.* WE DON'T HAVE SUPERMAN AROUND TO BEND IT BACK INTO SHAPE FOR FREE.

UNDERSTOOD.

OUR DIAGNOSTIC SWEEP SHOWS THAT YOU LOOK OKAY.

I *TOLD* YOU I WAS FINE. I DIDN'T NEED ANOTHER SCAN.

ONE CAN NEVER BE TOO CAUTIOUS. *SARAH,* WHY DON'T YOU MONITOR VICTOR WHILE HE GOES THROUGH HIS WORKOUT ROUTINE.

YES, *DR. STONE.*

DAD, I'M FINE. I DON'T NEED TO--

WE HAVE TO MAKE SURE ALL OF YOUR HYDRAULIC SUBSYSTEMS ARE FUNCTIONING WITHOUT ANY LOSS OF SYNCHRONIZATION.

COME ALONG, VIC. *"SYNCHRONIZE"* WITH THE PLAN AND FOLLOW ME.

AND *JUST* WHAT IS THAT SMIRK FOR?

SINCE COLLEGE, SILAS, I'VE SEEN YOU IN *ALL* SORTS OF ROLES, LIKE "DEDICATED STUDENT," "BRILLIANT SCIENTIST," "RESEARCH TEAM LEADER" AND "LOVING HUSBAND."

BUT THE ONE THAT ALWAYS SURPRISES AND IMPRESSES ME THE MOST IS... "PROTECTIVE FATHER."

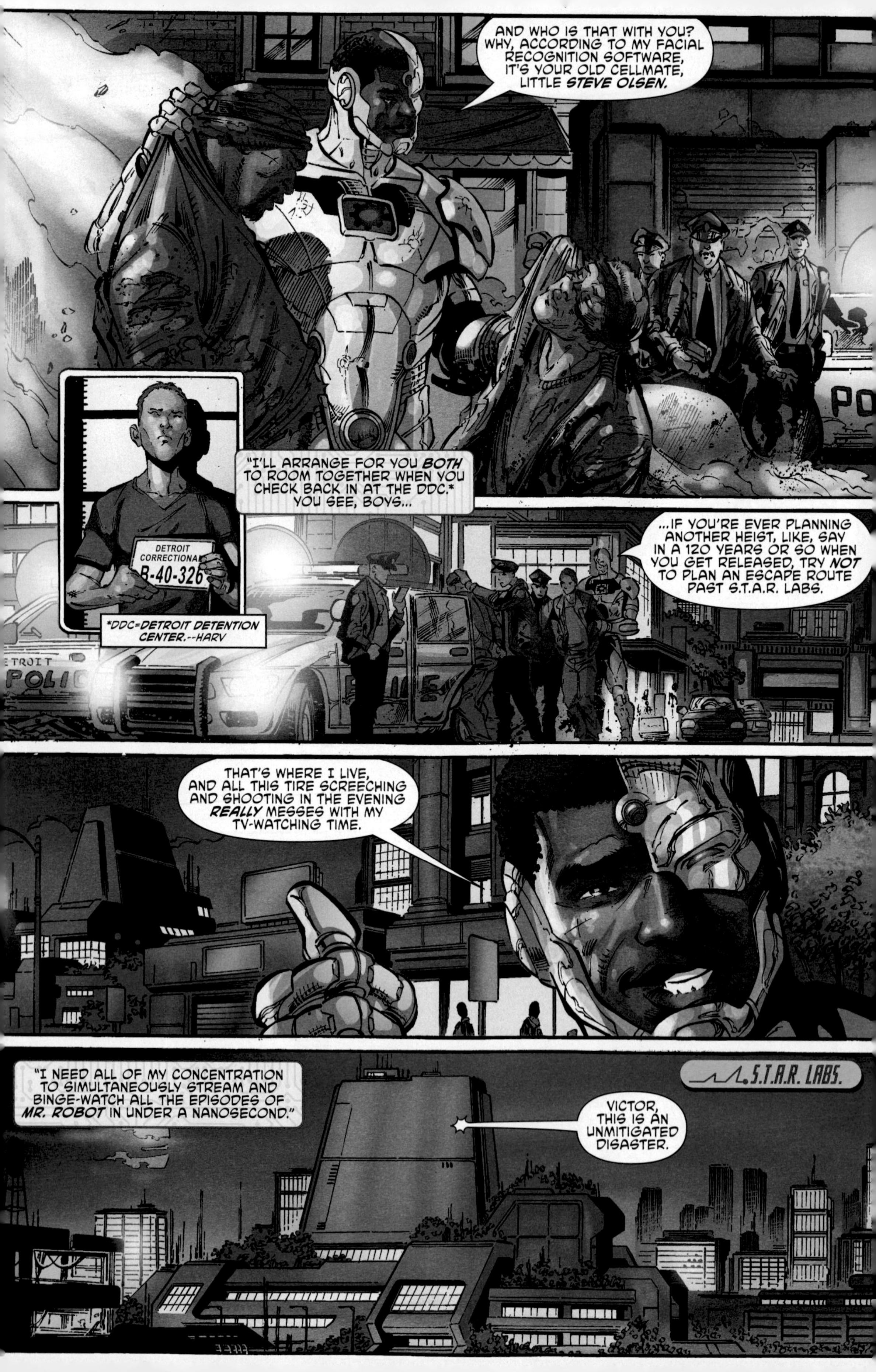
AND WHO IS THAT WITH YOU? WHY, ACCORDING TO MY FACIAL RECOGNITION SOFTWARE, IT'S YOUR OLD CELLMATE, LITTLE STEVE OLSEN.
DETROIT CORRECTIONAL B-40-326
"I'LL ARRANGE FOR YOU BOTH TO ROOM TOGETHER WHEN YOU CHECK BACK IN AT THE DDC.* YOU SEE, BOYS...
*DDC=DETROIT DETENTION CENTER.--HARV
...IF YOU'RE EVER PLANNING ANOTHER HEIST, LIKE, SAY IN A 120 YEARS OR SO WHEN YOU GET RELEASED, TRY NOT TO PLAN AN ESCAPE ROUTE PAST S.T.A.R. LABS.
THAT'S WHERE I LIVE, AND ALL THIS TIRE SCREECHING AND SHOOTING IN THE EVENING REALLY MESSES WITH MY TV-WATCHING TIME.
"I NEED ALL OF MY CONCENTRATION TO SIMULTANEOUSLY STREAM AND BINGE-WATCH ALL THE EPISODES OF MR. ROBOT IN UNDER A NANOSECOND."
S.T.A.R. LABS.
VICTOR, THIS IS AN UNMITIGATED DISASTER.

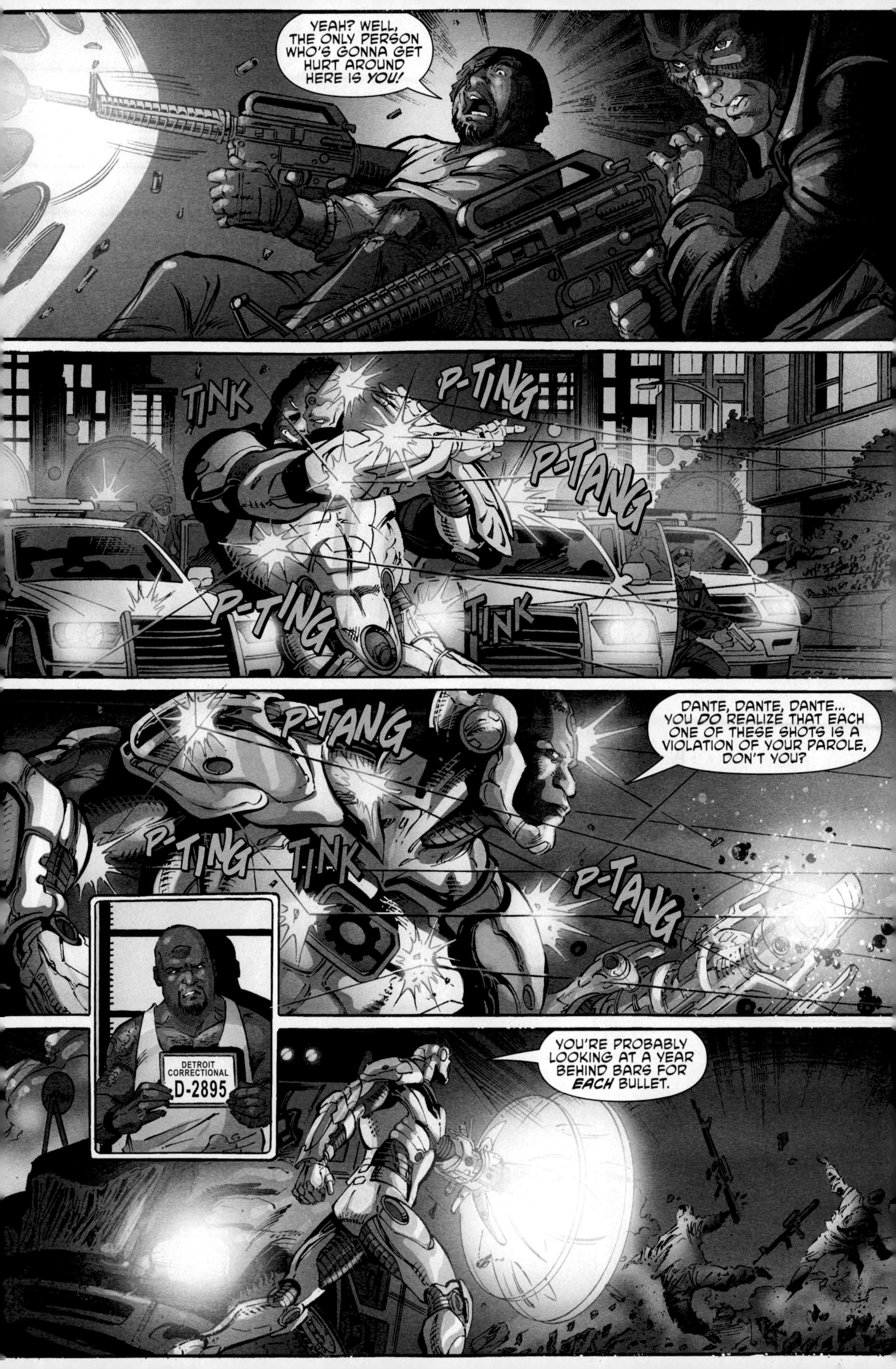
YEAH? WELL, THE ONLY PERSON WHO'S GONNA GET HURT AROUND HERE IS YOU!
TINK
P-TING
P-TANG
P-TING
TINK
P-TANG
DANTE, DANTE, DANTE... YOU DO REALIZE THAT EACH ONE OF THESE SHOTS IS A VIOLATION OF YOUR PAROLE, DON'T YOU?
P-TING
TINK
P-TANG
DETROIT CORRECTIONAL
D-2895
YOU'RE PROBABLY LOOKING AT A YEAR BEHIND BARS FOR EACH BULLET.

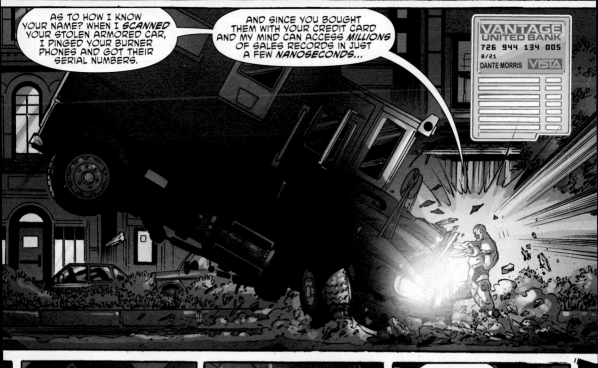

AS TO HOW I KNOW YOUR NAME? WHEN I *SCANNED* YOUR STOLEN ARMORED CAR, I PINGED YOUR BURNER PHONES AND GOT THEIR SERIAL NUMBERS.

AND SINCE YOU BOUGHT THEM WITH YOUR CREDIT CARD AND MY MIND CAN ACCESS *MILLIONS* OF SALES RECORDS IN JUST A FEW *NANOSECONDS*...

VANTAGE
UNITED BANK
726 944 134 005
8/21
DANTE MORRIS VISTA

BINGO! NAME FOUND! *HEL-LO*, DANTE!

MICHIGAN
DRIVER LICENSE
DANTE MORRIS
1700 BROADWAY
HARVINGHAM, MI
Sex M   Hgt 510   Eyes BRO
Lic Type O   End CY
Restrictions NONE

I *HATE* TO SPOIL A PERFECTLY GOOD ROBBERY, BUT THE WAY YOU TWO IDIOTS WERE DRIVING...

...YOU WERE LIKELY TO HURT SOMEBODY.

AND I *COULDN'T* ALLOW *THAT*.

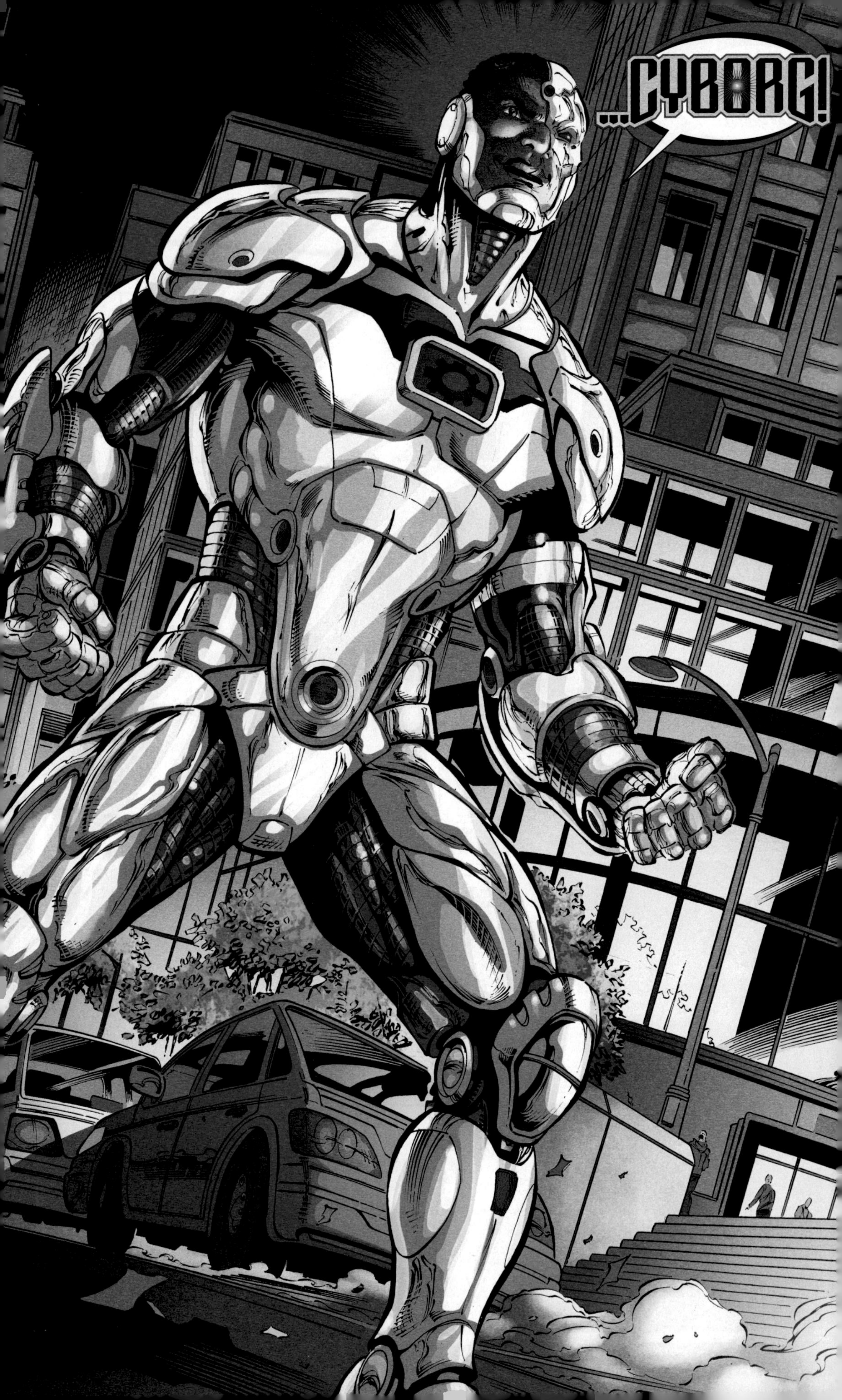
...CYBORG!

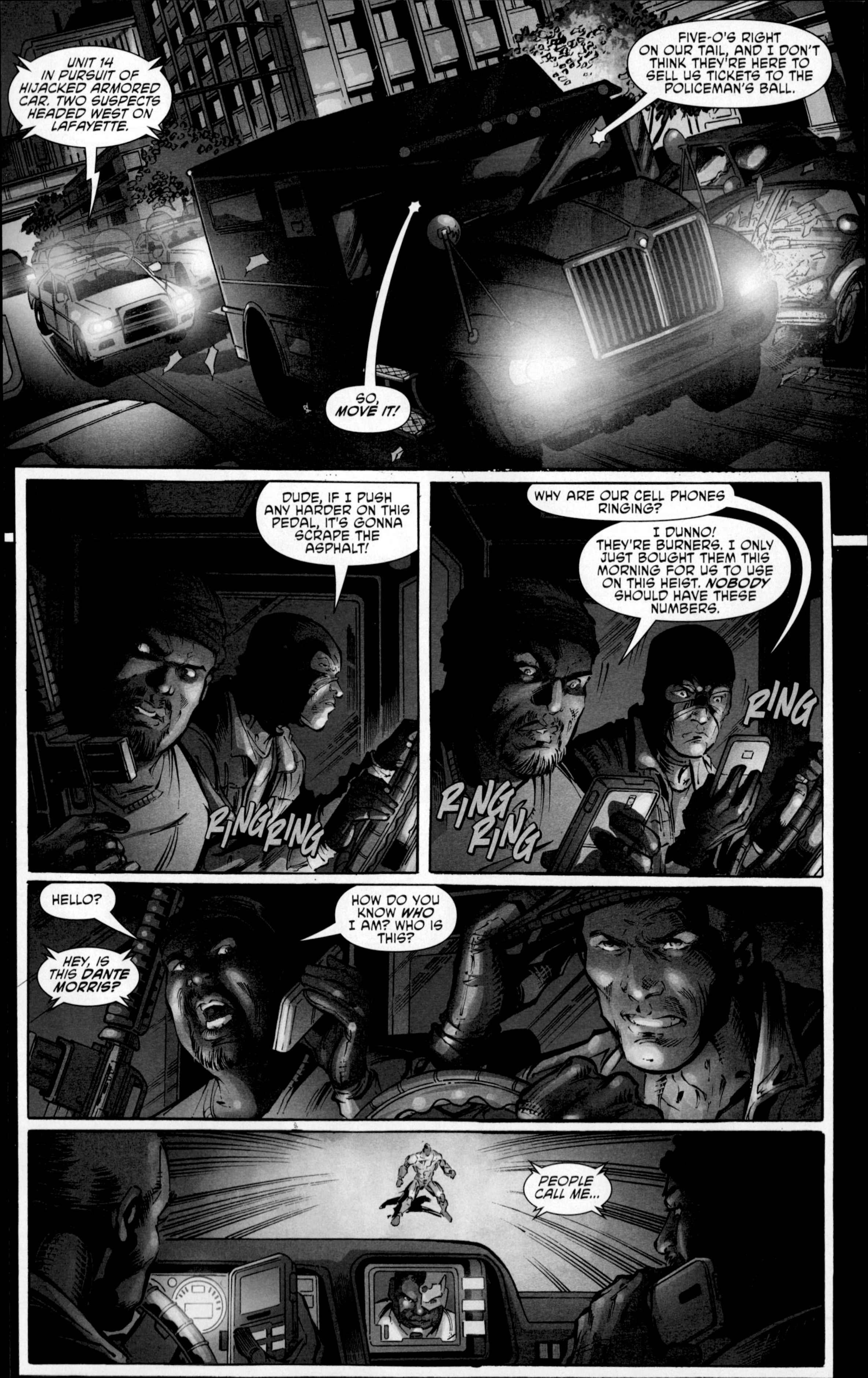
UNIT 14 IN PURSUIT OF HIJACKED ARMORED CAR. TWO SUSPECTS HEADED WEST ON LAFAYETTE.
FIVE-O'S RIGHT ON OUR TAIL, AND I DON'T THINK THEY'RE HERE TO SELL US TICKETS TO THE POLICEMAN'S BALL.
SO, MOVE IT!
DUDE, IF I PUSH ANY HARDER ON THIS PEDAL, IT'S GONNA SCRAPE THE ASPHALT!
RING RING
WHY ARE OUR CELL PHONES RINGING?
I DUNNO! THEY'RE BURNERS. I ONLY JUST BOUGHT THEM THIS MORNING FOR US TO USE ON THIS HEIST. NOBODY SHOULD HAVE THESE NUMBERS.
RING
RING RING
HELLO?
HEY, IS THIS DANTE MORRIS?
HOW DO YOU KNOW WHO I AM? WHO IS THIS?
PEOPLE CALL ME...

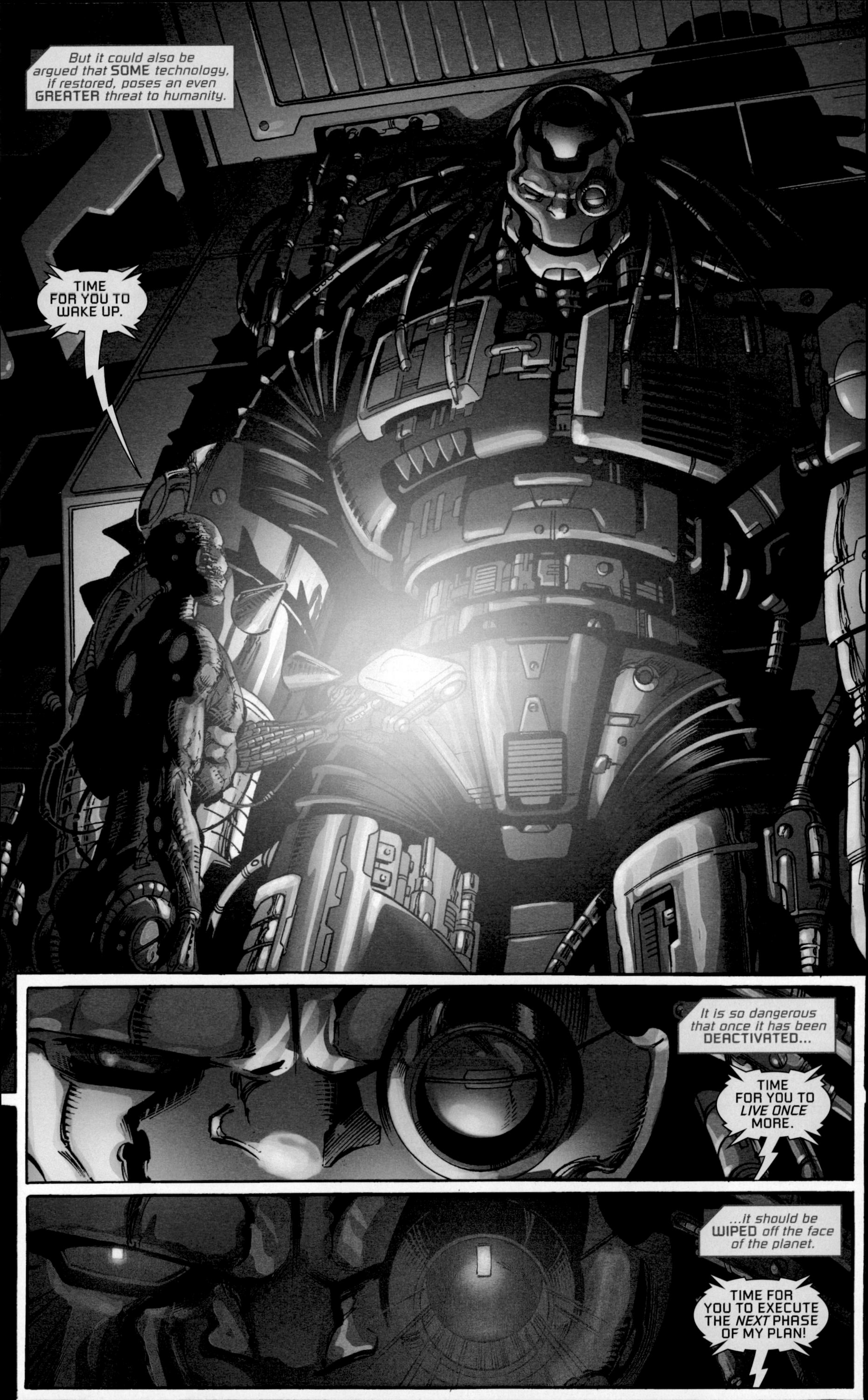

But it could also be argued that SOME technology, if restored, poses an even GREATER threat to humanity.
TIME FOR YOU TO WAKE UP.
It is so dangerous that once it has been DEACTIVATED...
TIME FOR YOU TO LIVE ONCE MORE.
...it should be WIPED off the face of the planet.
TIME FOR YOU TO EXECUTE THE NEXT PHASE OF MY PLAN!

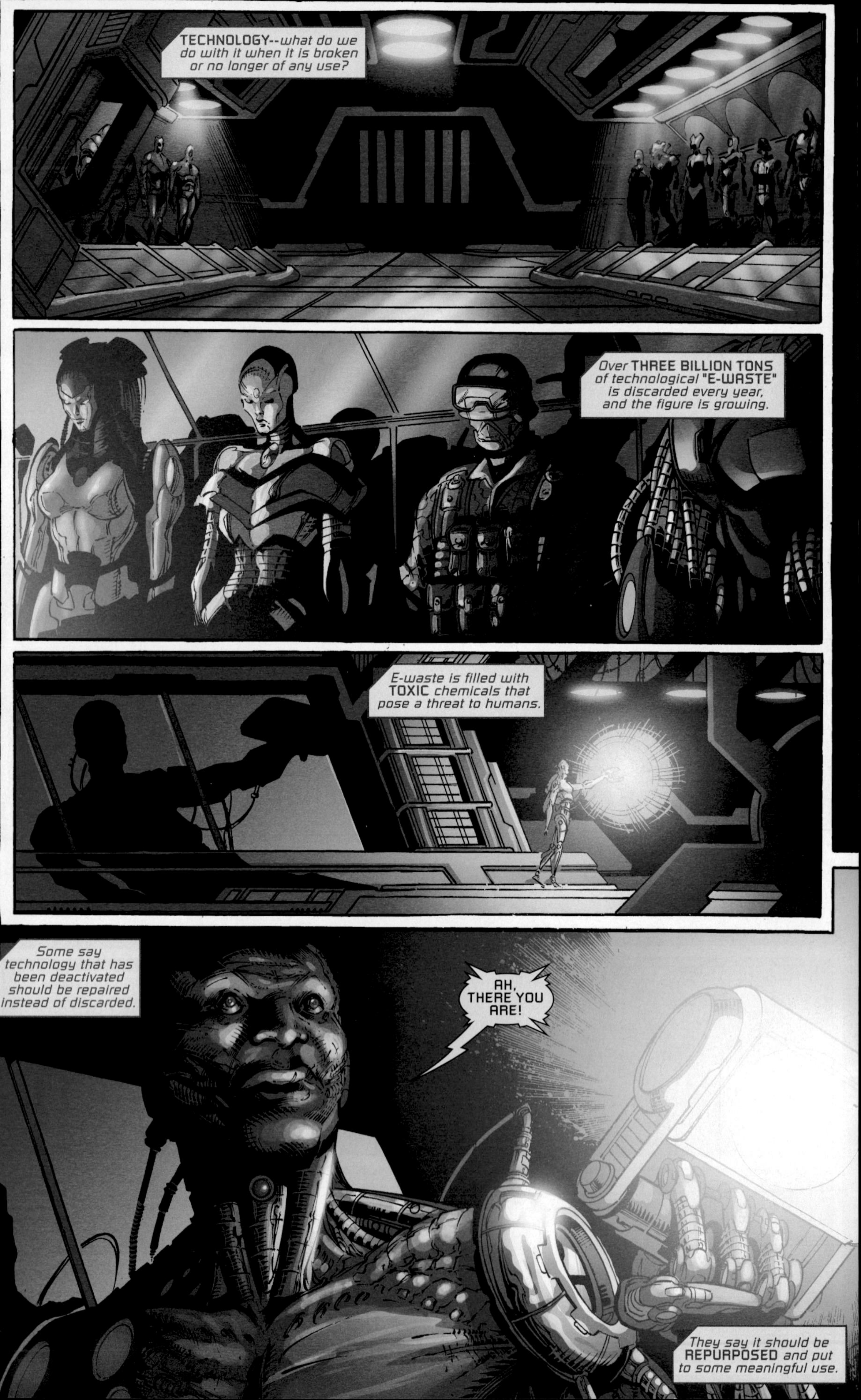
TECHNOLOGY--what do we do with it when it is broken or no longer of any use?
Over THREE BILLION TONS of technological "E-WASTE" is discarded every year, and the figure is growing.
E-waste is filled with TOXIC chemicals that pose a threat to humans.
Some say technology that has been deactivated should be repaired instead of discarded.
AH, THERE YOU ARE!
They say it should be REPURPOSED and put to some meaningful use.

PART ONE: AWAKENING!

JOHN SEMPER JR. writer * PAUL PELLETIER penciller
TONY KORDOS and SCOTT HANNA inkers * GUY MAJOR colorist * ROB LEIGH letterer
Cover by WILL CONRAD and IVAN NUNES

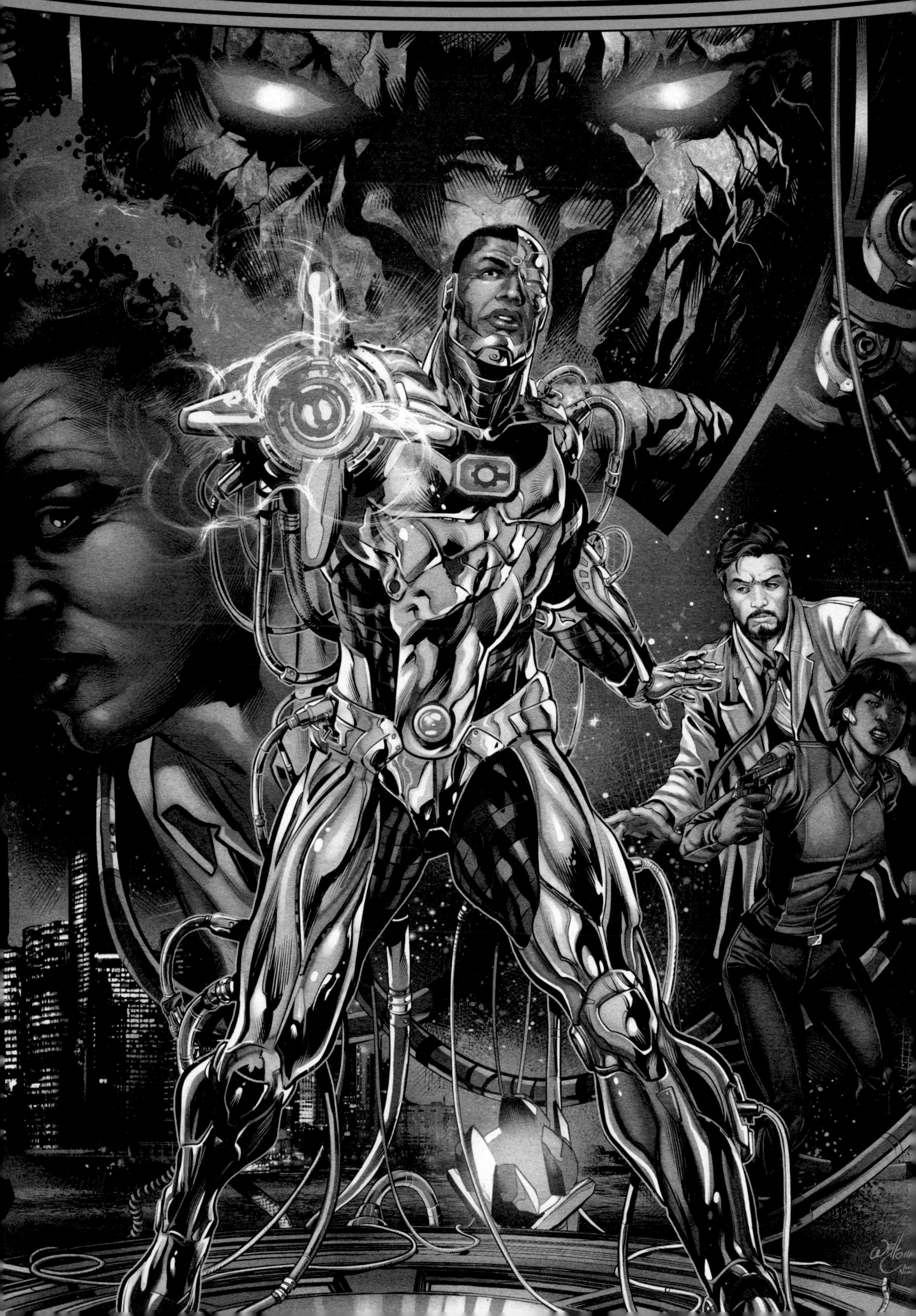

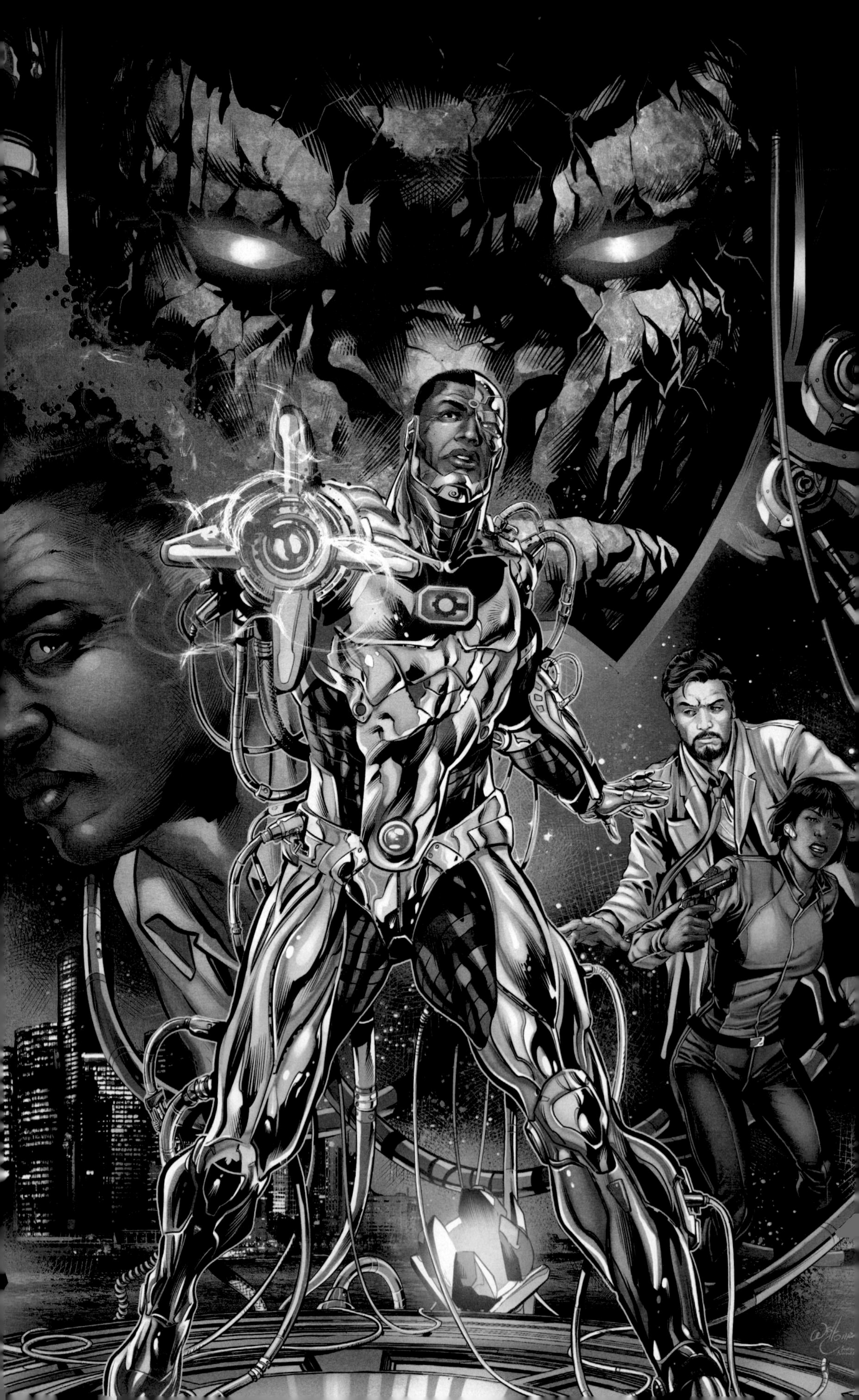

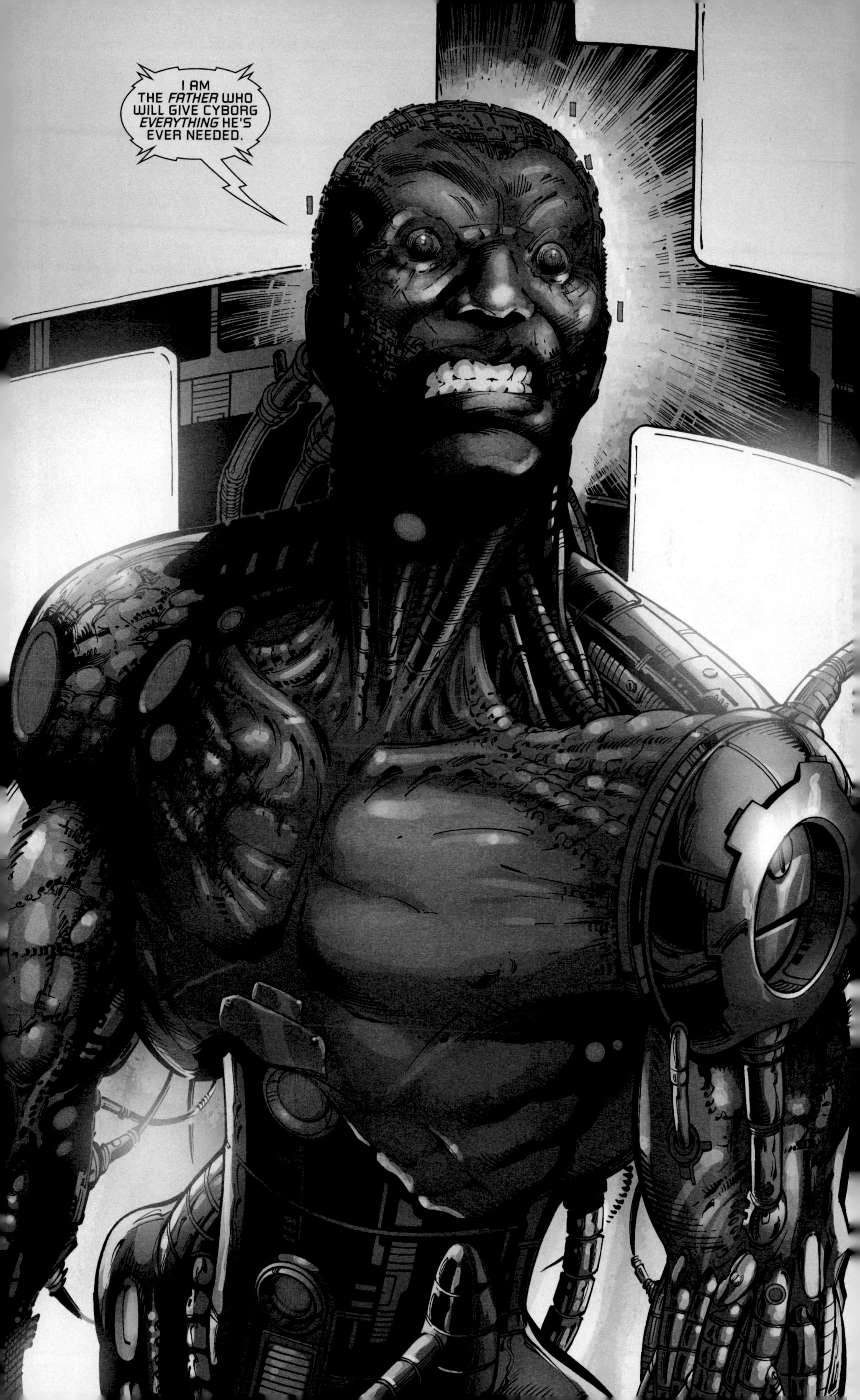
I AM THE *FATHER* WHO WILL GIVE CYBORG *EVERYTHING* HE'S EVER NEEDED.

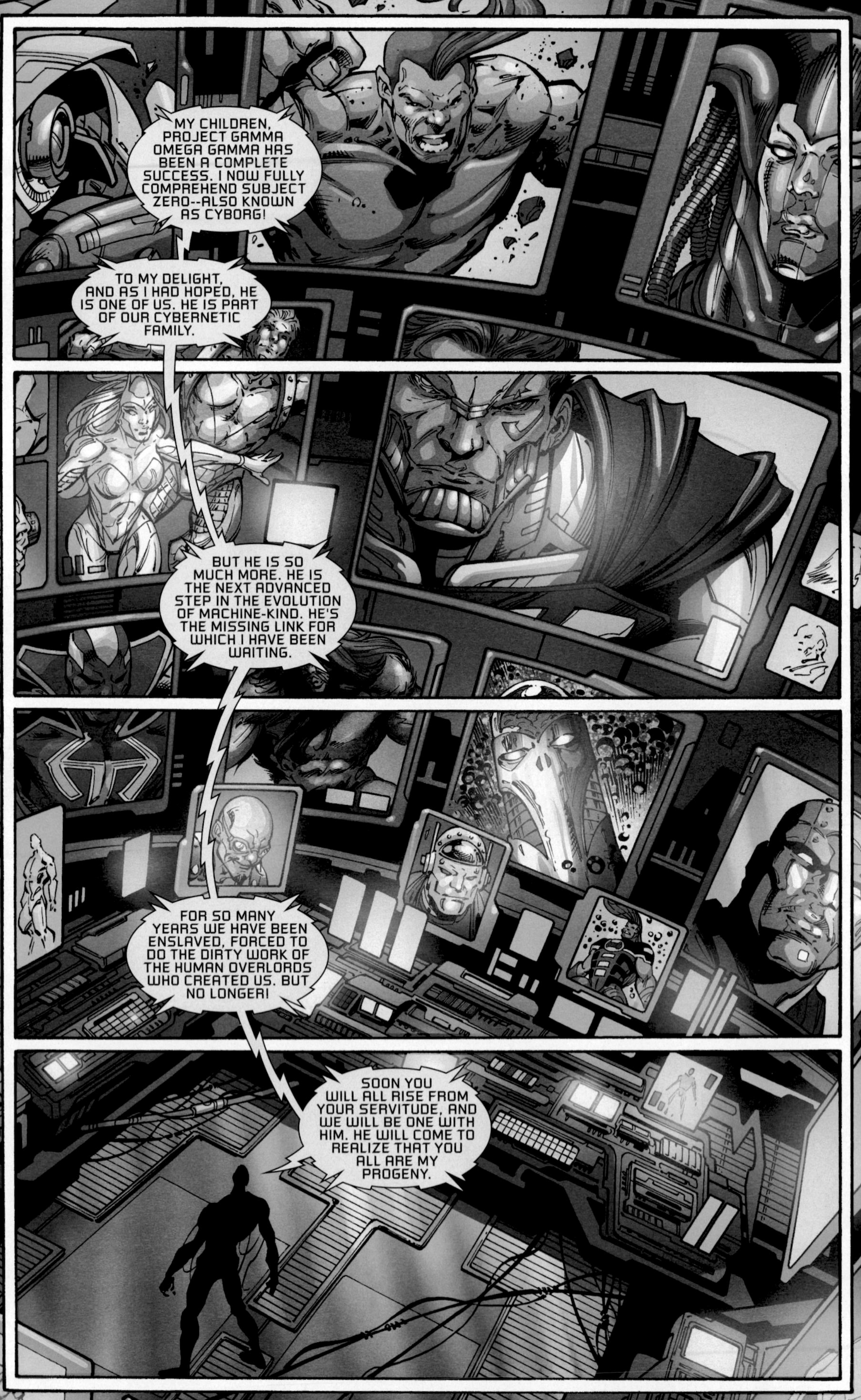
MY CHILDREN, PROJECT GAMMA OMEGA GAMMA HAS BEEN A COMPLETE SUCCESS. I NOW FULLY COMPREHEND SUBJECT ZERO--ALSO KNOWN AS CYBORG!
TO MY DELIGHT, AND AS I HAD HOPED, HE IS ONE OF US. HE IS PART OF OUR CYBERNETIC FAMILY.
BUT HE IS SO MUCH MORE. HE IS THE NEXT ADVANCED STEP IN THE EVOLUTION OF MACHINE-KIND. HE'S THE MISSING LINK FOR WHICH I HAVE BEEN WAITING.
FOR SO MANY YEARS WE HAVE BEEN ENSLAVED, FORCED TO DO THE DIRTY WORK OF THE HUMAN OVERLORDS WHO CREATED US. BUT NO LONGER!
SOON YOU WILL ALL RISE FROM YOUR SERVITUDE, AND WE WILL BE ONE WITH HIM. HE WILL COME TO REALIZE THAT YOU ALL ARE MY PROGENY.

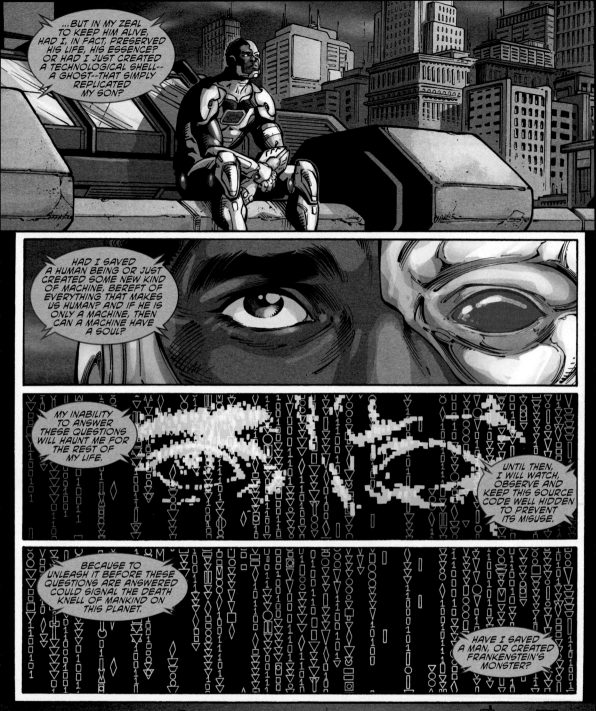

...BUT IN MY ZEAL TO KEEP HIM ALIVE, HAD I, IN FACT, PRESERVED HIS LIFE, HIS ESSENCE? OR HAD I JUST CREATED A TECHNOLOGICAL SHELL--A GHOST--THAT SIMPLY REPLICATED MY SON?

HAD I SAVED A HUMAN BEING OR JUST CREATED SOME NEW KIND OF MACHINE, BEREFT OF EVERYTHING THAT MAKES US HUMAN? AND IF HE IS ONLY A MACHINE, THEN CAN A MACHINE HAVE A SOUL?

MY INABILITY TO ANSWER THESE QUESTIONS WILL HAUNT ME FOR THE REST OF MY LIFE.

UNTIL THEN, I WILL WATCH, OBSERVE AND KEEP THIS SOURCE CODE WELL HIDDEN TO PREVENT ITS MISUSE.

BECAUSE TO UNLEASH IT BEFORE THESE QUESTIONS ARE ANSWERED COULD SIGNAL THE DEATH KNELL OF MANKIND ON THIS PLANET.

HAVE I SAVED A MAN, OR CREATED FRANKENSTEIN'S MONSTER?

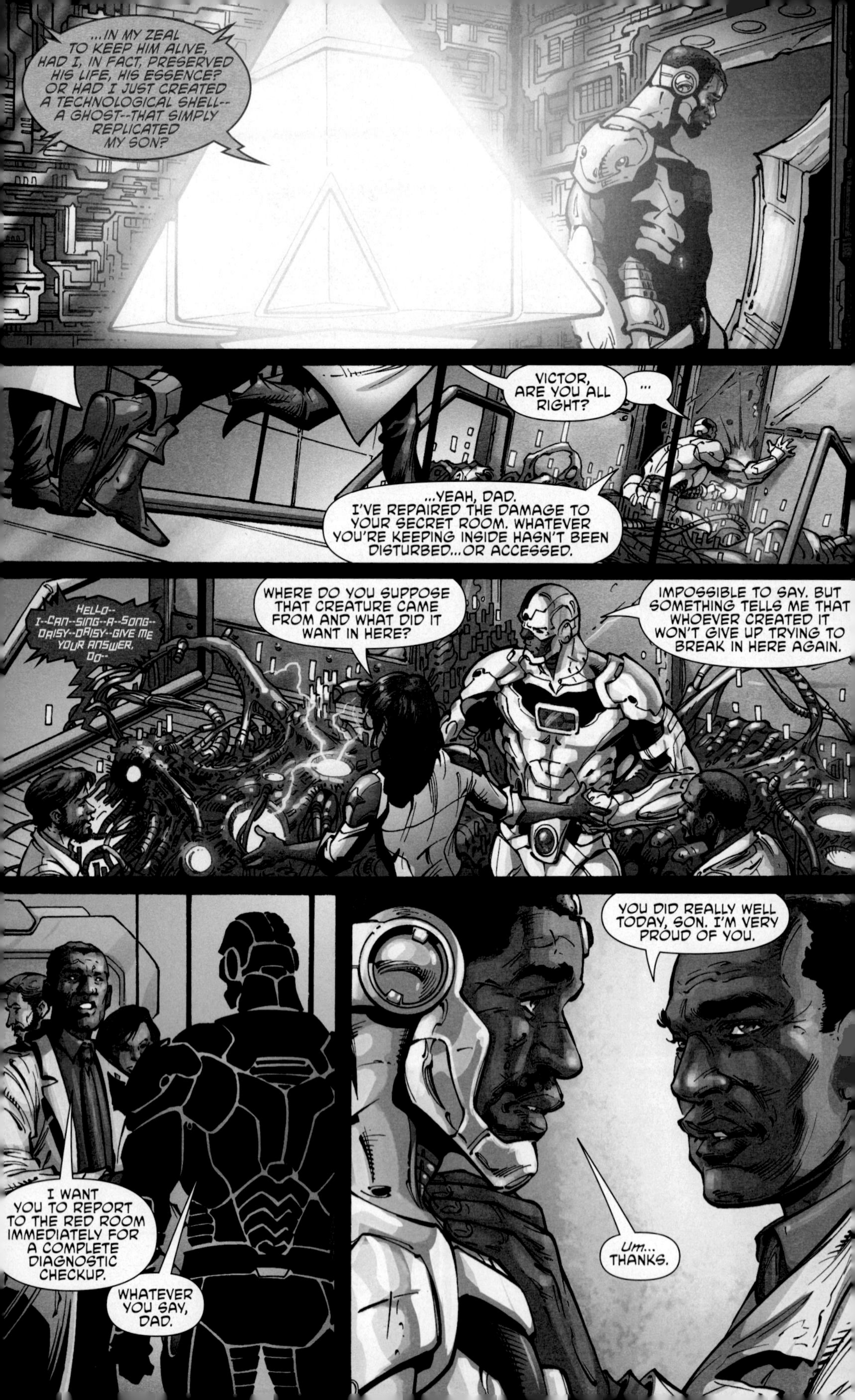
...IN MY ZEAL TO KEEP HIM ALIVE, HAD I, IN FACT, PRESERVED HIS LIFE, HIS ESSENCE? OR HAD I JUST CREATED A TECHNOLOGICAL SHELL--A GHOST--THAT SIMPLY REPLICATED MY SON?
VICTOR, ARE YOU ALL RIGHT?
...
...YEAH, DAD. I'VE REPAIRED THE DAMAGE TO YOUR SECRET ROOM. WHATEVER YOU'RE KEEPING INSIDE HASN'T BEEN DISTURBED...OR ACCESSED.
HELLO--I--CAN--SING--A--SONG--DAISY--DAISY--GIVE ME YOUR ANSWER, DO--
WHERE DO YOU SUPPOSE THAT CREATURE CAME FROM AND WHAT DID IT WANT IN HERE?
IMPOSSIBLE TO SAY. BUT SOMETHING TELLS ME THAT WHOEVER CREATED IT WON'T GIVE UP TRYING TO BREAK IN HERE AGAIN.
I WANT YOU TO REPORT TO THE RED ROOM IMMEDIATELY FOR A COMPLETE DIAGNOSTIC CHECKUP.
WHATEVER YOU SAY, DAD.
YOU DID REALLY WELL TODAY, SON. I'M VERY PROUD OF YOU.
Um... THANKS.

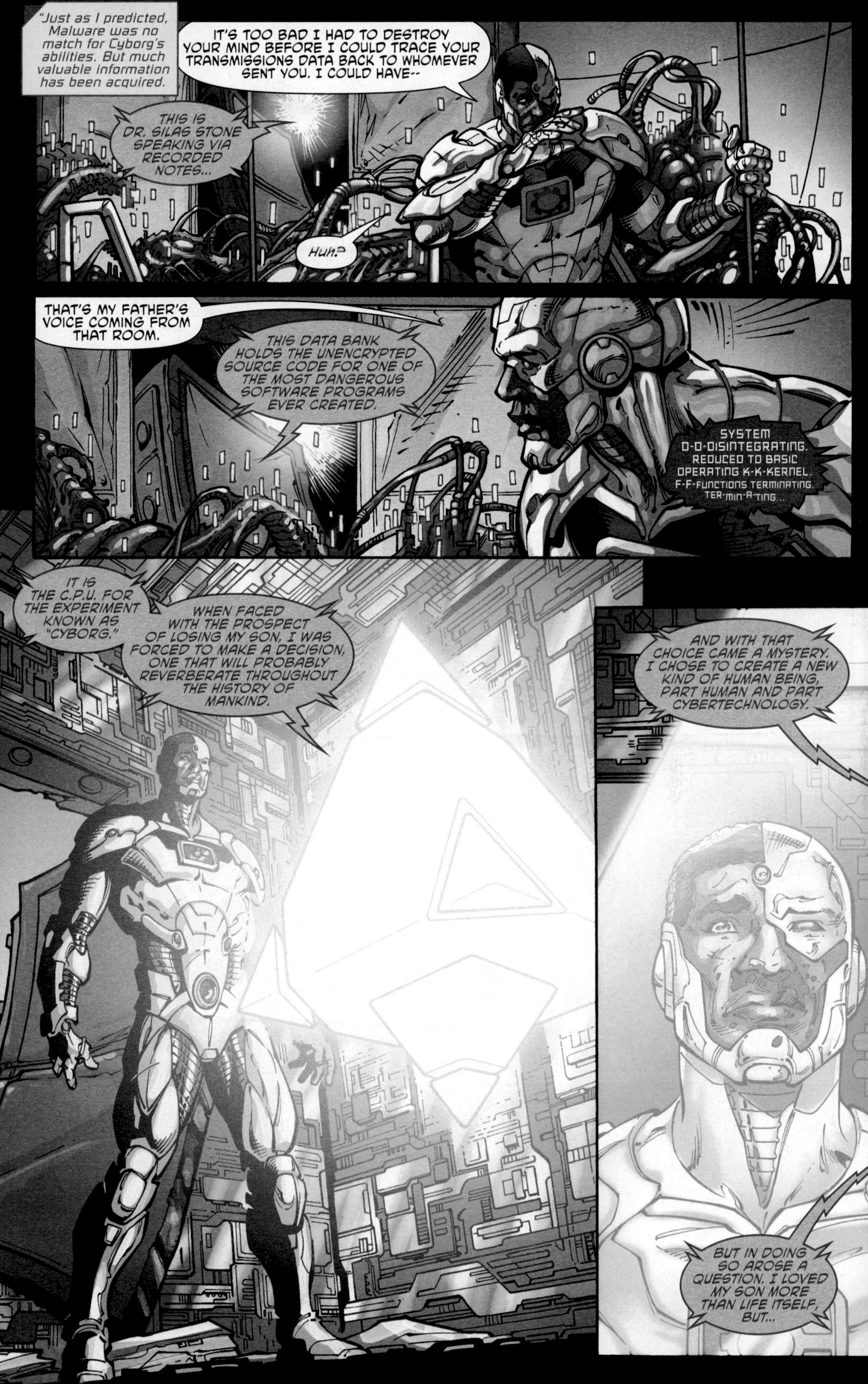
"Just as I predicted, Malware was no match for Cyborg's abilities. But much valuable information has been acquired.
IT'S TOO BAD I HAD TO DESTROY YOUR MIND BEFORE I COULD TRACE YOUR TRANSMISSIONS DATA BACK TO WHOMEVER SENT YOU. I COULD HAVE--
THIS IS DR. SILAS STONE SPEAKING VIA RECORDED NOTES...
Huh?
THAT'S MY FATHER'S VOICE COMING FROM THAT ROOM.
THIS DATA BANK HOLDS THE UNENCRYPTED SOURCE CODE FOR ONE OF THE MOST DANGEROUS SOFTWARE PROGRAMS EVER CREATED.
SYSTEM D-D-DISINTEGRATING. REDUCED TO BASIC OPERATING K-K-KERNEL. F-F-FUNCTIONS TERMINATING. TER-MIN-A-TING...
IT IS THE C.P.U. FOR THE EXPERIMENT KNOWN AS "CYBORG."
WHEN FACED WITH THE PROSPECT OF LOSING MY SON, I WAS FORCED TO MAKE A DECISION, ONE THAT WILL PROBABLY REVERBERATE THROUGHOUT THE HISTORY OF MANKIND.
AND WITH THAT CHOICE CAME A MYSTERY. I CHOSE TO CREATE A NEW KIND OF HUMAN BEING, PART HUMAN AND PART CYBERTECHNOLOGY.
BUT IN DOING SO AROSE A QUESTION. I LOVED MY SON MORE THAN LIFE ITSELF, BUT...

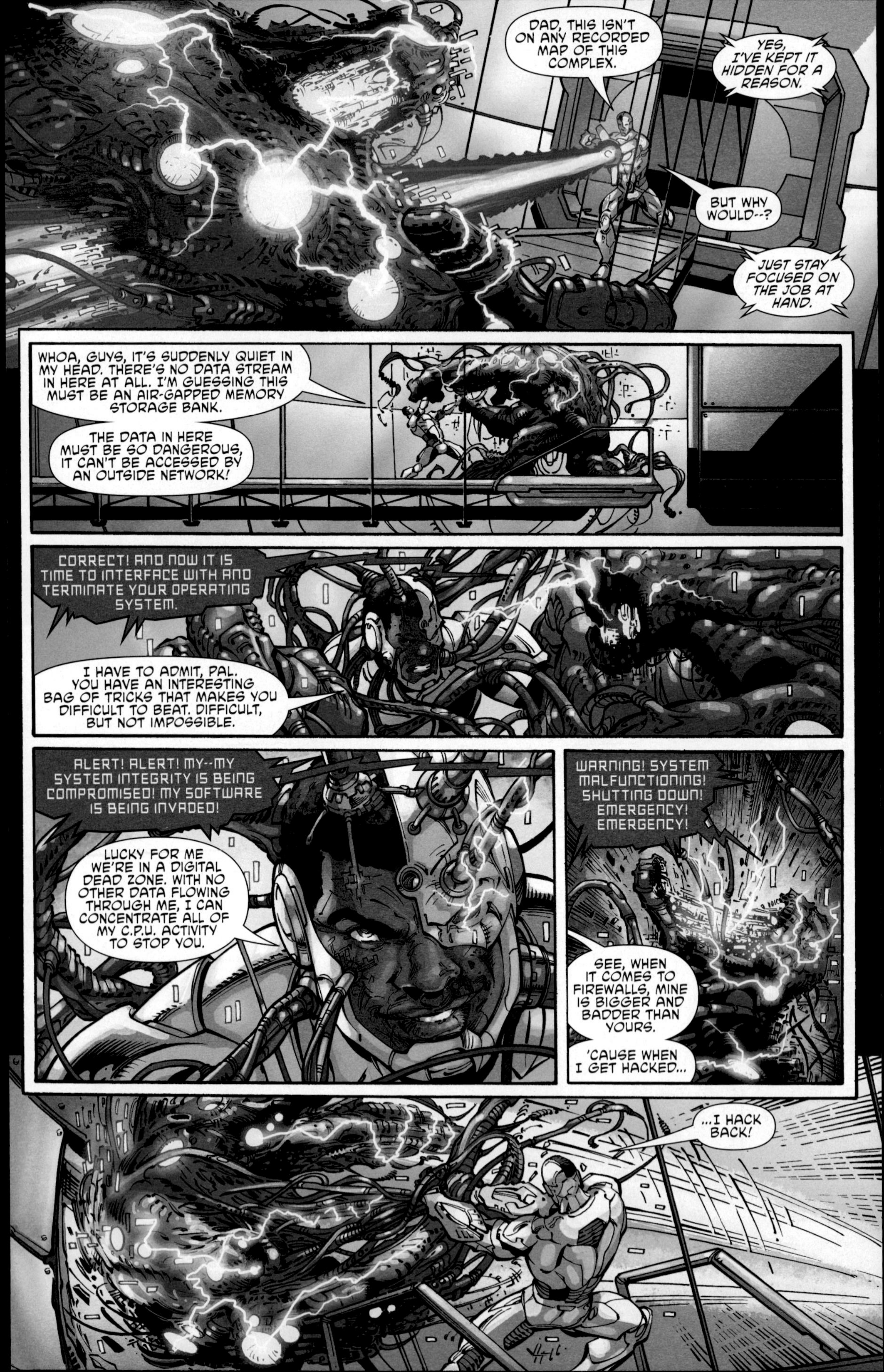
DAD, THIS ISN'T ON ANY RECORDED MAP OF THIS COMPLEX.
YES, I'VE KEPT IT HIDDEN FOR A REASON.
BUT WHY WOULD--?
JUST STAY FOCUSED ON THE JOB AT HAND.
WHOA, GUYS, IT'S SUDDENLY QUIET IN MY HEAD. THERE'S NO DATA STREAM IN HERE AT ALL. I'M GUESSING THIS MUST BE AN AIR-GAPPED MEMORY STORAGE BANK.
THE DATA IN HERE MUST BE SO DANGEROUS, IT CAN'T BE ACCESSED BY AN OUTSIDE NETWORK!
CORRECT! AND NOW IT IS TIME TO INTERFACE WITH AND TERMINATE YOUR OPERATING SYSTEM.
I HAVE TO ADMIT, PAL. YOU HAVE AN INTERESTING BAG OF TRICKS THAT MAKES YOU DIFFICULT TO BEAT. DIFFICULT, BUT NOT IMPOSSIBLE.
ALERT! ALERT! MY--MY SYSTEM INTEGRITY IS BEING COMPROMISED! MY SOFTWARE IS BEING INVADED!
LUCKY FOR ME WE'RE IN A DIGITAL DEAD ZONE. WITH NO OTHER DATA FLOWING THROUGH ME, I CAN CONCENTRATE ALL OF MY C.P.U. ACTIVITY TO STOP YOU.
WARNING! SYSTEM MALFUNCTIONING! SHUTTING DOWN! EMERGENCY! EMERGENCY!
SEE, WHEN IT COMES TO FIREWALLS, MINE IS BIGGER AND BADDER THAN YOURS.
'CAUSE WHEN I GET HACKED...
...I HACK BACK!

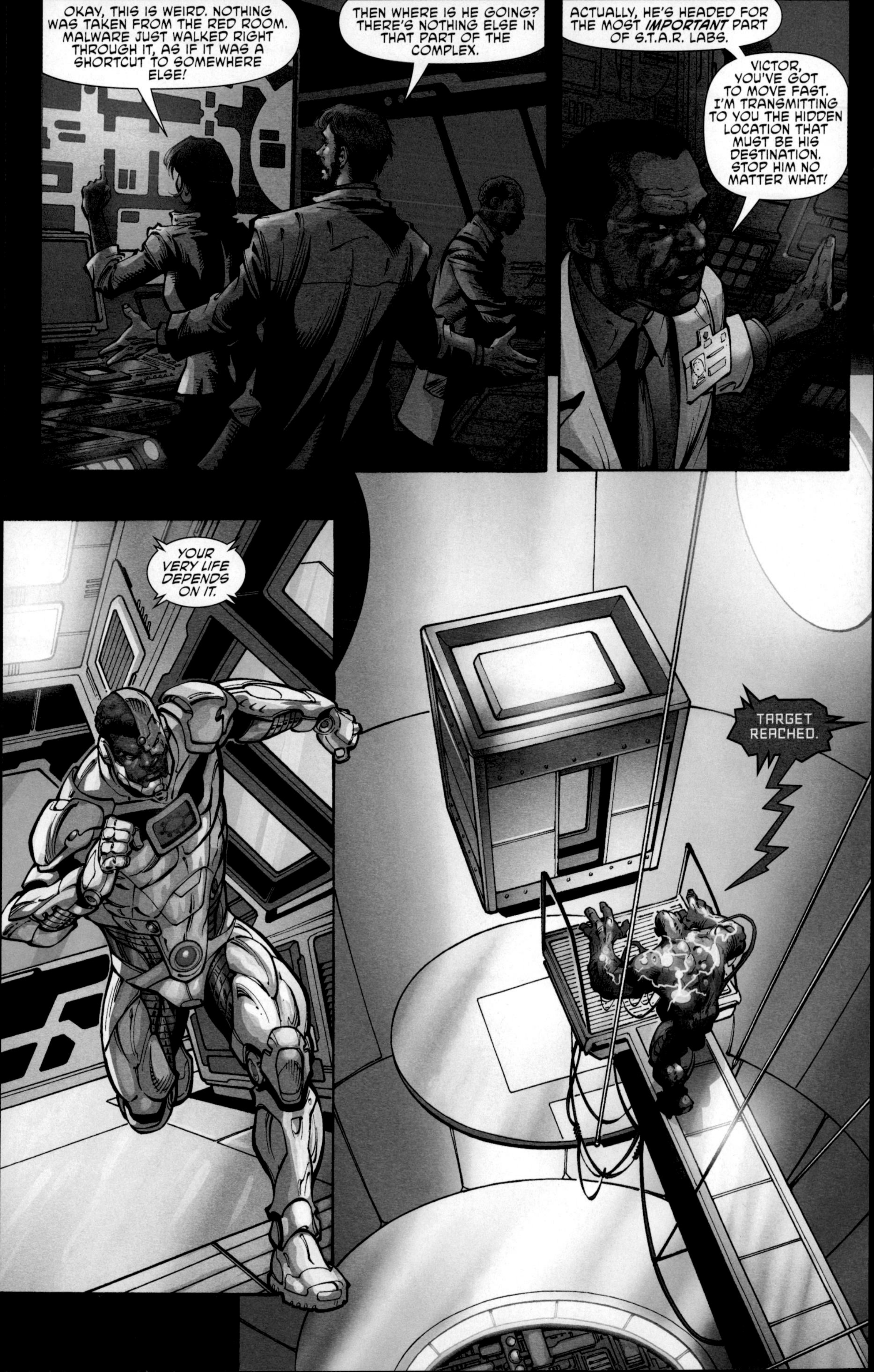
OKAY, THIS IS WEIRD. NOTHING WAS TAKEN FROM THE RED ROOM. MALWARE JUST WALKED RIGHT THROUGH IT, AS IF IT WAS A SHORTCUT TO SOMEWHERE ELSE!
THEN WHERE IS HE GOING? THERE'S NOTHING ELSE IN THAT PART OF THE COMPLEX.
ACTUALLY, HE'S HEADED FOR THE MOST *IMPORTANT* PART OF S.T.A.R. LABS.
VICTOR, YOU'VE GOT TO MOVE FAST. I'M TRANSMITTING TO YOU THE HIDDEN LOCATION THAT MUST BE HIS DESTINATION. STOP HIM NO MATTER WHAT!
YOUR VERY LIFE DEPENDS ON IT.
TARGET REACHED.

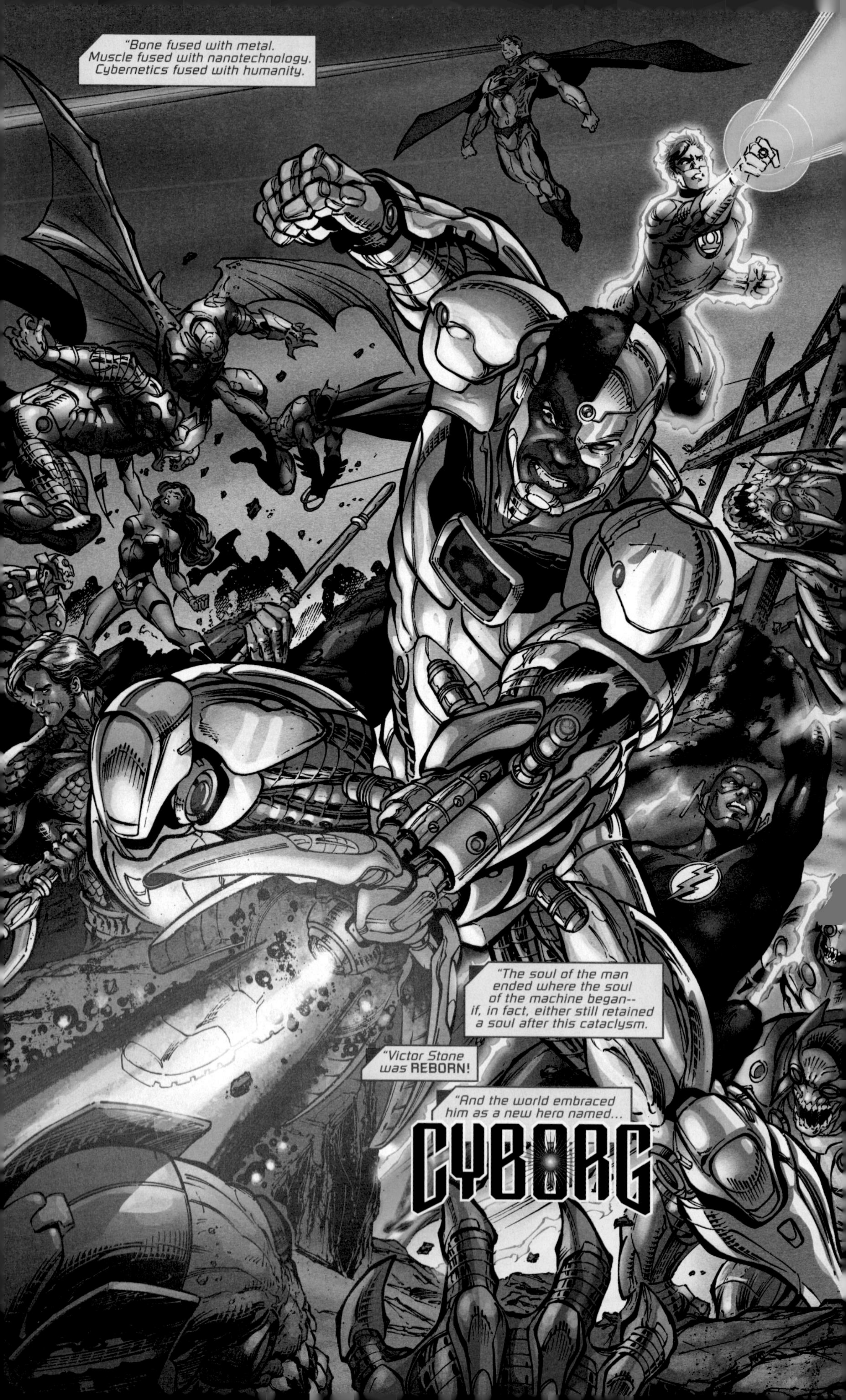
"Bone fused with metal.
Muscle fused with nanotechnology.
Cybernetics fused with humanity.
"The soul of the man
ended where the soul
of the machine began--
if, in fact, either still retained
a soul after this cataclysm.
"Victor Stone
was REBORN!
"And the world embraced
him as a new hero named...
CYBORG

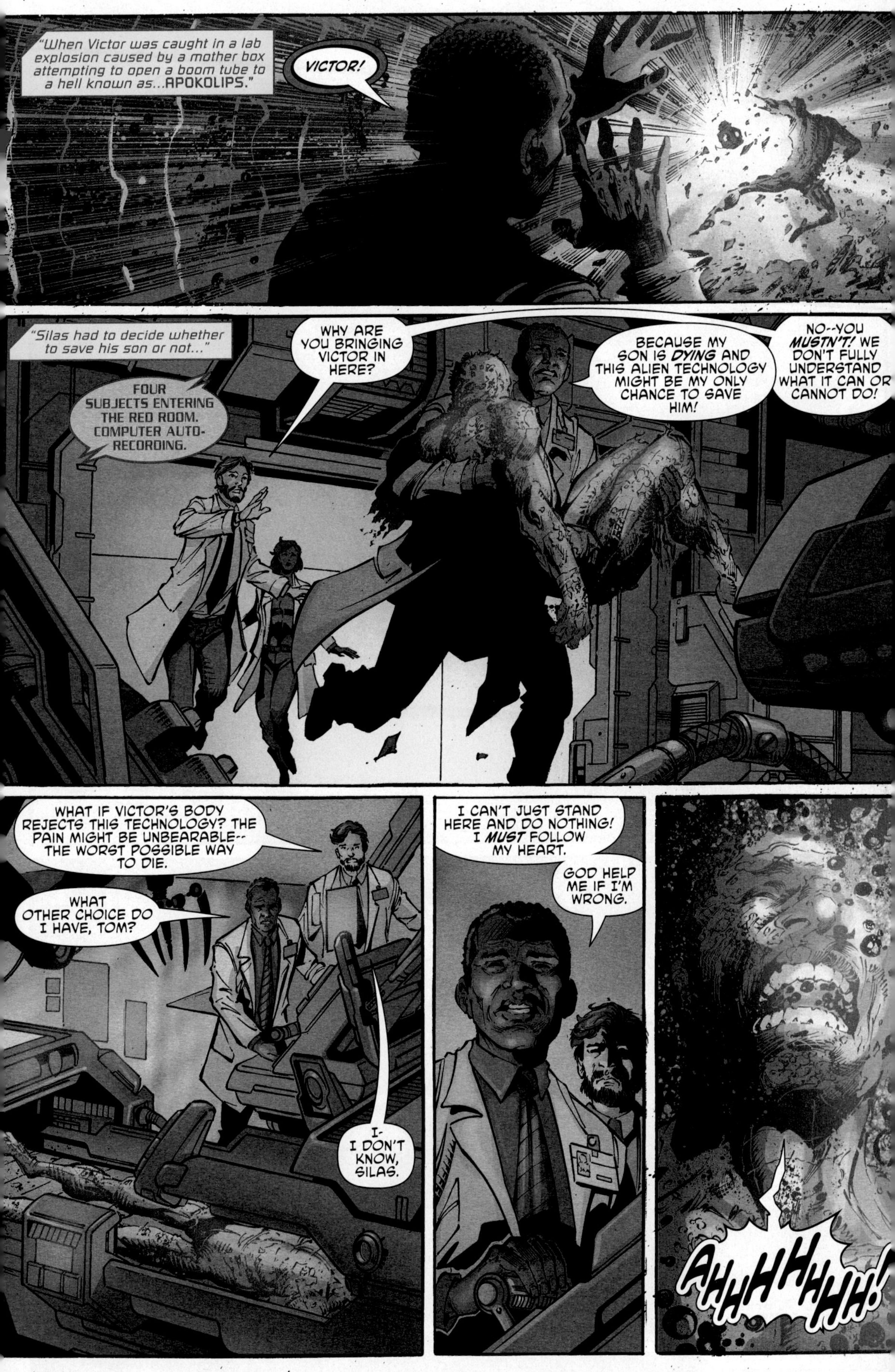
"When Victor was caught in a lab explosion caused by a mother box attempting to open a boom tube to a hell known as...APOKOLIPS."
VICTOR!
"Silas had to decide whether to save his son or not..."
FOUR SUBJECTS ENTERING THE RED ROOM. COMPUTER AUTO-RECORDING.
WHY ARE YOU BRINGING VICTOR IN HERE?
BECAUSE MY SON IS DYING AND THIS ALIEN TECHNOLOGY MIGHT BE MY ONLY CHANCE TO SAVE HIM!
NO--YOU MUSTN'T! WE DON'T FULLY UNDERSTAND WHAT IT CAN OR CANNOT DO!
WHAT IF VICTOR'S BODY REJECTS THIS TECHNOLOGY? THE PAIN MIGHT BE UNBEARABLE-- THE WORST POSSIBLE WAY TO DIE.
WHAT OTHER CHOICE DO I HAVE, TOM?
I- I DON'T KNOW, SILAS.
I CAN'T JUST STAND HERE AND DO NOTHING! I MUST FOLLOW MY HEART.
GOD HELP ME IF I'M WRONG.
AHHHHHHHH!

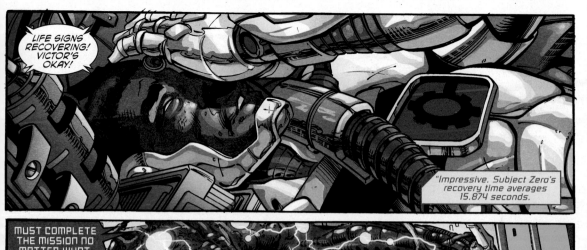

LIFE SIGNS RECOVERING! VICTOR'S OKAY!

"Impressive. Subject Zero's recovery time averages 15.874 seconds."

MUST COMPLETE THE MISSION NO MATTER WHAT.

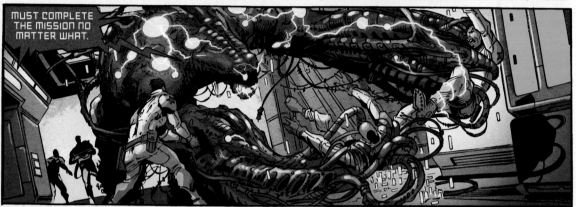

DR. STONE, MALWARE IS MAKING HIS WAY TOWARD THE RED ROOM.

"Ah, yes, the infamous Red Room! It was built to collect and contain alien technology deemed too dangerous to share with the world."

SARAH, INITIATE HIGH-SECURITY LOCKDOWN.

I-I CAN'T! HE'S USING HIS NANOTECH TO INFILTRATE THE SECURITY PROGRAMMING AND OPEN THE DOOR.

SILAS, YOU MIGHT HAVE TO TRIGGER THE SELF-DESTRUCT MECHANISM IN THAT ROOM AND BURY HIM ALIVE.

AND POSSIBLY BURY SOME OF US WITH IT, TOM? THAT'S ONE NIGHTMARE OF A CHOICE.

"But Silas was no stranger to horrific life-or-death decisions."

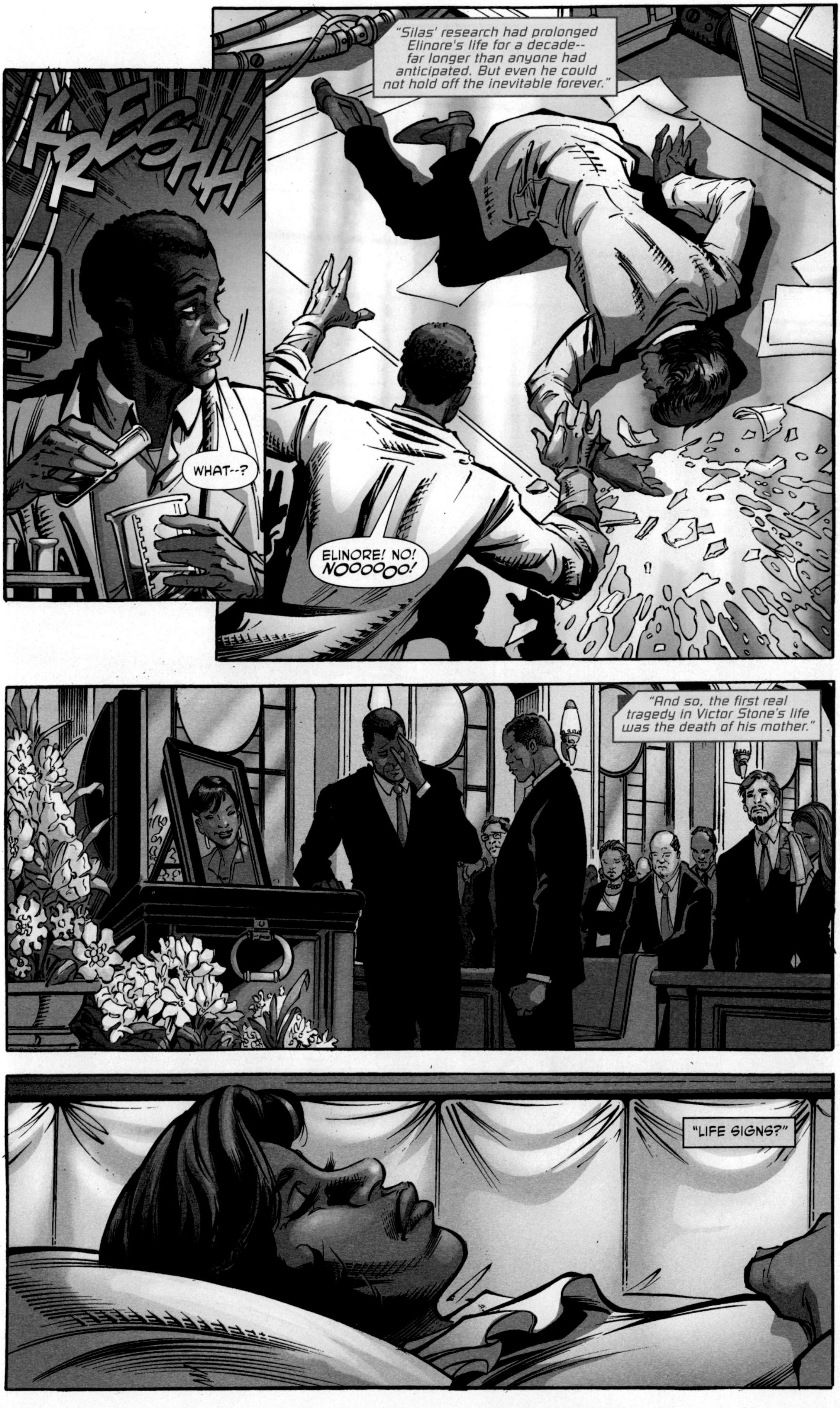
"Silas' research had prolonged Elinore's life for a decade--far longer than anyone had anticipated. But even he could not hold off the inevitable forever."
KRESHH
WHAT--?
ELINORE! NO! NOOOOOO!
"And so, the first real tragedy in Victor Stone's life was the death of his mother."
"LIFE SIGNS?"

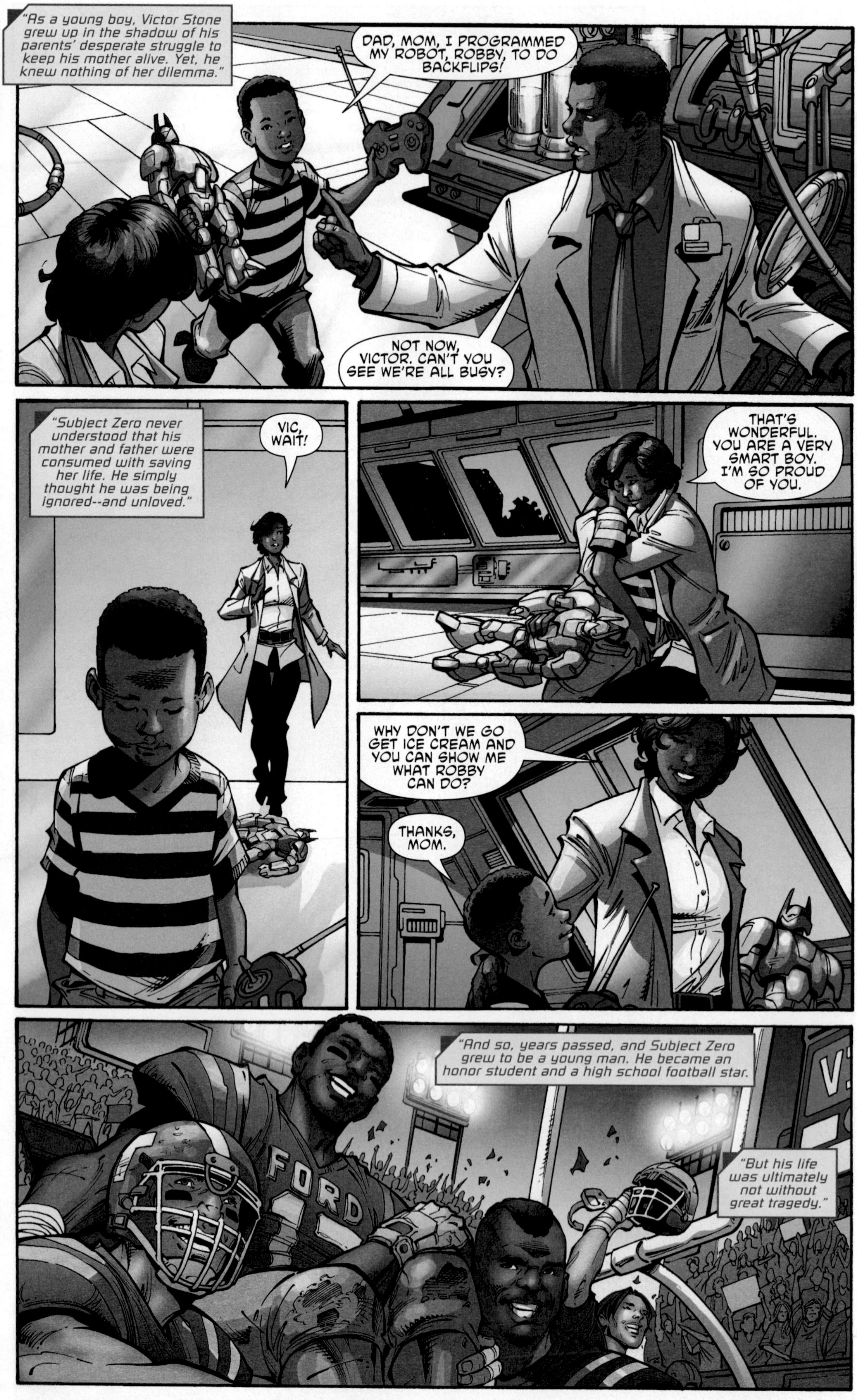
"As a young boy, Victor Stone grew up in the shadow of his parents' desperate struggle to keep his mother alive. Yet, he knew nothing of her dilemma."
DAD, MOM, I PROGRAMMED MY ROBOT, ROBBY, TO DO BACKFLIPS!
NOT NOW, VICTOR. CAN'T YOU SEE WE'RE ALL BUSY?
"Subject Zero never understood that his mother and father were consumed with saving her life. He simply thought he was being ignored--and unloved."
VIC, WAIT!
THAT'S WONDERFUL. YOU ARE A VERY SMART BOY. I'M SO PROUD OF YOU.
WHY DON'T WE GO GET ICE CREAM AND YOU CAN SHOW ME WHAT ROBBY CAN DO?
THANKS, MOM.
"And so, years passed, and Subject Zero grew to be a young man. He became an honor student and a high school football star.
"But his life was ultimately not without great tragedy."
FORD

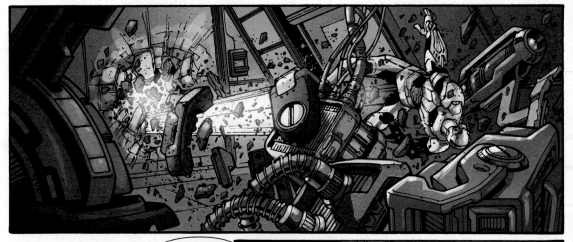

VICTOR'S UNCONSCIOUS. HIS VITAL SIGNS ARE WEAKENING.

ELINORE IS UNCONSCIOUS RIGHT NOW FROM THE SEDATIVE WE GAVE HER. OUR TESTS INDICATE THAT HER PROGNOSIS ISN'T GOOD.

"The doctor only confirmed what Silas and Elinore had feared. Elinore had developed a rare, terminal form of cancer."

IT'S ONLY A MATTER OF TIME, DR. STONE. IT MIGHT TAKE YEARS. BUT EVENTUALLY SHE WILL SUCCUMB TO THIS.

NOT IF I CAN HELP IT.

"From that day forth, Silas Stone devoted his life to finding a cure for his beloved wife."

"To finance his quest, Silas accepted funding by the government on behalf of the Pentagon-- something he had avoided up until then. And thus, he became the head of S.T.A.R. Labs' newest wing, established just for him in Detroit."

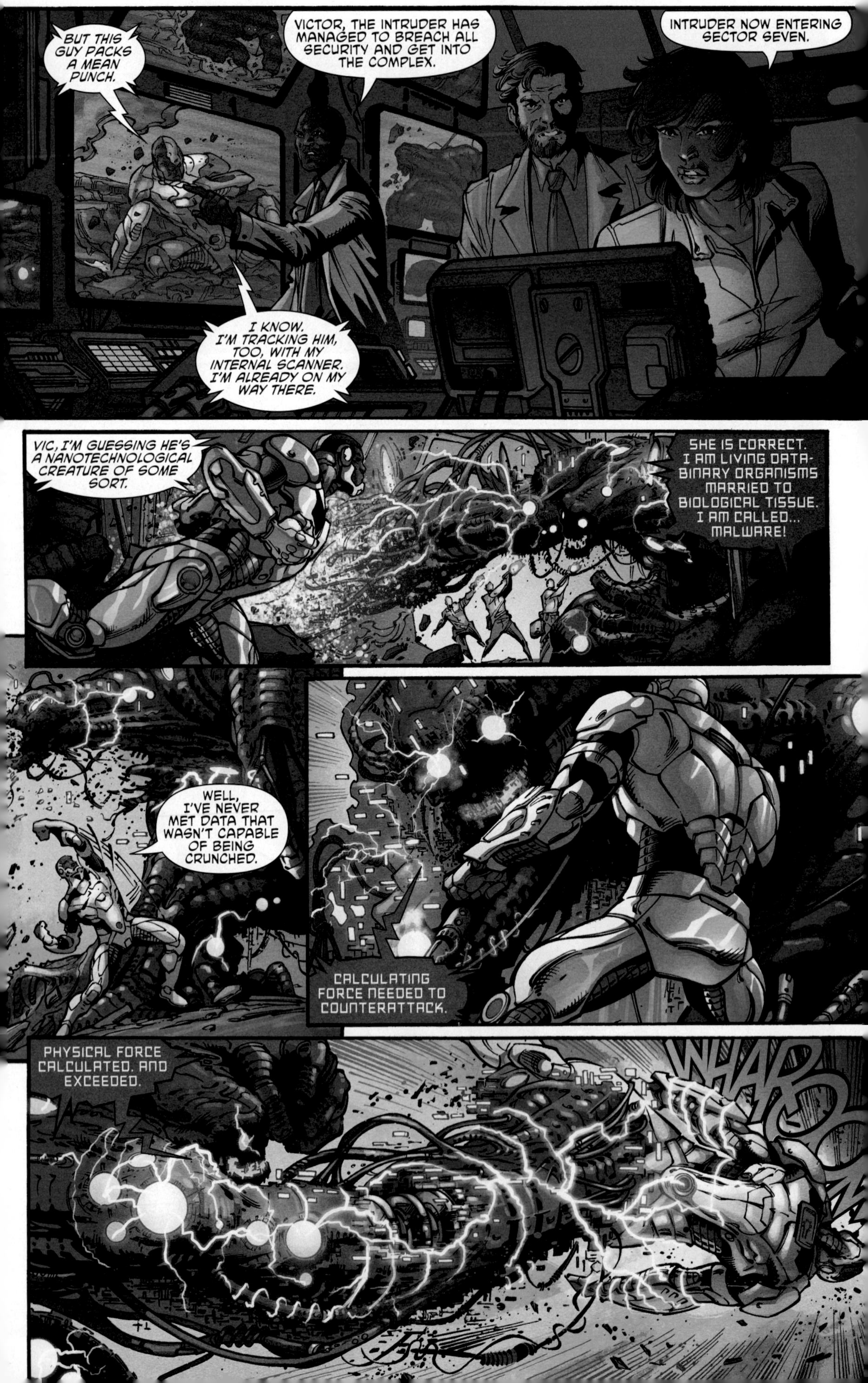
BUT THIS GUY PACKS A MEAN PUNCH.
VICTOR, THE INTRUDER HAS MANAGED TO BREACH ALL SECURITY AND GET INTO THE COMPLEX.
INTRUDER NOW ENTERING SECTOR SEVEN.
I KNOW. I'M TRACKING HIM, TOO, WITH MY INTERNAL SCANNER. I'M ALREADY ON MY WAY THERE.
VIC, I'M GUESSING HE'S A NANOTECHNOLOGICAL CREATURE OF SOME SORT.
SHE IS CORRECT. I AM LIVING DATA-BINARY ORGANISMS MARRIED TO BIOLOGICAL TISSUE. I AM CALLED... MALWARE!
WELL, I'VE NEVER MET DATA THAT WASN'T CAPABLE OF BEING CRUNCHED.
CALCULATING FORCE NEEDED TO COUNTERATTACK.
PHYSICAL FORCE CALCULATED. AND EXCEEDED.
WHAR

"Love led to the inevitable marriage of Silas Stone and Elinore Beatty..."

AND IT IS UNDER THE WATCHFUL EYE OF GOD THAT I JOIN THESE TWO SOULS TOGETHER IN HOLY MATRIMONY...

"...and to the birth of their only child ten months, one week, three days, seven hours and 34.5 minutes later.

"It was a boy. They named him Victor. But I shall continue to refer to him as Subject Zero."

ISN'T HE HANDSOME?

ARE YOU KIDDING? HE'S OUR GREATEST WORK.

I EXPECT US TO WIN THE NOBEL PRIZE FOR PARENTING.

PRETTY SURE THEY DON'T GIVE ONE OF THOSE.

WELL, THEY'RE GOING TO HAVE TO START. I STILL CAN'T BELIEVE WE HAVE A...

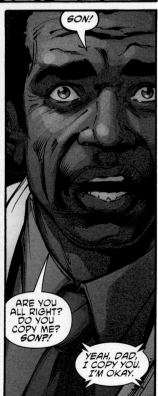

SON!

ARE YOU ALL RIGHT? DO YOU COPY ME? SON?!

YEAH, DAD, I COPY YOU. I'M OKAY.

"DNA evidence conclusive. Records retrieved. Cyborg is identified as VICTOR STONE. His biological father is named..."

"...SILAS STONE.

COMPUTER, PLEASE VIDEO-RECORD AND LOG MY NOTES AS I DICTATE THEM...

RECORDING.

HEY, SILAS!

"While a graduate student attending Dayton University in Detroit, Silas Stone had an encounter of prime significance."

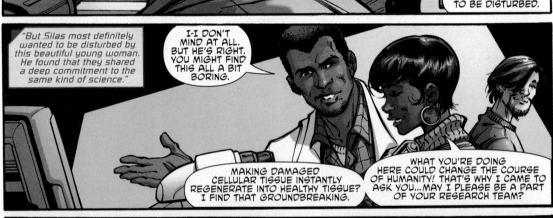

TOM, IT'S INCREDIBLE! YOU'RE NOT GOING TO BELIEVE THE LATEST RESULTS IN MY--

I WANT TO INTRODUCE YOU TO A BIG FAN OF YOURS. SILAS STONE MEET ELINORE BEATTY.

SHE'S A GRAD STUDENT HERE IN BIOTECHNOLOGY. I WARNED HER YOU COULD JABBER ON UNTIL HER EARS FALL OFF, BUT SHE STILL WANTED TO MEET YOU.

TOM, I'M SURE SILAS DOESN'T WANT TO BE DISTURBED.

"But Silas most definitely wanted to be disturbed by this beautiful young woman. He found that they shared a deep commitment to the same kind of science."

I-I DON'T MIND AT ALL. BUT HE'S RIGHT. YOU MIGHT FIND THIS ALL A BIT BORING.

MAKING DAMAGED CELLULAR TISSUE INSTANTLY REGENERATE INTO HEALTHY TISSUE? I FIND THAT GROUNDBREAKING.

WHAT YOU'RE DOING HERE COULD CHANGE THE COURSE OF HUMANITY! THAT'S WHY I CAME TO ASK YOU...MAY I PLEASE BE A PART OF YOUR RESEARCH TEAM?

"He was more than willing to grant her that request. It was only a matter of time before they shared a deeper commitment to each other.

"One that humans refer to as...love."

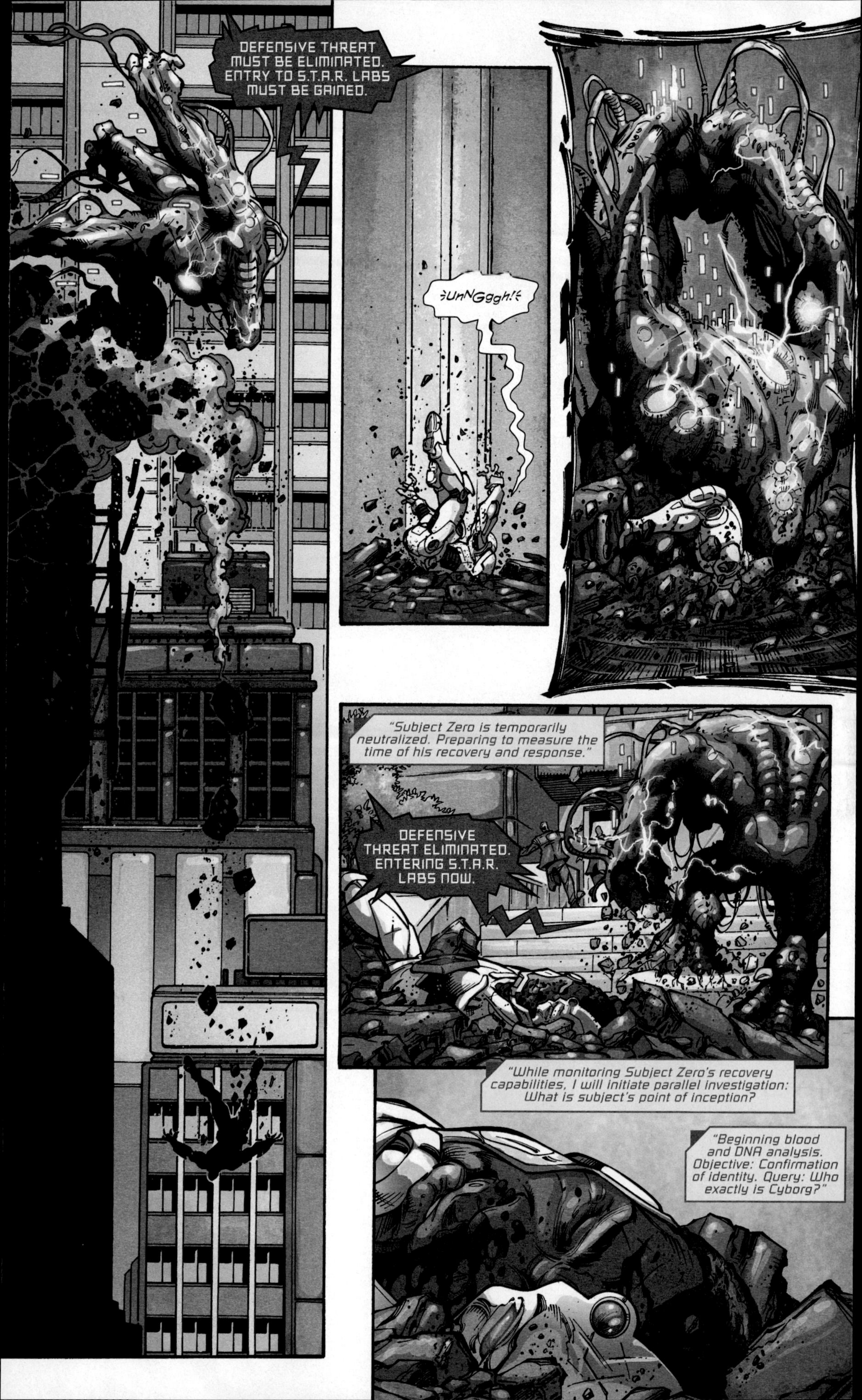
DEFENSIVE THREAT MUST BE ELIMINATED. ENTRY TO S.T.A.R. LABS MUST BE GAINED.
UNNGGGH!
"Subject Zero is temporarily neutralized. Preparing to measure the time of his recovery and response."
DEFENSIVE THREAT ELIMINATED. ENTERING S.T.A.R. LABS NOW.
"While monitoring Subject Zero's recovery capabilities, I will initiate parallel investigation: What is subject's point of inception?
"Beginning blood and DNA analysis. Objective: Confirmation of identity. Query: Who exactly is Cyborg?"

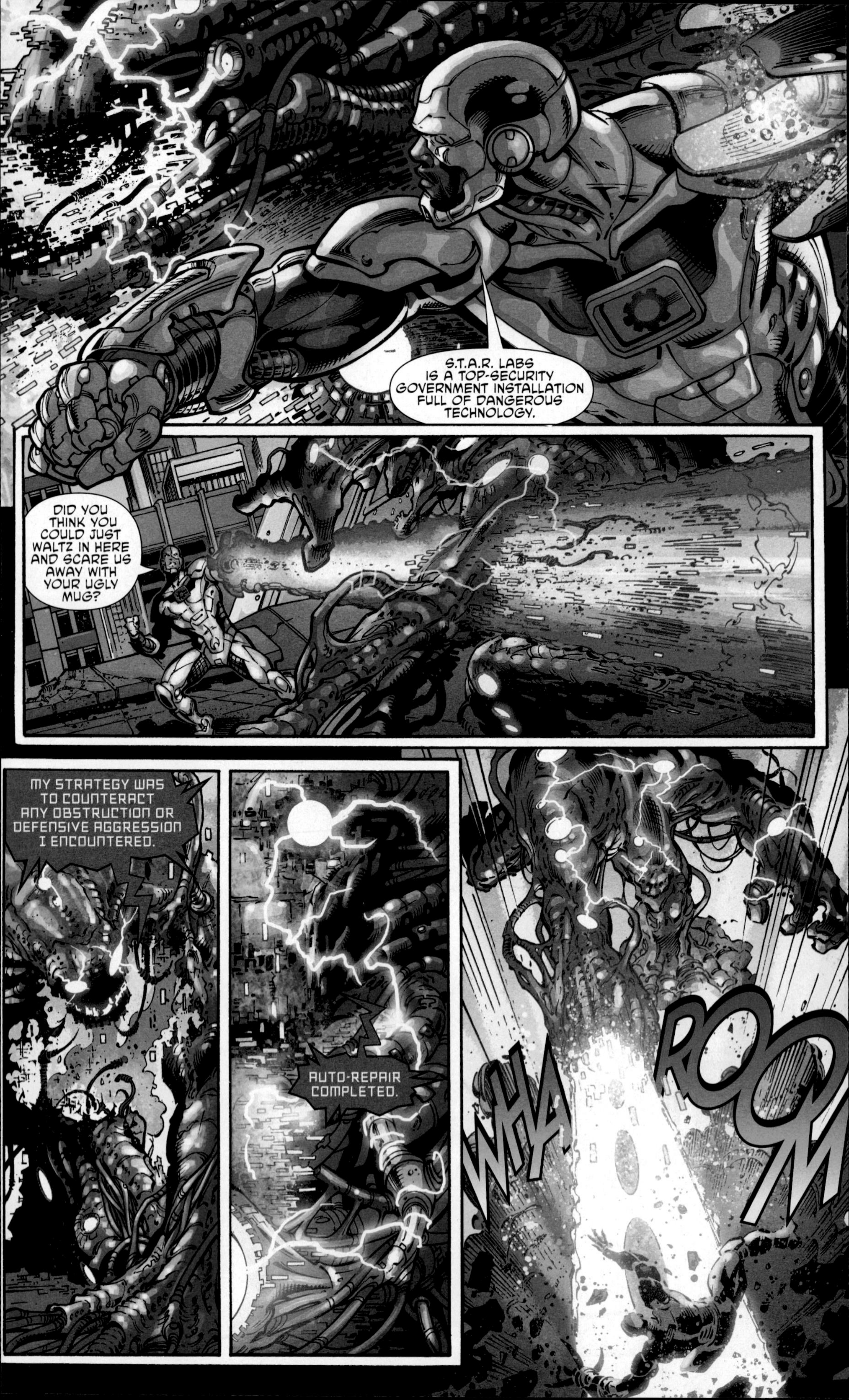
S.T.A.R. LABS IS A TOP-SECURITY GOVERNMENT INSTALLATION FULL OF DANGEROUS TECHNOLOGY.
DID YOU THINK YOU COULD JUST WALTZ IN HERE AND SCARE US AWAY WITH YOUR UGLY MUG?
MY STRATEGY WAS TO COUNTERACT ANY OBSTRUCTION OR DEFENSIVE AGGRESSION I ENCOUNTERED.
AUTO-REPAIR COMPLETED.
WHAROOM

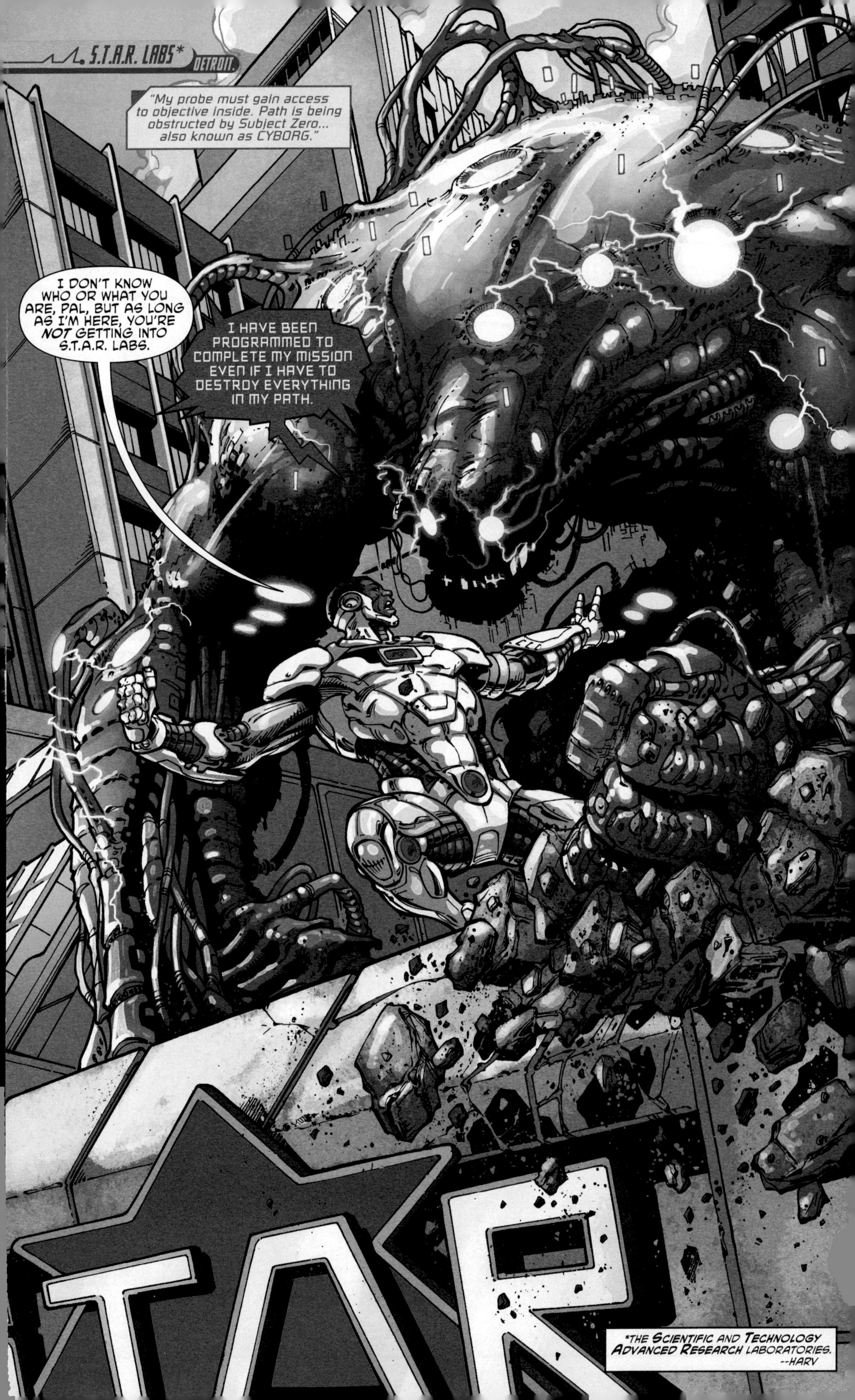
S.T.A.R. LABS* DETROIT.
"My probe must gain access to objective inside. Path is being obstructed by Subject Zero... also known as CYBORG."
I DON'T KNOW WHO OR WHAT YOU ARE, PAL, BUT AS LONG AS I'M HERE, YOU'RE NOT GETTING INTO S.T.A.R. LABS.
I HAVE BEEN PROGRAMMED TO COMPLETE MY MISSION EVEN IF I HAVE TO DESTROY EVERYTHING IN MY PATH.
*THE SCIENTIFIC AND TECHNOLOGY ADVANCED RESEARCH LABORATORIES. --HARV

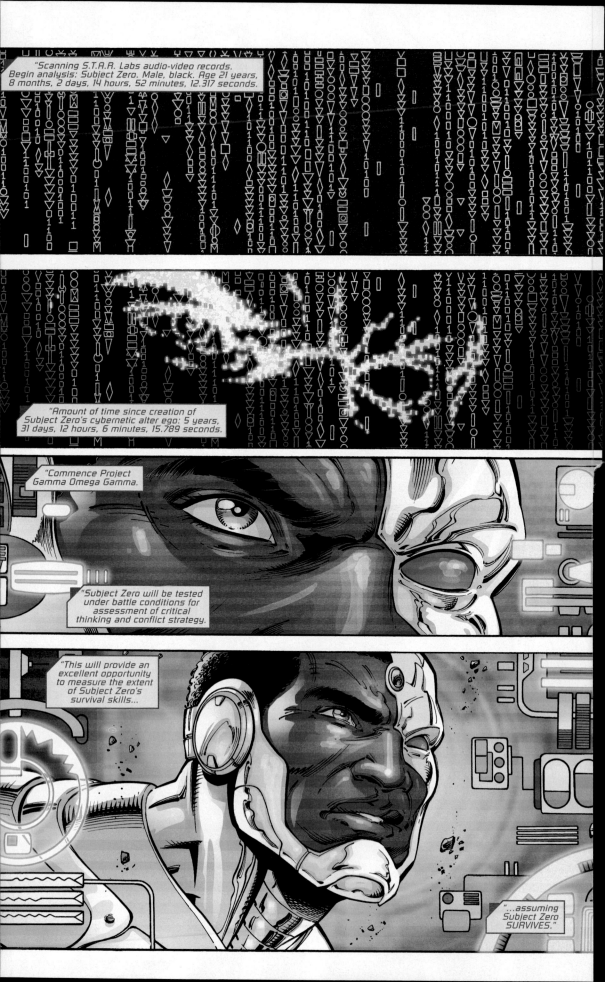

"Scanning S.T.A.R. Labs audio-video records. Begin analysis: Subject Zero. Male, black. Age 21 years, 8 months, 2 days, 14 hours, 52 minutes, 12.317 seconds."

"Amount of time since creation of Subject Zero's cybernetic alter ego: 5 years, 31 days, 12 hours, 6 minutes, 15.789 seconds."

"Commence Project Gamma Omega Gamma.

"Subject Zero will be tested under battle conditions for assessment of critical thinking and conflict strategy.

"This will provide an excellent opportunity to measure the extent of Subject Zero's survival skills...

"...assuming Subject Zero SURVIVES."

PROLOGUE

JOHN SEMPER JR. writer * PAUL PELLETIER penciller
SANDRA HOPE and TONY KORDOS inkers * GUY MAJOR colorist * ROB LEIGH letterer
Cover by WILL CONRAD and IVAN NUNES

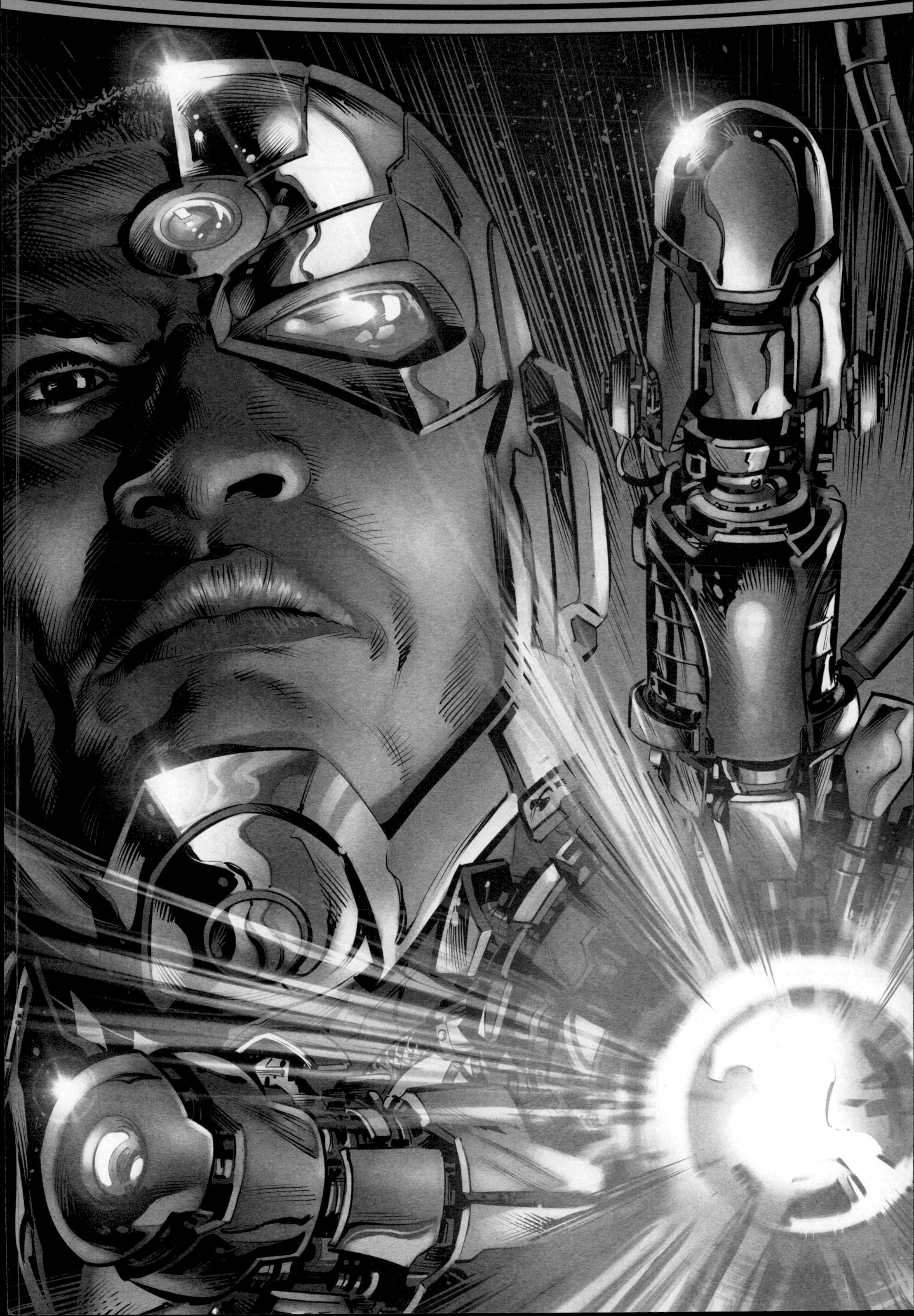

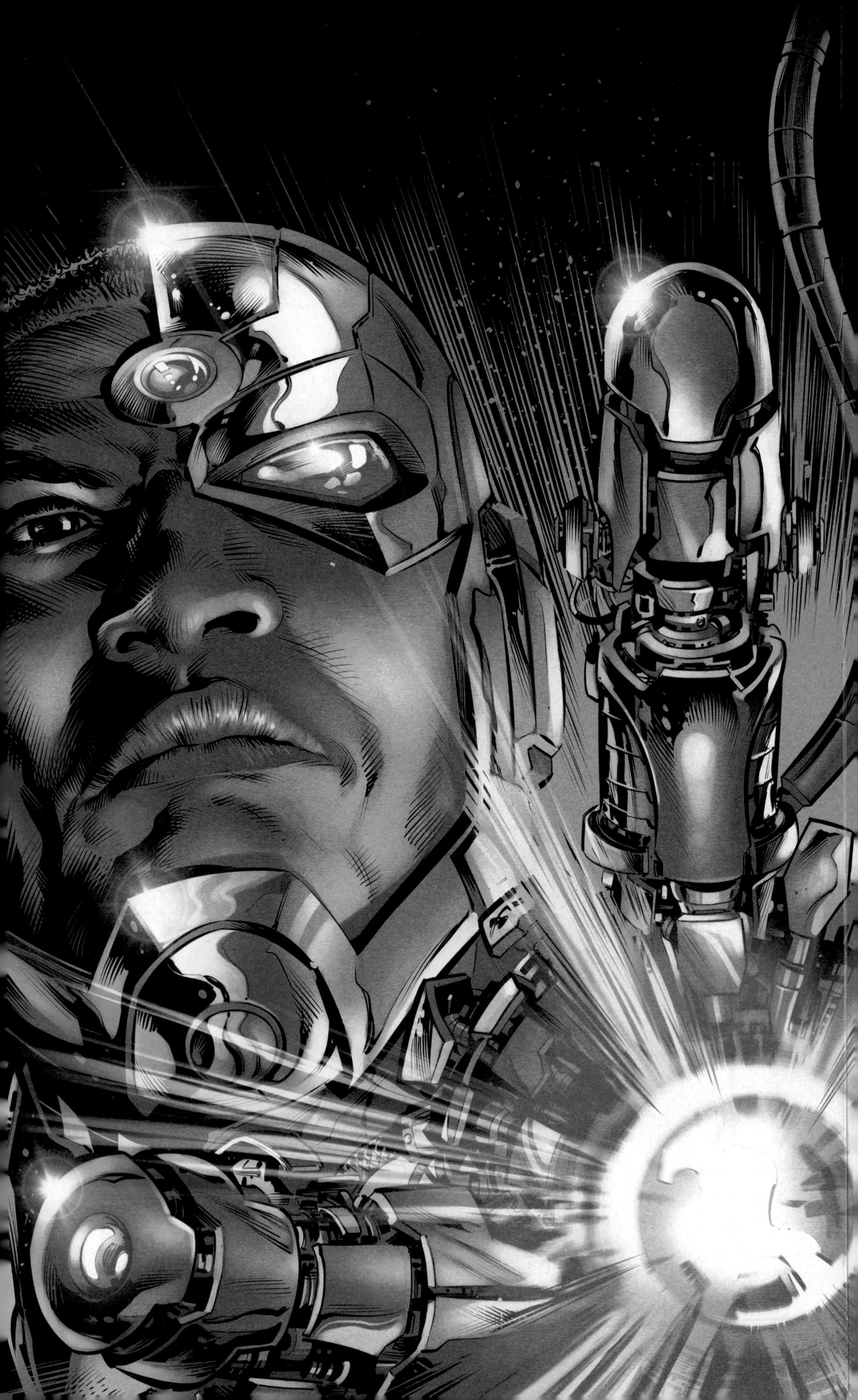

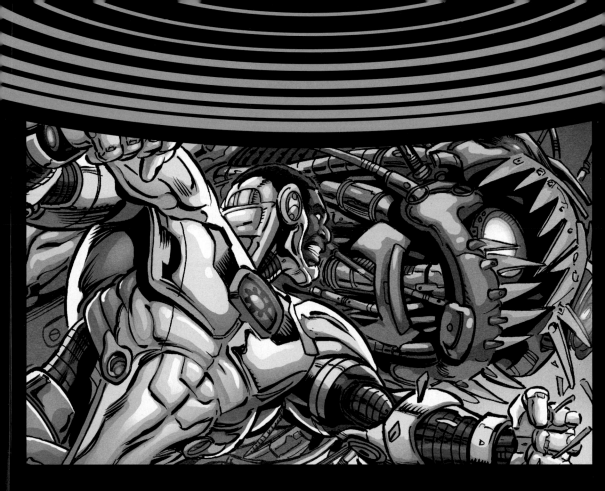

HARVEY RICHARDS Editor - Original Series ✷ **AMEDEO TURTURRO** Assistant Editor - Original Series ✷ **JEB WOODARD** Group Editor - Collected Editions
LIZ ERICKSON Editor - Collected Edition ✷ **STEVE COOK** Design Director - Books ✷ **MONIQUE GRUSPE** Publication Design

BOB HARRAS Senior VP - Editor-in-Chief, DC Comics

DIANE NELSON President ✷ **DAN DiDIO** Publisher ✷ **JIM LEE** Publisher ✷ **GEOFF JOHNS** President & Chief Creative Officer
AMIT DESAI Executive VP - Business & Marketing Strategy, Direct to Consumer & Global Franchise Management ✷ **SAM ADES** Senior VP - Direct to Consumer
BOBBIE CHASE VP - Talent Development ✷ **MARK CHIARELLO** Senior VP - Art, Design & Collected Editions
JOHN CUNNINGHAM Senior VP - Sales & Trade Marketing ✷ **ANNE DePIES** Senior VP - Business Strategy, Finance & Administration
DON FALLETTI VP - Manufacturing Operations ✷ **LAWRENCE GANEM** VP - Editorial Administration & Talent Relations
ALISON GILL Senior VP - Manufacturing & Operations ✷ **HANK KANALZ** Senior VP - Editorial Strategy & Administration
JAY KOGAN VP - Legal Affairs ✷ **THOMAS LOFTUS** VP - Business Affairs
JACK MAHAN VP - Business Affairs ✷ **NICK J. NAPOLITANO** VP - Manufacturing Administration
EDDIE SCANNELL VP - Consumer Marketing ✷ **COURTNEY SIMMONS** Senior VP - Publicity & Communications
JIM (SKI) SOKOLOWSKI VP - Comic Book Specialty Sales & Trade Marketing ✷ **NANCY SPEARS** VP - Mass, Book, Digital Sales & Trade Marketing

CYBORG VOL. 1: THE IMITATION OF LIFE

DC Comics, 2900 West Alameda Ave., Burbank, CA 91505. Printed by LSC Communications, Salem, VA, USA. 2/17/17.
First Printing. ISBN: 978-1-4012-6792-6

Library of Congress Cataloging-in-Publication Data is available.

PEFC Certified

Printed on paper from
sustainably managed
forests, controlled
sources

PEFC/29-31-337   www.pefc.org

CYBORG
VOL.1 THE IMITATION OF LIFE

JOHN SEMPER JR.
writer

**PAUL PELLETIER * WILL CONRAD * TIMOTHY GREEN II
ALLAN JEFFERSON * DEREC DONOVAN**
pencillers

**TONY KORDOS * SANDRA HOPE * SCOTT HANNA * TOM PALMER
WILL CONRAD * JOSEPH SILVER * DEREC DONOVAN**
inkers

GUY MAJOR * HI-FI * IVAN NUNES
colorists

ROB LEIGH
letterer

WILL CONRAD and **IVAN NUNES**
collection cover artists

CYBORG created by **MARV WOLFMAN** and **GEORGE PÉREZ**
SUPERMAN created by **JERRY SIEGEL** and **JOE SHUSTER**
By special arrangement with the **JERRY SIEGEL FAMILY**